CW01494360

VARIORUM COLLECTED STUDIES SERIES

The Crusades and Latin
Monasticism, 11th–12th Centuries

The Reverend H.E.J. Cowdrey

H.E.J. Cowdrey

The Crusades and Latin Monasticism, 11th–12th Centuries

Aldershot · Brookfield USA · Singapore · Sydney

This edition copyright © 1999 by H.E.J. Cowdrey.

Published in the Variorum Collected Studies Series by

Ashgate Publishing Limited
Gower House, Croft Road,
Aldershot, Hampshire GU11 3HR
Great Britain

Ashgate Publishing Company
Old Post Road,
Brookfield, Vermont 05036–9704
USA

Ashgate website: http://www.ashgate.com

ISBN 0–86078–795–8

British Library Cataloguing-in-Publication Data
Cowdrey, H.E.J. (Herbert Edward John), 1926–
    The Crusades and Latin Monasticism, 11th–12th Centuries.
    (Variorum Collected Studies Series: CS662).
    1. Crusades. 2. Monasticism and religious orders–History–
    Middle Ages, 600–1500.
    I. Title.
    270. 5

US Library of Congress Cataloging-in-Publication Data
Cowdrey, H.E.J. (Herbert Edward John)
    The Crusades and Latin Monasticism, 11th–12th Centuries/H.E.J. Cowdrey.
    p. cm. – (Variorum Collected Studies Series: CS662).
    1. Crusades–Inflluence. 2. Monasticism and religious orders–History–
    Middle Ages. 3. Monasticism and religious orders–History–
    Middle Ages, 600–1500.
    I. Title. II. Series: Variorum Collected Studies: CS662.
    D160. C68. 1999   99–29850
    270. 4–dc21   CIP

The paper used in this publication meets the minimum requirements of the American National Standard
   for Information Sciences – Permanence of Paper for Printed Library Materials,
   ANSI Z39.48–1984. ∞ ™

Printed by Galliard (Printers) Ltd., Great Yarmouth, Norfolk, Great Britain.

VARIORUM COLLECTED STUDIES SERIES CS662

CONTENTS

LATIN MONASTICISM

vii

This volume contains x + 274 pages

PUBLISHER'S NOTE

The articles in this volume, as in all others in the Variorum Collected Studies Series, have not been given a new, continuous pagination. In order to avoid confusion, and to facilitate their use where these same studies have been referred to elsewhere, the original pagination has been maintained wherever possible.

Each article has been given a Roman number in order of appearance, as listed in the Contents. This number is repeated on each page and is quoted in the index entries.

PREFACE

This is the first of two volumes in the Variorum Collected Studies series which will bring together articles published during the past fifteen years which directly or indirectly bear upon the subject of my book *Pope Gregory VII, 1073–1085* (Oxford, 1998). It concentrates upon two subjects: the coming of the Crusade and the contemporary and later development of the monastic order. The Crusade articles are particularly concerned with the transformation in western attitudes to the bearing of arms and in the quest for internal and external peace and security which are associated with Gregory VII and which help to give his pontificate an epoch-making significance in the history of Latin Christendom and its relations with the Byzantine and Islamic worlds. The articles on monasticism reflect the view that the relation between the Gregorian papacy and the Cluniacs was particularly close, but that such newer monastic families as the Carthusians and the Cistercians were also of importance in transmitting papal aspirations to the twelfth-century church and world. As is the general custom of the series, the pagination of the original publications is normally retained. The only exception is no. VIII, which for reasons of format has been reset and repaged; the page numbers of the original were 75–85.

St Edmund Hall, Oxford
March 1999

H.E.J. COWDREY

ACKNOWLEDGEMENTS

Grateful acknowledgement is made to the following publishers, journals, and editors for their kind permission to reproduce the eighteen articles included in this volume: M. François-Charles Uginet and the École française de Rome (I); Professor Luis García-Guijarro Ramos (II); Frau Ilse Neuhoff on behalf of B.G. Teubner, Stuttgart and Leipzig (IV); Professor Claudio Leonardi on behalf of *Studi Medievali* (V); P.W. Edbury (VII); Mrs Judith Loades on behalf of Headstart History (VIII); La Ville de Cluny (IX); Dr Christophe Lebbe on behalf of Brepols Publishers (X); M. André Pelletier on behalf of Presses Universitaires de Lyon (XI); M. Bernard Yon on behalf of Université de Saint-Étienne Publications (XII); Wilhelm Fink GmbH & Co., Munich (XIII); The Rev. Dom Daniel Misonne on behalf of *Revue Bénédictine* (XIV); Peter Lang Publishing, New York (XV); Dr James Hogg and Analecta Cartusiana (XVI, XVIII); Dr Richard Barber on behalf of Boydell & Brewer (XVII).

I

THE REFORM PAPACY
AND THE ORIGIN OF THE CRUSADES *

The contribution of the reform popes from Leo IX (1049-54) to Urban II (1088-99), and especially of Gregory VII (1073-85), in preparing the minds of the clergy and laity of Western Europe for the Crusade that Urban preached with such effect at Clermont nine hundred years ago has been a major subject for inquiry and debate since Carl Erdmann published in 1935 his monograph *Die Entstehung des Kreuzzugsgedankens*[1]. It is not my present purpose to consider the subject comprehensively; rather, I shall concentrate upon four particular ways in which, among others, the reform popes and their circles at Rome may have contributed to the eventual emergence of the Crusade. I have selected them because, at least as I shall present them, they perhaps deserve greater attention than scholars have given them.

The first topic is the conception that the Roman church formed of its relation with, and responsibility towards, the Byzantine empire and church. The year 1054 saw the journey to Constantinople of Leo IX's legates, Cardinal Humbert and Frederick of Lorraine. The most notorius episode of their stay at Constantinople arose from their antipathy to the patriarch, Michael Cerularius : their visit concluded with their placing of a bull of excommunication against him on the altar of Sancta Sophia, and with his calling of a synod at which Humbert and his companions were anathematized in return. Now,

---

* The following abbreviations are used in the footnotes to this paper :

Epp. vag. = *The Epistolae vagantes of Pope Gregory VII*, ed. and trans. H.E.J. Cowdrey (Oxford, 1972).
GCS = *Grieschischen christlichen Schriftsteller der ersten drei Jahrhunderte*.
MGH = *Monumenta Germaniae Historica*.
–, *Font. iur. Germ. antiq.* = –, *Fontes iuris Germanici antiqui*.
–, *Libelli* = –, *Libelli de lite imperatorum et regum*.
–, *SS* = –, *Scriptores*.
PL = *Patrologia Latina*, ed. J.P. Migne.
    [1] C. Erdmann, *Die Entstehung des Kreuzzugsgedankens* (Stuttgart, 1935); Eng. trans. *The Origin of the Idea of Crusade* by M.W. Baldwin and W. Goffart (Princeton NJ, 1977).

Leo IX had already died when these events occurred, and in 1058, the patriarch also died, under a cloud. Neither at Rome nor at Constantinople did these events find much record or leave any serious trauma[2]. But, at Rome, documents that were written in anticipation of the legates' mission, and some of Humbert's own reactions at Constantinople when he was not at loggerheads with the patriarch, gave rise to positive thoughts about Byzantium which led the papacy in the long run to express its duties towards it in ways that did much to prepare for the Crusade. Above all, in preparatory documents, the relation of the pope to the eastern emperor was expressed as one of father to son, and that of the see of Rome to that of Constantinople as one of mother to daughter. In a letter, perhaps of Humbert's drafting, which the legates were to take from Leo to the Emperor Constantine IX Monomachus (1042-54), Leo addressed Constantine as his beloved son and went on to refer to him as 'most glorious son and serene emperor'. If the pope was his father, the Roman church was his mother, who should not be despised because she was old but, rather, revered by him, so that he might be the more beloved of the Father of all as he became better disposed and humbler towards Rome as the supreme mother (*eidem principali matri*)[3].

Before the legates set out for the east, Leo addressed another long letter, commonly known as the *Libellus* and probably again owing much to Humbert's drafting, to the patriarch, Michael Cerularius, and to Archbishop Leo of Ochrida. It was a reply to Byzantine polemic about supposed Latin errors and a vindication of the *regale sacerdotium* of the Roman church. Much of it (caps 23-36) was devoted to insisting that Rome and Constantinople were mother and daughter – a relationship that the Byzantines had disregarded and should respect :

> You have hitherto yourselves abounded in so many and such great schismatics and heretics, who have assailed and striven to rend the catholic and apostolic church, that the Latin and western church might well complain of you like the bridegroom in the Canticle : My mother's sons have fought against me (S. of S. 1 : 5). Truly so : for is not the Roman and apostolic see, which conceived in the gospel the Latin church in the west, also the mother of the Constantinopolitan church in the east[4]?

Wayward children do not as a rule take kindly to parental exhortations that they should be dutiful; it was, therefore, well that

---

[2] J.M. Hussey, *The Orthodox Church in the Byzantine Empire* (Oxford, 1986), p. 129-38.

[3] C. Will, *Acta et scripta quae de controversiis ecclesiae Graecae et Latinae saeculo undecimo composita extant* (Leipzig and Marburg, 1861), p. 85-9.

[4] Will, *Acta et scripta*, p. 65-85; citation from p. 78.

the *Libellus* probably did not reach Constantinople in 1054 to cause resentment there. It was also well that not all the impressions that the legates in 1054 brought back to Rome were adverse ones. Cardinal Humbert had got on quite well with emperor. In his *Adversus simoniacos*, he recalled his talks with Constantine Monomachus, *orthodoxae memoriae imperator*. The talks confirmed his own observation that, in Byzantium, neither the emperor nor laymen disposed of churches or of ecclesiastical ordinations and resources. The easterns thus did not fall into simony, and in important respects their churches were free[5]. From Humbert, that was praise indeed. Assisted by such favourable impressions, the notion that Rome and Constantinople were mother and daughter persisted at Rome, without its being too heavy-handedly imposed upon Constantinople. Good mothers never forget their children, and they acknowledge their children's claim upon them when they are in trouble. Therefore, when, in 1071, the Seljuk Turks' defeat of the Byzantine army at Manzikert left the empire right up to Constantinople open to pagan invasion and ravaging, the mother-and-daughter relationship that had been insisted upon in the days of Leo IX was remembered at Rome, above all by Gregory VII. Soon after becoming pope, he wrote to the Emperor Michael VII Ducas of his desire to renew the ancient concord between the Roman church and its daughter of Constantinople[6]. These were no idle words, for, in 1074, Gregory was concerned to raise and himself to lead to the east a military expedition which would cross to Constantinople in aid of Christians who, being vexed beyond measure by incessant Saracen harassment, were urgently seeking his aid. Ultimately it would go to the Lord's sepulchre at Jerusalem[7].

A first way, then, in which papal circles contributed to the emergence of the Crusade was by the heightened awareness, aroused in Leo IX's last years, that Rome and Constantinople were mother and daughter, and that Rome had a mother's duty of care for a daughter's welfare when she was in dire need. When, in 1095, envoys from the Emperor Alexius Comnenus came to the council of Piacenza and suppliantly implored the pope and all Christians to

---

[5] Humbert, *Libri III adversus simoniacos*, 3. 8, ed. F. Thaner, *MGH Libelli*, l. 206-7.

[6] *Reg.* l. 18, to the Emperor Michael, 9 July 1073, p. 29-30.

[7] *Reg.* l. 46, to Count William of Burgundy, 2 Feb. 1074, p. 69-71, l. 49, general summons to all who were willing to defend the Christian faith, 1 Mar. 1074, p. 75-6, 2. 31, to King Henry IV of Germany, 7 Dec. 1074, p. 165-8, 2. 37, to all the faithful of St Peter, especially those beyond the Alps, 16 Dec. 1074, p. 172-3.

help a church that pagans had almost destroyed in eastern parts, up to the very walls of Constantinople, the plea was calculated to strike a chord in Pope Urban, both at Piacenza and, a few months later, at Clermont[8].

My second topic arises naturally from my first : it is the memory of the founder of Byzantium, Constantine, as it was enshrined in the buildings of papal Rome and in the minds of those who inhabited and visited them[9]. The topic has many ramifications, but the events of 1054 again provide a starting-point. For the emperor whom the legates met and liked was Constantine IX Monomachus. The letter from Pope Leo which the legates took to him addressed him as as the successor of the great Constantine in blood, name, and empire. The present bearer of his name should manifest the constancy which it encapsulated; like him, he should uphold the rightful prerogatives of the apostolic see of Rome[10]. The eleventh-century papal estimate of Constantine the Great was wholly favourable, even eulogistic. I can only now list four of the many written sources that contributed to making it so. The *Constitutum Constantini* – the 'Donation of Costantine', a fresh recension of which was made in the circle of Leo and Humbert, presented Constantine as exalting the prerogatives of the Roman church, as making over to the pope the Lateran palace at Rome, and as reverentially transferring the seat of earthly rule to Byzantium[11]. The *Constitutum Constantini* owed much of its dissemination to its place in – my second source – the Pseudo-Isidorian Decrees, where it was preceded by an account of Constantine's exemplary behaviour at the council of Nicaea in 325 : he had proclaimed the exemption of the clergy from human judgement, thereby foreshadowing the liberty of the church so dear to eleventh-century reformers[12]. Behind the *Constitutum Constantini*, and in the age of Gregory VII perhaps more influential, lay, thirdly, the so-called *Actus Silvestri*, which has justly been called 'the Constantinian foundation-legend of Christian Rome'[13]. It retailed

[8] Bernold, *Chronicon, aa.* 1095, 1096, *MGH SS* 5. 462, 464.

[9] For fuller discussions, see H.E.J. Cowdrey, 'Eleventh-century Reformers' Views of Constantine', in : *Conformity and Non-conformity in Byzantium*, forthcoming, *Byzantinische Forschungen*.

[10] Will, *Acta et scripta*, p. 85-9, esp. 86, 88.

[11] *Das Constitutum Constantini (Konstantinische Schenkung) : Text*, ed. H. Fuhrmann, *MGH Fontes iur. Germ. Antiq.* 10 (Hanover, 1968); for the Leo-Humbert recension, see p. 15-17, 30-32.

[12] *Decretales Pseudo-Isidorianae et capitula Angilramni* ed. P. Hinschius (Leipzig, 1863), p. 247-54.

[13] The only printed text of the *Actus Silvestri* which is at present available is that in B. Mombritius, *Sanctuarium seu Vitae sanctorum*, new ed., 2 vols (Paris, 1910), 2. 508-31. A new edition is in preparation; see W. Pohlkamp,

the legends surrounding Constantine's conversion and baptism by Pope Silvester, and it triumphantly unfolded how, as the centre of Roman religion, the pagan Capitol yielded to the Christian Lateran. But Constantine was not only the pious emperor; he was also the warrior emperor. There was, above all, the story from my fourth source, Rufinus' Latin translation of Eusebius' *Ecclesiastical History*, of Constantine's vision before his victorious battle against Maxentius of the cross of Christ, and of the angels' words, 'Constantine, in this sign conquer'[14]!

There is no need for speculation about how the legends of the good Constantine impinged upon the reform papacy; they are epitomized in the so-called *Descriptio basilicae Lateranensis*, a pilgrims' guide to the Lateran that underwent several recensions. The original version dates from between 1073 and 1118, but probably from soon after 1073[15]. It took from the *Actus Silvestri* the story of Constantine's conversion and recognition of the papal prerogatives. Having alluded to his vision of the cross before his victory and to the angels' words, it told how he sent his mother Helena to Jerusalem, where she found the true cross and brought a section of it to him at Constantinople, together with a wealth of other relics. Constantine sent all this treasure to Rome, and the Lateran became its principal repository; some was placed in the Lateran basilica, but the most precious items were kept in the papal chapel of St Lawrence in the palace itself.

A striking feature of the two relic lists in the *Descriptio* is that so many relics were either of Christ himself as he lived in the Holy Land, or else were very, tangible pieces of the Holy Land and of Jerusalem. I confine my examples to the chapel of St Lawrence. There were three principal reliquaries, containing respectively the foreskin of Christ's circumcision, a portion of the holy cross, and

---

'Textfassungen, literarische Formen und geschichtliche Funktionen der römischen Silvester-Akten', *Francia*, 19 (1992), 115-96; see also ibid. *'Privilegium ecclesiae Romanae pontifici contulit* : Zur Vorgeschichte der Konstantinischen Schenkung', in : *Fälschungen im Mittelalter*, 2 : *Gefälschte Rechtstexte. Der bestrafte Fälscher, MGH Schriften*, 33/2 (Hanover, 1988), p. 413-90; citation from p. 425.

[14] Eusebius, *Historia ecclesiastica*, 9. 8. 15, edd. E. Schwartz and T. Mommsen, *GCS* 9 (Leipzig, 1903-8), p. 827-9.

[15] The edition of the *Descriptio* in : *Codice topografico della città di Roma*, edd. R. Valentini and G. Zucchetti, Fonti per la storia d'Italia, 81, 88-91, 4 vols (Rome, 1940-53), 3. 319-373, is based upon its ultimate, twelfth-century form. The only printed text of the original version is in : D. Georgi, *De liturgia Romani pontificis in solemni celebratione missarum libri duo*, 3 vols (Rome, 1731-44), 3. 542-55, no. 14. For the recensions and a stemma of MSS, see C. Vogel, 'La *Descriptio ecclesiae Lateranensis* du diacre Jean', in : *Mélanges en l'honneur de Monseigneur Michel Andrieu* (Strasbourg, 1956), p. 457-76.

Christ's sandals in which he trod the Holy Land. There were relics of Holy Week – a loaf, and thirteen beans, from the Last Supper; the reed and the sponge of the Passion. And there was a plethora of the wood and the rock of the Holy Land. There was wood from Christ's cradle and from the sycamore tree which Zacchaeus climbed; there was more wood of the holy cross and also of the holy lance. Above all, there were pieces of rock – of the rock on which Jesus sat when he was baptized in the Jordan, of the rock of Mount Sion and of the mount of the Transfiguration, of the rock of Gethsemane, of the rock where Christ was tried and scourged and of Calvary, of the holy sepulchre, and so forth.

No one who trod the Lateran palace, whether it was the pope who alone could officiate liturgically at the main altar in the chapel of St Lawrence or whether it was the least pilgrim who came (in the words of the *Descriptio*) to pray to Christ 'for the peace of holy church, for the remission of all sins, to win the glory of the everlasting vision of God, and for the society of the citizens above and of the holy souls'[16], could well fail to be mindful of the Holy Land and of Jerusalem. The relics of these places which Constantine transmitted to the Lateran from the treasure that Helena brought to him were no museum pieces, but pledges of divine power derived from the places where Christianity began. Students of how the Crusading mentality was formed should not overlook how, in the Lateran palace and thanks to Constantine and his mother, the popes lived in the midst of relics of the Holy Land and of Jerusalem. They were an ever-present and a potent reality.

In one particularly noteworthy respect, the memory of Constantine was strong in the genesis of the First Crusade. During Urban II's travels in France of 1095-6, he dedicated a number of churches. A comparison between the relics that he used and the relic-lists of the *Descriptio* suggest that he had brought relics from the Lateran treasure, with relics of the true cross among them[17]. His dedications to the holy cross had Constantinian overtones. In February 1096, for example, he dedicated the matutinal altar of the abbey of la Trinité at Vendôme in honour of the most victorious cross (*in honore victoriossimae crucis*)[18]. In March, he dedicated the new abbey church at Marmoutier, near Tours, and its primary dedication was to the holy cross. The principal relic that he assigned to the so-called Dominical altar was a fragment of the most

---

[16] Georgi, *De liturgia*, p. 542.

[17] For details, see Cowdrey, 'Pope Urban II and the Idea of Crusade', *Studi medievali*, 3rd ser., 36 (1995), 721-42, esp. 737-42.

[18] *Ouvrages posthumes de D. Jean Mabillon et de D. Thierri Ruinart*, ed. V. Thuillier, 3 vols (Paris, 1724), 3. 386, cf. p. 245.

victorious cross (*particula ... victoriosissimae crucis Christi*)[19]. The manifest allusion to Constantine's vision of victory is paralleled in a charter of the abbey of Saint-Maixent, near Poitiers, which declared that, while Urban was keeping Easter at Saintes, the sign of the cross was seen in the sky[20]. The theme of Constantine's victorious cross helped with the recruiting of knights for the expedition to the east. The cross that they sewed on their clothing was the banner (*vexillum*) of the holy cross, evidently referring to the labarum of Constantine. Thus, during Urban's stay at Marmoutier, many knights in Urban's presence sewed upon their garments the banner of the holy cross (*sancte crucis vexillum*); among them was Count Hugh of Chaumont-Amboise, who was a benefactor of Marmoutier[21]. Such evidence lends colour to Ekkehard of Aura's statement about the Crusading host which captured Jerusalem, that 'this truly cross-bearing army displayed upon its garments the sign of cross in token of death, believing that, according to the vision long ago revealed to Constantine the Great, the army would triumph in this sign over the enemies of the cross of Christ'[22].

The traditions about Constantine which gathered about the Lateran and the relics, especially those of the holy cross, for which it was believed to be indebted to him, seem to have added authority to Urban as he progressed through France and to have contributed to the response that he evoked. The prominence of relics of the Holy Land and of Jerusalem in the Lateran treasuries may help to explain the centrality of Jerusalem in Urban's alleged perspective when, in Lent 1096, according to Count Fulk *le Réchin*, he came to Anjou 'and urged its people to go to Jerusalem and attack the gentile peoples who had seized that city and all the lands of the Christians up to Constantinople'[23]. Jerusalem came first and centrally; then followed the other Christian lands, up to Constantinople.

So far, our concern has been with matters which, on a well established and continuing basis, prepared the minds of the reform

[19] 'Textus de dedicatione ecclesiae huius sancti Maioris nostri monasterii', in : *Ouvrages posthumes*, 3. 397-90.
[20] See the charter in : *Analecta juris pontificii*, x^e sér. (Rome, 1869), no. 93, col. 551.
[21] *Ouvrages posthumes*, 3. 390-1; *Gesta Ambaziensium dominorum*, in : *Chroniques des comtes d'Anjou et des seigneurs d'Amboise*, edd. L. Halphen and R. Poupardin (Paris, 1913), p. 100-1.
[22] *Ekkehardi Chronica*, a. 1099, in : *Frutolfi et Ekkehardi Chronica necnon Anonymi Chronica imperatorum*, edd. F.-J. Schmale and I. Schmale-Ott (Darmstadt, 1972), p. 138.
[23] *Fragmentum historiae Andegavensis*, in : *Chronique des comtes d'Anjou*, 2. 330.

popes to call forth the Crusade : the papal recognition of Constantinople as a daughter with whose tribulations Rome, as mother, should be duly concerned; the papal estimate of Constantine as the most religious emperor who at Constantinople, but more still at Rome, did right by the church and by St Peter and, in particular, endowed the Roman church with relics of the holy cross, of the Holy Land, and of Jerusalem which made them palpably part of the papal environment. My other two ways in which concerns of the reform popes led to the Crusade have to do with, not standing, but developing and dynamic papal concerns. Let us consider next the burning issue of what authority upon earth should sovereignly provide for peace and order in Christian societies. The test case is Germany, and I should like to suggest that German affairs demand more consideration with regard to the origins of the Crusade that they have sometimes received. For they posed a key question – that of by whom, and in what ways, the peace that God purposed should be promoted upon earth. To that question, Urban's success in preaching the Crusade at Clermont was the papacy's decisive answer.

We may begin in the middle of things – in the Germany of the late 1070s and early 1080s, with the three-sided struggle of the partisans of pope, king, and princes which brought with it the devastation and miseries attendant upon all civil wars[24]. After Gregory's freeing Henry IV of Germany from excommunication at Canossa in January 1077 and the princes' election of Duke Rudolf of Swabia as anti-king at Forchheim in the following March, Gregory set himself to be arbiter and peacemaker. He hoped to intervene in Germany personally, but if not by means of legates who represented his authority. His preferred forum was an assembly of the whole of the German kingdom. Peace should be established, if possible by way of general concord and agreement, but if not by determining which of the rival kings was favoured by divine righteousness (*iustitia* – God's all-disposing power in action). Gregory thus sought to end the *lis et perturbatio regni*; for he grieved that Germany was being wasted and destroyed by fire, slaughter, and rapine, and he feared that its ills would overflow to the limits of Christendom. The remedy was that the pope should promote and uphold peace, while

---

[24] For the threefold character of the German struggle, see esp. I.S. Robinson, 'Pope Gregory VII, the Princes and the *Pactum*', *English Historical Review*, 94 (1979), 721-56; K. Leyser, 'The Crisis of Medieval Germany', *Proceedings of the British Academy*, 69 (1983), 409-43, repr. *ibid.*, *Communications and Power in Medieval Europe : The Gregorian Revolution and Beyond* (London and Rio Grande, 1994), p. 21-49.

the king should act in obedience to him as not its source but its executor[25].

In Germany, Gregory's bid thus to be the bringer of peace excited challenge. Some of it was virulent, as when in 1080 Henry IV, having been again excommunicated and deposed by Gregory at his Lent synod, held a synod of his own at Mainz as a step towards his synod of Brixen in June at which he decided upon the supersession of Gregory by a new pope. After the synod of Mainz, a number of bishops wrote down their impressions of Gregory. Here, for example, are some words of Bishop Huzmann of Speyer :

> Like all the princes of the realm I deeply bewail the disturbance of the kingdom (*perturbatio regni*), the destruction of the king's power, and, not less, the ruinous condition of the church. At Mainz, therefore, all of us were determined that the disturbance of the kingdom should be stilled and the king's power restored, and that we should help holy mother church so that she did not suffer shipwreck. We could not see how this might possibly be done, unless the head of the poisonous serpent [by which he meant Gregory] were wholly cut off, by whose poisoned breath these ills have hitherto been fanned. While the cause remains, how can a stop be put to the effects? All present at Mainz accordingly decreed that Hildebrand [that is, Gregory, unpoped by the use of his pre-papal name], the crafty invader of the apostolic see, should by God's help be totally repudiated. Let another, more worthy than he, be elected to the apostolic see, who will gather what has been scattered and heal what has been broken, and who, as a good shepherd, will foster, not discord and wars, but peace[26].

Whereas Gregory had sought to remedy the *perturbatio regni*, for Bishop Huzmann he was the author of it. Nevertheless, Huzmann looked for another pope who would foster, not discord and wars, but peace, thereby restoring Christian society.

Another challenge which began in Gregory's lifetime was more substantial than was Huzmann's. From the early 1080s, the kind of self-help against violence that, a century or so earlier, had manifested itself in first southern and then northern France in the Peace and the Truce of God, was attempted in Germany[27]. It

---

[25] The following among Gregory's letters are particularly relevant : *Reg.* 4. 23-4, p. 334-8, 5. 7, p. 356-8, 5. 14*a* (6), p. 370-1, 5. 15, p. 374-6; *Epp. vag.* 25, p. 64-7, 27, p. 70-3, 31, p. 82-3. For further discussion, see H.E.J. Cowdrey, 'The Papacy and the Origins of Crusading', *Medieval History*, 1 (1991), 48-60.

[26] *Udalrici Codex*, no. 60, cf. nos 61-2, in : *Monumenta Bambergensia*, Bibliotheca rerum Germanicarum, ed. P. Jaffé, 5 (Berlin, 1869), p. 126-30.

[27] For the German peaces and for further literature, see E. Wadle, 'Heinrich IV. und die deutsche Friedensbewegung', in : *Investiturstreit und Reichsverfassung*, ed. J. Fleckenstein (Sigmaringen, 1973), p. 141-73.

emerged in both Henrician and Gregorian circles. Some early examples are the peace instituted at Cologne in 1083 by Henry's supporter Archbishop Siegwin. It was renewed in 1085 at Mainz in Henry's presence by a synod of imperialist bishops[28]. On the Gregorian side, in the same year the *fideles domini papae* established a similar peace in Saxony[29]. In the mid-1090s, German peaces were increasingly formulated under lay rather than episcopal auspices, and to benefit temporal *provinciae*[30]. In due course, the king himself became directly responsible. As early as 1079, this had been foreshadowed at Gregory's Lent synod when Henry IV's envoy spoke of the king's sending other envoys 'to make peace between his kingly and your priestly authority (*ad componendam pacem inter ipsius regnum et sacerdotium vestrum*)'[31]. It was a challenge to Gregory's view that, in establishing peace in whatever social context, the *regnum* should be the obedient instrument of the *sacerdotium*; for Henry, each had its separate and comparable standing and mode of acting. From the late 1070s, Henry began to show in Germany that he had mastered his *métier de roi*. This was above all proven when, in 1103, the most important peace that was established during his long reign was the peace that he himself proclaimed at Mainz for his whole kingdon. This is how it was described :

> In 1103, the Emperor Henry established a peace at Mainz by his own hand, and the archbishops and bishops confirmed it by their hands. The king's son swore to it, as did the leading men of the whole kingdom – dukes, marquises, counts, and many others. Dukes Welf, Bertold, and Frederick [of Bavaria, Zähringen, and Swabia] swore the same peace until Pentecost and for four years thereafter : they swore, I say peace to churches, to clergy, monks, and laity – to merchants, to women lest they be seized by force, and to Jews[32].

Its impact may best be judged from the anonymous Life of Henry, written soon after his death. Its appraisal of the peace represented Henry as the hope of a Germany exhausted by decades of feuds and civil war : at last it was offered peace by a king who, unlike the pope, was at hand, who commanded sanctions, and who had an impressive array of ecclesiastical and lay princes at his side[33].

---

[28] *MGH Const.* 1, nos 424-5, p. 662-8; *Frutolfi Chronica, a.* 1085, in : *Frutolfi et Ekkehardi Chronica*, p. 98-9.

[29] Bernold, *Chron. a.* 1085, p. 440; the *Pax Dei incerta* : *MGH Const.* 1, no. 426, p. 608-9, may date from this occasion.

[30] Bernold, *Chron. a.* 1093, p. 458; *MGH Const.* 1. nos 427, 429, p. 609-10, 611-13.

[31] *MGH Const.* 1, no. 388, p. 512.

[32] *MGH Const.* 1, no. 74, p. 125-6.

[33] *Vita Heinrici IV imperatoris*, 8, in; *Quellen zur Geschichte Kaiser Heinrichs IV.*, edd. F.-J. Schmale and I. Schmale-Ott (Darmstadt, 1963), p. 438-40; cf. the

Three further features of the German peaces have been noticed by historians as indicating advances in legal remedies for violence. First, they prescribed strict limits for the feud as a means of vindicating wrongs; they thereby increased the role of rulers, including lay ones, in providing for peace. Secondly, they extended the range of capital and corporal punishments rather than of financial compositions, often doing this without regard to social rank or condition; they thus accentuated the criminal nature of violent acts and the duty of their public prosecution. Thirdly, they increased the part of communities in the guaranteeing and imposing of peace[34].

Urban preached his sermon at Clermont a little more than seven years before Henry IV issued his peace at Mainz, and therefore while these developments were in mid-course. He was able, in effect, to pre-empt Henry by drawing upon them to exhibit the papacy, not the empire, as the guiding force in the order and direction of western society. One may recall that, during the winter of 1084-5, as Cardinal Odo of Ostia he had travelled widely in Germany to rally Gregory VII's supporters there[35]. At Clermont, his concern with the peace and the truce of God is established by the conciliar canons[36]. The theme of peace was prominent in early twelfth-century versions of his preaching[37]. Like Gregory VII before him, he was concerned to vindicate papal leadership in the securing of peace and order in human society; going beyond Gregory, he was seen to owe a debt to current forms of peace legislation[38]. The peace for which Huzmann of Speyer had longed would, indeed, be fostered by a pope – and not by a Henrician anti-pope but by a successor of Gregory.

---

claim at the end of the record of the Mainz peace : '*Hoc iuramento utuntur amici regis pro scuto, inimicis vero nequaquam prodest'*.

[34] For the three points, see Wadle, *Heinrich IV. und die Friedensbewegung*, p. 162-4; cf. H.E.J. Cowdrey, 'Canon Law and the First Crusade', in : *The Horns of Hattin*, ed. B.J. Kedar (Jerusalem and London, 1992), p. 41-8, esp. 45-6. For illustrations of the three features, see : (1) *Pax Sigiwini*, cap. 12, p. 605; (2) *Pax Dei incerta*, caps 2-3, p. 608; (3) *Pax Alsatiensis*, Prol., p. 612; as well as the *Iuramentum* of the *Pax Moguntina* (1103), p. 125-6. (Page references are to *MGH Const.* 1.).

[35] For Odo in Germany, see A. Becker, *Papst Urban II. (1088-1099)*, MGH *Schriften*, 19/1-3 (Stuttgart, 1964), 1. 62-77.

[36] *The Councils of Urban II*, 1 : *Decreta Claromontensia*, ed. R. Somerville, *Annuarium Historiae Conciliorum*, suppl. 1 (Amsterdam, 1972), p. 143; see also p. 73-4, 94, 104-6, 108, 116, 124.

[37] D.C. Munro, 'The Speech of Pope Urban II at Clermont, 1095', *American Historical Review*, 11 (1906), 231-42, esp. p. 239-40.

[38] Urban had already legislated for the truce of God at the councils of Melfi (1089) and Troia (1093) : *Sacrorum conciliorum nova et amplissima collectio*, ed. J.D. Mansi, 31 vols (Florence and Venice, 1759-98), 20. 724-5, 790.

The presentation of Urban's preaching by the chronicler Fulcher of Chartres is particularly suggestive[39]. Fulcher was probably, but not certainly at Clermont. With due safeguards, he may be taken as indicating the impression that Urban made upon some who were close to his preaching, and as providing an early twelfth-century reconstruction of how he could be envisaged as drawing upon peace legislation that was beginning to criminalize human violence.

Fulcher represented Urban as giving two addresses. He directed the first especially to the bishops. Fulcher utilized the canons of the council to present Urban as promoting the peace of God in the west. He specified the acts of violence that were endemic, and he urged the bishops to be duly prompt to avenge them :

> Whoever has seized a bishop, let him be anathema. Whoever has seized monks, priests, nuns, and their servants, or pilgrims and traders, and despoiled them, let him be anathema. Let thieves and burners of houses, and their accomplices, be banished from the church and excommunicated. ... Perhaps owing to your own weakness in bringing to justice (*iustificatio*), scarcely anyone dares to travel on the road in safety for fear of seizure by robbers in the day or by thieves in the night.

Urban's second address was addressed to the laity, as well. His message was that those who had hitherto violated peace should redirect their energies against the Seljuks :

> Let those who in past times have been accustomed to spread private war so vilely among the faithful now advance against the infidels in a battle that should already have begun and that should end in triumph. Let those who formerly were brigands now become soldiers of Christ, those who once waged war against their brothers and blood-relatives now fight lawfully against the barbarians, those who have hitherto been mercenaries for a few coins now win eternal rewards.

Laudable warfare in the east should take the place of rapine in the west. But Urban's call was more than one merely to export violence. In lands that were also Christian, the Turks had perpetrated crimes of violence that cried out to be avenged. 'They have seized more and more of the lands of the Christians, ... have killed and captured many people, have destroyed churches, and have devastated the kingdom of God'. The whole Christian community must be mobilized to resist :

---

[39] *Fulcheri Carnotensis Historia Hierosolymitana (1095-1127)*, 1. 2-3, ed H. Hagenmeyer (Heidelberg, 1913), p. 123-38.

Wherefore I – no, not I but the Lord, exhort you as Christ's heralds insistently to urge men of all ranks whatsoever, knights as well as footsoldiers, rich and poor, to hasten to extirpate this vile race from the lands of our people (*de regionibus nostrorum*).

According to Fulcher, Urban described eastern Christians as 'our people'. Behind his summons lay the long-standing papal sense that the Roman church had a duty of maternal care for the eastern church which became the greater when Constantinople was under threat. The summons was also a decisive event in the long western quest for peace, especially in Germany and France, which was pursued as part of the contest between *regnum* and *sacerdotium* – between royal power and papal authority, about which was the source of peace and well-being in western society. By the response that he elicited, both in France and in Germany[40], Urban turned this contest decisively in the papacy's favour, despite the advantage that Henry IV could still draw in 1103.

The reform papacy also prepared for the emergence of the Crusade in more directly spiritual ways. I take as my fourth topic the concern with the practice of penance which led up to the most famous canon of the council of Clermont : 'Whoever shall set out to Jerusalem for devotion alone, not for the gaining of honour or money, to free the church of God, let that journey be reckoned to him for all penance'[41]. Earlier papal documents shed some light upon this ruling. In a familiar fragment, Pope Alexander II instructed the clergy of Volterra about the spiritual preparation of those intending to go to Spain – surely in order to fight the Saracens. All were duly to confess their sins to a bishop or other spiritual father and, lest the devil accuse them of impenitence (it should doubtless be understood, in the event of their being killed), a graded penance (*modus penitentiae*) should be imposed. But then, by the authority of Peter and St Paul, Alexander both relieved them from their penance and remitted their sins[42]. Whereas Alexander freed warriors from penances freshly imposed in prospect of a dangerous campaign, Urban in 1095 envisaged long-accumulated penances; but in either case, the reference was to the expunging of penances specifically imposed in respect of specific sins.

---

[40] For the response in Germany, see A.V. Murray, *Questions of Nationality in the First Crusade*, in *Medieval History*, 1 (1991), 61-73.

[41] *The Councils of Urban II*, ed. Somerville, p. 74 : *Quicumque pro sola devotione, non pro honoris vel pecunie adeptione, ad liberandam ecclesiam Dei Hierusalem profectus fuerit, iter illud pro omni penitentia ei reputetur.*

[42] S. Loewenfeld, *Epistolae pontificum Romanorum ineditae* (Leipzig, 1885), no. 82, p. 43.

There is another, less familiar document which illustrates the nature of the penances that the popes expunged, as well as other facets of the background to the Crusade[43]. In 1071, Peter Raymundi, son of Count Raymond Berengar I of Barcelona, murdered his step-mother, Almodis of la Perche. Early in his pontificate, Pope Gregory VII ordered the cardinals of the Roman church, by which he probably meant cardinal-bishops with senior urban clergy of Rome, to award an appropriate penance. They imposed twenty-four years of penance, for twelve of which Peter would be outside the church, without benefit of the kiss of peace or (save in the hour of death) of communion. They prescribed a regime, seemingly put together from penitential impositions customary at Rome, of rigorous fasts, abstinence, prayers, and vigils. Furthermore, he might not carry weapons, unless there were a special need to defend himself against enemies or to ride to battle against the Saracens (evidence of the Roman clergy's awareness of warfare against Moslems)[44]. When his father's wrath had died down, he was to embark upon a time of 'exile' in Jerusalem (evidence for another aspect of the Roman clergy's awareness of Jerusalem and of the anomaly that it was in pagan hands)[45].

But the most striking feature of Peter's penance is its burdensomeness; an eleventh-century penance was more than an Our Father and a couple of Hail Marys[46]. Not that Peter's penance was considered severe : to murder one's step-mother is, no doubt, an exceptionally grave sin which must attract a heavy penance; yet the cardinals claimed to be acting mildly (*magis misericorditer quam canonico rigore*), and there was also provision for the Roman pontiff to temper their provisions if Peter was conscientious in their fulfilment (*secundum fructum digne satisfactionis*). But it was a heavy burden that Peter bore. With it in mind, one can appreciate the appeal of Alexander II, when he ordered men to shoulder penances only that they might be removed from those who went on

[43] P.F. Kehr, *Das Papsttum und der katalanische Prinzipat bis zur Vereinigung mit Aragon*, in *Abhandlungen der preußischen Akademie der Wissenschaften, philosophisch-historische Klasse* (Berlin, 1926), no. 7, p. 80-1.

[44] 'Arma militaria nullo modo portare debebit, nisi forte se ab hostibus defendendo aut contra Sarracenos in prelium equitando'.

[45] 'Exilium quippe Ierusolimitanum, postquam placato patre in terra nativitatis sue secure manserit, arripiendum precepimus'.

[46] For an example of Urban II's recognition of the severity of penances to sinners' families as well as to themselves especially when they included a period of exile, and of his preparedness to mitigate them, see his letter to Archbishop William of Rouen in Loewenfeld, *Epistolae pontificorum Romanorum*, no. 132. p. 64.

a Spanish campaign. And how much more powerful must have been Urban's appeal at Clermont, when he raised the whole burden of penance from those whom he directed to Jerusalem, not as a place of exile, but as the goal in the noble work of freeing it militarily. With Peter's regime in mind, it is superfluous to introduce the notion of indulgence into Urban's thinking at Clermont; it sufficed that, like Alexander II before him, he should simply relieve the sheer burden of contemporary penances like Peter Raymundi's[47].

Peter Raymundi's penance may serve as the starting-point for another line of thought about the reform papacy's spiritual preparation for the Crusade. His penance was cumbersome, incoherent, and also rather mechanical. It is not surprising that one of Gregory VII's main concerns in his bid at his Roman synods, especially those of November 1078 and March 1080, to effect the moral re-armament of Latin Christendom, was to order and direct the system of penance. He was concerned to establish the difference between true and false penances. In 1078, his criterion was simple and based upon current penitential tariffs : false penances were those not duly imposed according to the gravity of the offence (*pro qualitate criminum*). Gregory attempted no definition of true penances. To the knight or merchant or steward whose daily business could not be engaged in without sin but who also fell into major offence, he could offer true penance only if he also effectively suspended his avocation. Lest such a one should despair, Gregory could offer only the provisional advice (*interim*) that he should do some good deeds so that God might enlighten his heart towards penitence[48]. It was an unsatisfactory canon which Gregory evidently intended to reconsider.

A letter of November 1079 to the clergy and people of Brittany suggests that, by a year later, he had begun to think how best to deal radically with what he called the ingrained custom of false penitence. He offered no such definition of false penances as he gave in 1078, but he clearly had in mind penances that were either lightly regarded or ignored. He turned his attention to 'unfruitful' penance, which he described as penance for a major sin which, because the penance was not taken seriously, left a man involved in the same sin or in some other which was about as bad. This was pretence, not penitence; Gregory took the decisive step, in principle, of breaking the parameters of the current penitential system and insisting upon total amendment of life :

---

[47] In derogation of my earlier opinion to the contrary in H.E.J. Cowdrey, *The Cluniacs and the Gregorian Reform* (Oxford, 1970), p. 126, n. 2.
[48] *Reg.* 6. 5*b*, 19 Nov. 1078, p. 401, 404.

Whoever would be worthily penitent must return to the beginning of faith. He must be careful vigilantly to keep what he promised in baptism : to renounce the devil and all his pomps, and to believe in God by discerning what is right about him and by keeping his commandments[49].

Following this line of thought, Gregory enacted a decree at his Lent synod of 1080 which had an altogether new theological sophistication, moral force, and clarity of expression. In a text which reads like a papal sermon, Gregory dismissed succinctly the false penance that men must avoid : as false baptism does not wash away original sin, so after baptism false penance does not erase a sin that has been committed. As regards true penance, the decree treated heinous sins like murder and perjury apart from the 'vocational' sins of merchants, warriors, and officials. It was upon heinous sins that the decree concentrated. It first demanded conversion : let each man turn to God. It then required that a man should so turn to God as to abandon all his iniquities and henceforth to continue in the fruits of good works. As the climax of his statement, Gregory cited the Lord's word by the prophet Ezekiel : 'If the unrighteous shall be converted from all his sins and shall keep the whole of my commandments, he shall surely die and not live' (cf. Ezek. 18 : 21). In what reads like an explanatory gloss rather than Gregory's own words, it is affirmed that warriors, merchants, and officials who continue in sinful ways cannot be held to have turned to God or to have done true penance. The decree as a whole reads as a warning that no man who deliberately remained in sins of any kind, whether by committing some grave offence like Peter Raymundi's, or whether in the course of of his avocation as warrior, merchant or official, or whether by regarding sins and penances with levity, could be deemed to have performed true penance[50].

There should be no mistaking the novelty, in terms of eleventh-century penitential practice, of what Gregory was now saying. True penance, true penitence, called for the complete inner conversion of a man's whole life – the life of the layman no less than the monk. Gregory was foreshadowing the moral theology of the twelfth and thirteenth centuries.

But our concern is with November 1095. When he became pope, Urban II professed a total commitment to follow in Gregory's footsteps : 'Believe about me', he wrote, 'just as about the blessed Gregory. I want to follow wholly in his footsteps. ... Whatever he

---

[49] *Reg.* 7. 10, 25 Nov. 1079, p. 471-2.
[50] *Reg.* 7. 14a, 7 Mar. 1080, p. 481-2.

deemed right and catholic, I affirm and approve'[51]. There are indications that, at the council of Clermont, this was the case as regards penance. According to one twelfth-century memorandum of its canons, Urban, too, insisted upon the necessity of inner conversion :

> Penance profits nothing save where there is compunction of heart. Therefore medicine cannot be given save to him who is penitent with his whole heart[52].

Other records confirm the testimony of this memorandum that Urban like Gregory insisted that penance for one sin does not profit unless there be penitence for all sins[53].

The Crusading canon of Clermont, too, may be set in the light of the development of thought that Gregory initiated in 1080. There is certainly a verbal similarity : Urban's requirement that a man should not set out 'pro *honoris* vel *pecunie* adeptione' uses language that Gregory used of the sin of perjury – 'periurii pro cupiditate *honoris* aut *pecunie* facti'. In two respects Urban seems in substance to have followed Gregory's line of thinking. First, Urban's requirement that a man set out for devotion alone (*pro sola devotione*) or, as he urged the citizens of Bologna in a letter dated 19 September 1096 which echoed the Crusading canon of Clermont, 'for the salvation of their soul alone and for the liberation of the church (*pro sola animae suae salute et ecclesiae liberatione*)'[54],

---

[51] *Ep.* 1, *PL* 151. 283.

[52] *The Councils of Urban II*, ed. Somerville, p. 115 : '*Nil igitur valet penitentia nisi ubi est cordis compunctio. Non ergo potest dari medicina nisi toto corde penitenti. Item si penitentiam agis de homicidio et in adulterio perseveras nil tibi prodest, nec salutis hoc modo potes invenire consilium. Non enim ex parte Dei et ex parte diaboli esse potes. Totum erit aut huius aut illius, Si ergo consilium queris de uno quiesce de ceteris; cum non sufficiat abstinere a malo nisi quod bonum est fiat : quiesce a malo et fac bonum* (cf. Ps. 33 (Vg.) : 14-15). *Et unde peccasti te retrahe : si per arma armorum abstine. Nam nec aliter veraciter est penitentia nec quis aliter consilium tibi potest prestare. Moneri tamen potes ut elemosinam facias quatinus veram invenias penitentiam*'. (This passage comes from Oxford, Bodleian Library, MS Selden Supra 90, fos 25ᵛ-27ʳ, in which the canons are presented as an allocution by Urban. The passage suggests the influence of both Gregory's canons).

[53] *The Councils of Urban II*, ed. Somerville, p. 79.

[54] H. Hagenmeyer, *Die Kreuzzugsbriefe aus den Jahren 1088-1100* (Innsbruck, 1901), p. 137-8 : '*... sciatis autem eis omnibus, qui illuc [to Jerusalem] non terreni commodi cupiditate sed pro sola animae suae salute et ecclesiae liberatione profecti fuerint, paenitentiam totam peccatorum, de quibus veram et perfectam confessionem fecerint, per omnipotentis Dei misericordiam et ecclesiae catholicae preces ... dimittimus, quoniam res et personas suas pro Dei et proximi caritate exposuerunt*'.

suggests the singleness of mind in pursuit of truth and salvation that Gregory regarded as the way of true penitence. Secondly, Urban's provision at Clermont that the journey to Jerusalem should be reckoned 'for all penance', when taken with his expansion of it in the letter to the Bolognese that there would be remission of all penance for sins of which they had made 'true and full confession (*veram et perfectam confessionem*)', is reminiscent of Gregory's insistence that men should abandon all their sins. In such respects, Urban's thinking at Clermont seems to have grown from Gregory's attempt of 1080 to revitalize the practice of penance, not least among the laity. A military expedition to Jerusalem which, subject to a right disposition in those who took part, would be reckoned for all penance was well calculated to appeal to knights who, in the words of contemporary charters, sought remission of their sins and purposed to save their souls[55]. Still more, it would appeal to those Gregorian-minded bishops and abbots upon whom Urban relied for the organization and success of his journey in France, and who were the willing agents of his purposes.

To sum up. After the battle of Manzikert, the reform papacy was impelled to respond to the afflictions of eastern Christians and to the predicament of Constantinople because it saw the church of Constantinople as the daughter of the church of Rome; Rome had a mother's duty to come to its rescue in its time of need. Its duty to respond was intensified by the prevailing appraisal of Constantine the Great as a model emperor and as the benefactor to whom it owed, among other things, the Lateran palace and its endowment of relics. These relics were a daily reminder of Jerusalem and of the saving events there which made its being in heathen hands an especial scandal among the misfortunes of the eastern churches. The holy cross, with its overtones of Constantine's assurance of victory in battle, was a powerful symbol in recruiting for and in warranting warfare rightly undertaken. In the conflict between *sacerdotium* and *regnum*, the imperial associations that, through Constantine's withdrawal to the east, gathered about the pope in the west, led the pope to claim a leadership in promoting peace in the Christian west and in extending it to the Christian east. This involved diverting the energies of the military classes to a warfare which was envisaged as centring upon Jerusalem and as extending to the walls of Constantinople. If it was for the pope thus to promote peace and order among Christians, so, by a duty that complemented

---

[55] See the examples cited by H.E.J. Cowdrey, *Cluny and the First Crusade*, in *Revue Bénédictine*, 83, 1973, p. 285-311, repr. *ibid. Popes, Monks and Crusaders* (London, 1984), no. XV, at p. 303.

this role, he took upon himself the task of so overhauling the system of penance as to stimulate the inner conversion of individual Christians from all acts of sin to following the commandments of God. Those who were directed to Jerusalem 'for devotion alone' appear to have been given to understand that their penances were set aside on account of a total conversion.

Such, it may be suggested, was the legacy from earlier reform popes, and especially Gregory VII, upon which Urban II drew at Clermont. The four subjects that have been discussed did not constitute the whole of the papacy's contribution in preparing for the Crusade; it also included such often-discussed matters as the changed moral evaluation of warfare and the concept of a *militia sancti Petri*. They are certainly not a full survey of the origins of the Crusade, the deeper roots of which lay, not at Rome, but more generally in western society[56]. But, considered together, they suggest a conclusion that I should like to draw. Especially through the part that Gregory VII plaved in revising papal ideas about penance, Urban's preaching at Clermont was probably able to derive much of its force from his anticipation of developments that historians have associated with St Bernard and the Second Crusade. The First Crusade as Urban proclaimed was, no less than the Second, intended both to free the east from the heathen and to free from sin the soul of the individual Crusader[57]. As Gregory VII's association in 1080 of inner conversion with true penance indicates, the time was ripe for such a combination of ideas. Gregory's final decree about penance helps to explain how the creative genius of Urban II was able to marshal the forces of the west for the novelty of an armed pilgrimage which would free the sepulchre of the Lord at Jerusalem and bring help to afflicted Christians from Jerusalem to Constantinople.

[56] See H.E.J. Cowdrey, *'The Genesis of the Crusades : the Springs of Western Ideas of Holy War'*, in *The Holy War*, ed. T.P. Murphy (Columbus, Ohio, 1976), p. 9-32, repr. *ibid.*, *Popes, Monks and Crusaders*, no. XIII.

[57] See H.E. Mayer, *The Crusades*, trans. J. Gillingham (2nd edn, Oxford, 1988), p. 96-7.

II

FROM THE PEACE OF GOD
TO THE FIRST CRUSADE[1]

In the days after he was elected pope in 1073, Gregory VII (1073-85) wrote to a number of powerful men, both clerical and lay, whose prayers and support he especially desired, in order to inform them personally of his elevation. It is ironic that, of the letters noted in Gregory's Register, the most paradigmatic is addressed to Archbishop Guibert of Ravenna; for by May 1085 when Gregory died at Salerno, Guibert had been enthroned in Rome as the anti-pope Clement III. To the formal notice of his election, Gregory added the personal assurance to Guibert that "we desire to join the Roman church and that over which by God's authorship you preside by such concord (*concordia*) and, so far as we shall be able saving their common honour, by such abounding charity (*caritas*), that in our own hearts as well the closest peace (*pax*) and entire love (*dilectio*) may be conjoined."[2]

The reason for citing these words of an eleventh-century pope is to draw attention to the Latin vocabulary that they embody. From classical times until the central middle ages, *pax* and *concordia*, often linked with each other, expressed two of the profoundest aspirations that were cherished for human societies. No visitor to Rome could fail to see, near the Colosseum, the temples of Peace and of Concord which had been built to enshrine these values in pagan Rome -Roman peace, as realised in the *pax Augusta* with its overtones of quiet at home and abroad which was guaranteed by strong and popular government, and Roman concord, as the harmony and agreement of the state or of bodies within the state. In the Latin Bible, the key-word *pax* found a new depth. It translated the Greek *eirēnē*, which in classical usage had betokened, negatively, an absence or termination of war; through the Septuagint, however, it had been filled out with the

---

1. The following abbreviations are used in the footnotes:
AQ   *Ausgewählte Quellen zur deutschen Geschichte des Mittelalters*
CCL   *Corpus Christianorum, series Latina*
Epp. vag.   *The Epistolae vagantes of Pope Gregory VII,* ed. and trans.H. E. J. Cowdrey   (Oxford, 1972)
MGH   *Monumenta Germaniae Historica*
__ Const.   __, *Constitutiones et acta publica*
__ Epp. sel. __, *Epistolae selectae*
__ SRG   __, *Scriptores rerum Germanicarum in usum scholarum separatim editi*
__ SS   __, *Scriptores*
Reg.   *Gregorii VII Registrum,* ed. E. Caspar, *MGH Epp. sel.* 2 (Berlin, 1920-4)
2. *Reg.* 1.3, 26 Apr. 1073, p. 6.

positive significance of the Hebrew *shalom*, as the total well-being, health, and strength of a community at one with itself. *Concordia* was not in the same way a key word of the Latin Bible. Yet it fitted well with the positive biblical idea of *pax*, and far into the middle ages few models of social order and motivation were more potent than that of the earliest church at Jerusalem in the Acts of the Apostles, 2: 44-47 and 4: 32-35, when amongst the multitude of believers there was *cor et anima una*, in effect, *concordia*. The Latin Bible associated with peace and concord the *caritas* and the *dilectio* of which Gregory VII wrote. For their part, the Latin fathers of the church combined the perspectives of imperial Rome with those of the Bible. In his *City of God*, for example, St Augustine of Hippo wrote of the peace of men as consisting in an ordered concord, while the peace of a city was an ordered concord of citizens in command and obedience (*pax hominum ordinata concordia, ... pax civitatis ordinata imperandi et oboediendi concordia civium*).[3] Such ideas underlay the capitularies and the political treatises of the Carolingian age. Thus, for Jonas of Orleans, it was the concern of kings to govern and rule the people of God with equity and justice, and to be zealous in fostering its peace and concord (*Regale ministerium est populum Dei gubernare et regere cum equitate et iustitia, ut pacem et concordiam habeat studere*).[4] The eleventh century did not come afresh to the problems of peace and social order; it was heir to a millennium of thought and endeavour. Its language, objects, and actions were influenced by its inheritance, and were in major respects a prolongation of it.

By way of preface, it may, therefore, be suggested that, from attempts to establish the peace of God at the beginning of the eleventh century to the First Crusade at its end, developments that had regard to the internal peace of Christian society should not be studied as a novel succession of discrete events which may or may not have affected each other. It must also be asked how different circumstances, problems, and persons provided further examples of an age-long search for the peace and concord of which Gregory wrote. In this paper, consideration will be given to four conjunctures of events which led from the peace of God to the Crusade, less by forming a causal sequence than by continuing an age-long quest for peace and concord. They contributed to establishing in Latin Christendom a framework of papal direction and of internal peace which was sufficient to enable Urban II successfully to preach the Crusade.

The first conjuncture that calls for comment is the attempts to establish the peace and truce of God which were made, mostly in Aquitaine but also in Burgundy and Northern France, beginning in the 970s and 980s until they lost momentum in the mid-1030s.[5] As a matter of definition, the peace was an attempt to protect from violence at all times the persons and goods of certain vulnerable social classes, such as clergy, monks,

---

3. *De civitate Dei*, 19.13, CCL 47-48, p. 679.
4. Reviron, *Les Idées politico-religieuses d'un évêque du IXe siècle: Jonas d'Orléans et son "De institutione regia"* (Paris, 1930), cap. 4, p. 145.
5. The fullest survey remains H. Hoffmann, *Gottesfriede und Treuga Dei*, Schriften der MGH 20 (Stuttgart, 1964). For a brief account, see H. E. J. Cowdrey, "The Peace and the Truce of God in the Eleventh Century", *Past and Present*, no. 46 (1970), 42-67, repr. idem, *Popes, Monks and Crusaders* (London, 1984), no. VII. A good recent collection of papers is *The Peace of God: Social Violence and Religious Response in France around the Year 1000*, edd. T. Head and R. Landes (Ithaca and London, 1992).

the poor, women, and travellers like pilgrims and merchants; while the truce sought to stop all violence at certain times. In practice, the peace and the truce came to be blended together. As proclaimed by church councils, the peace and the truce were intended to set moral as well as physical limits to violence. They diverted the bearing of arms towards ends that were acceptable to churchmen; they were also directed towards enforcing order as imposed by rulers both ecclesiastical and lay.

In a recent monograph on knightly piety, especially in the Limousin and Gascony, the English historian Marcus Bull has powerfully and successfully argued that there was no direct connection between early eleventh-century peaces in Aquitaine and the First Crusade.[6] His main points are as follows. First, the Aquitanian peaces were of limited duration: after the mid-1030s, and so two full human generations before Pope Urban II's sermon at Clermont, the peace went into steep decline. Secondly, even in its heyday in Aquitaine, peace arrangements were territorially uneven in their impact, many northern and western parts being little affected. Thirdly, after c.1035, the whole region remained violent and disordered, with little to suggest that a change of lay outlook had occurred that might have prepared even remotely for a response to the Crusade. Fourthly, the laity most involved in the peaces were not a broad knightly class, so much as a small group of great nobles, notably two dukes of Aquitaine, William V (995-1029) and William VI (1029-38), whose successors in the duchy did and perhaps could have done little to perpetuate their involvement. By substantiating these four points, Bull has ruled out a direct, linear connection between the early peace and truce of God and the Crusade, especially at the social level of the knightly classes.

Finally as regards the early peace and truce, it may be well to suggest a caveat and then to underline the last, and perhaps the most significant, of Bull's conclusions. The caveat concerns the all-too-well-established convention of referring to an early eleventh-century "Peace movement". In so far as this phrase suggests an analogy with peace movements, especially in the English-speaking world, during the twentieth-century cold war between the former Soviet Union and the West, it may be doubly misleading. Arguably, modern peace movements had an internal continuity, an organization, a regular time-table of events, and a singleness of immediate objective, which were not matched nearly a millennium earlier. Yet, despite their greater coherence, modern peace movements had no such deep roots in widely accepted religious and social values as did the peace assemblies of Aquitaine in the quest for peace and concord from classical to Carolingian times. If the Aquitanian assemblies lapsed, the underlying aspirations of which they were temporary expressions continued. Modern peace movements finally lost much of their *raison d'être* with the sudden end of the Cold War and the collapse of European Communism; the eleventh-century concern for peace was more able to revive in new forms, because it was nourished by a richer and more ancient soil. The portmanteau phrase "Peace movement" as applied to the eleventh century is misleading and would be best abandoned.

Bull's conclusion to be underlined is that, in Aquitaine, the laymen most involved in peace assemblies were a small group of nobles and especially the dukes themselves.

---

6. M. Bull, *Knightly Piety and the Lay Response to the First Crusade: the Limousin and Gascony, c.970-c.1130* (Oxford, 1993), esp. pp. 21-69, 283-7.

For their prominence foreshadowed a development by which, for the rest of the eleventh century and beyond, those who claimed to be the sources of peace and concord in human society were its most eminent lay and ecclesiastical figures, who acted sometimes in concert but sometimes in competition. As time passed, the peace of God tended to become the peace of counts, dukes, and kings, who sought by monopolizing it to augment their political authority and material power. But the claims of lay rulers were matched by the counter-claims of bishops and popes, especially popes of the reform papacy after 1046, to be the peace-givers and public arbiters of Christian society. Because of this process, the way from the Aquitanian peace of God to the First Crusade must first and foremost be followed at the highest levels of society.

Indeed, the second conjuncture that calls for attention is at the very highest level; it is the concern for peace in 1043-4, especially, of the Emperor Henry III of Germany (1039-56). His concern may not have been unrelated to the earlier peace assemblies in France and Burgundy: in 1043, he married the deeply religious Agnes of Poitou, daughter of Duke William V of Aquitaine who was chief among the nobles who had been involved in the peace there, and he was a friend of Abbot Odilo of Cluny (994-1048) who sponsored the peace of God in Burgundy.[7] At a synod in Constance held just before his marriage to Agnes, Henry ascended a pulpit and not only exhorted his people to peace but also, having himself forgiven all who had transgressed against him, he begged and compelled his subjects similarly to forgive each other. A year later, Abbot Berno of Reichenau wrote of this occasion in a letter to Henry that "justice and peace (*pax*) have proffered kisses of fraternal charity, when in the whole of your kingdom they have established such treaties of concord (*concordiae*) as have been unheard-of in all times past."[8]

In 1044, Henry won a great but bloody victory over the Hungarians on the River Raab. Immediately afterwards, he and his leading followers, barefoot and in penitential garb, returned thanks to God for their victory by prostrating themselves before a relic of the Holy Cross and forgiving each other their trespasses. Before long, Henry restored to his regality King Peter of Hungary, deposed in 1041, whose rival's army Henry had defeated, and he sponsored a solemn reconciliation between Peter and his people. Commenting upon this occasion, Abbot Berno of Reichenau rejoiced that Henry had both himself shown exemplary forgiveness and also had repeatedly recalled everyone to a unanimity of peace and concord (*in unanimitatem pacis et concordiae*).[9]

---

7. For a brief account of Henry III and peace, see G. Ladner, *Theologie und Politik vor dem Investiturstreit. Abendmahlstreit, Kirchenreform, Cluni und Heinrich III.* (new edn, Darmstadt, 1968), pp. 70-8; for further discussion, E. Steindorff, *Jahrbücher des deutschen Reiches unter Heinrich III.*, 2 vols (Leipzig, 1874-81), 1.185-7, 195-6, 205-10.

8. The principal sources are: Hermann of Reichenau, *Chronicon, a.* 1043, in: *Quellen des 9. und 11. Jahrhunderts zur Geschichte der Hamburgischen Kirche und des Reiches*, ed. W. Trillmich, AQ 11 (Darmstadt, 1961), p. 676; *Annales Sangallenses maiores, a.* 1043, *MGH SS* 1.85; *Die Briefe des Abtes Bern von Reichenau*, no. 27, ed. F.-J. Schmale (Stuttgart, 1961), pp. 56-64, esp. p. 57. For another act of mutual forgiveness between the king and his delinquent subjects, and amongst his subjects, during the Christmas court of 1043 at Trier, see Lampert of Hersfeld, *Annales, a.* 1044, edd. A. Schmidt and W. D. Fritz, AQ 13 (Berlin, n.d.), p. 44.

9. The principal sources are: *Annales Altahenses maiores, a.* 1044, ed. E. L. B. von Oefele, *MGH SRG* (Hanover, 1891), pp. 36-7; Hermann of Reichenau, *Chron. a.* 1044, pp. 676-9. The Niederaltaich Annals indicate that Henry made a further act of forgiveness in Rome *ante limina sancti Petri* during his visit of 1046-7: *a.* 1047, p. 44.

Too much should not be made of Henry's zeal for peace; warfare and feuds were endemic in Germany during his latter years, and after his death there followed the long minority of his son Henry IV (1056-1106) and, from 1073, the horrors of the Saxon wars. Yet the elder Henry registered both the claim and the duty of the highest rulers in Latin Christendom to be the source of peace and to seek for concord. Abbot Berno of Reichenau's letter to him illustrates how he renewed the vision that kings might, indeed, provide the peace and the concord that were the ancient and constantly reviving hopes of all grades of society.

The intervention of Henry III at Rome in 1046 led in due course to a further extension of the quest for peace. Its result was to revive in a reformed papacy a claim to leadership in human society which was facilitated by the civil wars in Germany. In 1073, the year in which the civil wars began, Gregory VII commenced his twelve-year pontificate. It may be regarded as the third conjuncture in the development from the peace of God to the First Crusade; for it is, perhaps, insufficiently recognized how deeply his dealings with the regions of Europe were coloured by the language and the aspirations that are associated with the peace of God.

His dealings with the French kingdom in the second half of 1074 provide a partial illustration. They represent the nadir of his relations with the Capetian king, Philip I (1060-1108), about whose shortcomings he wrote, first, to the French bishops, then to Count William of Poitou who was also Duke William VIII of Aquitaine (1058-86), and finally again to Archbishop Manasses I of Rheims.[10] He described Philip as not a king but a tyrant who was ruling his people *inutiliter*. The offences that Gregory described as being endemic, both through the king's unrestrained subjects and through his own misgovernment, were familiar as those against which the peace of God had been directed. Private warfare went on unchecked, and the result was slaughter and arson, rapine, perjury, sacrilege, incest, and mutual betrayal, and the capturing and torturing of even men's close families and neighbours. The unprotected whom the peace had been intended to protect —pilgrims and merchants, in particular— were suffering at the hands of the king and of powerful men. Gregory feared the spread of such evils from France to other lands. To seek the king's amendment or, if necessary, to impose the requisite sanctions, Gregory sought, first, a council of the French bishops, then pressure by right-minded magnates like the count of Poitou, and perhaps ultimately the intervention of papal legates. Gregory looked for peace to be kept by strong rulers who obeyed the admonitions of the apostolic see; such a ruler was Count Centullus IV of Béarn, whom Gregory acknowledged to have been a true Christian prince who was "a lover of righteousness, a defender of the poor, and a propagator of peace".[11] In France, Gregory settled for a *modus vivendi* with Philip that lasted throughout his pontificate. But he made clear that, when a king was ruling *inutiliter*—there were overtones of the year 751—the pope himself must seek means of providing for the peace of regions and of Christendom.

---

10. *Reg.* 2.5, to the archbishops and bishops of France, 10 Sept. 1074, pp. 129-33, 2.18, to Count William VI of Poitou, 13 Nov. 1074, pp. 150-1, 2.32, to Archbishop Manasses I of Rheims, 8 Dec. 1074, pp. 168-9.
    11. *Reg.* 6.20, to Count Centullus IV of Béarn, 25 Feb. 1079, pp. 431-2.

In Germany, matters were worse than in France. The civil wars were intensive and prolonged. In 1077, the kingdom itself became divided, when Gregory restored Henry IV to communion at Canossa and the princes elected Rudolf of Swabia at Forchheim to be anti-king. Throughout, Gregory wrote of the effects upon German society in the terms that he had used of French: as early as December 1073, he deplored discord and hostile factions which gave rise to homicides, arson, plunderings of churches and the poor, and of wretched devastation of the land; by 1080, he said that almost the whole German kingdom was given over to desolation.[12] Moreover, he repeatedly expressed such fears as he expressed about disasters in France: if the situation were neglected and got worse, it would produce injuries, dangers, disorder, and incalculable sources of woe, not only for the German people and kingdom, but right to the farthest limits of Christendom (*quoad fines christianitatis sunt*).[13] Already, in 1074, Gregory's horizons had been similarly stretched in connection with his so-called "Crusading" plan, to help Eastern Christians whom the Seljuk Turks were slaughtering like cattle and devastating their lands, while he believed that the Eastern churches were minded to renew their concord with the West.[14] The *lis et perturbatio regni* — the quarrel and disruption in Germany, too, was no "little local difficulty": it fortified Gregory in his view that his concern was with the peace and concord of the whole of Christendom.

To begin with in Germany, Gregory urged King Henry IV to accept an armistice with the Saxon insurgents until he could send from Rome envoys who might establish the causes of dissension and establish peace and concord.[15] After his legates of 1074 had restored Henry to communion, Gregory hoped, as he hoped for King Philip of France, that he might abandon his youthful follies and be guided to a better mind. By September 1075, Gregory looked with some confidence for peace and concord between himself and Henry; he signalled his willingness to consider his imperial coronation. He congratulated Henry upon his recent victory over the Saxons, rejoicing for the peace of the church while deploring the shedding of so much Christian blood.[16] But by the Lent synod of 1076, matters were wholly changed: Gregory pronounced Henry's deposition and excommunication.

The sequel is familiar: Gregory's restoration of a penitent Henry to communion but not to the kingship at Canossa in January 1077; the princes' election of Rudolf of Swabia to be anti-king at Forchheim in March 1077; the renewal of civil war with its attendant feuding, violence, and desolation; Gregory's second excommunication and deposition of Henry in March 1080 and his recognition of Rudolf as king; Rudolf's death in battle

---

12. *Reg.* 1.39, to the Saxon bishops and magnates, 20 Dec. 1073, p. 62, 3.4, to Archbishop Siegfried of Mainz, 3 Sept. 1075, p. 248, *Epp. vag.* no. 27, to the anti-king Rudolf and his supporters, (Mar./Apr. 1079), p. 70, *Reg.* 7.14a, record of the Lent synod, 7 Mar. 1080, p. 486, 9.29, to all the faithful, (summer, 1083), p. 613.

13. *Reg.* 4.23, to Gregory's legates in Germany, 31 May 1077, p. 335, 4.24, to all the faithful in Germany, 31 May 1077, p. 337, 5.7, to Archbishop Udo of Trier, 30 Sept. 1077, p. 358, 5.14a(6), record of the Lent synod, 27 Feb.-3 Mar. 1078, p. 370.

14. *Reg.* 1.18, to the Emperor Michael VII Ducas, 9 July 1073, pp. 29-30, 1.49, to all the faithful, 1 Mar. 1074, pp. 75-6, 2.31, to King Henry IV of Germany, 7 Dec. 1074, pp. 165-8, 2.37, to all the faithful, 16 Dec. 1074, pp. 172-3.

15. *Reg.* 1.39, p. 62.

16. *Reg.* 3.7, to King Henry IV, (early Sept. 1075), pp. 256-9.

in October. Throughout these vicissitudes, to bring peace to Germany was Gregory's major concern.[17] It meant, first, to establish who should be the rightful king. But it also involved seeking to establish concord among the princes, and to bring to an end the strife that afflicted the population.

To begin with, he wished to come to Germany himself and to hold an assembly; late in 1076, he set out, as he put it, "to make peace for the honour of God and the benefit of the holy church".[18] After Canossa, he still hoped to come,[19] but it never proved possible. So he called upon many well disposed persons and religious communities to entreat God that he would avert civil war and domestic ruin, and he directed legates whom he sent and also bishops to take counsel for the avoidance of slaughter, arson, and other perils of wars by seeking to decide between the rival kings and so establish peace.[20] Moreover, the *lis et pertubatio regni* became a major item on the agenda of Gregory's Lent and November synods at Rome; at these well attended occasions, too, he was to the fore as the authority who aspired to bring peace and concord to disordered societies.[21]

After Gregory renewed his sentence against Henry IV at his Lent synod of 1080, Henrician propaganda embroidered the theme that, far from seeking to remedy the *perturbatio regni*, Gregory had caused it. "Far and wide", ran Henry's manifesto of 1082 to the Romans, "he has led the world astray, and he has stained the church with the blood of its sons when he has made children rise up against their parents and parents against their children, and has armed brother against brother." Henry called for a public debate: *Fiat discussio in conspectu aecclesiae.*[22] Apparently in the summer of 1083, Gregory responded. First, he wrote to faithful Christians everywhere that, in some safe place and therefore not at Rome, he wished to hold a general synod to which clergy and laity, both his friends and his enemies, would come from all parts. At it, Gregory would drag into the open who was the cause and author of the ills that vexed the Christian religion. His letter said outright that it was Henry IV's breach of his promise of obedience that had caused so many evils—homicides, perjuries, sacrileges, acts of simony, and treacheries. Let all whom such calamities moved, or whom fear of God roused to seek peace and concord worthy of God, strive for a synod that would bring relief and strengthening to the head and whole body of the church.

Secondly, evidently a little later, an encyclical letter to the prelates of France and Germany summoned them to a November synod to take counsel about establishing the

---

17. *Reg.* 5.7, pp. 356-8.
18. *Reg.* 4.23, p. 335.
19. *Reg.* 4.24, p. 337.
20. *Reg.* 5.7, pp. 356-7.
21. See esp., for Lent 1078: *Reg.* 5.14*a*(6), pp. 370-1, 5.15, to all the faithful in Germany, 9 Mar. 1078, pp. 374-6, 5.16, to Archbishop Udo of Trier, 9 Mar. 1078, pp. 376-8, 6.1, to all the faithful in Germany, 1 July 1078, pp. 389-91; for Nov. 1078, 6.5*b*, pp. 400-1, 6.14, to Duke Welf IV of Bavaria, 30 Dec. 1078, pp. 418-19, *Epp. vag.* no. 25, to the supporters of both parties in Germany, (late Nov. 1078), pp. 64-7, no. 26, to the anti-king Rudolf and his followers, (late Feb. 1079), pp. 66-9; for Lent 1079, *Reg.* 6.17*a*(2-3), pp. 427-8.
22. *Epistolae Heinrici IV*, no. 17, ed. C. Erdmann, in: *Quellen zur Geschichte Kaiser Heinrichs IV.*, edd. F.-J. Schmale and others, *AQ* 12 (Berlin, 1963), pp. 76-83; see also the letters of German bishops in 1080: *Udalrici Codex*, nos 60-2, in: *Monumenta Bambergensia*, Bibliotheca rerum Germanicarum, ed. P. Jaffé, 5 (Berlin, 1869), pp. 126-30.

peace of God and healing the schism.[23] It was Gregory's final attempt to claim for himself as pope the making of peace and concord, wherever in Christendom it was needful. In the event, his November synod met at Rome and was thinly attended.[24] But his encyclical letter, in particular, gave publicity to a vigorous expression of his claim.

While Gregory was expressing himself in this way, a further conjuncture of events in Germany gave fresh life to the peace and the truce of God. Although the attempts in Aquitaine and Burgundy thus to deal with the problem of violence had lost their impetus there some fifty years earlier, the intervening decades had seen a number of similar endeavours elsewhere, especially in more northerly regions of France like Flanders and Normandy where comital or ducal power was relatively strong.[25] In 1082, a peace on broadly the French model was proclaimed at Liège, and so for the first time within the empire; it was followed by others at Cologne in 1083 and at Mainz in 1085.[26] These peaces were initiated, in a war-torn and war-weary Germany, by prelates who were concerned for their own ecclesiastical dioceses or provinces. The prelates concerned were Henricians by loyalty, but they were quickly imitated by their Saxon opponents. In 1084, an assembly at Goslar established a similar peace: *maximae treuvae inter fideles domini papae factae sunt*, wrote the chronicler Bernold, who added with some exaggeration that they were confirmed throughout almost all Germany.[27] The exaggeration suggests widespread concern for the establishment, under episcopal auspices, of regional peace agreements.

The peaces of the mid-1080s concerned Lorraine and Saxony. The years 1093-4 saw Pope Urban II's supporters promoting peaces across South Germany in Swabia, Bavaria, Franconia, and Alsace.[28] They were similar to those of the 1080s in being cumulative: as the 1084 peace at Goslar led to similar meetings elsewhere, so did a major assembly at Ulm in 1093. In two critical respects, they differed. First, whereas the earlier peaces were promoted by bishops and archbishops, these were mainly the work of lay princes, like Dukes Welf of Bavaria and Berthold of Carinthia. Secondly, the peaces of the mid-1090s were not based upon ecclesiastical dioceses or provinces but upon *provinciae* in a temporal sense—Swabia, Bavaria, Franconia, Alsace. The peaces of God were becoming *Landfrieden*.

---

23. *Reg.* 9.29, to all clergy and laity not under excommunication, (summer 1083), pp. 612-13, *Epp. vag.* no. 51, to the loyal archbishops, bishops, and abbots in France and Germany, (summer 1083), pp. 122-5.

24. *Reg.* 9.35a, notice of the Nov. synod, 23 Nov. 1083, pp. 627-8.

25. See Hoffmann, *Gottesfriede*, esp. pp. 143-50, 166-74, 185-8.

26. For Liège, the source is the late but reliable testimony of Giles of Orval, *Gesta episcoporum Leodiensium*, cap. 13, *MGH SS* 25.89-90, and ibid. *Gesta abbreviata, MGH SS* 25.131. For Cologne, see *MGH Const.* 1.602-5, no. 224. The peace at Mainz is referred to by Frutolf of Michaelsberg, *Chronica, a.* 1085, in: *Frutolfs und Ekkehards Chroniken und die anonyme Kaiserchronik*, edd. F.-J. Schmale and I. Schmale-Ott, AQ 15 (Darmstadt, 1972), pp. 98-9; the so-called *Pax dioecesis Bambergensis, MGH Const.* 1.605-8, no. 425, may belong to it. For the German peaces in general, see E. Wadle, "Heinrich IV. und die deutsche Friedensbeweung", in: *Investiturstreit und Reichsverfassung*, ed. J. Fleckenstein, Vorträge und Forschungen 17 (Sigmaringen, 1973), pp. 141-73, with references to earlier literature; I am heavily indebted in what follows to this paper.

27. *a.* 1084, p. 440; the *Iuramentum pacis Dei, MGH Const.* 1.608-9, no. 426, is perhaps to be associated with this assembly.

28. Bernold, *a.* 1093, p. 457, notices the peace assembly at Ulm; for its sequel in Franconia and Alsace, see ibid. *a.* 1094, p. 458. For the terms of the Bavarian and the Alsatian peaces, see *MGH Const.* 1.609-10, 611-13, nos 427, 429.

And what of the Germany emperor, Henry IV? By the 1080s, bitter experience had taught him much about the *métier de roi*. He played only a marginal part in the peaces of the bishops at that time: he seems to have known about the Liège peace of 1082, and at Mainz in 1085 he was present although not, it would seem, in a leading capacity.[29] His own major initiative came as late as 1103, when at Mainz on the feast of the Epiphany and in connection with his plan to go on pilgrimage to the Holy Land, he issued a peace.[30] In line with the South German peaces of the mid-1090s, it was territorially based; but it extended to the whole kingdom of Germany. It marked out the claim of the king to be the source of peace in his lands. The peace of God, as such, was not quite extinct in Germany,[31] but the measures of 1093-4 and of 1103 effectively led to its supersession by the initiatives of kings as and when they were in a position to take them.[32]

Henry IV issued his peace for the kingdom nearly eight years after Urban II preached the Crusade at Clermont. Fragmentary though the surviving evidence for the canons of Clermont is, there can be no doubt that Urban made detailed provision for the peace and truce of God which would contribute to the stability of the west while the Crusaders were away in the east.[33] It was the first at all successful attempt by a pope to proclaim peace throughout Latin Christendom. It marked the reform papacy's determination that it, rather than the temporal power, should be the supreme source of peace there. In this respect it pre-empted Henry IV's peace of 1103.

When seeking to assess the contribution to Urban's preaching of the Crusade of the series of conjunctures which have been suggested as being mainly relevant, it is important to avoid claiming both too little and too much. On the side of their being significant, three points may be made. First, although they were in themselves largely discrete developments, all were aspects of an underlying, age-long quest for peace and concord in human society, and they urgently raised similar questions about who should be the source of these benefits. Urban's attempt at Clermont as pope to establish an overall peace was an answer to a debate which had developed during the past century, and which had increasingly been concerned with major issues in the relations of *sacerdotium* and *regnum*.

Secondly, due weight must be given to Gregory VII's fear, expressed in respect of public disorders in both France and Germany, that the homicides, arson, ravagings,

---

29. Liège: Giles of Orval, *Gest. abbrev.* p. 131; Mainz: Frutolf of Michaelsberg, *Chron. a.* 1085, p. 98-9, noted the emperor's presence at the synod, but commented that *Ibi etiam communi consensu et consilio constituta est pax Dei*, without specific reference to him.

30. For what is known of its terms, see *MGH Const.* 1.125-6, no. 74. For Henry's initiative, see esp. *Annales Augustani, a.* 1103, *MGH SS* 3.135; the statement that *Saxones rebelles sibi reconciliavit, cunctisque gratia sua carentibus commissa dimisit* suggests that, in part, he followed the example of his father in 1043-4. The impact upon Germany of Henry IV's peace is clear from the account in the anonymous *Vita Heinrici IV*, cap. 8, in: *Quellen zur Geschichte Heinrichs IV.,* pp. 438-41.

31. See the peace for the diocese of Constance (1105) in *MGH Const.* 1.615-16, no. 431.

32. Esp. Frederick Barbarossa: *MGH Const.* 1.194-8, 247-7, 380-3, 449-42, nos. 140 (1152), 176 (1158), 277 (1179), 318 (1186).

33. For the canons of Clermont, see *The Councils of Urban II*: 1, *Decreta Claramontensia*, ed. R. Somerville, *Annuarium Historiae Conciliorum*, suppl. 1 (Amsterdam, 1972); for a conspectus of those concerning the peace and the truce of God, see p. 143. For a discussion see Bull, *Knightly Piety*, pp. 56-69.

perjuries, and like evils to which they gave rise might not be contained within their original localities but that they might overflow to the whole of Christendom. For Gregory in 1083, when he was under severe military and propaganda pressure from Henry IV of Germany, the answer was a general synod of the whole church, not necessarily to be held at Rome but to be convened under papal leadership. It would deal radically and universally with the issues of peace and of the disorders by which Christendom was beset. At least so far as the well-being of Latin Christendom was concerned, Gregory was already envisaging something very like Urban's council of Clermont. It must be remembered that, in 1083, as cardinal-bishop of Ostia the future Urban was among Gregory's closest associates and observers.

Thirdly, so far as the peace and the truce themselves are concerned, their prominence in the surviving records of the council of Clermont is striking. It is the more so in the light of Bull's argument that the connection between the early eleventh-century peaces in Southern France and the events of the 1090s was tenuous.[34] So far as can be seen, the relevant canons of Clermont remained generally within the precedents of earlier French legislation about the peace and the truce; this is to be expected, since as a Frenchman and a Cluniac Urban will have known them, and since at Clermont he was mainly concerned with French localities on or near his itinerary of 1095-6. But there is a presumption that he was no less aware of the German peaces of the 1080s and 1090s, and that, as the most active implementations of the peace and the truce at this time, they contributed to his appraisal of their value. For, while still cardinal-bishop of Ostia, he spent the winter of 1084-5 in Germany in an attempt to rally the Gregorian cause, and visited Saxony. As pope, he was in touch with the South German dukes, and his legate, Bishop Gebhard of Constance, attended the peace assembly at Ulm in 1093. There was one marked similarity between Urban's procedure in 1095 and the German peaces which may not have been coincidental: both were cumulative, in that the initial canons of a major assembly were to be adapted and confirmed at further, local councils: as the meetings at Goslar and Ulm were so followed up, the council of Clermont is known to have been followed in 1096 by councils at Rouen (for Normandy) and in the Touraine.[35] It may also be that the marked tendency of the German peaces to criminalize violence and to visit upon its perpetrators capital and corporal punishments influenced Urban at Clermont. As regards the peace of God, there is more than a suggestion of such a tendency in the canon on the peace and truce as recorded in the *Liber Lamberti* at Arras: if on prohibited days anyone inflicted injury upon another person, he was to be held guilty (*reus*) of a breach of holy peace and to be punished as should be adjudged (*prout iudicatum fuerit puniatur*).[36] And Urban may have been similarly influenced when he represented Seljuk depredations upon Eastern Christians as a wrong to be avenged by the extermination of the Seljuks from Christian lands. Whereas, in 1074, Gregory VII

---

34. See above, p. 53.
35. Rouen: *The Ecclesiastical History of Orderic Vitalis*, 9.3, ed. M. Chibnall, 6 vols (Oxford, 1969-80), 5.20-1; the Touraine: R. Bonnaud-Delamare, "La paix de Touraine pendant la première croisade", *Revue d'histoire ecclésiastique*, 14 (1975), 749-57, text on pp. 756-7.
36. Canon 1, *The Councils of Urban II*, ed. Somerville, p. 73.

invoked a caritative and biblical motive when seeking support for his projected eastern expedition—that of preparedness to lay down one's life for one's brothers (1 John 3: 16),[37] in 1095, Urban seems to have made more of the duty of waging war against those who seized the lands of Christians, killed or captured them, destroyed their churches, and devastated their countryside.[38] While Gregory's caritative emphasis largely fell on deaf ears, Urban's juridical emphasis was effectual.

Yet too much should not be claimed for the contribution to the Crusade of the conjunctures that have been noticed. First, prominently though the peace and truce of God featured in the canons of Clermont, it cannot be argued that the ideas which they embodied contributed directly to Crusading thought as did those of pilgrimage or of holy war. Both at and after Clermont, the peace and the truce of God were envisaged as a condition for the expedition to the east; they were never integrated into thought or practice about it.[39] Secondly, the vitality that the peace and the truce had shown in the eleventh century was, in any case, declining; as developments in Germany illustrate, the peace of God merged into that of the temporal ruler, and the maintenance of peace and justice became increasingly the task of the stronger monarchies of the central middle ages. The church had still to provide for the protection of Crusaders' lands and goods, but it did so as a specific concern rather than as part of a wider peace. Thirdly, it was not by way of the peace of God that Urban mainly won the knights for the Crusade. He did so by offering such spiritual benefits to lay participants as they themselves desired— the remission of sins and the cancellation of penance, and by offering them what seemed a worthy and just object for which to fight in the freeing of the Holy Sepulchre at Jerusalem and in the relief of Eastern Christians from Seljuk violence from Jerusalem to Constantinople.

The progression from the peace of God to the First Crusade did much to provide the mental and institutional background for the Crusade. It led men to think about Christendom as a whole; it gave rise to a debate about how leadership in Christendom should be vested; and it stimulated reflection upon how age-long problems about the building of peace and concord might be addressed. But its direct contribution to the Crusade was limited; it set the stage but did not play a major role. It cannot, therefore, be compared to pilgrimage or holy war as a constituent part of Crusading motivation.

---

37. *Reg.* 1.49, to all the faithful, 1 Mar. 1074, pp. 75-6, 2.31, to King Henry IV of Germany, 7 Dec. 1074, pp. 165-8, 2.37, to all the faithful of St Peter, 16 Dec. 1074, pp. 172-3.

38. For the possible themes of Urban's preaching at Clermont, see D. C. Munro, "The Speech of Urban II at Clermont, 1095", *American Historical Review*, 11 (1906), 231-42.

39. E.g. Pope Paschal II: council of Troyes (1107), canon 2, in: U.-R. Blumenthal, *The Early Councils of Pope Paschal II, 1100-1110* (Toronto, 1978), p. 91, cf. pp. 84-7. Pope Calixtus II: First Lateran Council (1123), canon 15, in: *Conciliorum oecumenicorum decreta*, edd. J. Alberigo and others (3rd edn, Bologna, 1973), p. 193. Pope Innocent II: Second Lateran Council (1139), canons 11-12, in: ibid., pp. 199-200.

III

Pope Gregory VII and the Bearing of Arms

While discussing the origins of the crusades in his by now classic survey of crusading, Hans Eberhard Mayer pointed out that, when making his crusading plans, Pope Urban II could look back to his predecessor, Gregory VII, who paid a great deal of attention to the knightly classes and tried to win them over to fight in the service of the church.[1] The purpose of this paper is to consider some of the ways in which Gregory can be seen from his letters and from other evidence to have concerned himself with the bearing of arms and thus to have prepared the way for the crusade as preached by Urban.

The moral problems raised by the bearing of arms arose in an acute form in connection with the administration of penance, which was among Gregory's most pressing concerns. For it is well to remember how seriously the great popes of the Middle Ages took the pastoral responsibilities of their office, and not least that of overseeing penance. A century or so after Gregory's lifetime, when Pope Alexander III was on his travels, someone acclaimed him as a good pope. 'If I judge well,' he replied, 'if I preach well, and if I award penance, I shall be a good pope.'[2] Gregory would probably have agreed. It is, therefore, instructive to notice an occasion at the beginning of his pontificate which illustrates the awarding of penance as then customary. In 1071, Peter Raymundi, son of Raymond Berengar I, count of Barcelona, had murdered his stepmother, Almodis of la Marche. In 1073, Gregory referred to the cardinals of the Roman church, by which was probably meant a cross-section of the Roman clergy headed by cardinal-bishops, the task of determining his penance.[3] They were said to have acted mercifully rather than with canonical rigour. Nevertheless, they awarded twenty-four years of graduated, but complex and burdensome, penance, which was set out in detail. One provision was that Peter Raymundi should on no account carry military arms, except in two contingencies: to defend himself against enemies, and to ride to battle against the Saracens.[4]

---

[1] Mayer, *Crusades*, p. 19.

[2] 'Si scirem, "Bien jujar, et bien predicar, et penitense donar, je seroie boene pape":' Peter Cantor, *Verbum abbreviatum*, cap. 65, PL 205:199C.

[3] Bishops were key figures in awarding penance: *Gregorii VII Registrum*, 6.5b(6), ed. Erich Caspar, MGH Epp. sel. 2:404. One would envisage such a body as is seen in *Il regesto di Farfa compilato da Gregorio di Catino*, ed. Ignazio Giorgi and Ugo Balzani, 5 vols. (Rome, 1883–1914), no. 1010, 5:9–11.

[4] Paul F. Kehr, 'Das Papsttum und der katalanische Prinzipat bis zur Vereinigung mit Aragon,' *Abhandlungen der Preußischen Akademie der Wissenschaften, phil.-hist. Klasse* 1 (Berlin, 1926), no. 7, pp. 80–81. For the murder, see *Gesta comitum Barcinonensium*, cap. 4, ed. L. Barrau Dihigo

Here was penance being awarded conscientiously but along traditional lines for public sin. It posed the obvious problem of being cumbersome: it imposed a heavy penance for a single grave sin, rather than taking into balanced account all of a man's sins; it also left a man unduly hampered in pursuing his work in life and in providing for the well-being and security of himself and his family.[5] But much other contemporary penance was open to the opposite criticism of being excessively lax. Writing in 1079 to the clergy and people of Brittany with the unreformed papacy of before 1046 evidently in mind, Gregory deplored that through ignorance and negligence there had been a lack of guidance about Christian discipline so that a custom of false, that is of insufficient, penances, or of penances that were simply disregarded, had become endemic.[6]

Between the extremes of severity and laxity, there was a need for an overhaul of the system of penances. In the period between his November synod at Rome in 1078 and his Lent synod there in 1080, the evidence of his Register suggests that Gregory was concerned on a broad front to raise the standards of clerical and lay life.[7] A major item of his agenda was the problem of true and false penance.

It was first raised in 1078, when a decree was made which kept largely within the lines of practice which Peter Raymundi's penance illustrates.[8] False penances were defined as insufficient penances which were not imposed by the standards of the best authorities of the past according to the gravity of the offence. To ensure that a penance was sufficient, if a man were guilty of a major sin and if his profession were one which could not be followed without incurring sin — the decree instanced the knight, the merchant, and the steward — he must accept that he could not perform a true penance, that is, one which would lead to eternal life, unless he abstained from his profession. In the case of a knight, he must, like Peter Raymundi, normally lay aside his arms; although, with the counsel of religious bishops, he might use them 'pro defendenda iustitia', that is, to defend his own or others' rightful interest.[9] The decree explained that the sins inescapable for the knight and the other professions named were hatred and the wrongful seizure

---

and J. Massó Torrents (Barcelona, 1925), pp. 6–7, and for its background, Bernard F. Reilly, *The Contest of Christian and Muslim Spain* (Oxford, 1992), p. 119. However, according to the *Gesta*, Peter Raimundi died *sub penitentia* in Spain, while his half-brother, Count Berengar Raymond II, died *sub penitentia* as a *peregrinus* to Jerusalem. (Berengar Raymond was deemed responsible for the murder in 1082 of his brother Count Raymond Berengar II, but he was convicted and deposed only in 1096; he died en route for Jerusalem in 1097).

[5] See, e.g., Urban II's ruling of 1089 to a plea of the archbishop of Rouen about hardship to families when penances included periods of exile: *Epistolae pontificum Romanorum ineditae*, ed. Samuel Loewenfeld (Leipzig, 1885), no. 132, p. 64.

[6] *Reg.* 7.10, to all bishops, clergy, and laity in Brittany, 25 Nov. 1079, pp. 471–472.

[7] See the records of the synods of Nov. 1078, Feb. 1079, and Mar. 1080: *Reg.* 6.5b, pp. 400–406; 6.17a, p. 425; 7.14a, pp. 480–482.

[8] *Reg.* 6.5b, p. 404.

[9] This represents a development upon Peter Raymundi's penance but is consistent with Gregory's letter to the Bretons: *Reg.* 7.10, p. 472, lines 10–12.

of others' goods. The decree ended by recognizing that this penitential regime carried the danger of inducing despair; as an interim measure for reducing the danger, the decree urged the sinner to do what good works he could, 'so that God might enlighten his mind to penitence.'[10] The last phrase recalls the provision in Peter Raymundi's penance that the pope and the apostolic see should grant an alleviation (*remedium*) if they discerned in the penitent 'a contrite and humbled heart, for according to the prophetic word a troubled spirit is approved by God as an acceptable sacrifice' (Ps. 50 [Vg.]. 19).

This decree was patently not intended to be the papacy's last word about penance. It still envisaged a heavy burden for one sin, rather than taking into balanced view all a man's sins. It did not satisfactorily define what constituted a true penance. It seriously hampered a man in pursuit of his livelihood. It recognized the danger that the uncertainty in which it left a man might plunge him into despair.

That Gregory soon gave further thought to the problems is apparent in his letter to the Bretons of about a year later.[11] It seems to embody rulings intended for widespread circulation. While its directions in general match those of 1078, the emphasis was moved from false penances, which were not now even defined, to true penances. The consequence for knights was that, in one sense, the position of those whose professions 'can scarcely be performed without sin' was made worse, for persisting in such avocations was now equated outright with homicide, adultery or perjury. In another sense, the knight's position became better; for so long as he followed the advice of religious men well versed in counsel leading to salvation, he might carry arms not only to protect his own right (*iustitia*) but also that of his lord, his friend, or the poor and in defence of churches. Good works were not now loosely attached extras but they were recognized within the penance itself. More important still, in 1079 Gregory brought to the forefront two deeper requirements about penance which had hitherto been understated. The first was that penance should be complete, in the sense of relating to all sins committed. This, no doubt, explains why the hatred of one's neighbour involved in warfare, like the predations on others' goods inherent in business or administration, was placed on a level with murder or adultery or perjury. A penance was, therefore, unfruitful — a fresh concept in 1079 — if it were so discharged that a man persisted in his fault or in another of comparable gravity. Secondly, a penance must be accompanied by complete conversion. Whoever would be worthily penitent must return to the beginning of faith. He must be careful vigilantly to keep everything that he promised in baptism: to renounce the devil and all his pomps, and to believe in God by discerning what is right about him and by obeying his commandments. For the penitent who carried arms, there was now, on the one hand, a heightened call to recognize the sins inherent in his everyday manner of life; but, on the other, there was a call to listen to 'religious

[10] It is to be remembered that the Latin word *penitentia* means both 'penance' and 'penitence'.
[11] *Reg.* 7.10.

24

men' for guidance in a widening range of ways in which he might rightly use his weapons. Here were the essentials of a contrast between warfare according to the purposes of man and warfare as directed by the church towards acceptable ends.

A decree of Gregory's Lent synod in 1080 carried matters further still.[12] It reads as though based upon a fervent address by Gregory himself. Conversion of life was its dominant theme. Those who wished to escape hell and to gain heaven must above all guard against false penances; for as false baptism does not wipe out original sin, so false penance does not cancel an offence committed after baptism. Thus, all who have committed grave sins should open their souls to wise and religious men so that by true penance they might secure sure pardon for their sins. True penance is seen when, after committing any grave wrong, a man turns wholly to God and repents of all his sins. To emphasize the word 'all', the decree cited the Lord's word by the prophet Ezekiel: 'If the unrighteous shall be converted from *all* his sins and shall keep *the whole of* my commandments, he shall surely live and not die' (Ezek. 18.21). It was clear to everyone, the decree continued, that no one who continued to bear arms against righteousness (*contra iustitiam*) or kept hatred in his heart, had turned wholly to God or done true penance. In this decree, Gregory did not expressly return to the circumstances in which a man might with justice bear arms. But he ended by reinforcing the point that, in accepting penance, recourse should be had only to righteous and experienced men whose religious and scriptural knowledge would guide penitents in the way of truth and salvation. The implication was that arms were justly borne when men were obedient to the guidance of right-minded clerical mentors.

There are indications that Gregory's rethinking between 1078 and 1080 of the subject of true and false penances set precedents for some elements in Urban's summons to the crusade in 1095. It should be remembered that he had moved from Cluny to Rome c.1080 and thereafter knew Gregory's mind from close and admiring familiarity. Gregory's insistence upon penance for all sins may be reflected in Urban's crusading canon, in which the expedition to Jerusalem was to be reckoned 'pro omni penitentia'; in his letter to the Bolognese of 1096, Urban expanded this into a promise that a crusader might expect release from all penance for sins concerning which he had made true and full confession ('veram et perfectam confessionem'). A twelfth-century record of the canons of Clermont attributed to Urban the outright statement that penance for one sin only was profitless; a man seeking relief from one sin must get rid of all the rest.[13] Gregory's emphasis upon complete inner conversion and a return to baptismal

---

[12] *Reg.* 7.14a(5), pp. 481–482.

[13] Robert Somerville, *The Councils of Urban II*, 1: *Decreta Claromontensia*, Annuarium Historiae Conciliorum, Supplementum 1 (Amsterdam, 1972), pp. 74 (Liber Lamberti, canon 2), 115 (Oxford, Bodleian Library, MS Selden Supra 90, canon 25); Heinrich Hagenmeyer, *Die Kreuzzugsbriefe aus den Jahren 1088–1100* (Innsbruck, 1901), no. 3, pp. 137–138. For Urban's insistence upon the need for penance for all sins, see also the first part of canon 16 of his council of Melfi (1089): Mansi, *Concilia* 20:724; repeated as canon 22 of Innocent II's Second Lateran Council (1139) in *Conciliorum oecumenicorum decreta*, ed. Giuseppe Alberigo and others, 3rd ed. (Bologna, 1973), p. 202.

purity may likewise have prepared the ground for Urban's requirement that a man go to Jerusalem 'pro sola devotione' and not for honour or money, as for the canon attributed to him that 'medicine can be given only to him who is penitent with his whole heart.'[14] Again, Gregory's extension of the reasons for which penitent knights might still bear arms to the protection of the poor and the defence of churches, together with his advice that penitents perform good works, can scarcely but have helped towards Urban's crusade with its objective of freeing the church of Jerusalem. In such ways, Gregory's presentation of true penance helped the preaching of the crusade by Urban as by the bishops, abbots and others who were of his mind.

Gregory's conciliar legislation also worked in what was, at least at first sight, a contrary direction so far as the moral acceptability of bearing arms is concerned. It is widely recognized that, despite his stature amongst the medieval popes, Gregory left relatively little mark upon the development of canon law or of Christian literature in general.[15] The principal exception is the decrees of the November synod of 1078, which were quite extensively cited in canon law collections up to and including Gratian's *Decretum* of c.1140.[16] There seems to have been a major publicity effort, and the circumstances for its success were more favourable than in the early 1080s, with the renewed breach between Gregory and King Henry IV of Germany. The result was that Gregory's decree of 1080 which expressed his developed and most forward-looking position about penitence in relation to the bearing of arms went largely unnoticed in the canonical tradition;[17] but the decree of November 1078, with its plain statement that the knight could not go about his business without committing sin, its requirement that a man doing penance must normally lay aside his arms, and its acknowledgement of a knight's liability to despair, was widely known under Gregory's name. Up to c.1140, a substantial number of canonical manuscripts survive which preserve it.[18] Most important of all for its survival in canon law, Gratian of Bologna included it in his *De penitentia*, whence it in due course passed into his *Decretum*.[19] It also appears outside the canon-law tradition. The German regular canon and polemicist Gerhoh of Reichersberg twice cited it in writings of c.1130.[20] No less

---

[14] Somerville, *Councils*, pp. 74, 115.

[15] See especially John Gilchrist, 'The Reception of Pope Gregory VII into the Canon Law,' *Zeitschrift der Savigny-Stiftung fur Rechtsgeschichte, kanonistische Abteilung* 90 (1973), 35–82; 110 (1980), 192–229.

[16] See especially Gilchrist's figures: 'Reception,' pp. 70–71, 223–224.

[17] Gilchrist notes a citation only in the uninfluential *Collection in Thirteen Books*, Berlin, Deutsche Staatsbibliothek, MS Savigny 3, fol. 148v; it is limited to Reg. 7.14a, p. 482, lines 12–18: Gilchrist, 'Reception,' p. 60. A version survives in the Volterra *Ordo officiorum: De Sancti Hugonis actis liturgicis*, ed. Mario Bocci (Florence, 1984), p. 79.

[18] See the MSS listed by Gilchrist, 'Reception.'

[19] *De penitentia*, D.5, c.6, in *Corpus iuris canonici*. Editio Lipsiensis secunda, ed. Emil Friedberg, 2 vols. (Leipzig, 1879–81), 1:1241.

[20] Gerhoh of Reichersberg, *Liber de edificio Dei*, marginalia to cap. 113, and *Epistola ad Innocentium papam*, ed. Ernst Sackur, MGH Libelli de lite 3:181, 231.

decisive for its long-term influence, Peter Lombard found a place for it in his principal work, the *Sententiarum libri quattuor*, written in the late 1150s.[21]

In this way, through the widespread and protracted circulation of what had been, on his part, a provisional and tentative decree upon which he quickly improved, Gregory himself contributed to the persistence far into the twelfth century of the opinion that a knight's arms could not be used without falling into sin. It is, however, unlikely that Gregory's decree of 1078 was a restraint upon crusade preaching; on the contrary, it probably facilitated it and complemented the revised decree of 1080 in promoting it. For the two strands in Gregory's legislation helped to establish the contrast, fundamental for early crusade preaching, between the everyday secular violence of the knight, and his rightful pursuit of warfare as directed by spiritual authority to a religious end. The contrast is already apparent in the chronicler Fulcher of Chartres's account of Urban II's preaching at Clermont. Urban contrasted the domestic warfare, soiled by robbery, slaughter and greed, in which knights had hitherto worn themselves out to their own detriment in body and soul, with the external warfare directed against pagans which would win remission of sins: 'Let those now become soldiers of Christ (*Christi milites*) who before were plunderers.'[22] The contrast was more elegantly stated by St Bernard of Clairvaux, when he set the *malitia* of worldly conflict with its accompaniment of anger, vain-glory and greed over against the new, crusading *militia* of those who, as *Christi milites*, might in all peace of mind fight the battles of the Lord.[23] It would be wrong to represent Gregory's two decrees as the direct inspiration of Bernard's antithesis. But by somewhat different routes, they prepared the way for his two kinds of warfare and service,[24] the one to be shunned but the other to be embraced, by the Knights Templar but also by other crusading warriors.

The most significant features of Gregory's concern between 1078 and 1080 to regulate penances were undoubtedly his desire for the complete conversion of the sinner and his gathering insistence that penitents should have recourse to truly religious men who would direct them, not least as regards the purposes to which they put their weapons. Inner conversion and properly guided warfare were to go hand in hand. The rapid mutation in Gregory's thought about penance did not stand alone; it arose from his wider concern, manifest from the earliest

---

[21] *Magistri Petri Lombardi Sententiae in IV libris distinctae*, 4.16.3, 2 vols., 3rd ed. (Grottaferrata, 1971–81), 2:339–340. For the interpretation of Gregory's decree by Gratian, Peter Lombard, and others, see Frederick H. Russell, *The Just War in the Middle Ages* (Cambridge, 1975), pp. 214–218. A description of trading, military service, and administration on behalf of lay authorities as avocations which 'sine admixtione mali non sunt administranda' also appears in the Pseudo-Augustinian tract *Liber de vera et falsa penitentia* 15.30: PL 40:1111–1130, at col. 1125. The date of the tract is uncertain, but the *terminus ante quem* is its citation in Gratian's *Decretum* of *c*.1140. While any date from the early tenth century is possible, its theological sophistication points to the early twelfth century. If this is so, it reflects rather than anticipates Gregory's rulings.

[22] FC 1.2–3, pp. 123–138.

[23] *De laude novae militiae*, caps. 2–3, in *Sancti Bernardi Opera*, ed. Jean Leclercq, C.H. Talbot, and H.M. Rochais, 8 vols. (Rome, 1957–77), 3:216–221.

[24] It should be remembered that the Latin word *militia* means both 'warfare' and 'service'.

days of his pontificate, to use the knightly classes for the service of the church in ways that would win them reward in this world and the next. In return, it in the long run served to invest warfare with a saving quality which raised it in itself into a means of conversion from iniquity and of fulfilling God's commandments, especially that of charity to one's neighbour.

One means by which Gregory might be expected to have raised the bearing of arms above the reproach of necessarily involving sin is the propagation of St Augustine of Hippo's doctrine of the just war.[25] However, this must be set aside. Gregory's cast of mind was not theoretical or speculative, and he shows little sign of being in any way directly indebted to Augustine. He cited him in his letters only once.[26] In none of his references to warfare or coercion is it possible to see any mark of Augustine's teaching.

More characteristically, Gregory set a stamp of his own upon military campaigns that were actually planned or fought. Campaigns under papal guidance or even leadership were a not infrequent feature of recent papal history.[27] They grew in frequency under Gregory, and there are signs that he aspired to raise at least some of them above the reproach of involving sin. His means were their close supervision, on his behalf, by bishops. Thus, in 1076, he heard that Count Roger of Sicily sought reconciliation with the Roman church before campaigning against the Saracens in Sicily. He forthwith ordered Archbishop Arnald of Acerenza to hasten to him and, if he found him truly penitent, to absolve him. He was also to absolve his knights who were about to fight the pagans, so long as they, too, were penitent. Such was accepted practice. Gregory then added two injunctions of his own which the archbishop was religiously to urge upon the count in respect of his prospective warfare in order that he might deserve victory over his enemies. First, he should keep himself from capital offences, and secondly he should strive to enlarge regard for the Christian name ('christiani nominis culturam') amongst the pagans. This, rather than Augustine's theory of a just war, was Gregory's way of moralizing armed conflict. His second injunction was similar to his advice to the Christian minority in Muslim North Africa, whom Gregory urged so to let their light shine before the Saracens that, seeing it, they would glorify the Christians' Father in heaven (cf. Matt. 5.16).[28]

In July 1080, and so a few months after his decree on penance at his Lent synod, Gregory wrote to all the bishops of Apulia and Calabria in anticipation of a campaign across the Adriatic by which he hoped that Robert Guiscard, the Norman duke of Apulia, would restore to the Byzantine throne the deposed

[25] For a summary of Augustine's teaching, see Russell, *Just War*, pp. 15–26.
[26] Gregory cited Augustine, *De doctrina Christiana* 1.23 in *Reg.* 8.21, to Bishop Hermann of Metz, 15 Mar. 1081, p. 556.
[27] See Carl Erdmann, *Die Entstehung des Kreuzzugsgedankens* (Stuttgart, 1935), pp. 21–24, 107–133, Eng. trans. *The Origin of the Idea of Crusade*, by Marshall W. Baldwin and Walter Goffart (Princeton, 1977), pp. 25–28, 118–140.
[28] *Reg.* 3.11, to Archbishop Arnald of Acerenza, 14 Mar. 1076, pp. 271–272; cf. 3.20, to the clergy and people of Bougie (May/June 1076), pp. 286–287.

Emperor Michael VII Ducas (1071–1077); for a Greek had arrived at Bari who gave himself out to be the ex-emperor.[29] As their office required, the bishops were most diligently to urge the knights who would cross the sea to perform appropriate penances. Again, so far, Gregory followed established usage. But, consonantly with his decree of 1080, he added moral demands: they must, as befitted Christians, keep true faith with the duke and with the *soi-disant* emperor; in all their deeds, they were to hold in view the fear and love of God; and they were to continue in good works. Upon these conditions, Gregory ordered the bishops on his own, or rather on St Peter's, authority to absolve them from all their sins.[30] Gregory's letter may be compared with Pope Alexander II's undated fragment addressed 'clero Vulturnensi', in which the clergy were to urge persons who purposed to travel to Spain whether as warriors or as pilgrims to give effect to their intentions. As in 1080, each was to confess his sins according to their gravity to his bishop or other spiritual father, and an appropriate penance was to be imposed. But whereas Gregory ordered the bishops to exhort the knights to good conduct before he absolved them, Alexander promised the raising of penance and the remission of sins, having made no reference to moral dispositions or good works.[31] Gregory's advance upon Alexander's practice seems to have

---

[29] For the circumstances, see Herbert E.J. Cowdrey, *The Age of Abbot Desiderius: Montecassino, the Papacy and the Normans in the Eleventh and Early Twelfth Centuries* (Oxford, 1983), pp. 143, 145.

[30] *Reg.* 8.6, to the bishops of Apulia and Calabria, 25 July 1080, pp. 523–524; cf. the instructions which Gregory's legate in Lombardy, Bishop Anselm II of Lucca, gave to his future biographer before the battle of Sorbaria in 1084 about the reconciliation of excommunicates and their absolution before fighting: '... hoc in mandatis praecipue commendans nobis, ut si cum excommunicatis communicassent, primitus illos absolveremus, et tunc pariter omnes auctoritate apostolica et sua benediceremus, instruentes eos, quo pacto quave intentione deberent pugnare, sicque in remissionem omnium peccatorum eorum instantis belli committeremus periculum:' *Vita Anselmi episcopi Lucensis,* cap. 23, ed. Roger Wilmans, MGH SS 12:20.

[31] For Alexander's letter, see *Epistolae pontificum*, ed. Loewenfeld, no. 82, p. 43. The see to which it is addressed is uncertain, though the suggestion of Volterra is attractive, since the names *Vulternensis, Wlturnensis,* and *Vulturnensis* occur: MGH Constitutiones et acta publica, 1:545, 572; since Volterra was directly subject to the apostolic see, a papal ruling about penance would be particularly likely. Historians have usually associated the fragment with warfare in Spain against the Saracens, and have sometimes had in mind the Barbastro campaign of 1064. But difficulties about this have recently been pointed out, with the suggestion that the fragment may relate, instead, to pilgrimage to Santiago de Compostela: Marcus Bull, *Knightly Piety and the Lay Response to the First Crusade: The Limousin and Gascony, c.970-c.1130* (Oxford, 1993), pp. 72–78. Bull's arguments are strong but less than compelling: (i) Alexander's advice to receive penance 'ne diabolus accusare de inpenitentia possit' may suggest a risk of imminent death which fits warfare more than pilgrimage; (ii) the phrase 'que divinitus admoniti cogitaverunt' is restrained and neither it nor anything else in the fragment necessarily implies a concept of divinely inspired holy war which of itself attracted spiritual benefits; and (iii) as addressed to pilgrimage, the fragment would imply a raising of penance and a remission of sins at the outset which would be hard to parallel. It is, perhaps, wise to leave open the question of warfare or pilgrimage but with a presumption remaining that Alexander had in mind the former. For the introduction of general absolutions in the eleventh century, see Paul Anciaux, *La théologie du sacrement de pénitence au XIIe siècle* (Louvain, 1949), pp. 50–51.

been to add to holy, or sacralized, warfare an expressly moral quality, with a requirement of right motives (the fear and love of God) and of the pursuit of good works.[32]

In campaigns that Gregory proposed to lead in person, the causes that he championed and the conviction that they were a service of St Peter likewise tended to raise the wielding of earthly arms above the reproach of sinful motives and human self-seeking. In the summer of 1080, he considered leading two expeditions. The first was to Spain, where he was persuaded that King Alfonso VI of León-Castile was complicit in crisis events which Gregory believed would bring back in his realms the Hispanic liturgical order; Gregory deemed that order to be gravely heretical. Gregory wrote to Abbot Hugh of Cluny that, if the king persisted, he would not think it excessive himself to go to Spain and bring to bear things hard and disagreeable ('dura et aspera moliri'), that is, to lead a military campaign, against the king as an enemy of the Christian religion. Writing as one monk to another, Gregory borrowed monastic language from the Rule of St Benedict. He adapted the spiritual service of the monastic way of life to set the tone for the earthly warfare that he envisaged and to give it moral acceptability.[33] Soon afterwards, Gregory prepared another letter calling upon clergy and laity faithful to St Peter to sponsor an autumn campaign that he would himself lead with the object of freeing the church of Ravenna from its archbishop, Guibert, whom King Henry IV of Germany at his synod of Brixen in June had chosen to be anti-pope. Gregory assigned high objectives to the campaign: the honouring of the duty of those who, like the Norman princes of South Italy, had sworn to defend the Roman church against its enemies; the fulfilling of the moral obligation to secure the return to St Peter of property — in this case, the church of Ravenna — which had been seized from him by godless men; a Christian's calling to humble the proud and to restore the peace and security of the church. By the elevation of its purposes, such warfare was calculated to justify those who took part.[34]

---

[32] It should, however, be observed that Gregory's use of 'religious men' to direct lay rulers and their knights in the use of arms could be exclusively temporal and without moral basis, as when he asked Abbot Desiderius of Montecassino to urge the Normans to depart from their customary abstention from warfare during Lent in order to protect the papacy's lands: *Reg.* 9.4, to Abbot Desiderius of Montecassino (early Feb. 1081), pp. 577–578.

[33] *Reg.* 8.2, to Abbot Hugh of Cluny, 27 June 1080, p. 518, lines 29–32, cf. Rule of St Benedict, 58.8, *La règle de Saint Benoît*, ed. Adalbert de Vogüé and Jean Neufville, 6 vols., Sources chrétiennes 181–185 (Paris, 1971–72), 2:628.

[34] *Reg.* 8.7, to all the faithful of St Peter (1080, summer), pp. 524–525. Cf. Gregory's further letters about Ravenna, 8.12, to all the faithful in the marches of Tuscany and Fermo and in the exarchate of Ravenna, 15 Oct. 1080, pp. 531–532; 8.13, to all the Ravennese, 13 Oct. 1080, pp. 532–534; and 8.14, to all the faithful in the dioceses of Ravenna and the Pentapolis, in the march of Fermo, and the duchy of Spoleto, 11 Dec. 1080, pp. 534–535. The campaign came to nothing.

30

The most remarkable expeditions that Gregory planned to lead in person were his so-called 'crusading' projects of 1074.[35] In so far as they were directed against the Seljuk assailants of the Byzantine empire, they, too, raised warfare to a lofty moral level as Gregory presented them. He repeatedly alluded to the fate of eastern Christians who were being slaughtered like cattle by the pagan ravagers of the Christian empire. He called for recruits 'by way of the faith in which you have been made one through Christ in the adoption of the sons of God (cf. Rom. 8.23).' They would be defending the law of Christ and the Christian faith, and would be serving the heavenly king. Whatever they volunteered to do would have been implanted in their minds by the divine mercy; Gregory accordingly wrote to King Henry IV of Germany that the will to rise up under the pope's leadership against the enemies of God and to press on with the pope to the Lord's sepulchre at Jerusalem had become firmly established in the minds of the knights themselves. Gregory's final call to arms in December 1074 was to warfare which was wholly pleasing in the sight of God:

> So, then, on behalf of St Peter we ask, urge, and invite to come to us an advance party of you who are willing to defend the Christian faith and to serve (*militare*) the heavenly king. With it, please God, we shall prepare the way for all who are willing, in defence of their heavenly birthright (*qui celestem nobilitatem defendendo*), through us to cross the sea, and who are not afraid to demonstrate that they are the sons of God. Therefore, most beloved brethren, be exceedingly strong to fight for the praise and glory that exceed all desire, since hitherto you have been strong to fight for things that you cannot hold on to or possess without vexation. For by a transitory labour you can win an eternal reward.[36]

Although such projected campaigns elicited from Gregory eloquent statements of how warfare for a noble end might rise above sinful human desires, they were occasional and they achieved little, if anything. At once more durable and more effective was Gregory's bid to mobilize the knights, especially of Italy, Germany and France, for papal purposes in the longer term, such as the coercion of clergy who persisted in simony and fornication, or, especially in the early 1080s, his warfare against the twice-excommunicated and now schismatic King Henry IV of Germany and his designated anti-pope, Archbishop Guibert of Ravenna.[37] Gregory built upon an established practice in Central Italy whereby spiritual sanctions as applied by the clergy were, if necessary, backed up by physical

---

[35] The principal relevant letters of Gregory are *Reg.* 1.46, to Count William of Burgundy, 2 Feb. 1074, pp. 69–71; 1.49, to all who are willing to defend the Christian faith, 1 Mar. 1074, pp. 75–76; 2.31, to King Henry IV of Germany, 7 Dec. 1074, pp. 165–168; 2.37, to all the faithful of St Peter, especially across the Alps, 16 Dec. 1074, pp. 172–173: *The Epistolae vagantes of Pope Gregory VII*, ed. and trans. H.E.J. Cowdrey (Oxford, 1972), no. 5, pp. 10–13. For the background, see H.E.J. Cowdrey, 'Pope Gregory VII's "Crusading" Plans of 1074,' in *Outremer*, pp. 27–40 = idem, *Popes, Monks and Crusaders* (London, 1984), no. 10.

[36] *Reg.* 2.37, p. 173.

[37] See especially Erdmann, *Entstehung*, pp. 134–211, Eng. trans. pp. 148–228; Ian S. Robinson, 'Gregory VII and the Soldiers of Christ,' *History* 58 (1973), 161–192.

coercion as applied by the faithful laity. Gregory's letters provide examples. In 1074, the clergy and people of Fermo were to act as the free and faithful sons of their mother church in helping by all means (*modis omnibus* — in Gregory's letters, a phrase implying coercion if necessary) to recover its despoiled property. In 1075, the clergy and laity of Pesaro were to help their bishop recover goods of the see from those who held them unjustly, bringing spiritual or secular aid as proved necessary ('quatenus episcopo Pensauriensi ad eos expugnandum spirituali et seculari auxilio, prout necesse fuerit, fideliter subveniant'). At the same time, Gregory told laity at Chiusi that those who helped to expel a perjured and adulterous provost and thereby to restore their church to its pristine condition would win salvation and remission of their sins.[38]

Gregory advanced upon such occasional use of those who bore arms in order to reinforce ecclesiastical sanctions in three, progressively more momentous, ways. First, as archdeacon and then as pope, he bestowed his approval and support upon the Patarenes of Lombardy, who used armed force against the simoniac and married or concubinous clergy whom it was a prime objective of Gregory to bring to heel.[39] In the early 1070s, their leader was the knight Erlembald, who engaged in bloody struggles at Milan against the ecclesiastical establishment. In Gregory's eyes, he was a *strenuissimus Christi miles*. Gregory wrote to Bishop William of Pavia that he could win favour with the Roman church by helping Erlembald in what he was doing by Gregory's counsel and from fear of God, and by joining him manfully in fighting God's warfare (*bellum Dei*) against the church's enemies.[40] In 1075, Erlembald met his end in savage rioting at Milan. At his Lent synod of 1078, Gregory treated him as a martyr and saint; according to the annalist Berthold of Reichenau, he had pursued the guilty with his military bands, compelling them to accept canonical correction or else putting them to flight and imprisoning them, and seizing and scattering all that they possessed.[41] In Gregory's eyes, Erlembald's bearing of arms was to be commended because it was in a worthy cause, and it could lead to a martyr's death.

Secondly, Gregory extended the bringing to bear of lay coercion against clerks guilty of simony and fornication across the Alps to Germany and France. He did so to Germany during his strenuous campaign against its errant clergy in 1074 and 1075. Early in 1075, he told the South German dukes, Rudolf of Swabia, Berthold of Carinthia and Welf of Bavaria, that he was now turning to them

---

[38] *Reg.* 2.38, to the count, clergy, and people of Fermo, 22 Dec. 1074, pp. 174–175; 2.46, to Abbots Gepizo of S. Bonifacio and Maurus of S. Sabas, 13 Jan. 1075, pp. 185–186; 2.47, to named and unnamed residents of the county of Chiusi, 13 Jan. 1075, pp. 186–187. See H.E.J. Cowdrey, 'Pope Gregory VII and the Bishoprics of Central Italy,' *Studi medievali*, 3rd ser., 34 (1993), 51–64, esp. pp. 59–61.

[39] See H.E.J. Cowdrey, 'The Papacy, the Patarenes and the Church of Milan,' *Transactions of the Royal Historical Society*, 5th ser., 18 (1968), 25–48 = idem, *Popes, Monks and Crusaders*, no. 5.

[40] *Reg.* 1.27, to Bishop-elect Albert of Acqui, 13 Oct. 1073, pp. 44–45; 1.28, to Bishop William of Pavia, 13 Oct. 1073, pp. 45–46.

[41] Berthold, *Annales, a.* 1077, MGH SS 5:305–306.

32

for energetic action, irrespective of the bishops, against clergy guilty of simony or fornication; whether in the king's court or whether in other localities and assemblies, they should prevent the ministrations of such clergy, even by force should it be called for ('etiam vi si oportuerit').[42] In France, Gregory turned to the knights (*milites*) for comparable service. By 1081, many of them had been giving his legates, Bishops Hugh of Die and Amatus of Oloron, their support and aid in coercing priestly fornicators and simoniacs; Gregory was anxious that their pressure should be maintained, even though they had fallen foul of the legates by not surrendering their tithes.[43] Since the legates were mainly operative in the south and west of France, Gregory's use of the armed force of the knights to advance his reforming purposes was fairly widespread.

Thirdly, after his breach in 1080 with King Henry IV of Germany, Gregory called on the military classes wherever he could find a response not to oppose only the abuses of simony and clerical fornication but also to defend the Christian faith itself at a time when he saw the time of Antichrist approaching with its threat of destruction for the Christian religion.[44] Early in 1075, in the shadow of disappointment at the lack of support from clergy and laity alike for his plans of the previous year, Gregory already adumbrated such a call in a letter to Abbot Hugh of Cluny:

And because we ought to use either hand as a right hand (Judg. 3.15) to subdue the violence of wicked men, it is needful, seeing that there is no prince who attends to such matters, for ourselves to protect the life of religious men. With brotherly charity we enjoin you to the best of your ability to extend your hand with watchful zeal by warning, beseeching and urging those who love St Peter that, if they would truly be his sons and knights (*milites*), they should not hold secular princes more dear than him. For secular princes reluctantly grant wretched and transient things; but he, by loosing from all sins, promises things blessed and eternal, and by the power committed to him (Matt. 16.19) he brings men to a heavenly home. I wish to know who are truly loyal (*fideles*) to him, and who love their heavenly prince for heavenly glory no less than to those to whom they are subject for an earthly and wretched hope.[45]

From 1082 onwards, Gregory in several letters developed a contrast between the large number of secular knights who, from motives of base reward, would lay down their lives for their lords, and the few who were prepared to stand firm in defence of the Christian religion.[46] In Gregory's last encyclical which he sent in 1084 from Salerno, the contrast was sharpened into a clarion call to the few who, for love of Christ's law, were determined to stand fast in face of the ungodly: 'We may not allow the sons of holy church to be made subject to

[42] *Reg.* 2.45, to the South German dukes, 11 Jan. 1075, pp. 182–185.
[43] *Reg.* 9.5, to Bishops Hugh of Die and Amatus of Oloron (1081), pp. 579–580.
[44] *Epistolae vagantes*, ed. Cowdrey, no. 54, pp. 132–135.
[45] *Reg.* 2.49, to Abbot Hugh of Cluny, 22 Jan. 1075, pp. 188–190.
[46] *Reg.* 9.21, to all bishops, abbots, clergy, and laity faithful to the apostolic see (1082), pp. 601–603; see also *Epistolae vagantes*, ed. Cowdrey, no. 51, pp. 122–125.

heretics, adulterers and intruders as though such men were their fathers, nor to be stigmatized through them as by the reproach of adulterous birth.' Gregory asked and commanded the few to help and succour their father (St Peter, the prince of the apostles) and mother (the Roman church, mother and mistress of all the churches), if through them they would have the absolution of all their sins, and blessing and grace in this world and in the world to come.[47] The call was for more than armed service, but it certainly included it. Like his decrees about penance, Gregory's last encyclicals divided those who bore arms into opposing camps — those who bore them from base motives in the corrupt service of this world, and those who bore them in the service of God and for the purposes of the Christian religion. Such service ennobled, and it raised their bearing of arms above the reproach of sinfulness. It pointed to the crusade.

Gregory also did much to raise the bearing of arms above the reproach that it of necessity involved sin by giving attention to the motivation of individual warriors. By so doing, he complemented the part of his concern with penance that had to do with the inner conversion of the individual. Once again, he had a foundation upon which he might build, for the century or so before he became pope had witnessed attempts to refine the motives and mentalities of those who bore arms. Perhaps the most pervasive attempt had been within the liturgical tradition of the West. The Romano-Germanic Pontifical, which was compiled c. 960 at Mainz and spread throughout Latin Christendom, provided a prayer for the army which asked both that those who fought might have a right motive in fighting (*proeliandi recta voluntas*) and that in the hour of victory they should imitate Christ the model victor, who by the humility of his passion triumphed on the cross over death and the prince of death.[48]

The twin concepts of a good will in warfare and of the imitation of Christ in battle and victory were powerful ones. The first of them was developed by Gregory's loyal follower Bishop Anselm II of Lucca in the thirteenth book of his *Collectio canonum*, in which he was at pains to assert the freedom from sin of those engaged in warfare that was, in his framework, just — that is, warfare against Christian heretics and schismatics. He found warrant, largely in the writings of St Augustine and of Pope Gregory the Great, for such *capitula* as 'that Moses did nothing cruel when, at the Lord's command, he slew certain men,' 'concerning punishment (*vindicta*), that it should be performed not from hate but from love,' and 'that those who fight can also be righteous (*iusti*), and that necessity not choice should be the reason for laying low an enemy.'[49] Such

---

[47] *Epistolae vagantes*, ed. Cowdrey, no. 54, pp. 128–135.

[48] *Le pontifical romano-germanique du dixième siècle*, ed. Cyrille Vogel and Reinhard Elze, 3 vols., Studi e testi 226–227, 249 (Vatican City, 1963–72), no. 245, 2:380. For discussion and examples of similar prayers, see Erdmann, *Entstehung*, pp. 334–335.

[49] The relevant material is best studied in Edith Pásztor, 'Lotta per le investiture e "ius belli": la posizione di Anselmo di Lucca,' in *Sant'Anselmo, Mantova e la lotta per le investiture: Atti di convegno internazionale di studi (Mantova 23–24–25 maggio 1986)*, ed. Paolo Golinelli (Bologna, 1987), pp. 375–421, esp. pp. 405–421. Anselm did not point up the question of the just war.

III

34

teaching was no doubt in the mind of Anselm's clerk who, before the battle of Sorbaria in 1084, instructed those who would take part 'on what grounds and with what intention they should fight.'[50] Theirs was to be, indeed, a *proeliandi recta voluntas.*

Gregory himself developed the other concept in the Pontifical — that of an imitation of Christ which raised warfare above the reproach of being sinful. He did so with especial force in his letters about his plan of 1074 to bring military help, which he himself would lead, to relieve Eastern Christians whom the pagan Seljuks were slaughtering like cattle. Gregory set before fighting men the supreme inner motive of self-sacrifice to the point of martyrdom which should direct their warfare.[51] The example of the Redeemer himself should be allied to the duty of brotherly love to recruit armed help, 'for as he laid down his life for us, so ought we to lay down our life for our brothers (1 John 3.16).'[52] Gregory's call to such self-sacrificial service under arms was the more compelling because he himself was willing to cross the sea and if need be to lay down his life for Christ which was the highest of human motives, 'for if, as some say, it is a noble thing to die for our country [Horace, *Carmina* 3.2.13], it is a far nobler and truly praiseworthy thing to give our corruptible flesh for Christ, who is life eternal.'[53] Papally-proclaimed warfare carried with it the possibility of a martyrdom which raised it to a wholly good and saving activity for those who shared its declared motive. During his last years, Gregory challenged those upon whom he called to resist Archbishop Guibert of Ravenna and King Henry IV of Germany by citing St Paul's words about sharing Christ's death and resurrection: 'If we suffer with him, we shall also reign with him (*Si compatimur, et conregnabimus*) (2 Tim. 12.2).' He also praised the few who for love of Christ's law were determined to stand fast to the death in the face of the ungodly.[54] For the individual who fought, being under arms was a following of Christ which required him to perfect his motive in fighting and which carried the promise of sharing Christ's death and resurrection. It was another route to a *proeliandi recta voluntas.*

It may be concluded that Gregory was responsible for profound changes in the Christian attitude to the bearing of arms. He set objectives for warfare which had the effect of making it without qualification morally acceptable; by directing those who took part to a spiritual commitment and to singleness of motive in terms of it, he proposed it as a sanctifying element in their own lives. In both ways, he prepared the ground for the crusade. He marked out the way in which

---

[50] See above, n. 30.

[51] For Gregory's estimate of martyrdom as the supreme aspiration of the Christian life, see his letter to Archbishop Cyriacus of Carthage, who had been imprisoned and beaten at the orders of the Muslim emir; Gregory praised the constancy of his faith, but said that the confession of his religion would have been still more precious if he had endured to the point of martyrdom: *Reg.* 1.23, 15 Sept. 1073, pp. 39–40.

[52] *Reg.* 1.49, p. 75, lines 22–26; 2.31, p. 166, lines 20–26; 2.37, p. 173, lines 12–14.

[53] *Epistolae vagantes*, ed. Cowdrey, no. 5, pp. 12–13.

[54] *Reg.* 9.21, pp. 602, line 28 to 603, line 2; *Epistolae vagantes*, ed. Cowdrey, no. 54, pp. 132–133.

Urban II in 1095 preached his expedition to Jerusalem. He also foreshadowed how, as Hans Eberhard Mayer has perceptively explained, the crusade in due course became both a means of freeing the East from the oppression of the heathen and also a means of freeing the crusaders' souls from sin.[55]

---

[55] Mayer, *Crusades*, p. 96.

IV

POPE VICTOR AND THE EMPRESS A.

In his *Annales Ordinis Sancti Benedicti*, Mabillon printed from a now lost manuscript source *(ex schedis nostris)* a letter which a pope named Victor addressed to a Byzantine empress as *gloriosae et dilectae filiae A. imperatrici augustae.*[1] His purpose was to secure an imperial edict which would relieve pilgrims and visitors to the Holy Sepulchre at Jerusalem of the excessive tribute which Byzantine officials imposed upon them (8–10, 13–15). Although grievances arose throughout the Empire, the pope referred especially to two places where a toll of three gold hyperpyra was imposed upon each horse and upon each pair of travellers by foot. Moreover, pilgrims' horses were requisitioned and misused (10–13). The letter dates from the second half of the eleventh century, for only then during the history of the Byzantine Empire were there popes with the name Victor. But the letter, which bears neither date nor place of origin, affords no direct evidence as to whether the pope concerned was Victor II (elected in late 1054, consecrated on 16 April 1055, died on 28 July 1057) or Victor III (elected on 24 May 1086, consecrated on 9 May 1087, died on 16 September 1087). Nor at any relevant date did a Byzantine imperial consort bear a name beginning with the letter A. There is, therefore, a problem about the identity of the pope and the empress, and so about the date of the letter, which it is the purpose of this paper to discuss.

Mabillon confidently, but with little argument, ascribed it to Pope Victor III; he also suggested that, after an emendation of the address, the recipient should be regarded as the Emperor Alexius Comnenus (1081–1118). This suggestion cannot be accepted, since the letter proceeds with a reference to a 'daughter most dear to us in Christ' (3). But the ascription to Victor III was generally accepted by scholars up to Philip Jaffé in the first edition of his *Regesta pontificum Romanorum.*[2] Thirty years later, in 1881, Count Riant argued forcibly that the pope concerned was Victor II. Proposing that the empress's initial A. should be emended to T., he identified her with the Empress Theodora, whom he noted as having reigned alone at Constantinople from 12 January 1055 until her death on 22 August 1056. He associated the pope's letter to her with the return to Europe from the Levant of Bishop Lietbert of Cambrai and his companions, who had been deterred at Laodicea from completing their pilgrimage to Jerusalem by the warnings of a returning pilgrim, Bishop Halinand of Laon, about the hardship which would be encountered *en route*. Lietbert met Victor II at Cologne in early December 1056.[3] Riant concluded that the pope then sent his letter to Theodora, in ignorance of her death some three months earlier.[4]

---

[1] J. Mabillon, Annales Ordinis Sancti Benedicti, 6 vols. (Paris 1709–39) 5.647 with discussion on 237; whence, with some minor misprints, J. P. Migne, Patrologia Latina 149.961–2. Mabillon's text is given in the Appendix to this paper.

[2] P. Jaffé, Regesta pontificum Romanorum (Berlin 1851) no. 4015.

[3] The main source for the pilgrimage of Bishop Lietbert in 1054–6 is Rudolf, Vita Lietberti episcopi Cameracensis, caps. 31–42, of which the best edition is now that by A. Hofmeister in MGH, SS 30. 838–68; the relevant chapters are at 854–8.

[4] Comte Riant, Inventaire critique des lettres historiques des croisades, Archives de l'Orient Latin 1 (1881) 1–224, at 50–53, no. 17. For Theodora, see J. M. Hussey, The Later Macedonians, the

Riant's redating of the letter commanded widespread acceptance; it was, for example, adopted in the second edition of Jaffé's *Regesta*, although within the date-range 1055–6 and without reference to Cologne.[5] It has not, however, passed unchallenged, notably by B. Leib and D. Lohrmann,[6] and I have myself had occasion briefly to concur in Leib's opinion that the pope concerned was Victor III.[7] The arguments for this view are even stronger than Leib stated; this paper will present more fully the reasons for assigning the letter to Victor III during his brief tenure of the papacy in 1086–7.

Besides the difficulty that the letter, if sent by Victor II in December 1056, was written some time after Theodora's death, Riant's case for Victor II's being the sender is open to several objections. It is difficult to see what Victor could have had in mind if he had referred to the Roman church as Theodora's 'prima et propria mater' (20–1); the phrase would hardly have been diplomatic so soon after the events of 1054. She was, it is true, of honourable, indeed imperial, line *(venerabilis genealogiae)* (17), having been born in the purple as the daughter of the Macedonian Emperor Constantine VIII (963–1025, sole ruler 1025–8); but, save as an honorific flourish, there was little substance in the final assertion that the Roman church 'venerated her family lineage' *(avitam prosapiam veneratur)* (22). If Michael Psellus is to be believed, there was no weakness of government during her sole rule which might have occasioned a papal approach to her.[8]

Moreover, Riant misread the letter when he represented the exactions of Byzantine officials (6–13) as being those of Byzantine guardians of the Holy Places at Jerusalem. The letter gave no indication of place, save that they occurred widely in the Byzantine Empire, and were especially objectionable at two localities. It is, therefore, unwarranted to argue for a date before the loss of Byzantine power in Syria and Palestine which occurred through the Turkish invasions of Palestine in the 1070s, the fall of Antioch in 1085, and the Seldjuk overrunning of Asia Minor.

Nor did the experiences of Bishop Lietbert of Cambrai provide so plausible a context for the letter as Riant maintained.[9] The long account in his *Life* of his pilgrimage gave no hint of harassment by Byzantine officials, apart from his need to purchase freedom from detention by the catepan of Cyprus (cap. 41); but it was not of such vexation that Pope Victor complained. Nor did Bishop Halinand of Laon warn Lietbert of difficulties that would await him at Jerusalem; he spoke only of unspecified hardships on the journey and made no reference to Byzantine officials (cap. 41). As

Comneni and the Angeli 1025–1204, in: The Cambridge Medieval History 4: The Byzantine Empire, pt. 1: Byzantium and its Neighbours, ed. J. M. Hussey (Cambridge 1966) 193–249, at 204–5. The probable date of her death was 21 Aug.

[5] P. Jaffé, Regesta pontificum Romanorum, 2nd ed. under the direction of W. Wattenbach, 2 vols. (Leipzig 1885–8) no. 4342. The date 1055/6 is followed, for example, by S. Runciman, The Eastern Schism (Oxford 1955) 56.

[6] B. Leib, Rome, Kiev et Byzanz à la fin du XIᵉ siècle (Paris 1924) 86–8; D. Lohrmann, Das Register Papst Johannes' VIII. (872–882) (Tübingen 1968) 91; A. Becker, Papst Urban II. (1088 bis 1099) 2: Der Papst, die griechische Christenheit und der Kreuzzug (Stuttgart 1988) 23 n. 41, suspends judgement, commenting that the pope's démarche had no known result.

[7] H. E. J. Cowdrey, The Age of Abbot Desiderius. Montecassino, the Papacy, and the Normans in the Eleventh and Early Twelfth Centuries (Oxford 1983) 209; The Gregorian Papacy, Byzantium, and the First Crusade, in: Byzantium and the West c. 850–c. 1200, ed. J. D. Howard-Johnston (Amsterdam 1988) 146–69, at 160.

[8] Michel Psellos, Chronographie, ou Histoire d'un siècle de Byzanz (976–1077), ed. E. Renauld, 2 vols. (Paris 1926–8) 2.72–82, esp. cap. 4, 73.

[9] For Lietbert, see Rudolf, Vita Lietberti (as Anm. 3).

regards Victor II's journey to Germany in 1056, Riant was wrong to state that he sought the Emperor Henry III's help against the Saracens of the Mediterranean. The statement of the *Annales Romani* that Victor travelled 'pro ea causa qua et praedecessor suus, ut eicerent Agarenos, quia clamor populi illius regionis non valebat sufferre'[10] unquestionably referred to the South Italian Normans, not to the Saracens, in accordance with the general usage of this source;[11] the pope was concerned to propose a renewal of the papal-imperial alliance against the Normans which had been the policy of his predecessor Leo IX (1049–54).

While it remains possible that the letter was written by Victor II to Theodora at some time during the latter's sole rule as Byzantine empress, the argument for its being written from Cologne in early December 1056 fails completely. There is no positive evidence to associate the letter with Victor II or Theodora; save for the latter's sole rule in the East during the pontificate of a pope named Victor, there is little in the circumstances of the time to commend a date in 1055–6.

To turn to the case for preferring an ascription of the letter to Pope Victor III, it may first be pointed that he was a more likely person than his predecessor to have written to a Byzantine ruler on the subject of the harassment of pilgrims. Victor II was a prelate of the German imperial church who, before becoming pope, had from 1042 been bishop of Eichstätt. Victor III, who was descended from the family of the Lombard princes of Benevento, had since 1058 been Abbot Desiderius of Montecassino; he had, therefore, passed his lifetime in proximity to the Byzantine sphere of influence in South Italy. The embellishment of his new basilica at Montecassino, dedicated in 1071, owed much to his direct or indirect contacts with Byzantium: in Constantinople its bronze doors had been cast; there, Desiderius commissioned its golden altar the making of which was supervised by the Byzantine Emperor, Romanus IV Diogenes (1067–71), himself; from there, Desiderius recruited craftsmen who executed the basilica's marvellous mosaics.[12] In 1076, the next emperor, Michael VII Ducas (1071–8), sought the prayers of Montecassino for himself and his children and for the well-being of the Empire; in return, he granted the abbey an annual pension of twenty-four pounds of gold and four cloths *(pallia)*.[13] Desiderius' buildings at Montecassino included a large hospice *(xenodochium maximum)* for guests and pilgrims which may well have been a forum for the ventilation of pilgrims' grievances against the Byzantine authorities.[14] Against this background, Victor III, whose pontificate was a more active one than has always been appreciated,[15] emerges as a credible pope to have been responsible for the letter under discussion.

Secondly, despite statements that have been expressed to the contrary,[16] there is ample evidence for the passage of western pilgrims through Byzantine lands during the early years of Alexius Comnenus, notwithstanding the depredations of Turks and

[10] Annales Romani, in: Le Liber Pontificalis, ed. L. Duchesne, Bibliothèque des Écoles françaises d'Athènes et de Rome, 2me série, vol. 2 (Paris 1886) 334.

[11] Cf. ibid., 333, lines 16, 21, 335, lines 12–21.

[12] Chronica monasterii Casinensis, 3.18, 27, 32, ed. H. Hoffmann, MGH SS. 34. 385, 396, 402–3.

[13] Ibid. 3.39, 4.112, pp. 415–16, 581; F. Trinchera, Syllabus Graecarum membranarum (Naples 1865) 62, no. 47.

[14] Chron. Cas. 3.33, 407–8.

[15] Cowdrey (as n. 7), 207–13.

[16] e.g. by Runciman (as n. 5).

Normans upon the Empire. Thus, in 1086, Bishop Pibo of Toul, accompanied by Count Conrad of Lützelburg, brother of the anti-king Hermann of Salm, and many German *principes*, went on pilgrimage to Jerusalem and passed through Constantinople.[17] Again, soon after the death of Archbishop Lanfranc of Canterbury (1070 –89), a monk of Christ Church, Canterbury, named Joseph made a similar pilgrimage with a body of companions, and made a detour to visit Constantinople on his journey back.[18] Both Pibo and Joseph were well received and were allowed to acquire precious relics, and the sources for Victor III's time as for Victor II's are silent about pilgrims' difficulties at the hand of officials.[19] But there is evidence for the passage of pilgrims in both the middle and the late eleventh century, and the state of the Empire in Alexius Comnenus's early years is likely to have made pilgrimage in the 1080s more, rather than less, fraught with difficulties than in the time of the Empress Theodora's sole rule, and so to have elicited the letter.

Thirdly, the mother of the Emperor Alexius Comnenus, Anna Dalassena (c. 1010 –1101/2), provides a more plausible identification for the Empress A. than does the Empress Theodora. Anna was, in Pope Victor's words, 'of honourable line' (*venerabilis genealogia*) (17), at least on the maternal side.[20] Her aristocratic antecedents match the word *venerabilis* better than does Theodora's more exalted, imperial descent.[21] Her mother's family was the Dalasseni, one of the great lines which emerged under the Emperor Basil II (963–1025). According to the probable construction of its genealogy, its fortunes were established by Damianus Dalassenus, who is attested as δούξ of Antioch from 995 until his death in 998. His sons, Constantine, Theophylact, and Romanus, were notable warriors, who all achieved the rank of κατεπάν. Anna's mother, of unknown name, was the daughter of Adrian, a son of Theophylact; c. 1030, she married Alexius Charon whom Nicephorus Bryennius described as a man of outstanding wisdom, who was called Charon because with whatever weapon he struck his enemy he at once slew him. Nicephorus further added that Alexius Charon was an imperial *chargé d'affaires* in South Italy, although nothing further is known about his rank or activities. Anna was the daughter of this marriage.[22] While there

---

[17] Gesta episcoporum Tullensium, cap. 48, MGH SS. 8.647; cf. G. Meyer von Knonau, Jahrbücher des deutschen Reichs unter Heinrich IV. und Heinrich V., vol. (Leipzig 1903) 21, n. 38.

[18] C. H. Haskins, A Canterbury Monk at Constantinople c. 1090, The English Historical Review 25 (1910) 293–5.

[19] Though the German pilgrims of 1064–5 made strong if unspecific complaints; thus, Bishop Gunther of Bamberg wrote home from Laodicea that 'Constantinopolitanos vidimus graece et imperialiter arrogantes, Romanitas perpessi sumus ultra omnem humanam et ferinam rabiem sevientes; gravia quidem perpessi sumus, sed adhuc gravia supersunt': Annales Altahenses maiores, a. 1065, (ed. E. L. B. von Oefele) MGH Scriptores rerum Germanicarum, 4, p. 67.

[20] As was recognized by Anna Comnena, the principal source of information about her grandmother: Anne Comnène, Alexiade, 3.8.1 (ed. B. Leib, 4 vols., Paris 1937–76).

[21] For Anna Dalassena's family, see C. Ducange's In Alexidem notae, in: Annae Comnenae Alexiadis libri XV (edd. L. Schopen and A. Reifferscheid, 2 vols., Bonn 1839–78) 2.482–3; N. Adontz, Notes Arméno-Byzantines, 5, Byz. 10 (1935) 171–85, repr. Études Arméno-Byzantines (Lisbon 1965) 163–77; A. P. Kazhdan and A. W. Epstein, Change in Byzantine Culture in the Eleventh and Twelfth Centuries (Berkeley/Los Angeles/London 1985) 63–5; J.-C. Cheynet/J.-F. Vannier, Études prosopographiques (Paris 1986) 75–115.

[22] Nicephorus referred to Alexius Charon "ᾧ τὰ κατὰ τὴν Ἰταλίαν ἐκ βασιλέως ἐγκεχείριστο πράγματα": Nicéphore Bryennios Histoire, 1.2 (ed. P. Gautier, Brussels 1975) 76–9. No Byzantine official with whom Alexius can be identified is recorded by either J. Gay, L'Italie méridionale et l'empire byzantin depuis l'avènement de Basil Ier jusqu'à la prise de Bari par les Normans (Paris 1904) or V. von Falkenhausen, Untersuchungen über die byzantinische Herrschaft in Süditalien vom 9. bis ins 11. Jahrhundert (Wiesbaden 1967).

is no positive evidence, Alexius Charon may have been known about at Victor III's abbey of Montecassino and thence in papal circles (22); for, as an 'external cardinal' of the Roman church from 1059, Desiderius was a familiar figure at Rome. In any case, both the greater lapse of time since the traumatic events of 1054 and the cordial relations that prevailed between Montecassino and Byzantium make it more likely that Victor III should refer to the Roman church as the empress's 'prima et propria mater' than that the German imperial bishop Victor II should have done so. Anna's place of birth is unknown, but it is not impossible that Victor III should have known it to have been in Italy.

Anna Dalassena married John Comnenus (died 1067); Alexius was the third of their eight children. In the *Alexiad*, their granddaughter Anna Comnena praised her as being of exceptional energy, skill, and experience in matters of government; in this judgement, Nicephorus Briennius concurred.[23] Anna wrote of her piety and moral probity,[24] her longing for the religious life,[25] and her regard for and patronage of monks.[26] As emperor, Alexius Comnenus had the highest confidence in his mother as a woman of affairs.[27] In 1081, he entrusted to her the civil side of imperial administration in order that he might concentrate upon military affairs, issuing a chrysobull to publish his decision.[28] Anna thus became virtually imperial vicegerent in all non-military respects, including fiscal matters.[29] She was, therefore, an appropriate person for Victor III to approach about the oppressions of imperial officials–the more so because, during Victor's pontificate, Alexius Comnenus remained subject to the excommunication under which Victor's predecessor as pope, Gregory VII (1073–85) had placed him. The address of Pope Victor's letter to an *imperatrix augusta* (1–2) may recall the usage of Gregory VII in referring to the western Empress-mother Agnes, widow of the Emperor Henry III (1039–56) and mother of the German king Henry IV(1056–1106) up to her death at Rome in December 1077.[30] Moreover, Anna Comnena referred to Anna Dalassena as δέσποινα (sovereign) and βασιλίς (empress).[31] Her position and authority since 1081 make an imperial address by the papal chancery understandable, and an association of Pope Victor's letter with her has the attraction of requiring no emendment of the reading *A. imperatrici augustae* (1–2). Finally, Victor III had a motive for paying Anna Dalassena courtly compliments (1–2, 3–4, 16–17, 22): he wished to win over her son Alexius Comnenus from supporting Henry IV of Germany and his antipope Clement III.

While the date and circumstances of composition of the letter of Pope Victor to the Empress A. cannot be definitely determined, the balance of probability is that it was dispatched in 1086/7 by the South Italian Pope Victor III to the Emperor

---

[23] Alexiad, 3.7.2–3, 4.4.1; Nicephorus Bryennius, Hist. 1.6 (as n. 22) 84–7. Leib summarizes Anna's character and career in Alexiade (as n. 20), 1.xiii–xvii; see also C. Diehl, Figures byzantines, vol. 1 (Paris 1906) 317–342. Cheynet and Vannier (as n. 21) 95–9.

[24] Alexiad 2.5.1–2, 3.5.1, 3.8.2–8.

[25] Ibid. 3.6.1–2, 3.8.4.

[26] Ibid. 1.8.2, 3.8.3.

[27] Ibid. 3.6.1.

[28] Ibid. 3.6.3–8.

[29] Ibid. 3.7.1, cf. 3.7.4–5, 3.8.1, 10.4.5.

[30] Gregory VII, Registrum, 2.30, 44, 4.3, ed. E. Caspar, MGH Epistolae selectae 2, 163, 181, 299; Quellen und Forschungen zum Urkunden- und Kanzleiwesen Papst Gregors VII., 1: Quellen: Urkunden. Regesten. Facsimilia, ed. L. Santifaller, (Vatican City 1957) no. 98, 83.

[31] δέσποινα: Alexiad 2.7.7, 3.6.4, 10.4.5; βασιλίς: 3.8.10, 6.7.5.

Alexius Comnenus's mother and vicegerent Anna Dalassena, rather than in 1055/6 by Pope Victor II to the Empress Theodora, at that time sole ruler of the Byzantine Empire.*

APPENDIX

Pope Victor requests Empress A. to secure relief for pilgrims to the Holy Sepulchre from excessive exactions by Byzantine officials

MSS: none. Printed: Mabillon, *Annales OSB*, 5.647, no. 26. Migne, *PL* 149.961–2. *Pontificia Commissio ad redigendum codicem iuris canonici orientalis. Fontes III, 1.* Vatican 1953, p. 784 (nr. 373).

Victor episcopus, servus servorum Dei, gloriosae et dilectae filiae A. imperatrici augustae.

Apostolicae sedis debito compellimur, carissima nobis in Christo filia, majoribus et minoribus non subtrahere solitaria monita. In qua utique causa tanto magis insistere sublimioribus debemus, quanto eos temporaliter plus prodesse aut nocere posse 5 Christi pauperibus scimus. Unde cupiens tuam dignitatem in futuro non condemnari pro temporali oppressione peregrinorum et pauperum, sed glorificari pro revelatione eorum, denunciamus et obsecramus in Domino Jesu, ut ab oratoribus et visitatoribus sancti et gloriosi Sepulchri ejus facias cessare gravissimum et importabile tributum quod eis imponitur a tuis officialibus. Ut enim alia quae ubivis locorum imperii tui 10 patiuntur taceamus, in duobus tantum locis adeo angariantur, ut pro singulis equis tres aurei, et ex binis peditibus totidem tollantur. Insuper equos eorumdem oratorum violenter ablatos quandiu volunt angariant et vexant. Cujus quidem periculi malum, nisi quantocius imperiali edicto a regno tuo propellas, in animam tuam, quod absit, 15 redundaturum scias: quia ad majores respicit quicquid a minoribus delinquitur, et facientes et consentientes pari poena plectentur. Nos tamen, ut decet, semper in bono memores tui, et tuae venerabilis genealogiae, optamus te prae multis sic temet atque tuos regere, quatenus sic nomen bonum, quod melius est quam divitiae multae, acquiras, et in futuro gaudium domini tui feliciter introeas. Valere perpetuo tuam ex- 20 cellentiam et optamus et oramus; atque ut Romanae ecclesiae, scilicet primae et propriae matris tuae, sicut te decet, recorderis, eamque semper venereris admonemus. Equidem ipsa jugiter tui in bono recordatur, et avitam prosapiam tuam veneratur.

4 solitaria: *perhaps* salutaria   7 revelatione: *Migne reads* relevatione *but cf. 1 Pet. 4:13*

*   This paper was presented as a communication to the XVIIIth International Congress of Byzantine Studies, Moscow, 8–15 August 1991. I gratefully acknowledge the receipt of subsidies from St Edmund Hall, Oxford, and from the Society for the Promotion of Byzantine Studies towards the expenses of attending the Congress.

V

Pope Urban II and the Idea of Crusade

Like many churchmen during the period of the First Crusade, Abbot Geoffrey of Vendôme was adamant that monks should not as a rule go Crusading. «I am in a position to know», he wrote, «as one who heard with his own ears the words of the Lord Pope Urban, when he at once enjoined upon laymen the pilgrimage to Jerusalem and also prohibited this pilgrimage to monks» ([1]). After Urban's address at Clermont in November 1095, according to Count Fulk *le Réchin* he came to Anjou in Lent 1096, «and urged its people to go to Jerusalem and attack the gentile peoples who

This paper was read to the international conference *Geistliche und weltliche Gewalten in der Realität und der Ideologie des hohen und späten Mittelalters* held from 31 October to 1 November 1991 in the Humboldt University at Berlin in honour of the sixty-fifth birthday of Prof. Dr. phil. habil. Bernhard Töpfer. It is dedicated to him in respect and friendship.

The following abbreviations have been used in the footnotes:

LP	*Le Liber Pontificalis*, ed. L. DUCHESNE, 3 vols. Bibliothèque des Écoles françaises d'Athènes et de Rome, 2ème Ser, 3, Paris, 1886-1957
MGH	*Monumenta Germaniae Historica*
— Epp. sel.	*Epistolae selectae*
— Schriften	*Schriften der MGH*
— SS	*Scriptores*
PL	J. P. MIGNE, *Patrologia Latina*
RHC Oc.	*Recueil des historians des Croisades, Historiens occidentaux*
SG	*Studi Gregoriani*

(1) *Ep.* 4,21, *PL* 157,162B: *Quod novi ego ipse, sicut ille, cuius aures erant ad os domini Urbani papae, cum et eundo Hierusalem peregrinari praeciperet laicis, et ipsam peregrinationem monachis prohiberet.*

722

had seized that city and all the lands of the Christians up to Constantinople» (²). Both the abbot and the count bore eye-witness to Urban as not only naming Jerusalem from the beginning of his Crusade preaching but as also giving it the central place in the expedition that he envisaged: for the abbot, Jerusalem was the goal of the Crusade when seen as a pilgrimage; for the count, the Crusade as holy war was likewise directed to Jerusalem. Though Constantinople as well as Jerusalem was to be delivered from gentile oppression, the perspective was one with Jerusalem as the central point. In order that emphasis might fall upon the Holy City, geographical proximity to the west and the likely unfolding of military events were reversed: the Crusading host was to go to Jerusalem and attack the gentiles who had seized that city and Christian lands up to Constantinople.

Despite such evidence, the debate about Jerusalem's centrality in Urban's preaching and, indeed, about whether he so much as mentioned it at Clermont, continues. The plan of this paper is, first, to insist upon the strength of the evidence that Urban named the Holy City, making it from the first central to his plans and preaching, and then to discuss three considerations which make it likely to have been in his mind by 1095 so that he was disposed to give it emphasis.

There is no need again to assemble all the evidence in support of Jerusalem's having from the outset formed part of Urban's preaching of the Crusade (³); for continuing doubts on this

---

(2) *Fragmentum historiae Andegavensis*, in: *Chroniques des comtes d'Anjou et des seigneurs d'Amboise*, edd. L. HALPEN and R. POUPARDIN, Paris, 1913, pp. 237-238: *In fine cuius anni, appropinquante quadragesima, venit Andegavim papa Romanus Urbanus et ammonuit gentem nostram ut irent Jerusalem expugnaturi gentilem populum qui civitatem illam et totam terram christianorum usque Constantinopolim occupaverant.* Urban was also said to have named Jerusalem first among eastern cities in the account of his preaching at Clermont in the *Gesta Ambaziensium dominorum*: ibid., p. 100.

(3) For my own discussions, see H. E. J. COWDREY, *Pope Urban II's Preaching of the First Crusade*, in: *History*, 55 (1970), 177-188, repr. in: *Popes, Monks and Crusaders*, London, 1984, no. XVI; *The Mahdia Campaign of 1087*, in: *The English Historical Review*, 92 (1977), 1-29, repr. in: *Popes, Monks and Crusaders*, no. XII; *The Gregorian Papacy, Byzantium, and the First Crusade*, in: *Byzantium and the West c. 850-c.1200*, ed. J. HOWARD-JOHNSTON, Amsterdam, 1988, pp. 145-169; *The Papacy and the Origins of Crusading*, in: *Medieval History*, 1 (1991), 48-60. The two supposed letters of Urban II, the second of which concerns the First Crusade, published by J. RAMACKERS, *Zwei unbekannte Briefe Urbans II. Zugleich ein Beitrag zum Problem der Register dieses Papstes*, in: *Quellen und Forschungen aus Italienischen Archiven und Bibliotheken*, 26 (1935-6), 268-276, are in fact forgeries based upon letters of the first year of the pontificate of Pope Innocent III (1198-1216); see *Die Register Innocenz' III.*, 1 Bd., *1 Pontifikatsjahr: Texte*, edd. O. HAGENEDER and A. HAIDACHER, Graz and Cologne, 1964, pp. 9-12, 21-

score, it may suffice to refer to the general histories of Crusading by E. Zöllner and H. E. Mayer (⁴). Attention may, however, be especially directed to the landmark that was reached in the recent debate with the publication in 1988 of the second volume of Alfons Becker's magisterial study of Urban II; the new volume is entirely devoted to the pope in relation to Greek Christendom and the Crusade. Central to Becker's argument is the contention, which he abundantly documents, that Urban understood Christian history according to a fourfold *schema*: (1) in Christian antiquity, there was a flowering of the church with a high standard of Christian life in major churches; but (2), especially in the seventh and eighth centuries and on account of human sins, many of these churches became subject to Saracen supremacy and tyranny; however (3) *nostris temporibus* there had ensued the great turning-point of the Christian Reconquest which spread through the western, central, and ultimately eastern Mediterranean; the Reconquest carried with it (4) a Christian restoration effected through the renewed outpouring of God's mercy and grace. In this restoration, the pope acted as God's *co-operator* (⁵). In the light of this *schema*, Becker regards Jerusalem as having been from 1095 not the only but the principal goal of the military operation that Urban proclaimed: «Jerusalem war nicht das einzige, aber das höchste Ziel des Unternehmens» (⁶).

Becker's *schema*, in which Jerusalem is placed in the setting of a long view of Christian history, offers a suggestive context for the evidence, like the two sources with which this paper started, which indicates that Urban consistently placed Jerusalem at the centre of his statements about the Crusade. The canons of the council of Clermont refer to it as both the goal and the centre of Urban's project. Canon 2 as recorded by Bishop Lambert of Arras promised that, if a man set out with a right disposition of mind to set free the city of Jerusalem, the journey would be reck-

---

22, nos. 4,13. My citation of the second of these letters in the third of the above articles at p. 165 must, therefore, be excluded from the argument. See also H. ROSCHER, *Zwei angebliche Briefe Papst Urbans II*, in: *Zeitschrift für Kirchengeschiche*, 76 (1965), 149-152; I am grateful to Prof. Dr H. E. Mayer, Kiel, for information about this article.

(4) W. ZÖLLNER, *Geschichte der Kreuzzüge*, 4th edn, Berlin, 1983, p. 50; H. E. MAYER, *The Crusades*, trans. J. GILLINGHAM, 2nd edn, Oxford, 1988, pp. 10-11.

(5) A. BECKER, *Papst Urban II. (1088-1099)*, MGH Schriften, 19, Stuttgart, 1964 -, 2,352-362, 374-376, 398-399; the *schema* is summarized at pp. 352-353.

(6) Ibid., p. 397.

oned to him in place of all penance ([7]). Canon 9 in the so-called Polycarp-Cencius summary of the proceedings, which provided for the security of the property of those who went on the Crusade, declared that «an expedition was decided upon, made up of knights and footsoldiers, to deliver Jerusalem and the other churches of Asia from the power of the Saracens» ([8]). Since the canons were written down as memoranda, an emphasis that was not Urban's may have been introduced; yet the common reference to Jerusalem is striking.

The surviving versions of and references to Urban's sermon at the end of the council of Clermont were all written after the city's capture in 1099; they were undoubtedly coloured by the success of which Urban did not live to learn. Nevertheless, it is remarkable that, of the main versions of the sermon, only that by Fulcher of Chartres, who was probably at Clermont and who wrote very early in the twelfth century, made no mention of Jerusalem ([9]). As chaplain to Count Baldwin of Boulogne he had been diverted to Edessa from the main Crusade, and he may therefore have wished to play Jerusalem down. Baldric of Bourgueil, who wrote c. 1108 and who was certainly at Clermont, dwelt at length upon the Moslem occupation of Jerusalem and upon Moslem outrages here. He represented Urban as citing Ps. 78 (Vg.), 1-4 as a prophecy that had in his day been fulfilled:

O God, the heathen have come into your inheritance:
    they have defiled your holy temple;
    they have established Jerusalem as a fruit-store.
They have exposed the corpses of your servants as food for the birds of
    the air;
    the flesh of your saints, for the beasts of the field.
They have poured out their blood like water all round Jerusalem,
    and there was no one to bury them.
We are made a reproach to our neighbours,
    a mockery and a scorn to those round about us.

(7) R. SOMERVILLE, *The Councils of Urban II, 1: Decreta Claromontensia, Annuarium historiae conciliorum, Supplementum* 1, Amsterdam, 1972, p. 74: *Quicumque pro sola devotione, non pro honoris vel pecunie adeptione, ad liberandam ecclesiam Dei Hierusalem profectus fuerit, iter illud pro omni penitentia ei reputetur.*

(8) Ibid., p. 124: *Tunc etiam expeditio facta est, et constituta est equitum et peditum ad Ierusalem et alias Asie ecclesias a Sarracenorum potestate eruendas.*

(9) FULCHER OF CHARTRES, *Historia Hierosolymitana,* 1,3,2-8, ed. H. HAGENMEYER, Heidelberg, 1913, pp. 132-138.

According to Baldric, Urban dwelt upon the holiness of the land that had witnessed the events recorded in holy scripture ([10]). Robert the monk was also at Clermont and wrote before 1107. According to him, Urban pleaded the plight of the holy places; Jerusalem was the navel of the world, and Urban urged his hearers to take the road to the holy sepulchre ([11]). Guibert of Nogent was not in Urban's audience, but wrote before 1108; he concentrated heavily upon Jerusalem as the key to God's plan in history ([12]). Chroniclers who referred to Urban's preaching without elaborating it at length also commonly made Jerusalem its leading theme. For Peter Tudebode, it centred upon an appeal that his hearers «should not hesitate humbly to embark upon the way of the Lord and the holy sepulchre» ([13]). Chroniclers who used his History developed this view; thus, writing before *c.* 1126, the chronicler of Saint-Maixent (dioc. Poitiers) said that, wherever Urban had travelled, he ordered men to make crosses and to go to Jerusalem and free it from the Turks and other heathen ([14]). It was not only French chroniclers who maintained this emphasis. In Swabia, Bernold of St. Blasien was quick to record that a very great multitude from Italy and from all *Gallia* and *Germania* began to go to Jerusalem against the pagans in order to liberate the Christians, and that of this expedition the lord pope was the chief author ([15]). In the Abruzzi, the chronicle of the monastery of San Clemente at Casauria was written somewhat later. But it, too, attributed the Crusade to Urban's grief that the Saracens had seized the holy city of Jerusalem with the Lord's sepulchre, and to his desire to deliver it from the hands of the wicked and to restore it to its ancient liberty (*reddere pristinae libertati*) ([16]).

(10) BALDRIC OF BOURGUEIL, *Historia Jerosolimitana*, 1,4, *RHC Oc.* 4,12-15.

(11) ROBERT OF REIMS, *Historia Iherosolimitana*, 1,1-2, *RHC Oc.* 3,727-730.

(12) GUIBERT OF NOGENT, *Historia quae dicitur Gesta Dei per Francos*, 2,4, *RHC Oc.* 4,127-140.

(13) PETRUS TUDEBODUS, *Historia de Hierosolimitano itinere*, edd. J. H. and L. L. HILL, Paris, 1977, pp. 31-32: *Apostolicus namque Romanę sedis Urbanus ... cepit ... predicare dicens ut si quis animam suam salvam facere voluisset, non dubitasset viam humiliter incipere Domini et Sancti Sepulchri.*

(14) *La Chronique de Saint-Maixent, 751-1140, a.* 1096, ed. J. VERDON, Paris, 1979, p. 154: *Ubicumque fuit, precepit cruces facere hominibus et pergere Jerusalem et liberare eam a Turcis et aliis gentibus.*

(15) BERNOLD, *Chronicon, a.* 1096, *MGH SS* 5,464: *His temporibus maxima multitudo de Italia et omni Gallia et Germania Ierosolimam contra paganos, ut liberarent christianos, ire cepit. Cuius expeditionis domnus papa maximus auctor fuit.*

(16) *Chronicon Casauriense*, 5, in: L. A. MURATORI, *Rerum Italicarum scriptores*, 2/2, Milan, 1726, col. 872AB: *Hic dolens, quia Saraceni occupaverant sanctam civitatem Hierusalem et*

The Spanish chronicler Roderic of Toledo wrote in connection with Archbishop Bernard of Toledo, who had been at Clermont, that Urban preached the Crusade «because the city of Jerusalem was held by the Hagarenes» ([17]). Some of these references to Jerusalem have undoubtedly an *ex eventu* colouring; but the insistence upon it by so many persons in different places and at different times is impressive witness to the significance that Jerusalem was believed to have had for Urban.

It is the more impressive since, although only a few pieces of evidence remain to illustrate Urban's concern with the Crusade after he had proclaimed it at Clermont, references to Jerusalem are a characteristic feature of them. This is the case, first of all, with sources other than Urban's own letters. The chronicle of San Clemente at Casauria referred to a brief visit by Urban to Chieti, in the south-eastern marches of the duchy of Spoleto, perhaps as early as March 1097; there, he held a conference with bishops and lay magnates *de via Jerosolomitana* ([18]). A letter of October 1098 in which the clergy and people of Lucca gave general publicity to a report of the capture of Antioch concluded with a notice that, at the council of Bari, Urban was himself considering a journey to Jerusalem; this may itself have been in response to the appeal of the Crusading princes that he should go to the East ([19]). Finally, at the council which Urban held in St

sepulchrum Domini, volens eam eripere de manibus impiorum et reddere pristinae libertati, praedicavit remissionem peccatorum, et vice sibi tradita a Deo omnibus dedit quicunque Hierusalem tenderent, et civitatem et terram transmarinam, quae a Sarracenis possidebatur, liberarent, adiciens etiam hoc, ut si quisquam in via sive in pugna pro Christo moreretur, in numero martyrum absolutus ab omnibus peccatis suis computaretur. Et dum totus mundus post eum curreret avidus remissionem peccatorum accipere et in numero sanctorum martyrum esse, contigit, ut hoc praedicans praedictus summus pontifex devenerit Thyetum, ibique perendinans non multis diebus, cum episcopis et baronibus de via Jerosolomytana habuit commune colloquium.

(17) RODERIC OF TOLEDO, *De rebus Hispaniae*, 6,26, in: *Hispaniae illustratae ... scriptores varii*, ed. A. SCHOTT, Frankfurt, 1603-1608, 2,107.

(18) As n. 16. For the date, see BECKER (as n. 5), 2,379-380.

(19) H. HAGENMEYER, *Die Kreuzzugsbriefe aus den jahren 1088-1100*, Innsbruck, 1901, pp. 165-167, no. 17,12: *Notum quoque vobis facimus, quod Dominus papa Urbanus apud Barum tenet concilium, tractans et disponens cum multis terrae senatoribus ad Jerusalem profecto tendere.* The Norman leader Bohemond also referred to Urban's intention, which his death prevented, in a letter of 1106 or 1108 to Pope Paschal II: W. HOLTZMANN, *Zur Geschichte des Investiturstreits, 2: Bohemond von Antioch und Alexios I.*, in: *Neues Archiv der Gesellschaft für ältere deutsche Geschichtskunde*, 50 (1935), 280-282. For the letter of the Crusading leaders, dated 11 Sept. 1098, see HAGENMEYER, *Die Kreuzzugsbriefe*, pp. 161-165, no. 16; at 16,2 the Crusaders are described as *Hierosolymitani Iesu Christi*. For further comment, see BECKER (as n. 5), 2,198, 428.

Peter's at Rome in April 1099, he was said by the Swabian chronicler Bernold to have urged men to rally to the help of their brothers who were engaged upon the journey to Jerusalem ([20]).

Furthermore, Urban himself prominently named Jerusalem in his three surviving letters which directly concern the Crusade. Between December 1095 and February 1096, and so at a very early date, he announced to the Flemings his plans for the mustering of the Crusade. He explained his expedition in terms which gave Jerusalem emphasis at the Holy City of Christ:

We believe that you are already informed of the barbaric fury which, by its attacks which move us to compassion, has laid waste the churches of God in eastern parts and, moreover, what is shocking to mention, has delivered the Holy City of Christ, made illustrious by his passion and resurrection, together with its churches, into an intolerable servitude. Grieving as was due in face of such a calamity, we journeyed to France and in large measure stirred up the rulers and subjects of that land to seek the liberation of the eastern churches ([21]).

The «calamity» of the eastern churches was a «servitude» which, according to Becker's *schema*, began with the Moslem conquest of the seventh century but was intensified since the Turkish inroads of the eleventh; the plight of Jerusalem was particularly scandalous. When Urban wrote from Pavia on 16 September 1096 to inform the Bolognese of who might and who might not go on Crusade, he dwelt yet more intensively upon Jerusalem:

We have heard that some of you have formed a desire to journey to Jerusalem, and you are aware that this pleases us greatly. Know that we remit the whole penance due for their sins to all who set out, not from greed of this world's goods, but simply for the salvation of their souls and for the liberation of the church (*ecclesiae liberatione*) ([22]).

---

(20) BERNOLD (as n. 15), a. 1099, p. 466: *De Ierosolimitano itinere multum rogavit ut irent et fratribus suis laborantibus succurrerent*. The Chronicle of Saint-Maixent recorded that *Eo anno fuit factum Rome concilium quod novissime tenuit Urbanus papa ... in quo confirmavit et ceteri viam Sancti Sepulchri Domini Nostri Jhesu Christi*: (as n. 14), a. 1099, p. 168. Archbishop Anselm of Canterbury's presence at Bari and Rome goes far to account for the change of mind about the Crusade which issued in his enthusiasm at the setting up in 1100 of the Latin kingdom of Jerusalem under Baldwin I: *Epp.* 235, 324, in: SANCTI ANSELMI CANTUARIENSIS ARCHIEPISCOPI, *Opera omnia*, ed. F. S. SCHMITT, 6 vols, Edinburgh, 1964-1961, 4,142-143, 5,255.

(21) HAGENMEYER (as n. 19), pp. 136-137, no. 2,2-3.

(22) Ibid., pp. 137-138, no. 3,4.

A similar concentration marked the letter which Urban wrote on 7 October 1096 from Cremona to the monastic community at Vallombrosa, and which had the same purpose as that to the Bolognese:

> We have heard that certain of you want to set out with the knights who are going to Jerusalem for the sake of liberating Christendom. The sacrifice is proper, but the apportioning of it is not. It was the hearts of knights that we stirred up for this expedition since by their arms they can ward off the ferocity of the Saracens and restore the ancient liberty of the Christians (*Christianorum ... libertati prisinae restituere*) ([23]).

Urban's concern to restore the *pristina libertas* of Christians, which also impressed the Casauria chronicler, is noteworthy. Like the description to the Flemings of Jerusalem as «the Holy City of Christ, made illustrious by his passion and resurrection», it expresses Urban's concern with Jerusalem as the city where Christ redeemed mankind and where his church had its beginnings. The condition of its earliest Christian days was something that Urban intended to recover and renew. Count Fulk *le Réchin* of Anjou may well have been correct in assigning to Jerusalem a central place in Urban's preaching and perspective ([24]).

The case that Urban laid such emphasis upon Jerusalem is the stronger if, as Abbot Geoffrey of Vendôme recalled, Urban from the start included in his call to Crusade the theme of pilgrimage ([25]). It is Becker's opinion that the idea of the Crusade as a pilgrimage developed only gradually and secondarily as the movement gathered momentum ([26]). This view does not do justice to the frequency with which charters recording knights' early reactions to Urban's call referred to the projected expedition in pilgrimage terms, regarding the expedition as a *peregrinatio* and the individual's participation as going to Jerusalem *peregre* ([27]). It is significant that, in a letter which the Byzantine Emperor Alexius Comnenus wrote in 1097 to Abbot Oderisius I of Monte-

---

(23) W. WIEDERHOLD, *Papsturkunden in Florenz*, no. 6, in: *Nachrichten von der Königl. Gesellschaft der Wissenschaften zu Göttingen, ph.-hist. Kl.*, Göttingen, 1901, pp. 313-314.

(24) As n. 2.

(25) As n. 1.

(26) BECKER (as n. 5), 4,387-388, 396, but cf. 407.

(27) COWDREY, *Pope Urban II's Preaching* (as n. 3), pp. 181-183.

cassino in answer to the abbot's requests about his reception of
the Crusaders, Alexius referred to the Crusaders as *peregrini* ([28]).
At Piacenza in 1095, Alexius had asked Urban for military
help ([29]). That after Oderisius's approach he regarded the Crusaders as *peregrini* suggests that this was how they were regarded
officially in the circle of Urban's closest collaborators as well as
in popular response. A pilgrimage implies a precise and spiritual
goal. In so far as the Crusade was officially presented as a pilgrimage, the case for the naming of Jerusalem as its goal is
strengthened ([30]).

There is thus substantial evidence that Urban both named
Jerusalem from the earliest days of his Crusade preaching and
assigned it centrality as the goal alike of his military campaign to
free the eastern churches and of a pilgrimage the completion of
which would ensure the spiritual benefits that he held out. In the
second part of this paper, three factors will be discussed that
may help to account for the centrality of Jerusalem in Urban's
Crusade ideology, because by 1095 it was already a potent idea
in his mind. If the evidential basis is limited and in large part
circumstantial, it must be recalled that the loss of Urban's Register of letters has deprived the historian of such a source as is
available for Gregory VII; while many privileges and formal documents survive from Urban's pontificate, there are relatively few
letters which reveal his mind as do those of Gregory VII which
are of his own dictation.

The first factor is the possible impact of Jerusalem upon Urban as a result of his association with Cluny, where he became a
monk in the late 1060s and grand prior by 1076, before leaving
for Rome, probably in 1079, to become cardinal-bishop of Ostia
and, from 1088 to 1099, pope. Cluny's impressive round of liturgical worship is likely to have imprinted upon his mind the imagery of Jerusalem in the Psalms which may be illustrated by the

(28) HAGENMEYER (as n. 19), pp. 140-141, no. 5,4: *De his autem, quae de peregrinis dicen-
dum est, qualiter Deus prospere se habuit circa nos et circa illos usque ad praesens, novit im-
perium meum, quod audistis a plurimus.*
(29) BERNOLD (as n. 15), a. 1095, p. 462.
(30) The history of the Mahdia campaign of 1087 tells against the setting of too great a
contrast between holy war and pilgrimage: COWDREY, *The Mahdia Campaign* (as n. 9), pp. 22-
23. In the Introduction to their edition of Peter Tudebode, the Hills make the important observation that, in some charters from Languedoc, the words *iter* and *via* were currently used
of pilgrimage as well as of warfare: (as n. 13), p. 13.

picture of the city's desolation in Ps. 78(Vg.) which has already been cited ([31]). Nothing embeds religious imagery more deeply in the mind than regular liturgical recitation. The special uses to which the Cluniacs also put Jerusalem Psalms is illustrated by Abbot Hugh of Semur's decree of between 1090 and 1093, that there should regularly (*sine intermissione*) be chanted at Terce on behalf of King Alphonso VI of León-Castile, who was hard-pressed by Almoravid attacks, the Psalm *Exaudiat te Dominus* (Ps. 19(Vg.)). It was a prayer for God's support from his sanctuary at Zion, or Jerusalem:

The Lord hear you in the day of trouble!
The name of the God of Jacob defend you!
May he help you from the sanctuary,
and give you support from Zion! ([32])

Furthermore, in the impressive ceremonies of Holy Week and Pentecost, Cluny's Customs provided for the especially solemn commemoration of Christ's entry into Jerusalem on Palm Sunday, for the elaborate Veneration of the Cross on Good Friday, and for the no less solemn commemoration at Pentecost of the coming of the Holy Spirit upon the Jerusalem church ([33]).

That Cluny's abundant liturgical references to Jerusalem may have helped to form Urban's thinking in preparation for the Crusade has been suggested before. A second factor, which has not hitherto been given the discussion that it deserves, is the impact that the Holy City may have had upon Urban through his particularly lively understanding of the earliest, post-Pentecostal church at Jerusalem as a pattern of life for both monks and regular canons ([34]). Urban's special contribution as pope to the recognition of regular canons because they followed this pattern of life is in itself well documented. In five surviving charters, all or most of which date from between 1092 and 1095 and so from the three years immediately before Urban preached the Crusade,

---

(31) Above, p. 724.

(32) H. E. J. COWDREY, *Memorials of Abbot Hugh of Cluny*, in: *SG* 11 (1978), 159-160.

(33) ULRICH OF CLUNY, *Antiquiores consuetudines Cluniacensis monasterii*, 1,13, 23-4, 54, in: *PL* 149,661-662, 671-672, 698.

(34) For a wide-ranging discussion of the eleventh-century preoccupation with the primitive church, see G. MICCOLI, «*Ecclesiae primitivae forma*», in: ibid. *Chiesa Gregoriana. Ricerche sulla Riforma del secolo XI*, Florence, 1966, pp. 225-299.

there is a fresh appraisal of the canonical life which is likely to express Urban's own view of it ([35]). According to the earliest, and to modern historians most familiar, version in Urban's second charter for the regular canons of Rottenbuch (dioc. Freising), canons were seeking «to renew the praiseworthy life of the holy fathers and to revive the institutes of apostolic discipline in the earliest days of the church» (*vos estis, qui sanctorum patrum vitam probabilem renovatis et apostolice instituta discipline in primordiis ecclesie exorta, sed crescente ecclesia iam pene deleta instinctu Spiritus sancti suscitatis*). The parallel with the sequence of pristine excellence – subsequent decline – contemporary restoration which Becker observes in Urban's Crusading *schema* is striking. Urban went on to observe that, from its earliest days, the church had offered two institutes of life: a lowly one for everyday Christians, but for the strong a higher one, by which the life of blessedness might be perfected. At first, the strong had been divided between monks and canons, but whereas the monks had persisted in their fervour the canons had largely decayed. Yet in Urban's day, it should not be held less meritorious to observe «this life of the primitive church» – the canonical life – than to observe that of the monks (*Itaque non minoris estimandum est meriti, hanc vitam ecclesie primitivam .... perseverantia custodire*). Urban established a comparability of esteem between monks and canons because of their common origin in the earliest church of Jerusalem ([36]).

Urban is said in other sources, as well, to have expressed a commitment to the apostolic discipline of the earliest days of the church. A canon of the council of Piacenza (1095) which is ascribed to him grounded the canons' renunciation of private property upon the model of the primitive church at Jerusalem, in

---

(35) The list of them was first assembled by W. LEVISON, *Eine angebliche Urkunde Papst Gelasius II. für die Regularkanoniker*, in: *Zeitschrift der Savigny-Stiftung für Rechtsgeschichte, Kan. Abt.*, 8 (1918), 31-33.

(36) The best text of the Rottenbuch charter is in: J. MOIS, *Das Stift Rottenbuch in der Kirchenreform des XI.-XII. Jahrhunderts*, Munich, 1953, pp. 76-77, = *Ep.* 58, PL 151,337-9. The other charters are: (1) for Saint-Ruf at Avignon (date not known), U. CHEVALIER, *Codex diplomaticus ordinis Sancti Rufi Valentiae*, Collection de cartulaires Dauphinois 9, Valence, 1891, pp. 8-9, no. 5; (2) for Saint-Paul at Narbonne (1093), *Ep.* 79, PL 151,360-361; (3) for Saint-Quentin at Beauvais (1093), *Analecta juris pontificii*, X^e sér., Rome, 1869, cols 531-533, no. 75; (4) for Maguelonne (1095), *Ep.* 136, PL 151,408-10. *Ep.* 279, PL 151,535-536 has no independent evidential value.

which no one called anything his own (Acts 4,32) [37]. Another, but undated, decision that is attributed to Urban related the canons' life even more fully to the Jerusalem church of Acts 4,32-35, when Christians assembled together and had all things in common, and there was a single heart and mind amongst all believers [38]. In 1091, the chronicler Bernold cited a letter of Urban in praise of the canonical life, which was «the more worthy of perpetual observance because it is formed according to the pattern of the primitive church» [39]. This crescendo of approval during the years before 1095 for the «primitive life of the church» implies on Urban's part a lively awareness and admiration of the earliest church at Jerusalem as depicted in Acts 2,44-47 and 4,32-35.

The idea of the Crusade thus took shape in the mind of a pope who was already concerned to restore in the regular canons of the west the *instituta discipline in primordiis ecclesie* as established after Pentecost at Jerusalem. Having regard to the *schema* of his thought about the east, he seems to have sought through the Crusade a comparable renewal and restoration there of the Jerusalem church itself, by restoring the *Christianorum ... pristina libertas* of which he wrote to the monks of Vallombrosa and which the Casauria chronicler remembered as a theme of his Crusade preaching. The primitive church of Jerusalem which Urban saw as the model for the canonical life may also have been a stimulus to him in envisaging the church of Jerusalem as he hoped to restore it by means of the Crusade.

It should not escape notice that, although the renewal of the church *ad instar vitae apostolicae* was a widely entertained aspi-

---

(37) C. DEREINE, *Le problème de la vie commune chez les canonistes d'Anselme de Lucques à Gratien*, SG 3 (1948), 287-298, at p. 298: *De communi clericorum vita, novum quid nequaquam indicimus sed eos qui ecclesiae beneficiis potiuntur, propriis renuntiare ad exemplar primitivae ecclesiae in qua nemo aliquid suum dicebat, sed communione una vivere praecipimus...*

(38) H. FUHRMANN, *Papst Urban II. und der Stand der Regularkanoniker*, in: Sitzungsberichte der Bayerische Akademie der Wissenschaften, ph.-hist. Kl., Jahrgang 1984, Heft 2, Munich, 1984, pp. 42-44, no. 4: *Quicumque vivunt in congregatione, quamvis nondum fecerint votum nichil habendi, comunem tamen vitam habent susceptam, quia ad exemplum eorum, quibus sine proprietate erant omnia communia, convenerunt in unum. Omnes quippe congregationes et specialiter canonicę iuxta formam et exemplum primitivę ęcclesię sunt institutę, de qua scriptum est: Multitudinis credentium erat cor unum et anima una et cętera.*

(39) BERNOLD (as n. 15), a. 1091, p. 453, = *Ep.* 56, PL 151,336: *Nos autem eandem conversationem et consuetudinem, sicut oculis nostris inspeximus, laudabile et eo perpetua conservatione dignissimam, quo in primitivae aeclesiae formam impressa est.*

ration of Urban's day ([40]), his own advocacy of it may bear a Clu-
nic stamp. His abbot at Cluny, Hugh of Semur, appears to have
thought similarly. When in 1086 the Cluniac monk Bernard of
Sédirac became archbishop of Toledo, Abbot Hugh urged him to
adopt the canonical life for his household, whether or not its
members included monks. By this means the church of Toledo
might be revived and the new plantation of a barbarian people
might be cultivated. In his letter to Bernard, Hugh came near to
himself according comparable esteem to the canonical and the
monastic life, and he took as his model the primitive church of
the apostles at Jerusalem ([41]). The model was not unfamiliar at
Cluny. In his long poem the *Occupatio*, its second abbot, Odo,
had already urged his monks to be guided by «the becoming pattern of the new-born church» ([42]). Cluniac tradition may have led
Urban by 1095 to ponder the earliest church at Jerusalem as a
model for the church in the west, and so have prepared him to
assign to a renewed Jerusalem the central place in his plans for
the east.

A third factor, of a very different nature, that may help to account for the centrality of Jerusalem in Urban's Crusade ideology
is the abundance of relics and images at Rome itself, especially
in the Lateran, then the popes' normal residence, which had to
do with Jerusalem and the Holy Land.

For the relics and images of the Lateran as for the traditions
that were associated with it, historians have an excellent, though
somewhat neglected, source in the *Descriptio ecclesiae Lateranensis*, a work which underwent several recensions before it reached
the late twelfth-century form in which it was edited in 1946 by
Valentini and Zucchetti ([43]). Its earliest recension dates from be-

---

(40) See MICCOLI (as n. 34).

(41) COWDREY (as n. 32), *Ep.* 4, pp. 145-149, at p. 148: *Et illos probate vite officiales et com-
militones, clericos dico, vel si fieri posset nostri ordinis professores, in domo Domini vobis
commissa aggregetis quibus sit anima una et cor unum, et cum quibus vos ipse instar apos-
tolorum ac primitive ecclesie communem vitam agere valeatis. Qui non negotiis secularibus nec
commutandis commerciis nec congerendis pecuniis insistant, sed resuscitatam domum Domini
et novellam barbarice gentis plantationem voce et opere edificent et instruant.*

(42) ODONIS ABBATIS CLUNIACENSIS *Occupatio*, 6,567- 582, ed. A. SVOBODA, Leipzig, 1900, pp.
135-136: *Ecclesiae formam docet hoc nascentis honestam.*

(43) *Codice topografico della città di Roma*, edd. R. VALENTINI and G. ZUCCHETTI, 4 vols.,
Fonti per la storia d'Italia 81, 88-91, Rome, 1940-1953, 3,319-373. This edition follows a copy
of the late twelfth-century recension by the Roman deacon John which perhaps dates from
the time of Pope Honorius II (1216-1227). With the praise of the *Descriptio* may be compared
that of Cardinal Peter Damiani in 1057: *Die Briefe des Petrus Damiani*, ed. K. REINDEL, *MGH*

tween 1073 and 1118, but probably from soon after 1073, and survives in seven manuscripts ([44]). It therefore provides evidence for the Lateran which Urban knew as cardinal and as pope, and also for widespread public interest in its traditions and its relics.

It discloses why it was thought that there had come to be so many and such important relics in the Lateran. The answer went back to Constantine and his conversion when, having been miraculously cleansed from his leprosy in the Lateran palace, he confessed Christ and gave to the Roman pontiff headship over all the bishops of the western world ([45]). The now Christian emperor resolved that, whereas his predecessors had been the church's persecutors, he would by God's grace be its peace and defence. The cross became central to his life. In a dream he saw the glorified cross in the sky and heard the angels' words, «Constantine, in hoc vinces», Being himself preoccupied by wars, he sent his mother Helena to Jerusalem, where she sought and found the true cross. The empress had it cut vertically in two: one cross she left in Jerusalem, but the other she sent to her son at Constantinople, together with the nails by which Christ had been secured to it. She also procured for Constantine practically the whole treasury of Old and New Testament relics which had been hidden at Jerusalem before Christ's incarnation and renewed there after his ascension. All these relics Constantine sent to Rome, where some found a resting-place at the principal altar of the Lateran basilica, and the rest in a small chapel at the far north-west corner of the Lateran palace which was dedicated to St Lawrence. So precious were the relics of this little chapel that it was called (though not by the *Descriptio*) the *Sancta sanctorum*, the most holy place upon earth. It had some of the functions at the Lateran of the much later Sistine chapel of the Vatican; at its main altar, only the pope was allowed to say mass ([46]).

Briefe, 4/2.55-57: *Lateranensis aecclesia sicut salvatoris est insignita vocabulo, ita mater et quidem apex ac vertex est omnium per orbem aecclesiarum.*

(44) For the various recensions and a stemma of the MSS, see C. Vogel, *La Descriptio ecclesiae Lateranensis du diacre Jean: histoire du texte manuscrit*, in: *Mélanges en l'honneur de Monseigneur Michel Andrieu*, Strasbourg, 1956, pp. 457-476. The only printed edition of the earliest form of the *Descriptio* is in D. Georgi, *De liturgia Romani pontificis in solemni celebratione missarum libri duo*, 3 vols. Rome, 1731-1744, 3,542-555, no. 14, which gives the text as in Vatican Library, MS Reg. lat. 712. A list of the relics to which it refers is given in the Appendix to this paper.

(45) See the *Actus Silvestri* in: B. Mombritius, *Sanctuarium seu Vitae sanctorum*, new edn, 2 vols. Paris, 1910, 2,508-31, esp. pp. 513-14.

(46) For the history of the Lateran palace, see P. Lauer, *Le Palais de Latran. Étude his-*

These legends illustrate the debt that the eleventh-century popes felt that they owed to Constantine – *vir religiosissimus Constantinus primus* – for endowing the papacy with the Lateran palace and furnishing it with relics from Jerusalem. There were other reminders of the city on the Bosphorus. In the chapel of St Lawrence, there was a reliquary containing what was believed to be wood of the cross that the Emperor Heraclius (610-641) had brought to Rome after his defeat of the Persian emperor Chosroes II and recovery of the cross from him. Above all, over the main altar of the same chapel was a painting of Christ which St Luke had designed, though its face was the work of angels and made without human hands; it was thought to have been brought from Constantinople to save it from the iconoclasts ([47]). No one at the Lateran palace, whose *basilica sancti Salvatoris* was also known as the *basilica Constantiniana* ([48]), could well be unmindful of Constantinople.

And yet, as Constantine was believed to have intended, that city did not obtrude itself; the focus was upon Jerusalem. Only a few examples can now be given of the relics which were not only reminders of the Holy Land and of Jerusalem but tangible pieces of its holiest places and events which gave them a presence here and now at Rome. Below the image of the Saviour that was not made by hands was a plethora of relics of the very rock of the Holy Land – the rock upon which St Mary sat, the rock on which Jesus himself sat for his baptism, the rock of his transfiguration, and from Jerusalem the rock of the Mount of Olives on which he prayed to the Father, the rock of the column by which he was scourged, the rock of Calvary, and so forth. There were relics of Christ's earthly life, like the wood of his cradle, but especially of Holy Week and the Passion – loaves and thirteen beans from the Last Supper, the reed, the sponge, the napkin. In the cypress

torique et archéologique, Paris, 1911. For the chapel of St Lawrence, see LAUER, *Le Trésor du Sancta sactorum*, in: *Monuments et mémoires publiés par l'Academie des inscriptions et belles-lettres* 15, Paris, 1906; also H. GRISAR, *Die römische Kapelle Sancta sanctorum und ihr Schatz*, Freiburg im Breisgau, 1908. On the true cross, see A. FROLOW, *La relique de la vraie Croix. Recherches sur le développement d'un culte*, Paris, 1961. On the liturgical history of the Lateran, see P. JOUNEL, *Le Culte des saints dans les basiliques du Latran et du Vatican au douzième siècle*, Collection de l'École française de Rome 26, Rome, 1977. The name *Sancta sanctorum* first appears in 855: *LP* 2,142; but for its history, see LAUER, *Le Trésor*, pp. 29-30.

(47) Ibid., pp. 22-27 and Plate 5; GRISAR, *Die Kapelle* (as. n. 46), pp. 39-55.
(48) e. g. *Registrum Gregorii VII*, 3,10a, ed. E. CASPAR, *MGH Epp. sel.* 2, p. 268.

chest that was named after Pope Leo III (795-816) were relics of Christ himself in three special reliquaries ([49]). The first contained a cross with, at its centre, the foreskin of Christ's circumcision after his birth at Bethlehem; to preserve the relic, it was annually anointed with balsam on the feast of the Exaltation of the Holy Cross (14 September) during a solemn procession of the pope and cardinals ([50]).

The second reliquary, which was richly decorated with biblical scenes, contained a relic of the cross upon which Christ died at Jerusalem. In the third were Christ's sandals, in which he walked the Holy Land and the Holy City. Such were the relics of the chapel of St Lawrence; as the *Descriptio* goes on to relate, comparable relics were deposited under the high altar of the Lateran basilica, to which only the pope and the cardinal-bishops had liturgical access. They were believed to include the Ark of the Covenant and many relics of the Old Testament, as well as more relics of the Holy Land, of Jerusalem, and of Christ himself. By its relics, the Lateran was a reminder of Jerusalem for those with a mind to listen; the discussion could be extended to other churches like Santa Croce in Gerusalemme, which was established in the days of Constantine and Helena to receive the true cross ([51]).

Nothing is more difficult for the historian than to know in what ways, and how deeply, men's habitual surroundings impinge upon their lives and outlook. But it should be remembered that, during the middle ages, a prime concern of the *ecclesia Romana* and its clergy and people from the pope downwards was the performance of a liturgical round which took place in the basilicas and churches of the city. Into this liturgical round, the countless pilgrims to the city were drawn. The *Descriptio* in its original form, with its description of the relics of the Lateran, was intended to bring home to pious pilgrims that these relics formed a treasure with deep meaning for those who sought both the peace of the church and also the remission of their sins ([52]).

---

(49) For the cypress chest and its contents, see LAUER, *Le Trésor* (as n. 46), pp. 38-60, 81; GRISAR, *Die römische Kapelle* (as n. 46), pp. 15, 58-102.

(50) LAUER, *Le Trésor* (as n. 46), pp. 49-60 and Plate 8; GRISAR (as n. 46), pp. 92-97.

(51) FROLOW (as. n. 46), p. 177, no. 27; see *LP* 1,179-180.

(52) GEORGI (as n. 44), 3,542: *Et quoniam totus orbis terrarum huic matri ecclesiae debitum subiectionis exhibere debet obsequium, multi e diversis regionibus oratores huic conveniunt,*

Relics were meant to have an impact, and another part of this impact may have been to direct papal minds to the churches and the Christians of the east, and especially of Jerusalem. When Pope Gregory VII in 1074 planned that his so-called «Crusade» of that year should end by reaching the Holy Sepulchre, his wish to lead it there may have been inspired by the evidences of Jerusalem by which he had been surrounded from boyhood in the Lateran ([53]). According to the *Liber Pontificalis*, Gregory's plan for an expedition to Jerusalem, now said to have been for the defence of the faith and to free the Holy Sepulchre from its enemies, stimulated Urban II to preach the Crusade ([54]). As cardinal-bishop of Ostia and during his brief occupation of the Lateran as pope, Urban himself experienced its evidences of Jerusalem which may have helped to inspire in him the concern expressed in his letter to the Flemings for the servitude of «the Holy City of Christ, made illustrious by his passion and resurrection» ([55]). The relics of Jerusalem at Rome at least deserve consideration as a factor which may have served to focus Urban's mind upon Jerusalem and to form his idea of the Crusade.

Finally, just a little evidence may be found to suggest that, during his French itinerary, Urban brought relics from the Lateran. Little is known about the relics that an itinerant pope like Urban may have had in his *capella*, and it is probable that Urban's access to the Lateran before his departure was too restricted to allow of any selection of relics to meet his purposes in 1095 and 1096. Not suprisingly, therefore, there is no evidence of his bringing relics directly associated with Jerusalem or the Holy Land. Yet one, at least, of the consecrations of churches and altars for which he was responsible involved relics which may have

---

quibus nescientibus quantum et quam preciosissimum in hac praedicta ecclesia sanctuarium Dei sit reconditum, per istarum insinuationem literarum volumus esse manifestum, saltem quando hi veniunt ad exorandum Dei Filium Iesum Christum pro pace sanctae ecclesiae, pro remissione omnium peccatorum, pro adquirenda gloria aeternae visionis Dei, pro societate supernorum civium et sanctarum animarum.

(53) *Reg. Greg. VII*, 2,31, (as n. 48), p. 166. For the plan, see H. E. J. COWDREY, *Pope Gregory VII's «Crusading» Plans of 1074*, in: *Outremer. Studies in the Crusading Kingdom of Jerusalem Presented to Joshua Prawer*, edd. B. Z. KEDAR, H. E. MAYER and R. C. SMAIL, Jerusalem, 1982, pp. 27-40, repr. *Popes, Monks and Crusaders* (as n. 3), no. X.

(54) *LP* 2,293: *Audierat iste praeclarus et devotus pontifex praedecessorem suum Gregorium papam praedicasse ultramontanis Iherosolimam pro defensione christianae fidei pergere et Domini sepulchrum e manibus inimicorum liberare...*

(55) Above, p. 727.

been derived from the Lateran collections. In March 1096, he
came to the abbey of Marmoutier near Tours, whose church he
dedicated to the Holy Cross, St Mary, the apostles Peter and
Paul, and St Martin ([56]). The principal relic that he caused to be
placed in the so-called Dominical altar was a fragment of the
most victorious cross (*particula ... victoriosissimae crucis Christi*);
it was one of several such dedications during his journey ([57]).
The placing of a frament of the cross at Marmoutier establishes
the possibility that Urban had with him fragments of the true
cross from the Lateran, particles of which he used for his dedications. This appears to have been effective as Crusade propaganda, for while Urban was at Marmoutier many knights were
moved to sew on their clothing the *vexillum* of the holy cross.
One who did so, Count Hugh of Chaumont-Amboise, was a benefactor of Marmoutier when Urban dedicated the Dominical altar
with its relic of the *victoriosissima crux*; the Constantinian overtones are apparent ([58]). Events at Marmoutier show that Urban
promoted the Crusade not only by his eloquence but also by giving relics of the cross which may have come from the Lateran
collection and which were reminders of both Christ and Constantine.

Other relics that were used at the dedication of the Dominical
altar at Marmoutier may also have had Lateran associations, for
they recall the lists in the *Descriptio ecclesiae Lateranensis*. Particles of St Peter's hair and beard recall his head which, with St
Paul's, was kept at the Lateran. A piece of the garment of St
John the Evangelist appears to refer to this saint's thaumaturgic

(56) The *Textus de dedicatione ecclesiae huius sancti Maioris nostri* is printed in the Appendix to T. RUINART, *Beati Urbani papae II Vita*, in: *Ouvrages posthumes de D. Jean Mabillon
et de D. Thierri Ruinart*, ed. V. THUILLIER, 3 vols., Paris, 1724, 3,387-390, whence *PL* 151. 273-
276. For events at Tours, see BECKER (as. n. 5), 2,446-447.
(57) e. g. Urban's dedication of the matutinal altar at the monastery of la Trinité at Vendôme *in honore victoriosissimae crucis*: RUINART (as n. 56), 3,386. In the light of the *Descriptio
ecclesiae Lateranensis*, such phrases evoke the memory of Constantine, as does the evidence
of a charter of Saint-Maixent that, during Urban's keeping of Easter at Saintes, the sign of
the cross was seen in the sky: *An. jur. pont.*, X[e] sér. (as n. 36), col. 551, no. 93. Urban's use of
the cult of the holy cross should be compared with that of the early Salian rulers of Germany: see S. WEINFURTER, *Herrschaft und Reich der Salier. Grundlinien einer Umbruchzeit*,
Sigmaringen, 1991, pp. 56-57, and the literature there cited.
(58) According to the *Gesta Ambaziensium dominorum*, many *in presentia pape ... vestibus
super amictis sancte crucis vexillum consuerunt*: (as n. 2), pp. 100-101; for Count Hugh's gifts,
see RUINART, *Beati Urbani ... Vita*, cap. 251 and Appendix, (as n. 51), 3,247, 390-391, whence
PL 151,198-199, 286.

tunic. Of the eighteen martyrs, confessors, and virgins whose relics are named, three with the unusual names Nereus, Achilles, and Praxedes appear in the Lateran lists ([59]). Such evidence is insufficient to prove that Urban used relics from the Lateran, but it establishes a possibility that he travelled with relics, including portions of the true cross, which were drawn from its treasures; that he used them as gifts when churches and altars were consecrated; and that relics of the holy and victorious cross formed part of his repertoire on occasions when he preached and recruited for the Crusade. With their Constantian overtones, they may have suggested Jerusalem and the Holy Land ([60]).

In conclusion, the evidence that, from the beginning at Clermont of his Crusade preaching, Urban both named Jerusalem and gave its liberation and renewal a central place in his plan for the Crusade is strong. Jerusalem may already have impinged upon his mind in several ways. At Cluny, he was familiar with liturgical references to it. In the years immediately before he launched his Crusade to the east, probably with the intention of restoring Jerusalem to its pristine liberty, he was concerned in the west to renew and propagate through the regular canons the life of the earliest church at Jerusalem. His concern for the Holy Land and the Holy City may have been the greater because the Lateran palace possessed a treasure of relics which evoked Christ's life upon earth. There was a wealth of the very rocks of the Holy Land, as well as of relics of Christ's life, passion, and resurrection with their Jerusalem associations. Urban's mind and experience were surrounded by tangible evidences of Jerusalem which are likely to have assured for it a central place in the *schema* of his Crusading ideology. By 1095, Jerusalem had in all probability assumed in Urban's own mind the significance that it was to retain for all the popes of the Crusading centuries.

---

(59) Cf. the Appendix to this paper, nos. 13, 15, 39, 60.

(60) Urban II's successor as pope, Paschal II (1099-1118), was also so aware. In 1100 he sent relics from Rome to the French abbey of Conques with an inscription that may refer to relics from the Lateran treasury: DOMINVS PASCALIS II PAPA A ROMA HAS MISSIT RELIQVIAS DE † (CRUCE) XR(IST)I ET SEPVLCHRO EIVS ATQVE PLVRIMORVM SANCTORVM: FROLOW (as n. 46), p. 306, no. 286.

APPENDIX

The relics of the Lateran according to the first recension of the Descriptio ecclesiae Lateranensis

I In the chapel of St Lawrence

    a In a gold cross-reliquiary in the cypress chest that Pope Leo III made
      1 the Lord's umbilical cord ([61]) and the foreskin of his circumcision
    b In another, gold and silver cross-reliquary in the chest
      2 the cross of our Lord Jesus Christ
    c In a third, silver reliquary in the chest
      3 the Lord's sandals, or shoes
    d In another, gilded reliquary
      4 of the wood of the holy cross, which Heraclius brought to Rome after his victory over Chosroes II
    e In the altar of St Lawrence
      5 the body of St Anastasius, martyr
      6 the arm of St Cesarius, martyr
      7 two bones of St John the Baptist
      8 a bone of St Jerome
      9 the shoulder-bone of St Dionysius the Areopagite
      10 a bone from the shin of Pope Stephen
      11 of Pope Damasus
      12 of Sts Primus and Felicianus
      13 the head of St Praxedes
      14 of St Anastasia and many others
      15 of Sts Agape, Chonia, Irene, Pistis, and Elpis, virgins, Nereus and Achilles, Prisca and Aquila
      16 of the knee of St Tiburtius, son of Cromatius
    f In the cypress chest
      17 a loaf from the Lord's supper
      18 of the cane, or reed (Matt. 27,29-30 or 48)
      19 thirteen of the beans of the Lord's Supper
      20 of the sponge with vinegar which was placed by the Lord's mouth (Matt. 27,48)

---

(61) The reference to the *umbilicus Domini* rested upon a misunderstanding. The relic of the circumcision was placed in a capsule affixed to the central point (*umbilicus*) of the cross; the word *umbilicus* was taken as referring to a second relic: Grisar (as n. 46), pp. 95-96.

21 wood from the sycamore tree that Zacchaeus climbed (Luke 19,1-10)

g Below the painted likeness of the Saviour that is over the altar

22 of the rock upon which St Mary sat

23 of the rock in the River Jordan upon which Jesus sat when he was baptised

24 of the rock of Bethlehem

25 of the rock of the Mount of Olives, where the Lord prayed to the Father (Matt. 26,36-46)

26 of the rock upon which the angel sat at the sepulchre (Matt. 28,2)

27 of the column to which the Lord was bound when he was scourged (Matt. 27,26)

28 of the Lord's sepulchre

29 of the lance with which the Lord's side was pierced (John 20,34)

30 of the wood of the Lord's cross

31 of the place which is called Lithostratos (John 19,13)

32 of the rock of Calvary

33 of the rock in which the Lord was buried

34 of the rock of Mount Zion

35 of the rock upon which the Lord was transfigured (Matt. 17,1.8)

36 wood from the Lord's manger in which he was laid (Luke 2,7)

37 rock from Mount Sinai, where the law was given

38 of the rock of the sepulchre of St Mary

h In another altar of the same chapel

39 the heads of the apostles Peter and Paul

40 the heads of Sts Agnes and Euphemia, virgins

i In a third altar

41 coals sprinkled with the blood of St Lawrence, and fat from his body

42 relics of the forty holy martyrs, and of many others

II In the Lateran basilica

a At the main altar

43 the ark of the covenant of the Lord (Exod. 25,8-22)

44 many other relics whose description was unknown

b Within the altar

45 the seven candelabra of the first tabernacle (Exod. 37,23-24, cf. Heb. 9,2)

46 Aaron's rod that budded (Num. 17,1-11)

47 the tables of the testimony (Exod. 31,18)

48 Moses's rod with which he twice struck stone and waters flowed (Exod. 17,1-6, Num. 20,2-13, cf. Ps. 77(Vg.),20

49 relics of the Lord's cradle

742

50 of the five barley loaves (John 6,9) and two loaves from the Lord's table
51 the towel with which he wiped his disciples' feet (John 13,1-5)
52 the seamless tunic that the Virgin Mary made for her son, the Lord Jesus Christ (John 19,23-24)
53 the Saviour's purple vestment (John 19,1-5)
54 two flasks of the blood and water from the Lord's side (John 19,34)
55 the napkin that was upon his head (John 20,7)
56 of the place of his ascension into heaven (Acts 1,6-11)
57 of the blood of St John the Baptist, and of the dust and ashes of his cremated body
58 his sackcloth of camel's hair (Matt. 3,4)
59 a flask filled with manna from the burial-place of St John the Evangelist
60 the tunic of this apostle, which was placed upon the bodies of three youths who had drunk poison and restored them to life

VI

Canon Law and the First Crusade

At the Cardiff Conference in 1983, Professor John Gilchrist presented a paper on "The Erdmann Thesis and the Canon Law, 1083-1141," which was then, and has since been, regarded as of the utmost importance for the study of the canonical preparation for the First Crusade.[1] It is far from my purpose to challenge this paper, for with most of it I am in basic agreement. I would like simply to suggest some questions that, in the light of it, call for further investigation and discussion.

The first, and perhaps the most pressing, is how far and in what form St. Augustine of Hippo's teachings about the just war were current and influential during the eleventh century. Here, one might wish to query a very few of Gilchrist's statements, as when, in speaking of the canonical tradition from Burchard of Worms to Anselm of Lucca and beyond, he postulates that "these collections... maintained a traditional Augustinian concept of the just/holy war directed mainly at the internal enemies of the church," and, again, when he asserts that, after Anselm's canonical collection was compiled, "the traditional Augustinian, Burchardian ethos lived on."[2] But how well formed or traditional was the Augustinian concept in the eleventh century? Augustine himself dealt with the subject of war occasionally and incidentally in writings primarily devoted to other topics.[3] By no means all of these writings remained generally known and read; even with those that did, it cannot be assumed that passages relating to war were often noticed. As F.H. Russell has pointed out, from the fifth century onwards, what were taken to be Augustine's ideas sometimes came from spurious works, and, in general, "the genuine Augustinian opinions in all their complexity were neglected, and even his formula for the just war disappeared from view."[4] In the eleventh century, references to Augustine were, on the whole, relatively few. For example, in all his letters, whether registered or

---

*   This paper was written and delivered before the appearance of J. Gilchrist's further important paper "The Papacy and War against the 'Saracens', 795-1216," *The International History Review* 10 (1988), 174-197.

1   CS, pp. 37-45.
2   Ibid., pp. 38, 41.
3   F.H. Russell, *The Just War in the Middle Ages* (Cambridge, 1975), pp. 16-26.
4   Ibid., pp. 26-27.

not, Pope Gregory VII, whom scholars rightly consider especially important in changing ideas about warfare, cited Augustine but once, in a context having nothing to do with war.[5] Again, in the *Libelli de lite*, some authors — Manegold of Lautenbach, the *Liber canonum contra Heinricum IV*, and Guy of Ferrara are the main early examples — cited Augustine frequently, but others, like Cardinal Humbert and Bonizo of Sutri, did so very seldom.[6] One would not deny the generally Augustinian character of the Christianity that the eleventh century inherited. But, so far as direct familiarity with and use of Augustine's writings were concerned, some authors and circles were assiduously studying and referring to them so far they were available; others were not. It was a time of rediscovery. There was no single tradition; each author and his circle must be looked at as a separate case.

How was it with the major canonists? Burchard of Worms is a good example of a figure who seems to have been little acquainted with Augustine or schooled in his writings. True, he held Augustine in the highest regard as one of the Latin doctors, and he dropped his name quite often. But he usually made the imprecise ascription *ex dictis Augustini*; many of his citations are apocryphal. As for Burchard's chapters on war,[7] they contain no direct reference to, or citation of, Augustine, genuine or spurious, save a single *dictum Augustini*.[8] Furthermore, Burchard's most detailed rulings about homicide in warfare come within his *Corrector*, or penitential;[9] this treatment stands wholly within the tradition of ninth-century penitentials which shows little directly Augustinian influence.[10] With Anselm of Lucca, matters are very different, both in his canonical collection and in his *Liber contra Wibertum* which has much material in common with it.[11] In general, he cited Augustine often, and almost always directly and accurately.[12] With regard to coercion and warfare, in Books XII, *De excommunicatione*, and XIII, *De vindicta et persecutione iusta*, he expounded the church's powers with the Wibertine schism as his background. According to A.M. Stickler's analysis,[13] these books contain forty *capitula* of especial

5 *Reg.* 8.21, ed. E. Caspar, MGH Epp. Sel. 2:556, cf. p. 552.
6 See the Index auctoritatum to MGH Libelli de lite 1:656-658.
7 Listed by Gilchrist, "The Erdmann Thesis," p. 44, n. 66, from the text of Burchard's *Decretum* in PL 140:537-1058.
8 6.43 in PL 140:776A.
9 19.5 in PL 140:952.
10 Russell, *Just War*, pp. 30-32.
11 Anselm's collection, up to 11.15, was edited by F. Thaner, *Anselmi episcopi Lucensis Collectio canonum* (Innsbruck, 1906-15). The *capitula* of the whole collection are in PL 149:485-534. The *Liber contra Wibertum* was edited by E. Bernheim in MGH Libelli de lite 1:517-528. For comment, see esp. A.M. Stickler, "Il potere coattivo materiale della Chiesa nella Riforma Gregoriana secondo Anselmo di Lucca," *Studi Gregoriani* 2 (1947), 235-285.
12 For example, in Thaner's edition the forty-nine *capitula* of Book IX, *De sacramentis*, are supported by twenty-three identifiable and one non-identifiable Augustinian citations; the forty-four *capitula* of Book X, *De coniugiis*, are supported by eleven identifiable and no non-identifiable citations.
13 "Il potere coattivo," table facing p. 248.

relevance, all save seven of which passed into Gratian's *Decretum*. In nineteen of them, all but one of which Gratian preserved, Anselm cited identifiable passages of Augustine, together with a single non-identifiable passage. With regard to war as to other matters, Anselm's citation of Augustine seems to have been unusually full and direct. Augustine's handling of the use of force against the Donatists provided him with a quarry of material that he exploited with hitherto unexampled thoroughness in order to serve his principal political purpose — to promote the just and holy war of Catholic Christians against Wibertine schismatics and simoniac heretics. If Anselm thus made a pioneering use of Augustine in order to develop the power of the church to wield the material sword itself and to direct the lay power in so doing, the possibility remains open that there may be truth in Erdmann's and Stickler's view of his work as representing a turning point.[14]

My second question is, to some extent, complementary to my first. We need to elucidate just what it was about the committing of homicide even in legitimate warfare that, until the age of Gregory VII and the First Crusade, made Christians reluctant to accord it complete moral acceptability. A common answer has been that such homicides almost inevitably involved human passions that were themselves sinful and deserving of penance — anger, avarice, currying the favor of temporal lords, and the like.[15] But this is not the whole answer, and for contrary reasons. On the one hand, the awarding of penance for homicide in war became a common feature of penitentials of the mid-ninth century and later that expressed clerical disapproval of lay violence of every kind. Although churchmen never quite made a general attack upon all warfare, all killing in the course of it was treated as a sub-division of homicide which, in every manifestation, was evil in itself.[16] Like Burchard of Worms's *Corrector* later on, such ninth-century penitentials as the *Poenitentiale pseudo-Theodori* and the *Poenitentiale Arundel* betrayed little direct acquaintance with Augustine and regarded homicide in war as in itself gravely sinful.[17] Even in the mid-eleventh century, the penitential ordinance that followed the Battle of Hastings seems to reflect a similar view.[18] It is significant that when Anselm of Lucca discussed penances, in a sub-section *De omni genere homicidiorum et de poenitentia eorum*[19] he avoided reference to homicide in war; the omission indicates that the notion of such homicide as being in itself sinful was at last being set aside.

14   C. Erdmann, *The Origin of the Idea of Crusade*, trans. M.W. Baldwin and W. Goffart (Princeton, 1977), pp. 241-248; Stickler, "Il potere coattivo," pp. 274, 282-284.

15   E.g., Hrabanus Maurus, *Liber poenitentium*, cap. 15 in PL 112:1411-1413; *Penitential Articles issued after the Battle of Hastings*, in *Councils and Synods with other Documents relating to the English Church*, pt. 1: *A.D. 871-1204*, ed. D. Whitelock, M. Brett, and C.N.L. Brooke, pt. 2: *1066-1204* (Oxford, 1981), pp. 581-584, No. 88, esp. caps. 2, 5.

16   Russell, *Just War*, pp. 30-33.

17   *Poenitentiale pseudo-Theodori* 1.4, *Poenitentiale Arundel* 11, in H.J. Schmitz, *Die Bussbücher und die Bussdisciplin der Kirche*, 2 vols. (Mainz and Düsseldorf, 1883-98), 1:441, 528.

18   E.g., in its insistence upon number: caps 1, 7.

19   *Collectio canonum* 11.34-55 in PL 149:526.

On the other hand, at the beginning of his book *De vindicta et persecutione iusta*, Anselm was at pains to assert the freedom from sin of those who engaged in warfare that was, within his framework, just. One needs only cite his first five *capitula*:

1. That Moses committed no cruelty when, at the Lord's order, he slew certain men.
2. That punishment (*vindicta*) should be performed from love, not hatred.
3. That wars are waged with good will.
4. That those who fight may also be righteous (*iusti*); and that an enemy should be resisted of necessity, not by choice.
5. That we should pray for one about to fight.[20]

Anselm of Lucca gives the impression of seeking to free at least some warfare from an inherent stigma of sinfulness and of wrong motivation. However, particularly in liturgical and devotional sources, Anselm was anticipated by much material that exhibited warfare in a positive and morally acceptable light. It is not difficult to compile a list of examples of the sanctification of armies before battle by penance, prayer, preaching, and communion.[21] The Romano-Germanic Pontifical contains an *Oratio pro exercitu* which included an intercession for a *proeliandi recta voluntas*—a right will in fighting.[22] A prayer of self-preparation by a warrior before battle that was current in Anglo-Saxon England addressed God as him by whose hand every victory was secured and every battle waged; God was besought to strengthen the warrior's courage so that he might fight well and manfully in God's strength.[23] In face of such a devotional tradition, one wonders why the notion of the inherent sinfulness of warfare persisted for so long. The Norman penitential ordinance after Hastings provokes the suggestion that the doing of penance by warriors for homicides and woundings may have been of value in appeasing feuds and vengeance, and so in promoting peace and order when battle was over.[24] Whatever the considerations

20 13.1-5 in PL 149:533; for all of these *capitula* Anselm cited true or apocryphal Augustinian authorities: Stickler, "Il potere coattivo," table facing p. 248. By *vindicta* and *persecutio*, Anselm meant material coercion; with the former term, the emphasis is upon vindictive punishment including death, and with the latter upon the use of force, including armed force, to restrain evil and to compel virtue: ibid., p. 239.

21 E.g., the pious preparation for the battle of Hastings by the Norman host according to William of Malmesbury, *Gesta regum Anglorum* 3.242, ed. W. Stubbs, RS 90 (London, 1887-89), 2:302; also such preparations as are recorded by historians of the First Crusade like the anonymous *Gesta Francorum et aliorum Hierosolimitanorum*, ed.R. Hill (London, 1962), pp. 67-68, 90, 95.

22 *Le Pontifical romano-germanique du dixième siècle*, sect. 245, cf. 242-244, ed. C. Vogel and R. Elze, 3 vols., Studi e testi, 226-227, 269 (Città del Vaticano, 1963-72), 2:378-80.

23 See the prayer *Domine Deus omnipotens, rex regum* in London, British Library, MS Cotton Nero A.II, fols. 11v-12v, and Cotton Galba A.XIV, fols. 3r-6r, where the Latin text is followed by an Old English translation: *A Pre-Conquest English Prayer Book*, ed. B.J. Muir, Henry Bradshaw Society, 103 (Woodbridge, 1988), nos. 6. 11-12, pp. 21, 29-30.

24 As note 15 above. In this connection it is noteworthy that William I's provisions for the security of his Norman followers in England distinguished between those who crossed the Channel with him in 1066 and those who had settled in England in the days of King Edward the Confessor: *Statutes of William the Conqueror*, caps. 3, 4, in *Select Charters*

that guided the moral appraisal of warfare up to the end of the eleventh century, one is left with the impression that they were various, mixed, and inconsistent. But the time was now ripe for the recognition of a general *proeliandi recta voluntas*, at least as a possibility.

Given this picture, my third question is, how and why were the inhibitions of the church's penitential discipline against wounding and homicide in warfare so far overcome as to permit of an enterprise like the crusade? The revival of Augustine's ideas by such a canonist as Anselm of Lucca is likely to provide only part of the answer. For Anselm's use of Augustine was, as we have seen, in his day exceptional, and it was directed against those in internal schism within Latin Christendom. Perhaps at least as much of the answer may be sought more widely, in changes in secular as well as canon law which affected the whole range of society, both clerical and lay. I cannot now attempt to set out fully the details and the synchronization of these changes. But the points that need to be considered are primarily suggested by that most stimulating of legal monographs, Julius Goebel's *Felony and Misdemeanor*, first published in 1937.[25] In the background is the long and fundamental process whereby acts of violence producing homicides and woundings ceased to be matters for settlement by financial composition between individuals and their kindreds, and became the concern of feudal or public authorities punishing often by financial penalties but increasingly by afflictive ones—by mutilation and capital punishment. One might single out the following points:

(a) The decay of financial emendation as a means of settling feuds, and also as a legal remedy in the courts for settling cases of violence.[26]

(b) The consequent development of a feudal justice that, in the interests of seignorial power, nevertheless began by combining concentration upon profits with procedural exclusiveness. Goebel emphasized the resulting "drive in the direction of penalty." "Until this concept," he wrote, "is completely embedded in the law and the court's interest in dealing with wrongdoers thereby made paramount, the shift from tort to crime cannot take place."[27]

(c) As it did take place, and as the concept of felony emerged, there was an increasing use of afflictive penalties involving life and limb.[28] This may have

and other Illustrations of English Constitutional History, ed. W. Stubbs, 9th ed. rev. by H.W.C. Davis (Oxford, 1913), p. 98.

25   J. Goebel, *Felony and Misdemeanor. A Study in the History of Criminal Law*, 1, repr. with Introduction by E. Peters (Philadelphia, 1976). (No further volumes were published.)

26   Ibid., pp. 195-199.

27   Ibid., pp. 222-224.

28   Thus, at least as a straw in the wind, in England King William I (1066-87) forbade capital punishment for any offense but prescribed exoculation or castration: *Statutes*, cap. 10, p. 99; his son Henry I (1100-35) imposed all three penalties: Florence of Worcester, *Chronicon ex chronicis*, a. 1108, ed. B. Thorpe, 2 vols., English Historical Society (London, 1848-49), 2.57.

been of particular importance for our subject: a society whose rulers increasingly inflicted judicial penalties of mutilation and death without incurring for themselves and their agents the canonical reproach of homicide could scarcely continue to countenance any such reproach in those who maimed or killed in legitimate warfare.[29]

(d) This shift in lay jurisdiction and sanctions must be studied in the light of the wider development of the eleventh century whereby lay rulers, such as the Norman dukes and kings and the Salian king of Germany, were successful, if in differing ways and degrees, in transmuting the peace of God into the peace of the secular prince. They thus built a system of law enforcement firmly lodged in princely hands.[30] This represented a further enhancement of the role of the lay power—first feudal lord and ultimately sovereign ruler—in determining both the legal form and the moral evaluation of measures to combat crime and of the sanctions by which to avenge it.

(e) Finally, Goebel draws attention to the long-term concern of the canon-law tradition in face of these developments to promote the collaboration of clergy and princes and the complementarity of spiritual and temporal sanctions, with the latter reinforcing the former.[31] The critical text for the canon lawyers was a forged canon, drawn up at some time after the synod of Tribur (895) to ensure that a man who fell under the *bannus episcopalis* should also be subject to the discipline of the king. Burchard of Worms cited it under the heading *De homicidiis, et calumniis episcoporum et reliquorum ordinum*,[32] and in due course Ivo of Chartres included it in his *Decretum*.[33] Such material seems to have been influential, for example providing the background for William the Conqueror's judicial measures in both England and Normandy.[34]

When Urban II preached the crusade in 1095, momentous and long-standing changes were taking place in secular as in canon law, and the two developments were interacting. The themes of crusade preaching, that princes and knights should uphold the peace that church and lay rulers were promoting within Latin Christendom, and that they should avenge the crimes of the Muslims against the churches and the Christians of the East, invite consideration against the background of both kinds of law, not just of one.

---

29 Goebel, *Felony and Misdemeanor*, pp. 236-238, 409-413.
30 Ibid., pp. 280-335; for Germany, see esp. MGH Const. 1:125-126, 605-617, Nos. 74, 425-432, and comment by J. Gernhuber, *Die Landfriedensbewegung in Deutschland bis zum Mainzer Reichslandfrieden von 1235* (Bonn, 1952).
31 Goebel, *Felony and Misdemeanor*, pp. 309-320.
32 *Decretum* 6.6 in PL 140:767-768.
33 *Decretum* 10.135 in PL 161:732-733.
34 *Ordinance of William I on Church Courts*, in *Councils and Synods* (note 15 above), pp. 620-624, No. 94; Canons of the Council of Lillebonne, in *The Ecclesiastical History of Orderic Vitalis* 5.5, ed. M. Chibnall, 6 vols. (Oxford, 1969-80), 3:26.

VI

My fourth and final question is one that has been put by Gilchrist, and also by many others; but it is a cardinal question. Why—to borrow Gilchrist's imagery—was there a "great silence," and a "gulf," between the crusade and the canonical tradition, so that not until the thirteenth century did the canonists even begin seriously to take account of the crusade?[35] The answer may lie partly in the canonical tradition itself, and partly outside it. Inside it, we have to reckon with (as J.A. Brundage has put it) "a transition from the consideration of war as primarily a moral and theological problem to a conception of war as fundamentally a problem of law. Likewise, as the Church's enforcement power increased, theological moralizing tended to be replaced by a more rigorous categorization of hostile actions."[36] The early stages of this development took place in a context of the restraint and correction of heresy and schism within the boundaries of Latin Christendom. It was in this context that Anselm of Lucca somewhat belatedly revived the direct study of Augustine's doctrine of the just war. In this sense, Erdmann and Stickler were correct to see in Anselm a turning-point in the Western appraisal of warfare. But, as Gilchrist has rightly argued, Anselm's direct legacy was not to the crusade tradition; like him, the canon lawyers, especially Gratian, who developed the canon law of war, did so above all with an eye to the destruction of heresy within Latin Christendom.[37] The thinking of canon lawyers was for long simply not directed towards the kind of warfare that we call the crusade.

In so far as the answer to my question lies outside the canonical tradition, it is germane to recall that Pope Urban II in 1095 made a direct address to the princes and knights of Latin Christendom. They were experiencing changes in secular law that were leading to wrongdoing being envisaged as crime that deserved afflictive punishment, and they saw no wrongfulness in the deeds of those who avenged it. In the eleventh and twelfth centuries, crusaders for the most part set out as individuals or groups who were engaged upon a particular purpose, that of fighting the external foes of Christendom, and their activities had their own momentum. Only with the great crusading measures of Pope Innocent III, like his bull *Quia maior* (1213) and his decree *Ad liberandam* (1215),[38] did the crusade became a function of the whole of Christian society. At the same time, crusades were increasingly directed towards heretics and schismatics within Christendom. The stage was at last set for the canonical tradition as it had been established by Gratian and his successors to take direct account of the crusades and of the problems to which they gave rise.

35   *CS*, p. 39; for the general problem of canon law and the crusades, see esp. J.A. Brundage, *Medieval Canon Law and the Crusader* (Madison, 1969), and "Holy War and the Medieval Lawyers," in *The Holy War*, ed. T.P. Murphy (Columbus, 1976), pp. 99-140.
36   "Holy War and the Medieval Lawyers," p. 100; cf. pp. 105-106, 123-124.
37   Gratian, *Decretum*, C.23, in *Corpus iuris canonici*, 2 vols., ed. E. Friedberg (Leipzig, 1897), 1:889-950; see Brundage, "Holy War," pp. 107-109.
38   *Quia maior*: G. Tangl, *Studien zum Register Innocenz' III.* (Weimar, 1929), pp. 88-97; *Ad liberandam: Conciliorum oecumenicorum decreta*, ed. J. Alberigo et al., 3rd ed. (Bologna, 1973), pp. 267-271.

48

It has been the purpose of these remarks to pose questions, not to draw conclusions. But it may in summary be noticed that there seems to be no reason to challenge Gilchrist's main argument, that the canonical tradition remained, into the twelfth century, within the conservative lines regarding warfare that Burchard of Worms had laid down. What is not so certain is that those lines were strongly Augustinian, in the sense of being the result of hard contemporary thought about Augustine's own writings. Such thought had largely to await Anselm of Lucca, and by it he, too, made a major contribution to Gratian. But, since Anselm's concern was schism and heresy within Latin Christandom, he may not have made a major direct contribution to the idea of the crusade. However, since he stood so near to Gregory VII, he is likely to have contributed to it indirectly and considerably. Finally, if in Anselm of Lucca canon law may have made an indirect contribution to the crusade, we should take into account the indirect but powerful contribution of secular law, as well.

VII

Martyrdom and the First Crusade

IN THE aftermath of Pope Gregory VII's death in exile on 25 May 1085, and therefore only some ten years before Pope Urban II preached at Clermont, Bonizo, the exiled and afflicted bishop of Sutri, replied to a friend who in perplexity had put two questions to him: Why did a righteous God seem deaf to all the cries of a persecuted Church? and, Was it indeed licit for a Christian to strive for the faith with the weapons of earthly warfare? Historians have been much concerned with how the Gregorian papacy affirmed the second question, and with the Crusade as the novel combination of holy war and pilgrimage that arose from Urban's preaching. But Bonizo's comments upon the first question are also of significance for the origin of the Crusade. He cited Christ's words: 'If a man would come after me, let him deny himself and take up his cross and follow me'. Christians, said Bonizo, were members of one head whom they should imitate and follow. Christ had been mocked, scourged, and crucified, and so had come to His resurrection; then He had been crowned with honour at His Father's side. 'So we also', Bonizo concluded, 'through earthly afflictions must die with Christ to rise and reign with Him'. He noticed how the apostles had thus triumphed and been made rulers over all lands, and how after them there followed the white-robed army of martyrs – the *martirum candidatus exercitus* – who likewise suffered torments, died, and won eternal life.[1] According to the author of the *Gesta Francorum*, it was Christ's same words that prompted the Crusade – the 'great stirring of heart throughout all Frankish lands, so that if any man, with all his heart and all his mind, really wanted to follow God and faithfully bear the cross after him, he could make no delay in taking the road to the Holy Sepulchre as soon as possible'.[2] I wish to illustrate how the theme of martyrdom, as Bonizo presented it, may have helped to prepare the way for the Crusade and may have enabled contemporaries to accept and to understand it.

For them, the idea and the ethic of martyrdom were all-pervasive, as part of the framework of Christian thought and at all levels of official and popular devotion. In a standard definition, Isidore of Seville had declared that martyrs were witnesses: as Christ's witnesses they bore sufferings (*passiones*) and strove for the truth even to death. The first martyr was St Stephen, whose name meant 'crowned'; the faithful might be martyrs in two ways: by public sufferings (*in aperta passione*) or by secret, heroic virtue (*in occulta animi virtute*).[3] For the eleventh century, the papacy, too, had a certain leadership in martyrdom: Bonizo asserted to his friend that, at the beginning of Christian times, the thirty-three earliest popes headed the public martyrs in unrelenting strife until Constantine – *pius Constantinus* – adopted the Christian faith and, however precariously, the Church received its freedom.[4] The ancient canticle *Te Deum laudamus* proclaimed to all Christian generations that the glorious company of apostles – themselves deemed to have all been martyred – and the noble fellowship of prophets were joined in their praise of God by the *martyrum candidatus exercitus* which impressed Bonizo's imagination.[5]

From Carolingian times such popular devotions as the Litany of Saints located the martyr-saints even more precisely in the upper ranks of the Christian order. The saints had a hierarchy. After the Blessed Virgin at its summit came the angels and archangels with Michael as their chief; next was John the Baptist and after him the apostles and evangelists; then followed the martyrs. Below them came the confessors and the virgins, the widows, the innocents, and the penitents.[6] Martyrs thus stood high in the ranks of heaven; but through their relics they were also widely present throughout Christendom. Apostles and martyrs were sought by pilgrims at the places of their burial, like St James at Compostela and – above all – St Peter and St Paul at Rome. Local centres also multiplied. The eleventh century, moreover, witnessed the growth of an urban self-consciousness that further encouraged the cult of patron saints, many of whom were martyrs of pre-Constantinian times. Their cult was often accompanied by a quest for standards of Christian life *ad instar vitae apostolicae*: the public sufferings of the martyrs of old were to be complemented by heroic private virtue now. To take only random examples, in Italy poets like Cardinal Peter Damiani and Archbishop Alfanus I of Salerno composed hymns and liturgical offices to commemorate martyrs and to commend their lives.[7] At Châlon-sur-Saône Abbot Hugh of Cluny preached his only extant sermon, with its message that 'summa ... felicitas pro Deo mori est', in an annual public commemoration of the martyr-bishop Marcellus.[8] Such annual festivals with their processions, ceremonies, and sermons celebrated martyrs in the greater churches. Their relics penetrated the awareness of Christian people everywhere, for it was customary to place relics in every altar that was consecrated.[9] In Sir Richard Southern's words,

> When the machinery of government was simple or non-existent, these tangible agents of spiritual power [i.e. relics] had an importance in public life which they lost in a more complicated age. The deficiencies in human resources were supplied by the power of the saints. They were the great power-houses in the fight against evil; they filled the gaps in the structure of human justice.[10]

The memory of the martyrs who were thus proclaimed and resorted to throughout Christendom was indelibly imprinted upon the minds of two key classes of western society – the monks and the knights. Every day at the office of Prime, monks heard a portion of the Martyrology which brought home in stark and memorable terms the witness of the martyrs of old.[11] In the 'political allegory' that he addressed to Countess Matilda of Tuscany, the monastic writer John of Mantua interpreted the pomegranites (*mala punica*) of the Song of Songs as martyrs: they were *mala* in the sweetness of their lives and *punica* because red with the blood of their sacrifice.[12] In his eyes martyrdom was like a new baptism to be not feared but embraced; for it was sanctified by the blood of Christ.[13] As for the knights, Orderic Vitalis related how, in the England of the Norman conquest, a chaplain of Earl Hugh of Chester named Gerold of Avranches addressed the comital court:

> To great lords, simple knights, and noble boys alike he gave salutary counsel; and he made a great collection of stories of the combats of holy knights, drawn from the Old Testament and more recent records of Christian achievements, for them to imitate. He told them vivid stories of the conflicts of Demetrius and George, of Theodore and Sebastian, of the Theban legion and Maurice its leader, and of Eustace, supreme commander of the army and his companions, who through martyrdom deserved to be crowned in heaven.[14]

The Song of Roland suggests that such stories sank deeply into the consciousness of lay feudal society. Archbishop Turpin promised just such a reward to the Franks before battle:

> Barons, my lords, Charles picked us for this purpose;
> We must be ready to die in our king's service. ...
> If you should die, blest martyrdom's your guerdon;
> You'll sit on high in Paradise eternal.

Charlemagne and his companions fought and died in the confidence that this was so.[15] Similarly, in Abbo of Fleury's *Life of St Edmund*, written in the late tenth century and circulated quite widely during the eleventh, a Christian king who fought the heathen Danes and died at their hands was repeatedly called a martyr, and was compared to St Sebastian and St Laurence.[16] Edmund aspired to die for his country: 'honestum michi esset pro patria mori'; and 'as king and martyr he entered with the palm of victory and the crown of righteousness into the senate of the holy court'.[17]

The status of Christian fighting men was also made clear in the so-called *Laudes regiae* which were festally chanted in the greater churches and monasteries. They included the refrain *Christus vincit, Christus regnat, Christus imperat*, and they related the hierarchy of heaven as in the Litany of Saints to the human ranks of popes, emperors and kings, bishops and abbots, and *principes* with the armies of Christians. In some texts the *exercitus Christianorum* had as its patrons such martyr-saints as Gerold of Avranches extolled: George, Martin, Maurice, and Sebastian – all believed to have once been soldiers. They were invoked to bring *salus et victoria* to fighting men.[18] It was not unknown for saints themselves to appear on the field of battle as helpers of armies. In early ninth-century Spain St James had appeared on the field of Clavijo against the Moslems; the incident is the subject of a sculpture in the cathedral at Compostela which must have been as conspicuous to eleventh-century pilgrims as it is today.[19] According to Benzo of Alba, during the Cadalan schism of the early 1060s God gave an army victory through his apostles St Peter and St Paul together with St Maurice and St Carpophorus.[20] A little later the Norman leader Robert Guiscard carried on his last campaigns some relics of the apostle St Matthew.[21]

These examples illustrate how the theme of martyrdom was familiar in the Christian West as part of its general religious outlook. In more specific ways, too, it was brought home to those who, like Bonizo of Sutri, shared the concerns of the reform papacy. Four, often interrelated developments are especially significant for the understanding of the First Crusade. The first is the occasional treatment as martyrs of those who died, or might die, in military endeavours pleasing to the papacy. So long ago as the ninth century, Popes Leo IV and John VIII extended the promise of everlasting life to those killed by Muslims or Northmen in defence of the Church.[22] In 1053 German troops who perished at Civitate during Pope Leo IX's Norman campaign were said to have been at once raised to highest heaven.[23] In connection with his 'crusading' plans of 1074 against the Seljüks, Pope Gregory VII urged upon Countess Matilda of Tuscany that 'if, as some say, it is a noble thing to die for our country, it is a far nobler and more praiseworthy thing to give our corruptible flesh for Christ, who is life eternal.'[24] And in 1087 the Pisan *vicecomes* Hugh, who fell in battle against Saracens during the Mahdia campaign, died for Christ and at the Last Judgement he would shine as a martyr.[25]

Secondly, the papacy had grown to see in a similar light the clerical and lay leaders of the Patarenes at Milan who suffered in urban strife. The Patarenes themselves claimed as a martyr their early leader Ariald, killed in 1066: in 1075 when Andrew of Strumi wrote his Life he described it as a *beati martyris Arialdi passio*, and told how his hero had desired to die for Christ and to bear witness by his own blood.[26] At his Lent council of 1078, Gregory VII in effect canonised the ruthless and aggressive Erlembald who perished in 1075. Gregory linked with him the Roman city prefect Cencius who 'pro iustitia et fide fausto triumphans martyrio vitam finivit temporalem' and was at once exalted to Paradise.[27] More emphatically still, late in 1075 Gregory congratulated as a martyr the hideously mutilated Patarene priest Liutprand:

> So, martyr of Christ, be strong in the Lord. Be sure that the office of priesthood is now yours more strongly than ever: before, it was yours by anointing, but now it is yours by the sprinkling of blood. ... We know that you are for ever assailed and afflicted by the enemies of holy Church. You should not fear or dread them, for you and your possessions are under the protection and the great love of ourselves and of the apostles.[28]

Urban II shared Gregory's opinion that the Patarene leaders were martyrs. In 1095, *en route* for Clermont, he was present when the relics of Erlembald – *miles Christi reverendus* and *vir beatus* in the words of his epitaph – were given burial in the Milanese monastery of San Dionisio.[29]

The Patarenes showed especial zeal against simony, and other aspects of the struggle against it provide a third way in which the theme of martyrdom was propagated. Especially in south Italy, publicists attacked simony by using the legends that had gathered about St Peter and his struggle with the heresiarch Simon Magus. Such legends found eloquent expression in the poem *In honore beati Petri apostoli* which a monk of Montecassino named Amatus dedicated to Gregory VII.[30] It culminated in the contest at Rome that led to Simon Magus's ignominious death and so to St Peter's own martyrdom at Nero's hands, thus ending what St Peter was made to call 'hoc bellum pro Christi nomine gestum'.[31] The eleventh-century Church was engaged in a like warfare. When commenting upon St Peter's encounter in Samaria with Simon Magus (Acts 8: 9-24), Amatus addressed Gregory as the Church's champion in it, and he alluded to St Peter's faith which would never fail again and by virtue of which Gregory would command obedience from this world's kings.[32] Similarly, in 1068 the anti-simoniac party at Florence, in a letter that circulated widely, urged upon Pope Alexander II the example of St Peter's martyrdom (*passio*) as an incentive to zeal in the *sancta bella* against Simon Magus's latter-day adherents.[33]

Fourthly, after the synod of Brixen (1080) and the consecration in 1084 of the antipope Clement III, much of the impetus of the warfare against simony was directed as well against the Guibertine schism. Gregory VII himself helped this redirection,[34] which found particularly clear expression in the writings of the Roman cardinal-priest Deusdedit.[35] In letters of his last years Gregory passionately sought in the struggle against the antipope and against Henry IV of Germany the support of those 'who for love of Christ's law are resolved to stand firm to the death in the face of the ungodly'. Again, he wrote, 'Consider, my beloved people, consider how many of this world's knights are every day induced by vile reward to incur death for their own lords. And we – what do we do for the king of all, and for an eternal reward?'[36] Similar words were attributed to Urban II at Clermont; and in the meantime Bonizo of Sutri, a zealot for the Patarenes and against simony and the antipope, dealt with his friend's two questions. In concluding his *Liber ad amicum* he had no doubt that the times called for steadfastness unto death upon the battlefield against Christendom's internal foes. He pointed to latter-day martyrs – Leo IX's troops at Civitate now crowned with glory and honour, and also Erlembald and Cencius:

> Therefore let the most glorious martyrs of Christ fight for the truth, strive for righteousness, and fight with a true heart against the heresy that exalts itself against every so-called god or object of worship. Let them emulate in good the most excellent Countess Matilda, a daughter of St Peter who with a man's heart has put aside all worldly goods and is ready to die rather than break God's law, and to fight by every means with all the powers at her command against the heresy that now rages in the Church.[37]

When such calls were sounding to warfare against Simon Magus and Clement III, and when at Pisa a death in battle against the Muslims was also represented as a glorious martyrdom, the preaching of the Crusade against Christendom's external foes was being well prepared.

It is time to turn to the sources for the Crusade itself. In them, references to martyrdom are quite, but not very, common; by and large they confidently continue ideas propagated earlier by the reform papacy and its sympathisers in warfare against Muslims, simoniacs, and schismatics. Thus martyrdom is referred to in a recruiting manifesto for the journey to Jerusalem, the so-called 'Encyclical of Pope Sergius IV', with its summons: 'Venite, filii, defendite Deum et regnum acquirite aeternum', with its appeal to the heroes of faith in the first days of the Church, and with its promise: 'Et nos si taliter fecerimus, sine dubio in vitam eternam permanemus'.[38] So, too, in 1098 Count Stephen of Blois as a matter of course informed his wife Adela of his confidence that the souls of the slain had passed to the joys of Paradise.[39]

For the most part, however, the theme of martyrdom must be pursued in the historians of the Crusade.[40] Of those who offered versions of Urban II's address at Clermont, four had him allude to martyrdom. He did so after the manner of Gregory VII and Bonizo of Sutri. According to Guibert of Nogent, he urged his audience henceforth to fight wars that carried in themselves the glorious reward of martyrdom. Baldric of Bourgueil made him present the more spiritual plea that it was fitting to die for Christ in Jerusalem; then he made him extend the hope that His warriors would despoil their enemies and either return home victorious or else, purpled with their own blood, receive an eternal reward. Robert the Monk had Urban see in everyone willing to take the cross a living sacrifice, holy and acceptable to God. William of Malmesbury developed the spiritual motive a little: the motive of men's labours should be charity, leading them to lay down their lives for their brothers; and they were to hope after death for the reward of blessed martyrdom.[41]

In their narratives, some historians alluded to martyrdom more often than others. Guibert of Nogent, Robert the Monk, Albert of Aix, and the unknown author at Montecassino of the *Historia peregrinorum*, none of whom took part in the Crusade, on the whole referred to it more frequently than did Raymond of Aguilers, Fulcher of Chartres, the anonymous author of the *Gesta Francorum*, Tudebod, and Richard the Pilgrim, author of the oldest parts of the *Chanson d'Antioche*, who had first-hand experience.[42] This suggests that martyrdom may have been of less significance as a formative influence upon the Crusade itself than as a means whereby it was accepted and interpreted. Of all the historians, Raymond of Aguilers was the most reticent on the subject. Fulcher of Chartres referred in his Prologue to the many kinds of martyrdom that men suffered for love of Christ; 'O quot milia martyrum in hac expeditione beata morte finierunt!'[43] The author of the *Gesta Francorum*, too, followed by Tudebod, referred to martydom only occasionally and in comment upon particular happenings.[44] Caffaro, who went to the East in 1101, spoke of Genoese *martires* at Antioch in 1097; angels received them into heaven where they were given places beside the Maccabees.[45] Among the non-participants, Baldric of Bourgueil and Ralph of Caen also made few references; although the latter concluded with an appeal for *constantia martyrialis*.[46] Others had more to say. Guibert of Nogent saw martyrdom as a discipline, a glory, and a reward; it was a main incentive to the Crusade.[47] For Robert the Monk, the expedition was itself a *martyrium*.[48] Albert of Aix took a similar view; but he often used the word of violent death as such while restricting its use to Christians, and martyrdom could be expressly suffered in God's name.[49]

The allusions to martyrdom throughout the narrative sources can be given a fourfold classification. First, many occur in addresses and sermons attributed to crusading leaders, both clerical and lay, at critical junctures and before major engagements. Thus the *Chanson d'Antioche* and – following it – Albert of Aix related, in slightly different forms, how in 1094 Peter the Hermit had been instructed in Jerusalem that the gates of Paradise were open to those who surmounted difficulties and temptations.[50] According to Guibert of Nogent, before the battle of Dorylaeum in 1097 the Frankish leaders reminded their followers of the strength that willingness for martyrdom brought, whether the outcome of battle were death or life.[51] Before Antioch fell in the following year, Robert the Monk ascribed similar words to Bishop Adhemar of Le Puy, together with an assurance that, purged from their sins by recent fasts and penances, those who died would enter eternal joys.[52] Albert of Aix had Bishop Adhemar at

Nicaea promise eternal life to those crowned with martyrdom in battle. In 1098 Duke Godfrey of Bouillon and Count Robert of Flanders reminded those who feared to storm the walls of Antioch of the rewards of dying for Christ. A Lombard priest later comforted the Franks with a sermon about a vision in which St Ambrose had promised glory to the fallen and prophesied victory for the expedition. In 1099 Duke Godfrey explained to the Muslim governor of Ramla that the Frankish attackers approached the town with songs and rejoicing, since they were confident that those who fell would receive a martyr's reward. Soon after, at the siege of Arsuf, he exhorted his troops to offer their souls for the name of Jesus, and to purge their sins so that they might perform their vows.[53] In Baldric of Bourgueil, before the capture of Jerusalem the clergy preached a long sermon with the concluding assertion that it was appropriate to die where Christ himself had died.[54] At 'Arqa in the same year, Raymond of Aguilers narrated a vision of Peter Bartholomew about Christ's five wounds in which he regarded as the highest orders of crusaders those who most fully shared Christ's passion and death.[55] An idiosyncrasy of Robert the Monk is his making the Norman leader Bohemond several times use the theme of martyrdom when recruiting and addressing his followers.[56] The *Gesta Francorum* attributed to his half-brother Guy, who was serving in the Emperor Alexius Comnenus's army, the wish that he could have suffered martyrdom with Bohemond, after Count Stephen of Blois had given an over-pessimistic account of Frankish fortunes at Antioch.[57]

Secondly, the historians tended particularly to associate two junctures in the Crusade with the reward of martyrdom. One was the seven-week siege of Nicaea in June 1097. The *Gesta Francorum* commented that many gained martyrdom there in battle, while many of the poor died of hunger in Christ's name; all alike entered heaven in the robe of martyrdom, crying upon the Lord to avenge the blood shed for His name.[58] Tudebod borrowed these words but omitted the cry for vengeance.[59] Robert the Monk piously regarded the restoration to the Catholic Church of so historic a Christian city as an achievement whose providential character was proved by the consecration of martyrs' blood.[60] In Albert of Aix, Bishop Adhemar preached at Nicaea on the rewards of martyrdom.[61] The *Historia peregrinorum* gave in full the text of the *Gesta Francorum*, including the plea for vengeance.[62] The other juncture was the testing time in the spring and early summer of 1098 before the fall of Antioch. According to the *Gesta Francorum*, on 6 March 'more than a thousand of our knights or foot-soldiers were martyred and, as we believe, ascended to heaven where, clad in white, they received the robe of martyrdom'.[63] Tudebod added their plea to Christ: 'Why, Lord, do you not avenge our blood which has today been shed for your name?'[64] Fulcher of Chartres by contrast emphasised the long-term sufferings of the whole body of living Franks who for love of God sustained starvation, cold, heat, and storm:

> I believe that the elect were tried by the Lord and by such sufferings were cleansed of their sins. For a long time they strove – although the sword of the smiter was also not lacking. Many willingly completed the course of martyrdom, perhaps taking encouragement from the noble example of holy Job who through bodily torments purged his soul and kept God always in his thoughts. They fought against the pagans, and they toiled for God.[65]

Robert the Monk made martyrdom a theme of Bishop Adhemar's sermon, which he delivered clad in a hauberk and clasping the Holy Lance.[66] The *Historia peregrinorum* repeated Tudebod's account of the martyrdom of Frankish warriors with the plea that God would avenge their blood; it added the cries of Christian hostages burned to death by the Muslims. It alone proceeded to declare that the merciless slaughter of the Muslim population of Jerusalem in 1099 was a Christian retaliation for the accumulated debt of martyrs' blood:

Who can express the gladness of the Christians [at Jerusalem], when those who once had rent Christ asunder in his members now in their own bodies received payment in kind (*taliones*) from them? For they rejoiced to see that the course of the pilgrim journey that they had vowed was now complete...[67]

Thirdly, the historians associated martyrdom with the sufferings and the witness of individual persons and groups of persons. Usually it involved death, whether in battle or at sieges.[68] Armies, too, were collectively exposed to martyrdom.[69] Likewise the bishops, priests, and monks who went out before Christian armies to aid by their prayers the warriors who were about to fight, also expected a martyr's reward if they were killed.[70] A like reward awaited individual priests who died saying mass in circumstances of danger.[71] A knight killed at Antioch in 1104 when he intervened after hearing a pagan blaspheme God's name was assuredly a martyr: 'still lying upon the ground he was already glorified in heaven'.[72] Refusal to apostatise to Islam, if sustained to the point of death, was another way to martyrdom,[73] as was the death of a hostage cruelly slain during a military assault.[74] Death was not always necessary for martyrdom. Fulcher of Chartres saw a way to it through fearful sufferings heroically borne by the living.[75] Exceptionally, the *Historia peregrinorum* regarded an eminent crusader's life as tantamount to martyrdom: in 1104 Bohemond was received in France 'tanquam verus miles martyrque Christi'.[76] In the strict sense of the term, the historians singled out some figures in particular as martyrs of the Crusade, especially in obituary notices. The outstanding example is the knight Anselm of Ribemont, killed at 'Arqa in 1099. Some were content to list him, with others, as a martyr.[77] But some related a vision that he experienced on the night before his death. In Raymond of Aguilers he saw the blessedness of those who die in Christ, as manifest in their risen beauty and in the especial splendour of their heavenly habitations.[78] However Ralph of Caen, followed by the *Historia peregrinorum*, said that Anselm was shown a great palace and a multitude of the blessed. He learnt that they were all the Frankish fallen:

'These are the pilgrims to Jerusalem (*Hierosolimipetae*) who from the beginning entered upon the way of God in which you too are still striving. They have departed this life and wear everlasting crowns. Unless perchance you yet refuse, you also will ascend to us; for you have fought the good fight, and you have completed your course.'[79]

Guibert of Nogent singled out for eulogy Hugh of Vermandois: at Antioch in 1098 he was desirous of a martyr's death, and in 1101 after the battle of Heraclea he was duly rewarded.[80] Robert the Monk instanced Gualo, constable of the king of France, whose wife prayed for him as a martyr after he was killed at Antioch in violation of a truce.[81]

Fourthly, on certain occasions martyr-saints actively aided crusading armies. Thus, as early as January 1098, in a letter addressed to the West the Greek and Latin bishops assembled near Antioch expressed their confidence that the crusading host was protected by St George, St Theodore, St Demetrius, and St Blaise, *militibus Christi nos vere comitantibus*.[82] Five months later, in a critical situation at Antioch when the Frankish army faced that of Kerbogha of Mosul, a strong and early tradition relates that the Franks were conscious of heavenly reinforcements amongst whom martyr-saints were prominent. According to the *Gesta Francorum* there appeared from the mountains a countless host on white horses and with white banners. The Franks realised that Christ had sent them help and that St George, St Mercurius, and St Demetrius were its leaders.[83] For Tudebod this intervention was presaged in a vision of a priest named Stephen, through which Christ promised the help of St George, St Theodore, and St Demetrius, together with 'all the pilgrims who have died in this journey to Jerusalem'.[84] Robert the Monk made Bishop Adhemar promise in a sermon that the Lord would send legions of his saints to avenge the Franks of their enemies; in the event the leaders were St George, St Maurice, St Mercurius, and St Demetrius.[85] Robert also accounted for the goodwill of Firuz – whom he represented as a Muslim – in his negotiations with Bohemond before the fall of Antioch by his having a vision of an army of martyrs led by St George, St Demetrius, and St Maurice who in life had borne weapons of war and had been beheaded for the Christian faith.[86] Another emir and many Muslims were converted to Christianity when they saw the *innumera albatorum equitum militia* that fought for the Christians.[87] The *Historia peregrinorum* laid much weight upon the intervention of martyr-saints, especially St Mercurius, St George, and St Theodore, who intervened at Antioch as upon other occasions.[88] Not surprisingly, when the Franks reached St George's traditional burial-place near Ramla they remembered his martyrdom and, according to Baldric of Bourgueil, his intervention at Antioch; and they established a bishopric.[89]

To what conclusions does this evidence point, bearing in mind its fairly small amount as well as its scattered and uneven dispersal through the sources? First, during the First Crusade there seems to have been little if any development beyond ideas current before 1095 in the understanding, appraisal, or propagation of the idea of martyrdom, except that it was set more fully in the context of warfare against Christendom's external enemy, Islam. Secondly, however, Bonizo of Sutri illustrates how, before the Crusade and in face of simoniacs and schismatics, attention could be concentrated upon Christ's words in the Gospels that were to inspire the crusaders to choose the way of self-denial, suffering, and death as a route to eternal life. Thirdly, the relative scarcity of references to martyrdom and their conventional character, especially in authors who themselves took part in the First Crusade, suggest that the idea of martyrdom did not make a direct and integral contribution to the *valida motio* as at first understood. In this respect it differed from the concepts of pilgrimage and holy war. As a familiar part of the world-picture, it seems to have acted as a catalyst in the strict sense, of something that assisted the fusion of these concepts while not itself undergoing substantial change or even being part of the change. Martyrdom was important because it enabled crusaders to understand how, with a view to the remission of their sins, they could at one and the same time deny themselves and follow Christ in pilgrimage to the city where He had suffered and died, and also fight a holy war that involved them in salutary suffering and death. So, fourthly, from the outset the theme of martyrdom helped the crusaders and those who recorded their fortunes to reflect upon what happened. But it was the writers like Guibert of Nogent who presented the Crusade from the standpoint of western Europe who most often referred to it. They prepared the way for many in the twelfth-century West to see martyrdom as an integral part of the crusading experience. The emergence of the military Orders was facilitated by this development; and the most eloquent exponent of the new warfare – 'Quam beati moriuntur martyres in proelio'[90] – was St Bernard of Clairvaux, who himself never set foot in the Holy Land.[91]

NOTES

1   Bonizo of Sutri, 'Liber ad amicum', i, ed. E. Dümmler, *MGH Libelli de lite*, i, 571-2.

2   *Gesta Francorum et aliorum Hierosolimitanorum*, ed. R. Hill (London, etc., 1962), 1.

3   *Isidori Hispalensis episcopi Etymologiarum sive originum libri XX*, ed. W.M. Lindsay (Oxford, 1911), 7.11.1-4. For the view that martyrdom like baptism cancelled all sins, see e.g. Bonizo of Sutri, *Liber de vita christiana*, ed. E. Perels (Berlin, 1930), 278, 332-3.

4   i, ii, pp. 573-5. For Gregory VII's promotion of the cult of martyr-popes, see Bernold of Constance, 'Micrologus', *PL*, cli, 1010.

5   *The Oxford Book of Medieval Latin Verse*, new edn. by F.J.E. Raby (Oxford, 1959), pp. 16-17, no. 14.

6   For examples, see *Le Pontifical romano-germanique du dixième siècle*, xl. 2, 23, ed. C. Vogel and R. Elze (Studi e testi, 226-7; Vatican City, 1963), i, 125-7, 134-5.

7   *L'opera poetica di s. Pier Damiani*, ed. M. Lokrantz (Stockholm, 1964); *I carmi di Alfano I, arcivescovo di Salerno*, ed. A. Lentini and F. Avagliano (Miscellanea cassinese, 38; Montecassino, 1974).

8   H.E.J. Cowdrey, 'Two Studies in Cluniac History, 1049-1126', *Studi Gregoriani*, xi (1978), 164-6.

9   *Le Pontifical romano-germanique*, xl. 48-50, i, pp. 48-50; cf. xxxv. 56, i, pp. 118-19.

10   R.W. Southern, *The Making of the Middle Ages* (London, etc., 1953), 137.

11   See e.g., J. Dubois, *Le Martyrologe d'Usuard. Texte et commentaire* (Subsidia hagiographica, 40; Brussels, 1965).

12   *Iohannis Mantuani In cantica canticorum et De sancta Maria tractatus ad comitissam Matildam*, ed. B. Bischoff and B. Taeger (Spicilegium Friburgense, 19; Freiburg, 1973), p. 97, lines 10-19; p. 140, line 24-p. 141, line 8; cf. p. 143, line 30-p. 144, line 5.

13   *Ibid.*, p. 53, lines 12-15; p. 80, lines 25-8; p. 136, lines 4-15; p. 144, lines 2-4.

14   *The Ecclesiastical History of Orderic Vitalis*, vi, 2, ed. M. Chibnall, iii (Oxford, 1972), 216-17.

15   *La Chanson de Roland*, ed. F. Whitehead (2nd edn., Oxford, 1946), p. 34, lines 1127-35 (the translation is by Dorothy L. Sayers); p. 55, lines 1854-6; p. 59, line 2016; p. 65, lines 2195-9; p. 66, lines 2240-1; p. 70, lines 2393-6; p. 85, lines 2898-9; p. 86, lines 2933-4.

16   *Three Lives of English Saints*, ed. M. Winterbottom (Toronto, 1972), cap. 10, pp. 78-9; cap. 16, pp. 85-6; and *passim*.

17   *Ibid.*, cap. 8, p. 75; cap. 10, p. 79.

18   For examples, see H.E.J. Cowdrey, 'The Anglo-Norman *Laudes regiae*', *Viator*, xii (1981), 72-8.

19   S. Alcolea, *La catedral de Santiago* (Madrid, n.d.), 114.

20   Benzo of Alba, 'Ad Heinricum IV imperatorem libri VII', ii, 18, *MGHS*, xi, 620-1.

21   *Das Register Gregors VII.*, viii, 8, ed. E. Caspar, *MGH Epistolae selectae*, ii (Berlin, 1920-3), 526-7; 'Chronica monasterii Casinensis', iii, 57, iv, 73, *MGHS*, xxxiv, 437-8, 539.

22   *Epistolae selectae Leonis IV*, no. 28 (853), *MGH Epistolae*, v, 601; *Iohannis VIII epistolae*, no. 150 (878), *MGH Epistolae*, vii, 26-7.

23   S. Borgia, *Memorie istoriche della pontificia città di Benevento*, ii (Rome, 1764), 321; see also Bonizo of Sutri, 'Liber ad amicum', v, ix, pp. 589, 620. Leo was believed to have had a death-bed vision of the slain: Bruno of Segni, 'Libellus de symoniacos', cap. 6, ed. E. Sackur, *MGH Libelli de lite*, ii, 550-1 (written during the mid-1090s).

24   *The Epistolae vagantes of Pope Gregory VII*, ed. H.E.J. Cowdrey (Oxford, 1972), no. 5, pp. 10-13.

25   H.E.J. Cowdrey, 'The Mahdia Campaign of 1087', *EHR*, xcii (1977), 27, stanzas 42-6.

26   'Vita sancti Arialdi auctore Andrea abbate Strumensi', *MGHS* xxx/2, 1047-75. See esp. Prol., p. 1049; cap. 19, pp. 1063-4; cap. 26, p. 1072. Cf. Bonizo of Sutri, 'Liber ad amicum', vi, p. 591.

27   Berthold, 'Annales', (a. 1077) *MGHS*, v, 304-6; cf. Bonizo of Sutri, 'Liber ad amicum', vii, ix, pp. 604-5, 620.

28   *Quellen und Forschungen zum Urkunden- und Kanzleiwesen Papst Gregors VII.: i, Quellen: Urkunden, Regesten, Facsimilia*, ed. L. Santifaller (Studi e testi, 190; Vatican City, 1957), no. 106, pp. 94-5.

29   G. Giulini, *Memorie spettanti alla storia, al governo, ed alla descrizione della città e della campagna di Milano ne'secoli bassi*, iv (Milan, [1760]), 319.

30   *Il poema di Amato su s. Pietro apostolo*, ed. A. Lentini, (Miscellanea cassinese, 30-1; Montecassino, 1958-9); for the dedication, see i, 60.

31   iv, 20; *ibid.*, i, pp. 139-40.

32   i, 18, ii. 7; *ibid.*, i. pp. 72-3, 83-4; cf. Lentini and Avagliano, *I carmi de Alfano I*, no. 37, pp. 183-4.

33   'Vita Iohannis Gualberti auctore Andrea abbate Strumensi', cap. 75, *MGHS*, xxx/2, 1096-9, esp. p. 1099, lines 29-42; cf. caps. 70-3, pp. 1094-5. This work was written c. 1092. For a critical edition of the letter, see G. Miccoli, *Pietro Igneo. Studi sull'età gregoriana* (Rome, 1960), 139-157, esp. pp. 156-7. Cf. Pope Alexander II's letter to the church of Cremona, in Bonizo of Sutri, 'Liber ad amicum', vi, pp. 597-8.

34   *Reg. Greg. VII*, viii, 5, pp. 521-3.

35   Deusdedit, 'Libellus contra invasores et symoniacos et reliquos scismaticos', ii, 11-12, ed. E. Sackur, *MGH Libelli de lite*, ii. 328-30; cf. 'Chronica monasterii Casinensis', iii, 70, pp. 452-3, also Pope Paschal II's letter to Count Robert of Flanders: *Ep.* 88, 21 Jan. 1102 (*recte*), *PL*, clxiii, 108.

36 *Epistolae vagantes*, no. 54, pp. 132-3; *Reg. Greg. VII*, ix, 21, pp. 601-3.

37 Bonizo of Sutri, 'Liber ad amicum', ix, p. 620.

38 A. Gieysztor, 'The Genesis of the Crusades: the Encyclical of Sergius IV (1009-12)', *Medievalia et Humanistica*, v (1948), 3-23; vi (1950), 3-34. The text is at pp. 33-4 of the second part; see nos. 17-18.

39 H. Hagenmeyer, *Die Kreuzzugsbriefe aus den Jahren 1088-1100* (Innsbruck, 1901), no. 10.6, pp. 149-52 at p. 150.

40 Sources are cited in the following editions. Raymond of Aguilers: *Le 'Liber' de Raymond d'Aguilers*, ed. J.H. and L.L. Hill (Paris, 1969). Fulcher of Chartres: *Fulcheri Carnotensis, Historia Hierosolymitana (1095-1127)*, ed. H. Hagenmeyer (Heidelberg, 1913). *Gesta Francorum*: as n. 2. Tudebod: Petrus Tudebodus, *Historia de Hierosolymitano itinere*, ed. J.H. and L.L. Hill (Paris, 1977). Bartolf of Nangis: 'Gesta Francorum expugnantium Iherusalem', *RHC Oc.*, iii, 491-543. Guibert of Nogent: 'Historia quae dicitur Gesta Dei per Francos, edita a venerabili domno Guiberto, abbate monasterii Sanctae Mariae Novigenti', *RHC Oc.*, iv, 117-263. Baldric of Bourgueil: 'Baldrici, episcopi Dolensis, Historia Jerosolimitana', *RHC Oc.*, iv, 5-111. Robert the Monk: 'Roberti monachi Historia Iheroslimitana', *RHC Oc.*, iii, 721-882. Ralph of Caen: 'Gesta Tancredi in expeditione Hierosolymitana, auctore Radulfo Cadomensi, eius familiari', *RHC Oc.*, iii, 602-716. *Chanson d'Antioche: La Chanson d'Antioche*, ed. S. Duparc-Quioc, (Paris, 1977-8). Albert of Aix: 'Alberti Aquensis Historia Hierosolymitana', *RHC Oc.*, iv, 269-713. Caffaro: 'Cafari, De liberatione civitatum liber', *Annali Genovesi di Caffaro e de'suoi continuatori*, i: *1099-1293*, ed. L.T. Belgrano (Fonti per la storia d'Italia, 11; Rome, 1890), 99-124. *Historia peregrinorum*: 'Tudebodus imitatus et continuatus, ex codice bibliothecae casinensis qui inscribitur, Historia peregrinorum euntium Jerusolymam ad liberandum Sanctum Sepulchrum de potestate ethnicorum', *RHC Oc.*, iii, 169-229.

41 Guibert of Nogent, ii, 4, p. 138E; Baldric of Bourgueil, i, 4, p. 15B-D, cf. Robert the Monk, cap. 2, p. 729FG; William of Malmesbury, *De gestis regum Anglorum libri quinque*, iv. 347, ed. W. Stubbs, ii (London: RS, 1889), 393-8.

42 Ekkehard of Aura, who travelled to the Holy Land in 1101, made no reference to it until the events of that year: *Ekkehardi Chronica, recensio I*, in *Frutolfs und Ekkehards Chroniken und die anonyme Kaiserchronik*, ed. F.-J. Schmale and I. Schmale-Ott (Ausgewählte Quellen zur Geschichte des Mittelalters, 15; Darmstadt, 1972), 130-78, esp. 170-2.

43 Prol. 4, p. 117.

44 e.g. their treatment of the death of Anselm of Ribemont and others: *Gesta Francorum*, p. 85; Tudebod, pp. 131-2.

45 p. 103, lines 9-17.

46 cap. 157, p. 716BC; cf. cap. 87, p. 667H.

47 iii, 8, p. 158JK; iii, 9, p. 159FG; iii, 10, p. 161H; vii, Praef., p. 221A,C; vii, 14, p. 321H; vii, 28, p. 247.

48 cap. 9, p. 734.

49 i, 21, p. 288C; i, 24, p. 291E; iii, 49, p. 373B; iii, 54, p. 376EF; iv, 14, p. 399B; v, 33, p. 453G.

50 lines 310-12, i, p. 33; Albert of Aix, i, 4, p. 273D.

51 iii, 10, p. 161C-F.

52 vii, 10, pp. 829-30.

53 ii, 27, p. 320B; iv, 18, pp. 401-2; iv, 38, pp. 415-16; vi, 43, pp. 492-3; vii, 4, p. 509D-F.

54 iv, 13, p. 101GH.

55 cap. 18, pp. 112-14.

56 ii, 4, p. 741E; ii, 16, pp. 747E-748A; iv, 10, p. 780E; cf. his dialogue at Antioch with Firuz: v, 8, pp. 796-7.

57 *Gesta Francorum*, pp.64-5; whence Tudebod, pp. 106-7. Cf. Guibert of Nogent, v, 27, p. 201.

58 p. 17.

59 p. 50.

60 iii, 6, pp. 758-9.

61 ii, 27, p. 320B.

62 cap. 24, p. 182.

63 p. 40.

64 p. 75.

65 i, 16, 1-4, pp. 224-7.

66 vii, 9-10, pp.829D-830A.

67 cap. 52, p. 192; cap. 57, p. 194; cap. 126, p. 223.

68 *Gesta Francorum*, p. 85; Tudebod, pp. 131-2; Robert the Monk, v, 12, pp. 799E-800A.

69 Guibert of Nogent, vi, 7, pp. 205I-206A; Baldric of Bourgueil, i, 27, p. 30F; Robert the Monk, iii, 15, p. 764A.

70 Guibert of Nogent, vi, 7, p. 205F.

71 Tudebod, p. 36; Robert the Monk, cap. 12, p. 735.

72 Fulcher of Chartres, ii, 27, 10-13, pp. 476-7.

73 Tudebod, pp. 79-81; Guibert of Nogent, ii, 10, p. 145B,G; vii, 49, pp.259-60.

74 Albert of Aix, vii, 2, pp. 507-8.

[75] i, 16, 1-4, pp. 224-7.

[76] cap. 140, p. 228.

[77] Fulcher of Chartres, i, 25, 8, p. 270; *Gesta Francorum*, p. 85; Tudebod, pp. 131-2; Guibert of Nogent, vi, 23, p. 219A-D; Baldric of Bourgueil, iv, 5, p. 93F-H. For his fame in the West, see Bishop Manasses II of Reims's letter of late 1099 to Bishop Lambert of Arras: Hagenmeyer, *Kreuzzugsbriefe*, no. 20, pp. 175-6.

[78] cap. 17, pp. 108-9.

[79] Ralph of Caen, cap. 106, pp. 680-1; *Historia peregrinorum*, cap. 104, p. 215.

[80] v, 25, p. 200B-D; vi, 5, p. 205D; vi, 11, p. 208 F-H.

[81] v, 7, p. 795E.

[82] Hagenmeyer, *Kreuzzugsbriefe*, no. 9, 3, pp. 147-8.

[83] p. 69. So Guibert of Nogent, vi, 9, p. 206GH; Baldric of Bourgueil, iii, 17, p. 77B-D.

[84] pp. 98-100, 111-12.

[85] vii, 10, p. 830AB; vii, 13, p. 832.

[86] v, 8-9, pp. 796-7.

[87] v, 18, pp. 835-6.

[88] Prol., p. 173; cap. 27, p. 183; cap. 82, p. 205. The story of an intervention by martyr-saints at the battle of Dorylaeum (1097) was anticipated by Raymond of Aguilers who did not name *duos equites* who intervened: cap. 5, pp. 45-6, cf. 2 Macc. 10: 29-31; and by Bartolf of Nangis who said that they were St George and St Demetrius, *martyres gloriosos*: cap. 9, p. 496DE.

[89] *Gesta Francorum*, p. 87; Tudebod, pp. 133-4; Robert the Monk, vii, 21, p. 859A; Baldric of Bourgueil, iv, 8, p. 96AB. In January 1099, according to Raymond of Aguilers, Peter Desiderius was instrumental in securing from Antioch relics, including those of St George, *vexillifer huius exercitus*: cap. 18, pp.131-4.

[90] 'De laude novae militiae', i. 1, *Sancti Bernardi Opera*, iii: *Tractatus et opuscula*, ed. J. Leclercq and H.M. Rochais (Rome, 1963), 215.

[91] I am grateful to Miss Shefali Rovik for reading and giving her criticisms of this paper.

William I's relations with Cluny further considered

William the Conqueror's dealings as king of England with the abbey of Cluny and with its abbot, Hugh of Semur (1049–1109), constitute a minor, but puzzling, detail of the events of his reign. There were three known occasions of contact between them. In order of probable importance though not necessarily of occurrence, Wiliam first sought from Hugh the dispatch of a group of professed Cluniac monks – six or twelve in number according to different sources – to advise and assist him with the reform of the church in England; but he encountered Hugh's firm refusal. Secondly, William sought and, in this case, received from Abbot Hugh the benefit of spiritual confraternity with his abbey; in return, William and Queen Matilda sent to Cluny generous gifts of ecclesiastical vestments. Thirdly, Abbot Hugh is on record as having met the king during a visit to Normandy. The principal evidence for these contacts is to be found in two sources, one considerably and the other very much later than the events that they record. One is a collection of material apparently made at Cluny after 1121 by an unknown Cluniac monk, which is usually referred to as Anonymous II.[1] It drew heavily upon earlier Lives of Abbot Hugh by Gilo of Tusculum, Hildebert of Lavardin, and Reynald of Vézelay; it also utilized other material, mostly written. The other is the longer, and forged, foundation charter of the Cluniac priory of St Pancras at Lewes. Sir Charles Clay established that, as it stands, its date of composition is almost certainly later than 1201 and that it was possibly drawn up and sealed fictitiously as late as 1396 × 1417.[2] However, it clearly

---

[1] *Bibliotheca Cluniacensis*, eds. M. Marrier and A. du Chesne (Paris, 1614), cols 447–62; most of the material relevant to this paper is reprinted in J. P. Migne, *Patrologia Latina* [hereafter *PL*], clix. 923–8. For discussions of the dates of the sources for Abbot Hugh of Cluny, see H. E. J. Cowdrey, 'Two Studies in Cluniac History, 1049–1126', *Studi Gregoriani*, xi (1978), pp 22–30; F. Barlow, 'The Canonization and Early Lives of Hugh I, Abbot of Cluny', *Analecta Bollandiana*, xcviii (1980), pp 297–334, repr. *The Norman Conquest and Beyond* (London, 1983), pp 257–95.

[2] The charter is printed in W. Dugdale, *Monasticon Anglicanum*, new edn. by J. Caley,

includes older material of historical value, perhaps derived from a foundation narrative.

The most recent substantial discussion of William I's relations with Cluny is a paper published in 1981 by Professor Frank Barlow.[3] In it, his most important suggestion is that the communications between the king and the abbot of Cluny about the dispatch of Cluniac monks should probably not be dated, as by recent commentators, to the very early years of the Conqueror's reign;[4] a date in the second half of it is more likely. The historical record preserved in the forged Lewes foundation charter provides a likely context during Abbot Hugh's visit to Normandy for which it is the principal source. Barlow's hypothesis is that Hugh came to Normandy at some time between 1078 and 1080 to confer with the king 'on some unknown business'. This visit was, according to the charter, the occasion of discussions about Lewes between Hugh and its founder, William of Warenne, later earl of Surrey. In 1076 William and his wife Gundrada had decided upon its foundation when they were diverted to Cluny while on a journey to Rome. The king was involved because Abbot Hugh insisted upon his written consent, but even so the foundation had run into difficulties which had involved the retention of the first prior, Lanzo, at Cluny for a whole year. William of Warenne was minded to transfer the church of St Pancras to the abbey of Marmoutier. But matters were resolved when Abbot Hugh's visit to King William in Normandy gave William of Warenne a chance to discuss matters with Hugh in person. Barlow concludes: 'The problems of Lewes could easily have led to a consideration [by the king and the abbot] of what part Cluny could play in the English, and possible Norman, Church at large or in the Conqueror's St Martin *de Bello* [Battle Abbey] in particular. In these circumstances the king's request for six or twelve monks . . . may have been little more than an uncalculated response to the impression that the saint made on him at their meeting'.[5] As for Hugh's grant of confraternity to William, Barlow concludes from Anonymous II that it was probably made while the intermediary, Warmund, abbot of Bourg-Dieu, Déols (dioc. Bourges) from *c*. 1074 and archbishop of Vienne from 1076, thereafter holding both offices, was abbot but not yet archbishop, that is, in 1075 or 1076.[6]

H. Ellis and B. Bandinel, 6 vols. in 8 parts (London, 1817–30) v. 12–13; also in *Recueil des chartes de l'abbaye de Cluny*, eds., A. Bernard and A. Bruel, Collection des documents inédits sur l'histoire de France, 6 vols. (1876–1903) [hereafter cited as Bruel with the number of the item], 3651. For the date, see *Early Yorkshire Charters*, viii, ed. C. T. Clay, Yorkshire Archaeological Society, Records Series, Extra Series, vi: Warenne Charters (1949), pp 59–62.

[3]F. Barlow, 'William I's Relations with Cluny', *Journal of Ecclesiastical History*, xxxii (1981), pp 131–41, repr. *The Norman Conquest and Beyond*, pp 245–56. (References hereafter are to the reprint).

[4]See Barlow (as n.3), p 254, n.1. A later date was proposed in older works, e.g. *PL* clix. 927B.

[5]Barlow (as n.3), p 254.

[6]*Ibid.*, pp 247, 253.

It is not the purpose of this paper to exclude Barlow's conclusions, which stand as a possible resolution of the problem as far as the scanty and unsatisfactory evidence allows. But further light may be shed on William's relations with Cluny if they are set in a fuller context than Barlow provides, especially from the Cluniac side. This context will first be outlined, and then the problem will be reconsidered in its light.

In part, the context is set in Normandy itself. It is well known that, especially through the reforming activity of William of Volpiano, abbot of Fécamp (1001–33), Cluny had an appreciable if indirect impact upon Norman monasticism during the first half of the eleventh century.[7] Less often noticed are the direct dealings between Cluny and the duchy that, according to Orderic Vitalis, took place in the ten years or so before the Norman conquest of England with regard to his monastery of Saint-Evroult, founded just before 1050 in the far south of the diocese of Lisieux. These dealings must have been ambivalent in their effects, encouraging Duke William to look to Cluny as a source of monastic reform but warning Abbot Hugh to caution in his response. The encouragement to Duke William was that Robert of Grandmesnil, abbot from 1059 to 1061, had, as a young man, received permission from Abbot Thierry (1050–7) to visit Cluny. When he had spent some time there, Abbot Hugh allowed him to bring back a distinguished monk of Cluny named Bernfrid, who later became bishop of an unknown see; Robert for some time retained Bernfrid at Saint-Evroult with honour, so that he could instruct its monks in the customs of the Cluniacs.[8] Abbot Hugh thus demonstrated his willingness to allow one of his monks who was of the calibre to be a bishop to travel as far as Normandy in order to instruct a favoured monastery in Cluniac monastic ways. The warning to Abbot Hugh came soon afterwards, when the future Abbot Mainer (1066–89), who had entered Saint-Evroult under Abbot Robert, received advice and leave from Abbot Osbern (1061–6) to go to Cluny. According to Orderic, Mainer went in a state of terror and shame because of Saint-Evroult's misfortunes since Abbot Robert had withdrawn to Italy and Duke William has intruded Osbern in his place, with the result that Osbern was excommunicated by authority of Pope Nicholas II. At Cluny, Mainer was a model subject of Abbot Hugh for a year during which he 'fervently learnt to undergo the discipline of the Cluniacs'. Osbern recalled him to become prior of Saint-Evroult only when Pope Alexander II had regularized the situation there.[9] Abbot Hugh must

---

[7] For recent summaries, see B. Golding, 'The Coming of the Cluniacs', *Proceedings of the Battle Conference on Anglo-Norman Studies, III, 1980* (Woodbridge, 1981), pp 65–77, at pp 65–6; D. Bates, *Normandy before 1066* (London/New York, 1982), pp 218–25.

[8] *The Ecclesiastical History of Orderic Vitalis*, ed. M. Chibnall, 6 vols. (Oxford, 1969–80), ii. pp 74–5.

[9] *Ibid.*, ii. pp 96–7, 107–8.

have learnt from Mainer about the spiritual and physical perils that might befall monks in the domains of William of Normandy.[10]

There is a wider context, too, in Cluny's ever-increasing willingness to answer the favour of reforming kings by sending monks to establish monasteries in their lands, to advise about ecclesiastical affairs, and possibly to serve as abbots and bishops. Although it was only under Abbot Hugh than Cluniac monks at all frequently became bishops,[11] Cluny began to assist well-disposed kings under his predecessor Odilo (994–1048). In Germany, the Emperor Henry II upon a visit to Cluny in 1022 gave it gifts including a jewel-studded golden crown and received confraternity; with Henry's support, Bishop Meinwerk of Paderborn successfully asked Odilo and his community for thirteen monks to establish a monastery at Abdinghof.[12] Odilo also had dealings with King Sancho II el Mayor of Navarre (1000–35).[13] A number of Spanish monks came to Cluny and learned its Customs, which they took back to Spain; c. 1021 one of their number, Paternus, became for a time abbot of the principal Aragonese monastery of San Juan de la Peña.[14] Abbot Odilo's letters refer to Sancho's admission to Cluny's confraternity and to his gifts, as well as to Odilo's wish to maintain contacts with his sons and successors.[15] By 1053 at latest, the train of events had begun by which the strongest of Sancho's sons, King Ferdinand I of León and Castile, came to pay an annual census or tribute to Cluny. The attestation of a charter by a 'Frater Galindus clunia(ce)nsis' suggests that by 1053 Abbot

---

[10] *Ibid.*, ii. pp 90–115, esp. pp 94–9.

[11] J. Mehne, 'Cluniacenserbischöfe', *Frühmittelalterliche Studien*, xi (1977), pp 241–87, esp. pp 254–63. The *Historiae Tornacenses* recorded that Gregory VII asked Abbot Hugh for monks whom he might duly make bishops, and that those whom he sent included the future Pope Urban II: iv. 11, *Monumenta Germaniae Historica* [hereafter *MGH*], *Scriptores*, xiv. pp 340–1; cf. Orderic Vitalis (as n. 8), ii. pp 298–301.

[12] *Vita Meinwerci ep. Patherbrunnensis*, cap. 28, ed. F. Tenckhoff, *MGH Scriptores rerum Germanicarum* (1921), p 32.

[13] For the complex and unresolved problems of Spanish history in the eleventh century, the following especially bear upon the subject of this paper: P. David, *Etudes historiques sur la Galice et le Portugal du vie au xiie siècle* (Lisbon/Paris, 1947), pp 341–439; H. E. J. Cowdrey, *The Cluniacs and the Gregorian Reform* (Oxford, 1970), pp 214–47; P. Segl, *Königtum und Klosterreform in Spanien. Untersuchungen über die Cluniacenserklöster in Kastilien–Leon vom Beginn des 11. bis zur Mitte des 12. Jahrhunderts* (Kallmünz, 1974); C. J. Bishko, 'Fernando I and the Origins of the Leonese–Castilian Alliance with Cluny', *Studies in Medieval Spanish Frontier History* (London, 1980), II; J. F. O'Callaghan, 'The Integration of Christian Spain into Europe: the Role of Alfonso VI of León–Castile', *Santiago, Saint–Denis, and Saint Peter. The Reception of the Roman Liturgy in León–Castile in 1080*, ed., B. F. Reilly (New York, 1985), pp 101–20; J. Williams, 'Cluny and Spain', *Gesta*, xxvii (1988), pp 93–101.

[14] Ralph Glaber, *Historiae*, 3.12, Raoul Glaber, *Les Cinq Livres de ses histoires*, ed. M. Prou (Paris, 1886), pp 61–2.

[15] *Epp.* 2–3, *PL* cxlii. 941–2; cf. Jotsaldus, *De vita et virtutibus s. Odilonis abbatis*, 1.7, *PL* cxlii. 902B.

Hugh was employing one of his monks, evidently of Spanish origin, as a legate in León.[16]

It was under Ferdinand's son and successor, Alphonso VI (1065–1109), that Cluny's relations with the kingdom of León–Castile became extremely close. In the troubled circumstances of his accession, Alphonso believed that he owed his escape from captivity by his brother to the intercessions of the Cluniacs. In 1077 he doubled his father's *census* to Cluny and in 1090 confirmed it in perpetuity; Abbot Hugh granted him exceptional liturgical commemorations. His reign saw the establishment by himself and by his nobility of a number of Cluniac houses which were subject to Cluny and which followed its Customs; they included San Isidoro de las Dueñas (1073), San Salvador de Bilafreda (1075), San Zoile de Carrión (1076), San Juan Battista de los Eremitas (1077), Santa Maria de Nájera (1079), and San Coloma de Burgos (uncertain).[17] From the mid-1070s it became usual for Alphonso to have at his court at least one Cluniac monk who advised him on ecclesiastical matters; such monks were often themselves promoted to high ecclesiastical office as abbots or bishops.[18] A critically important figure was the monk Robert, well established in Spain by 1077, who was Alphonso's intimate counsellor at court until, probably in 1080, he became abbot of Sahagún. He played a central part in the crisis that arose in 1080 between Pope Gregory VII and King Alphonso, attracting the pope's most extreme censure.[19] His successor at Sahagún was, however, another Cluniac monk, Bernard of Sédirac, who in 1086 became archbishop of the newly reconquered city of Toledo.[20]

For the present inquiry, the most significant document to survive from these events in Spain is the letter of 1077 that Alphonso VI addressed to Abbot Hugh in connection with his doubling of his father's *census*.[21] It was full of praise for the monk Robert, who was the king's constant counsellor and who had urged him to increase the *census*. To Alphonso, it said, he was the most excellent and dear of monks, and to Hugh he was a close and most faithful *confrater*; Alphonso thanked Hugh fulsomely for sending to his kingdom and for his particular benefit this portion of his monastic flock. He earnestly besought him that Robert, whom he held supreme and most

[16]For the *census*, see Bruel, 3443, 3509, 3638; Galindus is discussed by Bishko (as n. 13), pp 24–6, who cites the unpublished charter Madrid, Academia de la Historia, Colección Velázquez, IV, leg. 4, no. 1420.

[17]Bruel, 3452, 3481, 3492, 3507–8, 3540, 3582. For a survey of Alphonso's gifts, see Segl (as n. 13), pp 47–76, and for non-royal gifts, pp 128–47.

[18]Listed by David (as n. 13), p 362.

[19]Robert is referred to in Bruel, 3441, 3509, 3582. For the crisis, Cowdrey (as n. 13), pp 230–9.

[20]For Bernard, see esp. J. F. Rivera Recio, *El Arzobispo de Toledo Don Bernardo de Cluny* (1086–1124) (Rome, 1962), esp. pp 11–17; *ibid.*, *La Iglesia de Toledo en el siglo xii* (1086–1208), 2 vols. (Rome, 1966–76), esp. i. pp 125–34.

[21]Bruel, 3441 (misdated 1070).

dear in all his affairs, might stay with him throughout his life and help him by words and deeds. 'For you assuredly know how all the advice that he gives is of benefit to you. Consider me', the king pleaded, 'and for no cause whatever cease to allow his permanent residence in our land'. Alphonso's main plea, however, was that Hugh would increase his bounty by sending some more of his monastic family (*aliquos tue sanctissime religionis domesticos*) for their common benefit in a place – by *locum* Alphonso seems to mean his whole kingdom rather than a particular locality in it – which was both Alphonso's and Hugh's because Hugh had begun to water it from his most holy fountain of Cluny. He at once stipulated his own side of the bargain, which was to double the *census* and so provide wheat for the sustenance of the community at Cluny. It will be noticed that Alphonso wished to keep Robert with him as a familiar counsellor, as he did for the next three years; it is not stated that further monks who might come were destined for high ecclesiastical office as abbots or bishops, or even for settlement in existing or new monasteries. He made a general request on behalf of his kingdom; it was possible, but not stated, that any or all of the monks who came might, like Robert, eventually received ecclesiastical office. It is not known that Hugh sent more monks from Cluny in response to the letter.[22]

To return from the background in Normandy, Germany, and Spain, to King William I and Cluny: Alphonso's request of 1077 for the dispatch of more Cluniac monks may help to elucidate William's very similar request in Anonymous II. William's request has usually been understood thus,[23] hereafter interpretation A: wishing worthily to make appointments to (*ordinare*) the sees and abbeys of England, King William sent a letter to Abbot Hugh asking him to send six of his monks, by whose counsel he might carry out his duty in this matter of making appointments (*de ecclesiis ordinandis*), and when he had made them (the six monks) rulers (of churches), that is, abbots and bishops, he might be confident about the care and ruling of their flocks.[24] But, by analogy with Alphonso's request, this passage is patient of another translation, hereafter interpretation B: wishing in general sense fittingly to set in order (*ordinare*) the sees and abbeys of England, King William sent a letter to Abbot Hugh asking him to send six of his monks, by whose counsel he might carry out his duty of setting churches in order (*de ecclesiis ordinandis*), and then, when rulers (not necessarily the six) had been appointed for the churches, he might be confident about the care and ruling of their (the churches'?) flocks.

---

[22]But I have not been able to check Rivera Recio's reference to P. Sandoval, *Cronica de los cinco reyes* (Pamplona, 1615), lib. 18, c. 10: *El Arzobispo* (as n. 20), p 13.

[23]Including by the present writer: Cowdrey (as n. 1), p 143.

[24]*PL* clix. 924AB. The phrase *illius* establishes that, in Anon. II's view, William's plan was restricted to England and excluded Normandy.

According to interpretation A, the six Cluniacs were destined themselves to become abbots and bishops; according to interpretation B, this was not necessarily so: as in Spain, so in England they would be royal counsellors who might or might not eventually become prelates.

Interpretation B has three powerful arguments in its favour. First, it understands the verb *ordinare* in the sense of 'set in order', rather than 'ordain to ecclesiastical office', that it twice bears in Abbot Hugh's reply as excerpted by Anonymous II: Hugh at once seized upon William's good intention, according to interpretation B, of in general setting in order (*ordinare*) the people with whom God had entrusted him in the way of salvation: and he referred to his need of monks for places that he himself must set in order (*loca a me ordinanda*).[25] Secondly, however, if William's proposal to make payment for the monks is left for later discussion, Abbot Hugh's letter continued in exclusively monastic terms, of his responsibility for monks who had been professed to him and who in England would not be subject to any obedience or discipline. Hugh's objection that the monks would fear no chapter in a land where there was no Cluniac house to relieve or to constrain them, would lose force if they became bishops or abbots, or lived in a settled community; it was natural if they were to serve at large as long-term counsellors at the king's court. Thirdly, at no time in his reign did William greatly favour monk-bishops but preferred royal clerks and chaplains, while all save two of his new abbots came from Normandy or Maine. In this light, too, interpretation B makes the better sense.[26]

Historians read Abbot Hugh's reply to William, which Anonymous II cites verbatim,[27] very differently, some finding it angry, scornful, and rude, but others seeing only a forceful statement of Cluny's general policy blended with implicit pastoral advice. Unquestionably it can be read in several ways according to the reader's presuppositions, but there is a strong case for a relatively mild interpretation. Hugh addressed the king respectfully and cordially (*domine rex, karissime domine*), and without irony described himself as his friend (*amicus*). He began by genuinely applauding William's request in so far as it proceeded from his good intention in seeking the salvation of the English people, and he concluded by inviting the king to ask some other favour and to bear patiently with his refusal since it would be incompatible with a friend's salvation to do otherwise. In the body of the letter, Hugh took up William's offer to reimburse Cluny for the loss of personnel and their spiritual and temporal services by an annual payment of a hundred pounds of silver for each monk. The bargain that William proposed calls

---

[25] *PL* clix. 924B and D.

[26] For William's bishops, see J. Le Patourel, *The Norman Empire* (Oxford, 1976), pp 35–6, 49–51; for his abbots, D. Knowles, *The Monastic Order in England*, 2nd edn. (Cambridge, 1963), pp 112, 704, also Barlow (as n. 3), p 253.

[27] *PL* clix. 924–925A; Cowdrey (as n.1), pp 143–4.

for careful assessment. In all respects save a crucial one, it is reminiscent of the exchanges made or proposed with the Emperor Henry II's support in respect of Abdinghof, and in King Alphonso VI's letter of 1077. Such exchanges should probably be considered against the background of the gift-exchange of a diplomatic, not commercial nature that for centuries had been part and parcel of relations between great men and institutions, lay and ecclesiastical.[28] Accordingly, Anonymous II commented that William's proposal was advanced 'on the grounds of friendship and amity' (*sub titulo amicitiae et gratiae*).[29] The novel and shocking element in it was William's brash commercialism in putting a price upon each monk sent; this, according to the Anonymous, was what made the arrangement unacceptable to Hugh: 'he who wished to become a buyer (*emptor*) could not do so, because he did not find a seller (*venditor*) of monks'.[30] It was the diversion from the familiar conventions of aristocratic gift-exchange to the novel and brash language of the market-place at which the abbot bridled. The king's proposal also approached dangerously near to simony, although an express comment that Abbot Hugh refused the king 'because his petition was for a sale and seemed simoniacal' had to await the twelfth-century draftsman of the chapter-headings to Anonymous II.[31] This may express a later understanding of simony, for which William was not notorious during his lifetime. In any case, Abbot Hugh did not develop his objection in terms of resistance to the king's simony, but of his own obligation as abbot to safeguard the welfare of those who were, and would continue to be, his monastic subjects. Especially if interpretation B of Anonymous II's introduction to the letter is preferred, the king's stake in the matter was limited – the dispatch of six monastic counsellors, not the filling of as many major ecclesiastical offices. Hugh's letter bears the aspect of a forceful exposition of his own position in face of a royal proposal that ran counter to accepted diplomatic rules as between kings and churchmen, rather than of a personal and ill-mannered rejection of royal generosity. Anonymous II credibly recorded that William at first was extremely upset at being denied a request that he backed up with so generous a gift, but that, on reflection, he took Hugh's point and admired him the more for his integrity as abbot. This suggests that the letter caused no lasting trauma.[32]

---

[28]This subject needs further investigation, but see H. E. J. Cowdrey, 'Legal Problems Raised by Agreements of Confraternity', *Memoria. Der geschichtliche Zeugniswert des liturgischen Gedenkens im Mittelalter*, eds. K. Schmid and J. Wollasch (Munich, 1984), pp 233–54, at pp 236–7.

[29]*PL* clix. 934B.

[30]*Ibid.*

[31]Marrier and du Chesne (as n. 2), col. 453A.

[32]That William would hear and reverence ecclesiastics who addressed him plainly is suggested by whatever lies behind his exchange with Guitmund, monk of la-Croix-saint-Leufroi and

Although it is scanty and the result of several decades of Cluniac tradition, Anonymous II's account of William's request for monks and Hugh's
answer may well be judged to have the ring of basic reliability. If two interpretations of its account of William's request are possible, interpretation B has
a remarkably close parallel in Alphonso's request of 1077. The Anonymous
gives an intelligible account of Hugh's reaction, and it cites his letter in
reply at length. The next question to arise is how this version compares in
subject matter (the problem of date will come later) with that in the longer
version of the Lewes foundation charter.[33]
    Massive substantial differences between the two accounts leap to the eye.
According to Anonymous II, the king and the abbot were at a distance and
exchanged formal letters; in the charter, the king raised the matter in a
conversation that William of Warenne overheard when all three were together
in Normandy during the abbot's visit. For the Anonymous, William's request
was sent at the beginning of his reign in England; the charter locates it in
the course of negotiations about Lewes during the later 1070s. In the
Anonymous William requested six monks, but in the charter twelve. If the
Anonymous is open to different readings about how they were to be used,
the charter is unequivocal: William would make all twelve of them bishops
and abbots in the land of his inheritance that God had given him – that is,
in England. In the Anonymous, the story is told at length and in its own
right. The charter introduces it as an aside by which William of Warenne
justified his fear that Prior Lanzo of Lewes might quickly receive further
royal preferment: whereas for the Anonymous the king seems to have wanted
the monks to counsel him about the affairs of the kingdom and perhaps to
be prelates, in the charter William, in the middle of his reign, had already
appointed the better candidates in England to ecclesiastical dignities and
had perforce turned to Cluny![34] Unlike the Anonymous, the charter says
nothing about William's offer of payment, or about Hugh's reply to him, or
about his own reaction thereafter. In short, the contrast between the two
sources is so extensive and so detailed that the historian must follow either
the one or the other; it is unlikely that they can be reconciled or combined.
    The concluding section of the charter in which the reference to the king's
remarks to the abbot is to be found is riddled with improbabilities. Barlow
has sufficiently shown that Abbot Hugh's supposed concessions to William

---

later bishop of Aversa, about his promotion to ecclesiastical office in England: Orderic Vitalis
(as n. 8), ii, pp 270–81.
    [33]As n. 2.
    [34]'... timuimus', runs William of Warenne's supposed charter, 'ne dominus Lanzo cum
redisset, cito aufereretur nobis, quia rex quos meliores invenire potuit in dignitates ecclesiae
exaltavit, et nobis audientibus requisivit ab abbate quod mitteret ei duodecim de sanctis monachis suis, et eos omnes faceret episcopos et abbates in terra haerditatis suae quam ei dederat
Deus', *Monasticon* (as n. 2), v. 13a.

of Warenne are almost certainly unauthentic and William's alleged reasons for seeking them therefore implausible.[35] As regards William's request to Hugh for monks, there is no confirmation of the assertion that, by 1078, William had run out of suitable candidates for ecclesiastical promotion: between 1078 and 1087 there were only seven new bishops, all save one chosen from among royal clerks and chaplains; of sixteen or so new abbots, all seem to have come from houses in William's lands. Nothing suggests that he was scraping the barrel of clerical talent. Although the number twelve for the Cluniac monks whom William allegedly requested has been widely countenanced, or even preferred to Anonymous II's six, it is manifestly excessive in view both of the slow turnover of bishops and abbots and of William's policy for replacements. The known events of the foundation of Lewes leave scant room for a period of coolness on the king's part. Not only does the longer charter not mention it, but the genuine charter, surviving as an original, appears to have been quickly followed by royal *acta* that indicate friendly relations.[36]

There is nothing to impugn the acceptability of the longer charter, based perhaps on a foundation narrative, as evidence for a visit by Abbot Hugh to King William between 1078 and 1080 during which they met in William of Warenne's presence. But it seems likely that, when the charter was long afterwards put together, it introduced into its account of the visit a reference to negotiations about sending monks that may have occurred long before. There are two possibilities. One is that, whether by direct dependence or from another source, the charter follows with modification of detail the story as in Anonymous II, presenting it according to interpretation A. Indeed, it is the first evidence to survive for such an interpretation. Alternatively, it cannot be excluded that William of Warenne overheard in 1078/80 an authentically recorded conversation between king and abbot recalling negotiations by then long past that Anonymous II correctly located in the earliest years of William's reign. With his wounds long since healed, the king now felt able to jest to his friend about his continuing problem in finding good bishops and abbots with hyperbole about how many Cluniac monks he would need nowadays.

---

[35](As n. 3), pp 249–50.

[36]The documents are best edited by Clay (as n. 2), pp 54–7. No. 2 is the authentic foundation charter of Lewes which Clay dates c. 1078–82 but probably before Dec. 1081 (although Barlow points out that the *terminus a quo* could be earlier: (as n. 3), p 249, n. 14. No 3 is King William's notification to Archbishop Lanfranc of Canterbury and Bishop Odo of Bayeux that he has confirmed to the abbey of Cluny the land at Falmer (Sussex) given by William of Warenne and his wife. This act of goodwill to Cluny appears to come from, or very soon after, the date of no. 2 because (i) Falmer is mentioned in it, and (ii) the gift is said to be to *sanctus Petrus de Cluniaco* rather than to St Pancras. In no. 4, which Clay dates 1081–3, William I confirms to Lewes Priory the manor of West Walton, Norfolk.

What, then, may be concluded about the date of William the Conqueror's approach to Abbot Hugh for the dispatch of monks? Despite the fragility of the evidence in the longer Lewes foundation charter, the possibility of a date between 1078 and 1080 must be kept open because of the similarity of King Alphonso VI's request of 1077 for an unspecified number of Cluniac monks to be sent to his court as permanent counsellors. The case becomes a little stronger if it is thought that, in the light of interpretation B of Anonymous II, William indeed made a similar request. William could have heard of Alphonso's approach and have decided to follow suit; a channel of communication from Castile to England at about this time was Alphonso's negotiations with William about his possible marriage to one of the Conqueror's daughters.[37] This would sidestep a possible objection to a date in the 1060s for the Conqueror's approach to Cluny: that Alphonso, who was *au courant* with Cluniac affairs through the monk Robert and others, would scarcely have made in 1077 an approach of a kind that he knew Hugh to have rebuffed ten years or so earlier.

But Alphonso may have felt confident that his case in 1077 differed from William's in the 1060s because of the long-standing relations between Spain and Cluny and also of the magnitude and diplomatic propriety of Spanish gifts, and because of the established Cluniac monastic houses in León–Castile. And strong reasons can be advanced for preferring a date for William's request at the beginning of his reign. The much earlier source, Anonymous II, which claims to follow a written request from the king, unequivocally states that the approach took place then (*cum praefatae regionis potiri coepisset*), in the context of a general desire to do well for the English church (*volens digne episcopatus et abbatias terrae illius ordinare*);[38] only the very late and, as has been suggested, highly improbable account in the Lewes charter places it in the context of the foundation of Lewes. Moreover, however one reads the Anonymous, but especially if interpretation B is followed, it is hard to envisage the king's entertaining the idea of recruiting a group of Cluniac counsellors at a time when Lanfranc was well established as archbishop of Canterbury and as William's trusted right-hand man in ecclesiastical affairs. Lanfranc's view of Cluniac monasticism is unknown, though there is no evidence for such contact with Cluny as Anselm had while abbot of Bec.[39] But it is not likely that William would have sought

---

[37] *Vita Simonis Crespeiensis auctore synchrono*, cap. 5, *PL* clvi. 1215DE.

[38] *PL* clix. 924A.

[39] As young men, Lanfranc and Abbot Hugh are likely to have met at Pope Leo IX's council of Reims in Oct. 1049. For Anselm, see *Ep.* 37, *Sancti Anselmi Cantuariensis archiepiscopi Opera*, ed. F. S. Schmitt, 6 vols. (Edinburgh, 1946–61), iii. pp 144–8. In his Customs for Christ Church, Canterbury, Lanfranc shows that he had read and used Bernard's version of Cluny Customs: *Decreta Lanfranci monachis Cantuariensibus transmissa*, ed., D. Knowles, Corpus Consuetudinum Monasticarum, iii (Siegburg 1967), p xviii; but for the non-Cluniac nature of

the sending of six or twelve monks, especially if they were to become bishops and abbots, without consulting Lanfranc, or that Lanfranc would have been much in favour. So drastic a change in William's policy in mid-stream is barely credible, and an early approach is far more easy to envisage.

The use of the royal title in the Anonymous's account, and still more in Abbot Hugh's letter which it cites, points to a date after William's coronation on Christmas Day 1066, but his alleged reluctance to be crowned does not establish it:[40] Hugh may have been unaware of this reluctance. An exchange of letters soon after the battle of Hastings (14 October 1066) cannot be excluded. The way may have been prepared. Encouraged by Hugh's recent dispatch of his monk Bernfrid to Saint-Evroult, William may have begun to canvass means of ecclesiastical reform during his diplomatic preparations for the conquest of England. His envoy to Pope Alexander II may have discussed them with the pope and others like Archdeacon Hildebrand, and may even have visited Cluny during his journey.[41] But the most likely time for the exchange of letters is during William's stay in Normandy from late February to early December 1067, when the uncertainties surrounding the loyalties of Stigand of Canterbury and Aldred of York may have made him particularly anxious to strengthen his ecclesiastical entourage.[42] A date after the ecclesiastical measures of 1070 and the accession of Lanfranc to Canterbury is unlikely. If 1067 is the most likely date for William's approach, a powerful factor in Abbot Hugh's refusal may have been the warning that William's recent dealings over Abbot Osbern of Saint-Evroult provided. It may have reinforced the habitual caution that Hugh expressed in his letter. An early date for it, 1066 or more probably very soon after, cannot be proved but is very likely.

The two further occasions of known contact between King William and Abbot Hugh call for only brief comment. William's reception of spiritual confraternity is expressly referred to only in Anonymous II.[43] He is not

---

Bec's Customs up to Lanfranc's time, see *Consuetudines Beccenses*, ed., M.P. Dickson, CCM iv (Siegburg, 1967), pp xxx–xlii. Lanfranc is most likely to have obtained Bernard's Customs after 1078 from Prior Lanzo of Lewes – another argument for a late date (1079/89) for Lanfranc's compilation: M. Gibson, *Lanfranc of Bec* (Oxford, 1978), pp 240–1.

[40]Guillaume de Poitiers, *Histoire de Guillaume le Conquérant*, 2.28–9, ed., R. Foreville (Paris, 1952), pp 216–19.

[41]Orderic Vitalis (as n. 6), ii. 142–3.

[42]For the archbishops' actions after the battle of Hastings, see the Anglo-Saxon Chronicle D version, *a.* 1066: William of Poitiers, 2.38 (as n. 40), pp 242–5. William's conciliatory attitude to distant monasteries and his desire for spiritual benefits from them are exemplified in his charter of Apr. 1067 for Saint-Benoît-sur-Loire: *Regesta regum Anglo-Normannorum, 1066– 1154*, i: *Regesta Willelmi Conquestoris et Willelmi Rufi*, 1066–1100, ed. H. W. C. Davis (Oxford, 1913), p 2, no. 6a.

[43]*PL* clix. 923.

commemorated in any of the major Cluniac Necrologies.[44] According to the Anonymous, the gift occurred when William was king of England:[45] time must be allowed for any temporary estrangement that may have occurred after Hugh refused William's request for the dispatch of monks. The *terminus ante quem* depends on how the Anonymous is read. It names as Hugh's messenger '*dominus Warmundus*', who afterwards rose from abbot of Déols to be archbishop of Vienne.[46] The latest possible date is thus 1076, when Warmund became archbishop. The Anonymous is, however, ambiguous about whether Warmund came before or during his abbacy, that is, before or after *c.* 1074. Those who have argued for his travelling to Normandy while abbot of Déols have done so without regard to his having previously been a monk, and latterly, prior of Cluny itself.[47] The Anonymous's description of his as *dominus* (rather than *abbas*, or an equivalent), and the word 'afterwards', more naturally suggest that he travelled while still at Cluny; indeed, a mission to convey confraternity to a king would be a more likely task for a prior of Cluny than for the abbot of a distant abbey not now connected with Cluny. Thus, the most likely dates are 1073 or early 1074 – dates when William's presence in Normandy and Maine is attested.[48] The sending of rich presents by William and Matilda is also noticed in Gilo's *Life of Abbot Hugh*;[49] this time, the basis was a normal gift-exchange in the tradition of the munificence to Cluny of Henry II of Germany and the Spanish kings. Perhaps William had learnt the lesson of an earlier rebuff.

For Abbot Hugh's visit to King William in Normandy, the longer foundation charter of Lewes is the only, and very late and in many respects unreliable, source. Barlow has sufficiently established that such a visit would have taken place between 1078 and 1080;[50] it is credible as perhaps drawn from the fund of older material upon which those who drew up the charter depended. That such a visit took place is fairly securely attested by Cluny's own traditions, not only as recorded by Anonymous II but also by Gilo, according to whom William 'often honoured Father Hugh with embassies, self-commendation, and gifts, which proclaimed the pledge

[44]*Synopse der Cluniacensischen Necrologien*, ed. J. Wollasch, 2 vols. (Munich, 1982).

[45]The Anonymous II is not concerned with the relative chronology of events: Barlow (as n. 3), pp 248–9.

[46]See above, p 2. For Warmund, see N. Huyghebaert, 'Un légat de Grégoire VII en France: Warmond de Vienne', *Revue d'histoire ecclésiastique*, xl (1944–5), pp 187–200, subject to Barlow's comments: (as n. 3), p 246, n. 6.

[47]Bruel, 3003, 3282, 3439. For the imperfect state of knowledge about the succession of priors, see M. Chaume, 'Les grands prieurs de Cluny. Compléments et rectifications à la liste de la Gallia Christiana', *Revue Mabillion,* xxviii (1938), pp 147–52, esp. p 150.

[48]*Regesta* (as n.42), pp 18–20.

[49]2.15, ed., Cowdrey (as n. 1), pp 64–5.

[50]Above, pp 2, 10.

14

of his life'.[51] It is reasonably certain that Abbot Hugh's visit to Normandy occurred.

The conclusions of this inquiry may be summed up as follows: (i) Probably very soon after late 1066, with 1067 as the likeliest date, though just possibly in 1078/80, William asked for, and was refused, the dispatch of six Cluniac monks for his purposes as king of England. The figure of twelve is too suspect to be seriously entertained. (ii) Probably in 1073 or 1074, but possibly in 1075 or 1076, Prior, or Abbot, Warmund brought William from Abbot Hugh the gift of spiritual confraternity with Cluny; in return, King William and Queen Matilda made rich presents to it. (iii) Between 1078 and 1080, the king and the abbot almost certainly met in Normandy when the latter paid a visit to the duchy.

---

[51]Anon. II: *PL* clix. 923A; Gilo: as n. 49. Gilo's word *commendatione* should perhaps be translated 'self-commendation' as referring to William's seeking confraternity and spiritual benefits (cf. *PL* clix. 923BC), rather than, more generally, 'favour'.

IX

ST HUGH AND GREGORY VII

This paper will be limited to the personal relations and dealings of Abbot Hugh and Pope Gregory VII, both before and after he became pope in 1073* . It will not, save incidentally, be concerned with the wider relationships between Cluny and the later eleventh-century papal reform. Three topics will be discussed : first, contacts between Hugh and Hildebrand as recorded in the miracles appended by the Canterbury monk Alexander to his **Liber ex dictis beati Anselmi** ; secondly, Hugh's dealings with Gregory as pope between 1073 and 1085 ; and thirdly, their attitudes to each other as presented with hindsight by Abbot Hugh during the twenty-four years between Gregory's death in 1085 and his own in 1109[1].

By way of introduction, a word is called for about their respective ages and early careers. Hugh's date of birth can be placed securely in the year 1024[2], but Hildebrand's is far from certain. So far as written evidence is concerned, a pointer that has sometimes been followed is that he was made subdeacon by Pope Leo IX between 1049 and 1054[3] : because the canonical age for admission to the subdiaconate was twenty years, this suggests that he may have been born between 1029 and 1034 and therefore significantly Hugh's junior. An earlier range of dates has, however, often been proposed, and it has been reinforced by a recent medical examination of his physical remains which indicates his age at death as between sixty-five and seventy-five but probably about seventy[4]. This would place his date of birth between 1015 and 1025 but probably **c.** 1020, in which case he would have been Hugh's senior by some four years. Hugh nevertheless entered permanently upon high responsibility at a much younger age than Hildebrand. Hugh began his sixty years as abbot of Cluny in 1049, having been grand prior since 1047/1048[5]. It was in the winter of 1048-1049 that Hildebrand returned to Rome from his exile with Pope Gregory VI, to be made subdeacon by Leo IX ; not until 1058 did he become archdeacon at Rome [6]. On the other hand, despite his lowly position, he had occasionally made highly responsible journeys as papal legate - notably to France in 1054 and 1056[7]. When pope, in his **Dictatus**

papae of 1075 he was to make much of a legate's authority : « *a legate of the Roman pontiff takes precedence in a council of all bishops, even though he be of inferior rank, and he can pass sentence of deposition against them*« [8]. As legate, the young Hildebrand passed such sentences, and his reported vaunting of **Roma fide et armis semper invicta** suggests that he was already not behindhand in his statements of legatine authority[9]. During his visits to France, both this authority and his probable seniority by age may be envisaged as grounds which both men might have recognized for his having precedence over the young Abbot Hugh.

The evidence for their early contacts is the first three of the six Hildebrandine anecdotes in the section **De miraculis** which follows the **Liber ex dictis beati Anselmi**[10]. They were noted during a visit to Cluny of Archbishop Anselm of Canterbury, almost certainly between 1103 and 1105 during his second exile from England, by his companion Alexander, a monk of Christ Church, Canterbury. Alexander heard them amongst many miracle stories that the aged Abbot Hugh used to tell. He wrote his **Dicta** and **Miracula** in two recensions, probably of **c.** 1109 and 1115 ; the three stories about Hugh and Hildebrand occur only in the second recension[11]. Their subjects are :

i. How Hildebrand knew Hugh's inner thoughts about him as they were riding in the same party (cap. 25) ;

ii. How, during a joint visit to a monastery, Hildebrand had visions of Christ and of an angel with drawn sword, and how he foretold a pestilence (cap. 26) ;

iii. How Hildebrand at Cluny saw Christ overseeing the chapter of faults that Hugh was conducting (cap. 27). In the third section of this paper it will be argued that, like the other Hildebrandine anecdotes in this source, these stories primarily illustrate Abbot Hugh's current concerns at the very end of his life. Nevertheless, they have just a little to say about his relations with Hildebrand of half a century and more ago.

First, in the **Miracula** Hugh and Hildebrand are shown upon Hugh's testimony to have been together at various junctures in Hildebrand's travels as legate - on journeys **in parte Allobrogum** (the region of Lyon and Vienne) (cap. 25), during what was intended to be a few days' business visit to an unnamed monastery (cap. 26), and during a brief stay by Hildebrand at Cluny itself (cap. 27). In the latter story, reference was made to Hildebrand's being a monk as well as a legate (pp. 213/20).

Secondly, according to Alexander of Canterbury there were

IX

ST HUGH AND GREGORY VII

already longstanding bonds of especial affection between the two men on account of their having formerly lived together (**ex antiqua cohabitatione**) and of Hildebrand's respect for Hugh's well-known integrity (**nota probitate**) (pp. 211/28-30)[12]. The phrase *ex antiqua cohabitatione* presents difficulties. No place is indicated, though since Hugh is not known to have dwelt elsewhere than at Cluny after he entered it in 1039 it is likely that Cluny is intended. The phrase is, however, clearly a comment by Alexander which probably does not represent Hugh's **ipsissima verba** in 1103/1105. For Hugh would scarcely have spoken of his own **nota probitas** any more than of his coming to Hildebrand amongst a « *non parva multitudo* **sacrorum** *virorum* » (pp. 211/26-7), and other versions of the anecdote have no equivalent for the phrase *ex antiqua cohabitatione*[13]. Some other details that Alexander gives are highly suspect : Hildebrand's legatine activity probably occurred under Pope Victor II (1054-1057) not Alexander II (1061-1073), and if so Hildebrand is wrongly described as archdeacon[14]. As an **obiter dictum** of the monk Alexander, written down as late as 1115, it can bear no weight as evidence for Hildebrand's having been a professed monk at Cluny, which on other grounds is highly unlikely[15]. But it may be based upon a genuine memory of a visit by Hildebrand to Cluny during his absence from Rome in 1046-1048. No more can safely be said on this point.

Thirdly, the pattern of relationships between the two young men can dimly be perceived. The three anecdotes that concern them both place Hildebrand in a position of greater honour on account of his temporary legatine authority. When Hildebrand came **in partes Āllobrogum**, Hugh came to meet him as legate and it was the legate who received the abbot (pp. 211/25-8). There were tensions between the two men which, in the anecdotes, centre upon Hugh : Hugh secretly thought that Hildebrand was made inwardly proud by the honour and service that he was accorded (pp. 212/5-7, 11-12). But Hugh was easily satisfied in this account. When Hildebrand read his thoughts, he insisted that he received honour not on his own behalf, but on that of God and St Peter whose legate he was (pp. 212/12-14). This reply left Hugh astonished (*valde stupidum*) and manifestly gratified (p. 212/18-19), just as the story of Hildebrand's reading of the abbot's thoughts in chapter at Cluny left the two men united in reflection upon the goodness of a God who was present with his servants (*suis fidelibus*) even when they were unaware of him (p. 214/23-4). The earlier anecdote presents a picture of tensions resolved because, from Hugh's side, the honour due to Hildebrand in his Petrine capacity gave him a proper official pre-eminence. The imponderable factor here is how

175

far the aged Abbot Hugh's anecdote as told in 1103/5 was coloured by the benefits that Cluny had subsequently received from papal legates, especially Cardinal Peter Damiani in 1063 and Cardinal Peter of Albano in 1080[16]. Undoubtedly there may have been some colouring. But even in the 1050s Cluny's debt to the apostolic see, and especially to Popes Benedict VIII (1012-1024) and John XIX (1024-1032), was sufficient for Hugh to have revered Hildebrand as its accredited representative[17]. The anecdotes further suggest that Hildebrand reciprocated with a high regard for Hugh's prayers, to which he saw Christ himself more strongly drawn than to his own (p. 212/31-4), and for Hugh's pre-eminence as a monastic superior at whose side Christ manifestly assisted (pp. 213/28-30, 214/20-2).

Through memories of half a century ago as spoken by the aged Abbot Hugh and written down with editorial comment by the monk Alexander, the Hildebrandine anecdotes provide a dim but inherently credible picture of the abbot and Hildebrand enjoying a personal relationship that was already close. Hugh honoured Hildebrand, who was probably slightly the older man, for his exercise of apostolic authority, while Hildebrand honoured Hugh for the efficacy of his prayers and for his qualities as abbot of Cluny, a monastery at which they may earlier have come to know and value one another. There could be tensions between them, but they were capable of being resolved as a result of an underlying common monastic commitment and, no less, of mutual regard and friendship.

With Gregory's pontificate, the evidence for contacts between pope and abbot becomes more plentiful, at least from Gregory's side. No letter from Hugh to Gregory survives, and evidence in the twelfth-century Lives of Hugh is meagre. But, although Gregory in January 1079 complained to Hugh that « *if only Romans came to your part of the world as often as your people come to us, we could keep you better informed by letters or by word of mouth about how this-worldly and heavenly matters are going* » (6. 17), his Register includes as many as eight letters addressed to Hugh and another jointly to him and Bishop Hugh of Die ; five of them are probably of Gregory's own dictation[18]. Abbot Hugh is personally referred to, directly or indirectly, in twenty-one other items in Gregory's Register and **Epistolae vagantes**[19]. Such evidence survives from every year of Gregory's pontificate except 1076, 1081, 1084, and 1085 ; it points to regularity in their personal dealings and to Gregory's setting a high value on them.

Gregory several times gave expression to his esteem. Hugh was one of the select few to whom, according to the Register, Gregory

sent a notice of his accession with an appropriate personal tailpiece
(1. 4). At the end of April 1073 in a special message to Hugh,
Gregory alluded to the *caritas* in which the abbot had hitherto held
him and besought him to demonstrate it untiringly now that, as
pope, Gregory particularly needed it (1. 6). In an otherwise
querulous letter of March 1074, Gregory reminded Hugh of the
many and great affairs that he had entrusted to him and to
Cardinal-bishop Gerald of Ostia, the former grand prior of Cluny
who was currently a legate in Germany. Gregory hoped that, since
so much was now left in Hugh's sole hands, he would have to come
to Rome. « *Wherefore* », he continued, « *disturbed though we are,
we urge you with intimate affection* (**dilectionem vestram intimo
ammonemus affectu***) to be at pains to visit us as soon as possible,
placed as we are in many and great difficulties* » (1. 62). Twice, in
January 1075 and May 1079, Gregory poured out his personal
anguish to Hugh in terms that he used to no other correspondent
(2. 49, 5. 21). « *If it were possible* », he began the earlier letter, »
*I would like you fully to know what great tribulation vexes me, and
how much toil daily wearies me and as it increases greatly distresses
me, so that according to the tribulations of my heart brotherly
compassion might incline you to me and to pour your heart out in
a profusion of tears before God that the poor man Jesus, through
whom all things were made and who rules over all, would reach out
his hand and with his habitual mercy set free his wretched servant* ».
His later letter opened more succinctly : « *Worn out by the pressure
of so many peoples and by the thought of so much business, I write
a little to him whom I love much* ». In each letter he listed his
concerns and weighed the burden of the papal office. He despaired
of those near him : « *Regarding those amongst whom I live - I mean
the Romans, the Lombards, and the Normans, as I often tell them,
I convict them of being in their way worse than Jews and pagans* » ;
and again,« *We are oppressed by so many difficulties and wearied
by so many labours, that those who are here with us are not only
unable to share them ; they cannot even see them* ».

Failing consolation near at hand, Gregory's constant recourse
throughout his pontificate was above all to the prayers of Abbot
Hugh and his monks at Cluny (1. 6, 1. 62, 2. 49, 5. 21, 6. 3, 6.
17). His own pursuit of an active life as ruler of the church in a
time of exceptional danger made monastic intercessions, and
especially those of Hugh and his monks, in his eyes indispensable ;
« *Because praise is not seemly or prayer holy when hastily offered
upon the lips of a sinner whose life deserves [little] praise and whose
actions are worldly, I pray, beg, and beseech you to implore with
watchful zeal those who deserve to be heard for the excellence of*

their lives that they will pray to God for me with the charity and love that they owe to [the apostolic see], their universal mother » (2. 49). Not only was monastic intercession for the benefit of the church, it was also the fulfilment of the monastic vocation. Gregory ended the most querulous of his letters to Hugh in which he reproved him for receiving Duke Hugh I of Burgundy into the haven of Cluny (*in Cluniacensem quietem*) by making this point : the first of all virtues, the love of God and one's neighbour, should incite the abbot to hold up hands of prayer on Gregory's behalf and to provoke all his monks to do the same, so that they themselves might progress from virtue to virtue and attain the perfection of the highest charity (6. 17).

In his dealings with Abbot Hugh, Gregory thus recognized the primacy of prayer in the monastic life. Nevertheless, no doubt because of Hugh's wide-flung monastic empire and of his acceptability to churchmen and laymen alike, Gregory continually looked to him for active service as an adviser, as a legate, and in other ways. This was a development of Hugh's role in Pope Alexander II's latter years when Archdeacon Hildebrand was a power behind the papal throne. Only a few days after his election Gregory sought to restore the position of Cardinal Hugh Candidus, whom the Cluniacs had accused of simony at Alexander's Lent council of little more than a month before[20], in the eyes of Abbot Hugh and his monks. He also referred to Abbot Hugh's recent co-operation in promoting Count Ebolus of Roucy's dealings in Spain (1. 6). Gregory several times employed Hugh himself as a legate in France, in collaboration with others such as Hugh, bishop of Die and archbishop of Lyon, and the Roman subdeacons Roger and Hubert, to deal with problems concerning the French episcopate - William of Clermont (4. 22), Rainerius of Orléans (5. 20), Manasses I of Reims (5. 22, 6. 2-3), Ralph of Tours (**Epp. vag.** 23, 37), and Lambert of Thérouanne (9. 31, 33-4)[21]. Gregory consulted or employed Hugh in connection with further French business - matters concerning Manasses of Reims (1. 14, 7. 12, 20), his dealings with Berengar of Tours (5. 21), and monastic disputes at Toulouse (9. 30, **Epp. vag**. 50). Hugh's counsel was of value in Spanish affairs (5. 21). Gregory's use of him makes clear his appreciation of one whom he described in 1083 as *gravem et illustrem virum* (9. 34).

Hugh twice played an active part in Gregory's dealings with King Henry IV of Germany ; his life-long bond with the king as godfather was perhaps, though not expressly, here of significance[22]. At Canossa in January 1077 he was present and supported **ex parte**

regis the oath that the king took (4. 12, 12a). In May Gregory commented to Bishop Hugh of Die upon the abbot's probity : « *We trust in … his habit of life, for no man's entreaty, no man's favour or grace, nor any acceptance of persons whatever, could move him from the way of rightfulness*« (4. 22). In September he acknowledged to Archbishop Udo of Trier and his suffragans the sanction that Hugh's support of the king's oath at Canossa had provided (5. 7)[23]. These comments establish Gregory's approval of his role there. In 1083, Hugh attempted to mediate at Rome between the pope and the king. The sole source is Raynald of Vézelay's Life of Abbot Hugh. The initiative was Gregory's, and upon arrival Hugh insisted upon meeting him in Rome before he saw Henry at Sutri. Although Hugh was not able to create concord between pope and king, he was able to appease the king's wrath towards himself and to obtain his apology for the obstructiveness of Henry's supporter Bishop Ulrich of Brescia[24]. In 1083 as in 1077, Hugh's actions as an intermediary had Gregory's support and approval.

Raynald's account of events at Rome in 1083 is also noteworthy for the observation that Abbot Hugh regarded Gregory as a « *stern pope* » (**severus pontifex**) : Hugh would find it easier to secure forgiveness from St Peter and St Paul for making his first Roman call one upon the pope than to secure Gregory's forgiveness if he first made pilgrimage to the apostles under Henry IV's protection[25]. Hugh may have remembered how, if the report of the German chronicler Berthold is correct, his mediation in 1076 with the excommunicated king had necessitated his own absolution by Gregory[26]. It is, however, interesting that later Cluniac tradition remembered Gregory's reciprocal view of Hugh as a strict ruler. When Hugh's biographer Gilo retailed his version of the Hildebrandine anecdote about how Hildebrand had seen Christ at Hugh's side during the chapter of faults at Cluny, he recalled that, when he had become pope, Gregory used to dub Hugh « *the urbane tyrant* » (**blandus tirannus**) because he saw him to be as a lion to the fierce and as a lamb to the meek, and one who well knew how to spare the humble but to rebuke the proud[27]. Gilo referred the sobriquet to Hugh's domestic conduct as abbot, but the Virgilian echo suggests that, in Gregory's eyes, it was more widely applicable.

Given the force of their personalities and the intensity of their feelings about their respective vocations, it is not surprising that Gregory and Hugh occasionally clashed. Gregory's letters to Hugh record two occasions, in particular. The first (1. 62) was in March 1074, when Gregory blamed Hugh's remissness in not coming to Rome[28]. Gregory's rebuke was severe : « *Your words* », he chided

Hugh, « a*re pleasing to us and pleasant ; but they would fill us with far more abundant delight if your charity glowed more warmly towards the Roman church. For we see the flame of your love dying down when we are unable to take consolation in the visit by you that we have so often requested* ». Gregory put it to Hugh that his remissness came not from pressure of other concerns but from work-shyness and from seizing excuses to postpone serious business. Now that Gregory had dispatched Cardinal Gerald of Ostia to Germany, he expected Hugh to come to Rome as soon as possible. Having made this plea, however, Gregory ended his letter by opening his soul at length to Hugh and by beseeching the intercessory support of his monks : « *We carry, although we are weak and although it is beyond the powers of mind and body - all alone we carry in this most dangerous time a huge weight not only of spiritual but also of temporal cares. We daily dread that we shall fall beneath the burden that presses us down, for in this world we can find no support whatever to bear us up. So we ask through Almighty God that, just as we have asked ever since the beginning of our pontificate, you will urge your brother monks to pray continually to God on our behalf...* »

Gregory's final blessing was for the monks' continuance in their monastic vocation. Gregory's second querulous letter, that of January 1079 in which he reproved Hugh for admitting to the cloister Duke Hugh I of Burgundy (1075-8) (6. 17), is remarkable for the similarity of its tone and pattern, although the appeal to Hugh is even more personal and direct. It is addressed to him as **venerabili Cluniacensi abbati et carissimo fratri**. It opens with irony no less biting than before : « *You are very good at feeding those of your own household, but you care little for the rustics outside* ». Hugh was heedless of the perils of the time to the church at large, when so few laymen were willing to resist the godless and to face death in the cause of righteousness and truth. The shepherds and sheepdogs of Christ's fold were fleeing, while wolves and robbers attacked his sheep unhindered. It was in such circumstances, Gregory wrote, that « *you have attracted or at least received the duke into the haven of Cluny, and have brought it about that a hundred thousand Christians lack a guardian* ». The root of Gregory's grievance against Hugh is exposed when he insists that Duke Hugh was a **princeps**, a figure of high standing : « *By God's mercy, monks, priests, knights, and not a few poor men who fear God can be found in one place or another ; but as for **principes**, in the west scarcely any can be found who fear and love God* ». Having made the point that it was inappropriate for such great men to enter the cloister, Gregory's tone changed and, as in 1074, he concluded with a plea for prayers and with his own blessing upon the monastic life : « *We leave off from writing more about this affair, because we trust in God's mercy that the charity of Christ which has its habitual abode in you will prove me right by piercing your heart and bringing clearly home how great my grief should be when a good prince is wrested from his mother. If no one worse than he succeeds him in his reign, we can be comforted* ». Gregory urged Hugh in this letter to take greater care in future : « *Moreover, we urge you in the bond of brotherhood to behave more cautiously in such matters and to make the first of all your motives the love of God and your neighbour* ». If Bernold of St Blasien rightly reported Hugh's later refusal to admit King Alphonso VI of León-Castile to the cloister[29], Hugh did what Gregory asked.

During the eighteen months that followed Gregory's letter about the duke of Burgundy, correspondence about two very different, but in fact not unrelated, topics - Cluny's relations with its neighbouring bishops, and problems arising from its role in León-Castile - further illustrates Gregory's desire to settle matters concerning Abbot Hugh by resolving situations of tension and thus promoting a concord that was based upon his high regard for the abbot.

The years 1079-1080 saw a fresh outbreak of Cluny's quarrel with the bishop of Mâcon and the archbishop of Lyon which had been quiescent since Peter Damiani's legatine visit of 1063[30]. It had been re-opened by Bishop Landeric of Mâcon upon a visit to Rome. Gregory took up an initial stance of something very close to impartiality. In a letter to Abbot Hugh of April 1079, he urged him to leave the church of Mâcon in peaceful enjoyment of its just rights, and he named Bishop Hugh of Die and Abbot Bernard of Saint-Victor, Marseille, to make a legatine adjudication. His letter ended with a plea for concord (**concordia**) ; « *without concord* », he insisted « *we say that the mere forms of religion (***religiositas***) are of no worth, and every work , even if it seem good, is nothing* » (6. 33, cf. Epp. vag. 30). By March 1080, Cluny's enemies at Mâcon had engaged in high-handed actions that put them in the wrong. Gregory became Cluny's defender by dispatching Cardinal Peter of Albano to renew Peter Damiani's work in 1063. Gregory upheld his legate's rulings in favour of Cluny, first by reproving Bishop Landeric for disobeying his legate and urging him to make peace with Abbot Hugh (**Epp. vag.** 38), and then by pronouncing at his Lent council of 1080 the allocution in favour of Cluny that was, perhaps, the high-water mark of papal favour for it (**Epp. vag.** 39). Gregory did not name Abbot Hugh, but his statement that « *there* *has never been an abbot of it who was not a saint* » is eloquent of his personal regard. During the twenty-nine remaining years of his abbacy Hugh had no further major problem about Cluny's exemption[31].

During the summer of 1080, the activities in Spain of a Cluniac monk named Robert elicited from Gregory one of the most energetic responses of his pontificate[32]. Despite the potential threat to his relations with Abbot Hugh, a letter that he wrote to him in June 1080 (8. 2) concerning the outrage (**impietas**) that had issued from his monastery was redolent of the eulogy upon Cluny that Gregory had pronounced three months before. Not only did Gregory express his certainty that Hugh had not consented to his monk's iniquity, but he knew that Hugh would share his grief at the enormity of the crime and would be minded to impose condign retribution. Gregory alluded to his own unwavering staunchness in Hugh's cause throughout debates at Rome during recent months about Cluny and its neighbouring bishops. Almost alone Gregory had upheld Cluny's interests when many at Rome had murmured against it, and he had been unmoved by their allegations ; to mention no other service to Cluny upon his part, almost all his Roman brethren, unless restrained by his arguments, would have changed their love for Cluny into bitter enmity. This, Gregory said, happened « *before the time of our brotherly conversation* (**ante tempus fraterne collocutionis)** ». This phrase almost certainly implies a face-to-face meeting after Cluny's local affairs became an issue early in 1079 (6. 33), and so a hitherto unnoticed visit by Hugh to Rome later in a year when Gregory was continually at Rome and Hugh's movements are otherwise little known[33]. Indeed, in a letter of 1078/1079, Gregory had expressly told the archbishop of Tours that he was expecting such a visit (**praestolamur enim Cluniacensem abbatem ad nos in proximo perventurum**) (**Epp. vag.** 37). Their conversation must have been momentous. It would have gone far to satisfy Gregory's grievances in his two querulous letters - in that of 1074 (1.62) because Hugh had at last come to Rome, and in that of 1079 (6. 17) because a matter discussed is likely to have been the releasing of Odo, the grand prior of Cluny, to fill the cardinal-bishopric of Ostia that had been vacant since the death in December 1077 of the Cluniac Gerald : if Hugh had robbed Gregory by admitting the duke of Burgundy to the cloister, the gift of Odo - the future Pope Urban II - was indeed a generous repayment. What talks Gregory and Hugh may have had about Henry IV of Germany at a critical point before his second excommunication can only be a matter for speculation. But a visit would also go far to explain Gregory's change of attitude to Cluny's local dispute from the impartiality that he showed in April 1079 to the extravagant eulogy upon Cluny that followed in the Lent council of March 1080. In its afterglow, Gregory expressed his confidence in Hugh's fullest collaboration in the Spanish crisis as a whole, as well as in disciplining his own errant subject. In a parallel letter to King Alphonso VI (8. 3), he expressed his complete concord with Hugh : « *The abbot of Cluny will imitate us in what we do, for we walk by the same way, by the same mind, and by the same spirit* (**eadem enim via eodem sensu eodem spiritu ambulamus**) ».

This is but a succinct statement of an estimate that underlies all of Gregory's letters to Hugh, even his querulous ones with their final references to the excellence of the monastic vocation. That it extended to Hugh's activities in a wider sense was made clear when he urged him, and the trusted Hugh of Die, to « *act manfully and wisely and let all your deeds be in charity, so that the oppressed may find you their wise defenders and that the oppressors may acknowledge you to be lovers of righteousness* (**iustitia**) » (6. 3), and when, in retrospect from 1080, he assured him « *that you have given us longstanding proof* (**antiquum experimentum**) *of being of one mind with us concerning the honour of the holy Roman church, and of having kept your freedom of action for the performance of a righteousness* (**iustitia**) *which, since love has grown cold, has now all but departed from the earth* » (8. 2). Such pronouncements put beyond reasonable doubt Gregory's true estimate of Hugh.

For Hugh's estimate of Gregory, it is necessary to return to the Hildebrandine anecdotes as, according to Alexander of Canterbury, Hugh was telling them in the late evening of his life, a quarter of a century on from the last events to be discussed. The world changed, and men changed with it. By the first decade of the twelfth century, a network of friendship embraced three elder statesmen of the Gregorian church whose earlier careers had by no means always been harmonious : Anselm of Canterbury, Hugh of Lyon, and Hugh of Cluny, all of whom had enjoyed the confidence of Pope Urban II. They were brought especially closely together during Anselm's exiles of 1097-1100 and 1103-1106[34], and their friendships were consolidated by the exchange of letters[35]. It is against the background of this mellowed and intimate network of friendship, with its shared remembrance of Gregory VII and his profound admirer Urban II, that Abbot Hugh's Hildebrandine anecdotes, when shorn of the monk Alexander's comments, must be understood[36].

According to Alexander of Canterbury, Hugh told six anecdotes about Gregory : the three about Gregory and himself that have been discussed[37], and three more which were either about Hildebrand alone or about Gregory and Hugh after 1073 :

iv. How, while still acting as legate, Hildebrand had unmasked a simoniac French bishop who could not complete the Gloria Patri (cap. 28) ;

v. How, when pope, he saw a devil riding upon the back of a French nobleman who refused to forgive another who had slain his son in a tournament (cap. 29) ;

vi. How, while Abbot Hugh was travelling with Pope Gregory **in Appuliam**, the latter knew that a close supporter in Rome had committed fornication and discreetly used Hugh to bring him to a gentle but speedy repentance (cap. 30).

By way of introduction to his **De miraculis**, Alexander said that Hugh's conversations with Anselm had been upon three subjects : the Christian's true native land of the heavenly life, the ordering of this life by Christian virtues, and the holy and wonderful deeds of good men (**de caelestis vitae patria, de virtutis morum institutione, de bonorum virorum sancta et admirabili operatione**) (cap. 21). The six Hildebrandine anecdotes may be seen as edifying stories designed to impress upon Hugh's early twelfth-century hearers the distant memory of Gregory VII as an exemplar of these things, and especially of the last two. Gregory's holy and wonderful deeds as a good man were the heart of them. Each one of the six discloses Gregory as having been endowed with the gift of prophecy - in every case of prophetic insight so that he could discern the inner thoughts and dispositions of others, whether they were present (caps. 25-9) or absent (cap. 30), and in one case also of prophetic foresight, so that he could predict future events (the visitation of pestilence upon a monastery, cap. 26). To contemporaries, such prophetic gifts were a warrant of sanctity. This was the case in the Cluniac hagiographic tradition. In the Lives of Abbot Hugh himself, written with a view to his own canonization in 1120, they were claimed for him ; in Gilo's Life, for example, the first section of his miracles, comprising eight stories, presented just such evidence of prophetic insight and foresight[38]. In his anecdotes, Abbot Hugh was concerned to show that Gregory was a true exemplar of sanctity as the Cluniac tradition understood it.

Furthermore, it can fairly be claimed that each anecdote demonstrates Gregory as having exemplified an activity or quality upon which the Cluniac tradition as seen in its late eleventh and early twelfth-century literature set a high value. The first (cap. 25) refers to Hildebrand's activity as a papal legate. It demonstrates how much respect was due to a legate who acted for God and St Peter, and how every mouth should be stopped that saw in a legate's official honour any element of human pride. The high evaluation of a papal legate may be coloured by the debt that Cluny owed to the legatine interventions of 1063 and 1079-1080 by legates of the standing of Peter Damiani and Peter of Albano[39]. The second anecdote (cap. 26), in which Hildebrand saw Christ beside Hugh when both were praying, ends with the observation that Hildebrand indeed possessed the spirit of prophecy ; it was this spirit that Gilo was to place to the fore when he demonstrated Hugh's own sanctity[40]. In the third anecdote (cap. 27), Hildebrand was present in Cluny's own chapter as a monk among monks ; he fully approved of Hugh's performance of his abbatial duty of correcting faults which later Cluniac tradition about him was to esteem so highly, and he honoured its monastic values[41]. The fourth anecdote (cap. 28) illustrates Hildebrand's zeal against simony - a zeal that the young Abbot Hugh was remembered for, as well[42]. The fifth anecdote concerns Gregory as pope insisting that French noblemen should desist from the vendetta that arose in a homicide during a tournament (cap. 29). Not only did the Cluny of Abbot Hugh seek by propagating the Peace of God to promote peace by bringing powerful men to forgive their enemies[43], but Hugh himself set an example by forgiving his brother's slayers and by praying for his father's[44]. Cluny's endeavours to appease local vendettas were given the sanction of a similar act of peacemaking by a pope who bore the marks of sanctity. The final anecdote (cap. 30) illustrates the wise and gentle pastoral care for individual sinners that was a facet of Gregory's many-sided character as pope[45]. It shows him as a model of the good pastor that, once again, Cluniac tradition was to find in Hugh himself and, in Gilo's Life, to illustrate by similar stories[46].

The Hildebrandine anecdotes are thus above all important as showing the image of Gregory VII that the octogenarian Abbot Hugh was concerned to communicate in and through his abbey long after their subject was dead. As Gregory had spoken in 1080 of the sanctity of the abbots of Cluny, so Hugh now spoke of Gregory's sanctity. He did so in terms of a prophetic insight and foresight that constituted sovereign proof in Cluniac eyes. He chose activities or qualities of Gregory that were particularly charged with meaning for Cluny. Hugh's last reflections upon the great pope who was probably his senior in years and whom he had long outlived were no doubt highly selective. They excluded the tensions that there had been between Gregory and himself, and they threw into relief aspects of Gregory's life that were most akin to Cluniac values, interests, and concerns. But they are eloquent of the lifelong friendship and underlying compatibility, if not community, of purpose that bound the two men, and to which Gregory had given eloquent expression in his own letters. It is not only on Gregory's side but also upon Hugh's that there is first-hand evidence of walking **eadem via eodem sensu eodem spiritu**. It was such an impression that Abbot Hugh was at pains to leave as he shared his thoughts with the exiled Anselm of Canterbury.

Notes.

* The following abbreviations are used :

Cowdrey, **Cluniacs** : H.E.J. Cowdrey, **The Cluniacs and the Gregorian Reform** (Oxford, 1970).

Cowdrey, « Two Studies » : H.E.J. Cowdrey, « Two Studies in Cluniac History », **Studi Gregoriani**, 9 (1978), pp. 1-298.

Cowdrey, **Desiderius** : H.E.J. Cowdrey, **The Age of Abbot Desiderius. Montecassino, the Papacy and the Normans in the Eleventh and Early Twelfth Centuries** (Oxford, 1983).

Cowdrey, **Popes** : H.E.J. Cowdrey, **Popes, Monks and Crusaders** (London, 1984).

Epp. vag. : **The Epistolae vagantes of Pope Gregory VII**, ed. H.E.J. Cowdrey (Oxford, 1972).

Gilo : Gilo, **Vita sancti Hugonis abbatis** in : Cowdrey, « Two Studies », pp. 45-109.

Hugh the monk : Hugh, monk of Cluny, **Vita sancti Hugonis abbatis**, in Cowdrey, « Two Studies », pp. 121-139.

MGH : **Monumenta Germaniae Historica**.

BDK : **Die Briefe der deutschen Kaiserzeit**.

Epp. sel. : **Epistolae selectae**.

LdL : Libelli de lite imperatorum et pontificum.

SS : Scriptores.

P.L. : Patrologia Latina, ed. J.P. Migne.

References to items in Gregory VII's Register are to the book and number in **Gregorii VII Registrum**, ed. E. Caspar, **MGH Epp. sel. 2** ; references to his Epp. vag. are to the number of the letter. References to the **Miracula** in Alexander of Canterbury's **Liber ex dictis beati Anselmi** are to the chapter numbers in Southern and Schmitt, **Memorials of Saint Anselm** (as n. 1) or, where appropriate, to pages and lines.

1. Alexander's Liber is edited by R. W. Southern and F. S. Schmitt, **Memorials of Saint Anselm** *(London, 1969), pp. 19-30, 105-270. The Hildebrandine anecdotes from the* **Dicta** *were earlier edited, with discussion, by F. S. Schmitt, « Neue und alte Hildebrand-Anekdoten aus den* **Dicta Anselmi** *»,* **Studi Gregoriani**, *5 (1956), pp. 1-18. See also A. Stacpoole, « Hugh of Cluny and the Hildebrandine Miracle Tradition »,* **Revue Bénédictine**, *77 (1967), pp. 341-363.*

2. **Venerabilium abbatum Cluniacensium chronologia**, *in :* **Bibliotheca Cluniacensis**, *ed. M. Marrier and A. Duchesne (Paris, 1614), col. 1620.*

3. Desiderius of Montecassino, **Dialogus de miraculis sancti Benedicti**, *3. 1, ed. G. Schwartz and A. Hofmeister,* **MGH SS** *30/2, p. 1143.*

4. G. Fornaciari, F. Mallegni, and C. Vultaggio, « Il regime di vita e il quadro fisio-clinico di Gregorio VII », **Rassegna storica Salernitana**, *NS 2/2 (1985), pp. 31-90, at pp. 45-46.*

5. Gilo, 1. 4, pp. 51-53.

6. D. Jasper, **Das Papstwahldekret von 1059. Überlieferung und Textgestalt** *(Sigmaringen, 1986), pp. 39-45.*

7. T. Schieffer, **Die päpstlichen Legaten in Frankreich vom Vertrage von Meersen (870) bis zum Schisma von 1130** *(Eberings Historische Studien, 263, Berlin 1935), pp. 50-53, 55-58, n°s. 17, 19.*

8. Cap. 4, **Gregorii VII Registrum**, *2. 55a, ed. E. Caspar,* **MGH Epp. sel.** *2, p. 203.*

9. **Die Hannoversche Briefsammlung (3. Briefe Berengars von Tours)**, *n° 87, ed. C. Erdmann and N. Fickermann,* **Briefsammlungen der Zeit Heinrichs IV.**, **MGH BDK** *5, pp. 148-152, at p. 152.*

10. Southern and Schmitt, **Memorials of Saint Anselm**, *pp. 211-219.*

11. **Ibid.**, *pp. 19-30.*

12. For the term **probitas** *in Anselm's teaching, see* **ibid.**, *pp. 91, 141-142 ; cf. Gregory's own praise of Hugh's probity in his* **Reg.** *4. 22 : above, p. .*

13. William of Malmesbury, **De gestis regum Anglorum,** *3. 263, ed ; W. Stubbs (2 vols., London : Rolls Series, 90, 1887-1889), 2. 322-323 ; Paul of Bernried,* **Vita sancti Gregorii VII,** *cap. 18, in :* **Pontificum Romanorum ... vitae,** *ed. J.B.M. Watterich (2 vols., Leipzig, 1862), 1. 481.*

14. See Schmitt, « Neue und alte Hildebrand-Anekdoten » (as n. 1), p. 8.

15. Cowdrey, **Cluniacs,** *p. 148, n. 4 ; see also A. Müssigbrod, « Zur Necrologüberlieferung aus Cluniacensischen Klöstern »,* **Revue Bénédictine,** *98 (1988), pp. 62-113, at pp. 68-69.*

16. Cowdrey, **Cluniacs,** *pp. 47-57 ; Cowdrey,* **Popes,** *n° XI. But see Damiani's comment :* **Die Briefe des Petrus Damiani,** *n° 75 (1060), ed. K. Reindel, MGH BDK 4/2, pp. 375-377, at p. 376/14-18.*

17. Cowdrey, **Cluniacs,** *pp. 32-43.*

18. To Hugh : 1. 4, 28 Apr. 1073, p. 7 ; 1. 14, 30 June 1073, pp. 22-23 ; 1. 62, 19 Mar. 1074, pp. 90-91 ; 2. 49, 22 Jan. 1075, pp. 188-190 ; 5.21, 7 May 1078, pp. 384-385 ; 6. 17, 2 Jan. 1079, pp. 423-424 ; 6. 33, 14 Apr. 1079, pp. 446-447 ; 8. 2, 27 June 1080, pp. 517-518. To Bp Hugh of Die and Hugh of Cluny : 6. 3, 22 Aug. 1078, pp. 394-396.

19. 1. 6, to his legates Bp Gerald of Ostia and the subdeacon Rainbald, 30 Apr. 1073, pp. 8-10 ; 4. 12, to the German princes, cf. 4. 12 a, Henry IV's Iusiurandum, late Jan. 1077, pp. 311-316 ; 4. 22, to Bp Hugh of Die, 12 May 1077, pp. 330-334 ; 5. 7, to Abp Udo of Trier and his suffragans, 30 Sept. 1077, pp. 356-358 ; 5. 20, to Bp Rainer of Orléans, 24 Apr. 1078, pp. 383-384 ; 5. 22, to his legates Hubert and Teuzo, 22 May 1078, pp. 385-386 ; 6. 2, to Abp Manasses I of Reims, 22 Aug. 1078, pp. 391-394 ; **Epp. vag.** *23, to Abp Ralph of Tours, summer 1078, pp. 60-63 ;* **Epp. vag.** *30, to Bp Hugh of Die, Apr./May 1079, pp. 76-81 ;* **Epp. vag.** *37, to Abp Ralph of Tours, 1078/1079, pp. 92-95 ; 7. 12, to Abp Manasses I of Reims, 3 Jan. 1080, pp. 475-477 ;* **Epp. vag.** *38, to Bp Landeric of Mâcon, Mar. 1080, pp. 94-97 ;* **Epp. vag.** *39, Allocution in praise of Cluny, Mar. 1080, pp. 96-99 ; 7. 20, to Abp Manasses I of Reims, 17 Apr. 1080, pp. 495-496 ; 8. 3, to King Alphonso of León-Castile, 27 June 1080, pp. 519-520 ; 8. 4, to Abbot Richard of Saint-Victor, Marseille, 27 June 1080, pp. 520-521 ;* **Epp. Vag.** *50, to the same, ?1082, pp. 120-121 ; 9. 30, to the same, 1082/1083, pp. 615-617 ; 9. 31, to Oilardus and Eustachius of Thérouanne, 1083, pp. 617-618 ; 9. 33, to Abp Hugh of Lyon, 1083, pp. 619-620 ; 9. 34, to Count Robert I of Flanders, 1083, pp. 621-622.*

20. Bonizo of Sutri, **Liber ad amicum,** *6, MGH LdL 1. 600.*

21. Schieffer (as n. 7), pp. 95-96, 99-102, 108-109, 115-121, 132-134, n° 31.

22. See J.H. Lynch, « Hugh I of Cluny's Sponsorship of Henry IV : its Context and Consequences » **Speculum** *60 (1985), 800-826.*

23. Cf. the terms in which Berthold of Reichenau, who seems to have been familiar with a lost letter (litterae commonitoriae) of Abbot Hugh, wrote of his mediation with Henry IV to secure the release of Gregory's legate in Germany, Abbot Bernard of Saint-Victor at Marseille, and his companion the monk Christian from captivity by Count Ulrich II of Lenzburg : « Quos rex Heinricus captos comperiens, non, ut domno apostolico iureiurando pactum iam fecit, dimitti precepit. Cluniacensis autem abbas paulo post litteras ad eum commonitorias transmisit, in quibus satis superque illum pro periurio coarguit. Quippe nota ipsi tota reconciliationis et confederationis causa inter papam et regem fuerat, utpote qui precipuus mediator his presto intererat. Insuper ipsi facie revelata liberrimus demandavit, quod id certissimum perditionis illius indicium foret, quod tam magnos et sanctissimos Dei viros incarceratos propter iusticiam sedis apostolice contemptor inhumanus non liberaret, sed potius intrudi preciperet. Qua ille commonitione satis liberrime coargutus et vix confractus, etsi non pro Deo, tamen pro tanti monitoris importunitate, vinctos Dei, solutos et liberos, suis autem omnibus depredatos, abire consensit » : **Annales, a.** *1077,* **MGH SS** *5. 297-8. (I am grateful to Dr I.S. Robinson for permission to cite the text according to his forthcoming edition).*

24. *Raynald of Vézelay,* **Vita sancti Hugonis abbatis Cluniacensis,** *4. 25-6,* **PL.** *159, cols. 903-904, cf. Cowdrey, « Two Studies », p. 29, n. 42.*

25. **Ibid.**

26. *Berthold,* **Annales, a.** *1077,* **MGH SS** *5. 289.*

27. *Gilo, 1. 7, p. 57.*

28. *For contacts with earlier reform popes, see H. Diener, « Das Itinerar des Abtes Hugo von Cluny », in :* **Neue Forschungen über Cluny und die Cluniacenser,** *ed. G. Tellenbach (Freiburg, 1959), pp. 358-360, nos 15, 22, 25-6, 35-6, and with Urban II and Paschal II,* **ibid.,** *pp. 370, 372, nos 116-18, 138.*

29. *Bernold,* **Chronicon, a.** *1093,* **MGH SS** *5.457.*

30. *As n. 16.*

31. *But for Abp Hugh of Lyon's actions in 1087, see Cowdrey,* **Desiderius,** *pp. 187-188.*

32. *For the Spanish crisis of 1080, see Cowdrey,* **Cluniacs,** *pp. 230-239.*

33. *For Gregory, see P. Jaffé,* **Regesta pontificum Romanorum,** *2nd ed. by W. Wattenbach* **et al.** *(2 vols, Leipzig, 1885-1888), 1. 629-33 ; Hugh is known only to have been at Fleury before 4 Aug. : Diener, « Das Itinerar », p. 367, n° 87. He was probably at Cluny by 2 Feb. 1080 : ibid., p. 367, n° 88.*

34. *Alexander of Canterbury,* **Liber ex dictis,** *cap. 21, in : Southern and Schmitt,* **Memorials of Saint Anselm,** *p. 196 ; Eadmer,* **Historia novorum in Anglia,** *2, 3, ed. M. Rule (London : Rolls Series, 81, 1884), pp. 90-91, 114-15, 157-9 ; Eadmer,* **Vita sancti Anselmi archiepiscopi Cantuariensis,** *2.27, 39, 46, 52, ed. R.W. Southern (London, etc., 1962), pp. 103, 116-17, 123-4, 130.*

35. *Cowdrey, « Two Studies », pp. 151-152, 155-156, nos. 6, 8-9.*

36. *Upon becoming pope Urban wrote to his German supporters : « De me porro ita credite, sicut de beatissimo Gregorio ; cuius ex toto sequi vestigia cupiens, omnia quae respuit respuo, quae damnavit damno, quae dilexit prorsus amplector, quae vero rata et catholica duxerit confirmo et approbo » : Ep. 1,* **P.L.,** *151, col. 284A.*

37. *Above, p. .*

38. *Gilo, 1.13-21, pp. 63-70.*

39. *See, e.g., the title of the* **Carta Petri Albanensis episcopi et cardinalis Romani de immunitate Cluniaci** *: Cowdrey,* **Popes,** *XI. 487.*

40. *Gilo, 1.13, pp. 63-64.*

41. *Gilo, 1.13-14, 18, 22-3, 52, 2.3, pp. 63-64, 67-68, 70-71, 89, 93-94.*

42. *As n. 20, cf. Gilo, 1.8, pp. 57-58.*

43. *Hugh the monk, caps 4, 7, pp. 122-125.*

44. *Gilo, 1. 50-1, cf. 25, pp. 72, 88.*

45. *e.g. his pastoral care for the young Bp Hugh I of Grenoble : Guigo I,* **Vita sancti Hugonis Gratianopolitani**, *cap. 2. 6-7,* **P.L.** *153, cols. 766-767.*

46. *Gilo, 1.13-14, 18-19, 23, 52, pp. 63-64, 67-68, 71, 89.*

X

CLUNY AND ROME

The purpose of this paper is to review the problem of Cluny's relations with the papacy during the second half of the eleventh century in the light of some recent publications, and to suggest how it might be formulated for future study.

So far as Pope Gregory VII is concerned, the complexity of the problem is illustrated by two letters of his dictation with the date 2 January 1079 — a date which is near the beginning of an eighteen-month period when relations between Cluny and Rome are agreed to have been subject to periodic stress if not crisis. To the monks of Saint-Victor at Marseilles, he held Cluny up as a paradigm of the closest relationship in which a monastery could stand to Rome : he desired that their house, as Cluny had for long done, should cleave to the apostolic see and should rejoice in the special help and blessing of the Roman church (*Reg.* 6.15). But he severely censured Abbot Hugh of Cluny for admitting to the cloister Duke Hugh I of Burgundy (*Reg.* 6.17). On the same day, Gregory proclaimed Cluny's special relationship to the papacy, and also expostulated with its abbot about his recruiting a prince (*princeps*) into the quiet of the cloister, with adverse results for church and society. A study of Cluny and Rome must take account of both the ideas that the papacy entertained of Cluny, and the events which occurred in their dealings. I first focus on Cluny the institution as Gregory envisaged it.

X

At least from 1080, Gregory praised Cluny in terms of its *libertas Romana*. About this phrase, I would re-iterate two points which I made in my book (Cowdrey, 1970). First, the freedom from temporal obligations that the *libertas Romana* carried with it was intended to have as its complement a complete dedication to spiritual ends and to the purposes of the papacy. The quintessence of this dedication was an unhindered service of God in direct obedience to St Peter as the principal patron saint of the see of Rome. But, secondly, the *libertas Romana* was not a generalized or an abstract concept. Each instance of it had its particular character, determined by the ends which each institution sought and by the services that its members performed. I wish now to probe a little further Gregory's own reasons for his praise of Cluny as an institution.

Four reasons stand out. Two are expressed in letters to Abbot Hugh. First, Gregory shared the medieval view that the service of intercession to God was essential for society and its rulers ; monks, especially Cluniac monks, had an indispensable role in underpinning by their prayers the temporal and eternal ends of the church and its active rulers. "By Almighty God we beseech you, as we have asked from the outset of our rule, to urge your monks to pray continually to God ; for unless by the mediation of them and of other faithful people we gain divine help, we cannot escape danger to ourself and, what we more greatly fear, to the church" (*Reg.* 1.62). Secondly, Gregory also shared the view that the monastic life was the highest form of the Christian life. In more connections than one (it has been observed), Hildebrand the monk looked over the shoulder of Gregory the pope. Necessity compelled him to be active ; he contrasted his own, mean and tainted lot with the higher life of Hugh's monks, and he wanted at least an association with it : "Because praise is not precious, nor is prayer which entreats hastily holy, upon the lips of a sinner whose life deserves [little] praise and whose business is of this world, I pray, beg, and beseech you with watchful solicitude to ask those who, for the merits of their lives, do deserve to be heard, to intercede with God on my behalf..." (*Reg.* 2.49).

Gregory's conciliar allocution at Rome of 1080 in eulogy of Cluny (*Epp. vag.* 39) adds reasons specific to Cluny. A third reason : Cluny's liberty (*libertatis immunitas*) from all external authorities made it from its foundation in 910 an exemplar of the freedom from subjection to the powers of this world and of the unqualified subjection to St Peter which comprised Gregory's ideal for the church as a whole. It was an exemplar, not as an inert pattern, but as an active source. "Its abbots and monks have never in any way dishonoured their sonship of this (the Roman) church nor have they bowed the knee to Baal or the Baalim". Fourthly, and perhaps most important : Gregory asserted of Cluny that "there has never been an abbot there who was not *sanctus* — holy". His thought was close to that which, in *Dictatus papae* 23 and towards the close of his letter of March 1081 to Bishop Hermann of Metz (*Reg.* 2.55a, 8.21), he entertained of the popes themselves : "The Roman pontiff, if he has been canonically instituted, is indubitably made *sanctus* by the merits of St Peter". Gregory applied a parity of argument to the abbots and convent at Cluny, who "have always copied the liberty and dignity of this holy Roman see which they have enjoyed from the beginning, and from generation to generation they have nobly preserved for themselves its authority. For they have never bent their necks before any outsider or earthly power, but they have remained under the exclusive obedience and protection of St Peter and this church". There was a parallel between the exclusive dedication of Cluny to St Peter and that of the apostolic see of Rome. As St Peter's merits devolved upon a canonically elected pope and made him *sanctus*, the same merits devolved upon the abbots of Cluny *per successionis seriem*. I cannot now go into the problem of interpreting the word *sanctus* : official sanctity ? moral and spiritual sanctity ? the first leading to the second ? What I wish to highlight is Gregory's conviction that, because of the special character of Cluny's *libertas Romana*, its abbot possessed what might be called a "deduced sanctity" which of necessity followed from it. This deduced sanctity was one pole of Gregory's evaluation of an abbey's or an abbot's life and service which prejudged and might overrule the other pole — the impact of actual events or behaviour, like Abbot Hugh's tardiness in coming to Rome (*Reg.* 1.62) or the fracas of 1079 over the duke of Burgundy.

With these remarks about Cluny's liberty and how it coloured attitudes in mind, I turn to two scholarly discussions upon which I was asked to comment. The first is B. Szabó-Bechstein's monograph on *libertas ecclesiae* (Szabó-Bechstein, 1985). With what she says about Cluny I largely agree. Her work has the merit of placing the concept of *libertas ecclesiae* against its historical background from early Christian times. Perhaps the main limitations arise from the fact that, as I have indicated, Cluny's *libertas* cannot be comprehended only as a cold intellectual concept. Especially, perhaps, for a non-Cluniac like Gregory VII, it had an emotional colouring that came from the deepest springs of eleventh-century religious conviction. This makes it the more important to see the idea of *libertas* as only one pole of papal dealings with Cluny, the other being an empirical, Rankean *wie es eigentlich gewesen ist* : real men and real situations in their contingency and complexity.

But I welcome her insistence that, even under Gregory VII, the idea of Cluny's liberty and immunity was developing. The Cluniacs and the reforms associated with Gregory should not be approached as a succession in time, as A leading (or not leading) to B ; but as historical phenomena that developed together and interacted. Particularly illuminating is her observation that it was only from about 1079-1080 that Gregory referred to Cluny's *libertas* ; his privilege of 1076, for example, does not contain the term ; Cluniac monks served the Lord *semper sub tutela et emunitate Romana* (*QF*, 107). On Cluny's side, due notice must be taken of D. Iogna-Prat's suggestion that, from the second third of the eleventh century, there was a *grand tournant* in Cluny's self-awareness and sense of identity which may have included a touching up of the foundation charter of 910 to emphasize the Roman roots of Cluny's liberty. A cardinal feature was "les dispositions de l'acte de fondation de Cluny, en particulier le degré de souveraineté du monastère et la nature de ses liens avec Rome. Par petites touches, se forge ainsi l'image d'un monastère idéal, fortement ancré dans la légitimité apostolique, 'fille' de Rome, pas simplement métaphoriquement, mais dans la plénitude du pouvoir". The *grand tournant* was spread over a long period — 1050-1120 ; but for most of it, Hugh was abbot (Iogna-Prat, 1992). There seems to have been a convergence between Gregory's and Hugh's perceptions of Cluny's liberty as an idea, which calls for a fresh formulation and explanation.

The other work on which I was invited to comment is Hermann Jakobs's review article of my book (Cowdrey, 1970) which appeared in *Francia* (Jakobs, 1974). I am glad to do so, for it has always seemed to me a model of what such an appraisal should be — critical, penetrating, challenging, constructive.

Since 1970, my own mind has changed more on the side of the "Gregorian Reform" than of the Cluniacs. I should now be more cautions in using the post-Vatican-I term of art, Gregorian Reform, which Augustin Fliche popularized if he did not invent. Gregory VII himself now seems to me to have been more tentative, flexible, and exploratory in his definitions as in his exercise of the prerogatives of the apostolic see. This was reflected in his use of the term *libertas* as applied to Cluny, and also to Hirsau, Marseilles, Schaffhausen, and Sahagún — monasteries for which Cluny's *libertas* was in some sort a model. Few of Gregory's dicta now seem to me more revealing than one which he already used in January 1075 to caution the headstrong Bishop Hugh of Die, later archbishop of Lyons. Gregory drew on words of Pope Gregory the Great to caution Hugh of Die that "no one suddenly becomes uppermost, and high buildings are built by easy stages (*Nemo repente fit summus et alta edificia paulatim edificantur*)" (*Reg.* 2.43). So I welcome Jakobs's call for greater flexibility in interpretation. Hirsau, especially, must be set more firmly in the context of the three-cornered struggle in Germany between pope, king, and princes, and of the upward pushing of dynastic families anxious to consolidate their social power. And, in general, Germany was a very different place from France. Two respects in which Jakobs thinks that Cluny may have contributed to Gregory's outlook, and which he argues that I neglected, seem, however, to be exaggerated by him. The first is the quasi-monarchical position of the abbot of Cluny, as when Jakobs writes of the "Herrschaftsposition ... des koniggleichen Abtes" ; the second is Cluny's position as head of an institutionalized "Klosterverband" or of an *ecclesia Cluniacensis*. I do not doubt Gregory's awareness of both these tendencies. He used to call Hugh *blandus tirannus*, with the Virgilian echo that he was *haud ignarum parcere subiectis et castigare superbos*. Gregory's privilege of 1076 (*QF*, 107) shows him as well aware of Cluny's far-flung dependencies (although I would query Jakobs's assertion that "Die *ecclesia Cluniacensis* war zu einer Kirche in der Kirche geworden", least of all by 1076). But to say that Gregory recognized these things is one proposition ; to say that they were a model for him in ordering the church is another. I can see no evidence that they were.

A final point about Gregory's idea of Cluny. I once argued that, whereas the papacy needed Montecassino more than Montecassino needed the papacy, with Cluny matters were reversed (Cowdrey, 1983) : Cluny needed the papacy more than the papacy needed Cluny. I still think this is true. But it is also true that, for all the strengths of the institutions that they represented, both Pope Gregory and Abbot Hugh dealt with each other from positions of personal insecurity. For Gregory, this was not just because of the contest with Henry IV and the eventual Guibertine schism. At Rome, he felt alone and isolated ; hence his complaint to Abbot Hugh that "those among whom I live, the Romans that is, the Lombards, and the Normans, as I often tell them, I accuse of being worse even than Jews and heathen" (*Reg.* 2.49). Abbot Hugh was vulnerable to the claims of local bishops. Such personal insecurity made each man look to the other's institution for strength : Hugh to the papacy which could send legates, Peter Damiani in 1063, Peter of Albano in 1080, as nineteenth-century colonial powers could send a gunboat ; Gregory to Cluny which from its foundation had been so very close to St Peter as to be invested with his sanctity. Gregory could use Hugh as a kind of surrogate abbot to whom he could bare his soul (*Reg.* 2.49).

Small wonder that formulations of Cluny's liberty seem to the modern mind artificial and overdrawn. But, given the circumstances of the eleventh century, they could and did touch the springs of life, especially in so religious a pope as Gregory VII.

I now turn to the opposite pole of the problem of Cluny and Rome : what happened in historical reality. This will enable me to say a little about what is probably the most important event of 1993 in Cluniac studies : the publication of Armin Kohnle's monograph on Abbot Hugh (Kohnle, 1993). I preface certain criticisms by expressing my admiration of its thoroughness and of its judicious handling of many aspects of the abbot's life and activity. Like most historians, Kohnle regards 1079 and 1080 as critical years in relations between Gregory VII and Abbot Hugh. They are years in which every piece of evidence demands meticulous interpretation in order to seek what actually happened. I take two problems which call for deeper discussion than Kohnle offers. The first demands an extension of the inquiry beyond what has been customary : it is that raised by Gregory's letter to Hugh of 2 January 1079 about his admission to the cloister in 1078 of Duke Hugh I of Burgundy (*Reg.* 6.17). It has seemed to epitomize the difference of approach to the Christian life between the two men — between Hugh's ideal of monastic withdrawal from the world and Gregory's ideal of an active *militia Christi* in and through the affairs of the world. But it is misleading to consider Hugh of Burgundy's entry into the cloister apart from that of Count Simon of Crépy in 1077 which prompted it. Both events involved Pope Gregory, Abbot Hugh, and a French *princeps*, few of whose rank, according to Gregory, ruled justly in the world. Abbot Hugh admitted the duke to Cluny ; he also seems to have directed the count to the austerer monastery of Saint-Oyend. As for Gregory, one would have expected that, if he was angry about the duke of Burgundy, he would have been even angrier about the count of Crépy-Valois. Despite Gregory's complaint à propos Burgundy that a hundred thousand Christians now lacked a guardian, Duke Hugh handed on his duchy intact to his brother Odo ; whereas Count Simon had no son or kinsman to whom he could hand over his inheritance, and it quickly disintegrated. That mattered, for whereas the duchy of Burgundy was not all that important in the politics of Christendom, the principality of Crépy-Valois, especially if ruled by so valiant a Christian prince as Simon promised to be, was an important check upon the Capetian king Philip I, who was far from in the good books of Gregory VII or, later, of Urban II. Again, so far as is known, Duke Hugh's monastic conversion was not infectious among his lay contemporaries ; other great men did not copy his example. But Simon of Crépy inspired not only Hugh of Burgundy but also Count Guy of Mâcon to leave the world. True, as a hermit at Rome Simon was useful to Gregory in negotiating the renewed alliance with Robert Guiscard of Apulia which led in 1080 to the oath-taking at Ceprano. But, according to his *Vita*, during Simon's diplomatic journey to the Normans his preaching led to sixty Norman knights entering various monasteries ! He thereby reduced the Normans' capacity to help Gregory in his hour of need for allies against Henry IV of Germany and Archbishop Guibert of Ravenna. Yet Gregory was whole-hearted in his approval of every step in Simon's progress from prince to monk to hermit at Rome. Why did he reprove Duke Hugh's relatively innocuous entry into Cluny, while applauding Count Simon's more momentous changes of life ?

Just two comments on this seeming paradox. First, Gregory did not view matters as we would. He was not much interested in political consequences, like the break-up of the principality of Crépy-Valois. What did matter to him was whether, here and now, a ruler's actions fostered the peace and concord (Gregory's own preferred terms) which constituted his immediate objectives for human society. In Gregory's eyes, Simon's way of going about things ensured the peace of the people whom he left, and it still conduced to peace after he became a monk and hermit. As it seemed to Gregory, Duke Hugh with Abbot Hugh's connivance omitted similarly to provide for his people's peace. Secondly, over the duke of Burgundy, Gregory and Abbot Hugh seem quickly to have come to a *modus vivendi*. The air was somehow cleared. Duke Hugh stayed in the cloister ; but, as according to the statement of the chronicler Bernold the example of King Alphonso VI of León-Castile was to show, Abbot Hugh took care for the future to dissuade inappropriate lay rulers from entering Cluny on the grounds that they were needed in the world. Abbot Hugh knew when to defer. Gregory, on the other hand, was far from being opposed on principle to lay rulers entering the cloister — witness Count Simon of Crépy. What mattered were the circumstances in which it happened.

Another problem in what actually happened in the critical period 1079-1080 turns upon Gregory's immediate reaction in June 1080 to receiving from his legate in Spain, Abbot Richard of Marseilles, tidings of an outrage perpetrated by a Cluniac monk named Robert — an *impietas*, he told Abbot Hugh, "which has come forth from your monastery by the presumption of your monk Robert" (*Reg.* 8.2). I wish to focus upon just one issue : whether or not this letter lends support to the suggestion that, in mid-1079, Abbot Hugh may have visited Rome for a meeting with Gregory (Cowdrey, 1990). Kohnle's view that it does not (Kohnle, 1993) is insufficiently grounded, for he merely cites a single sentence of Gregory's letter out of context and points to the future tense of the verb. This letter is a classic example of evidence which demands a close reading. A possible interpretation with a view to the point at issue might be as follows. Having immediately confronted Hugh with his monk's act of iniquity, Gregory expressed confidence that Hugh in no way consented to it. He well understood that Hugh would be as saddened by it as he himself was, and would be minded to exact due vengeance. Gregory was particularly so persuaded "because you have given long-standing warrant to our confidence that you feel exactly as we do about the integrity of the Roman church (*de honore sancte R[omane] ecclesie*), and you have kept to the free path of equity in the performance of righteousness (*ad executionem iustitie... libertatem rectitudinis reservasse*) — of righteousness which, as love has grown cold, has now almost departed from the earth". Since January 1079, when Gregory castigated Hugh for lack of charity in depriving the Burgundians of their ruler, the air had been cleared. From the experience of the past, Gregory went on to draw two lessons for the future. First, "for a surety, from this settled certitude of mind, no rumour and no insinuation will be able (*poterit*) to shake us". Secondly, "and neither will those who murmur (*murmurant*) against you on many matters be able (*poterunt*) to give rise to outrage in us so that we suspect otherwise, before a time of brotherly talking together (*ante tempus fraterne collucationis*)". That there had lately been such a talking together which should be model for the future resolution of differences is suggested by a reference in the next sentence to Gregory's own past vindication of Cluniac interests at Rome. It must be remembered that, in 1078/1079, Gregory was confidently awaiting an imminent visit : *praestolamur enim Cluniacensem abbatem ad nos in proximo perventurum*, and had decided upon its agenda (*Epp. vag.* 37). By mid-1079, the potential agenda were many and from Hugh's side pressing : they included the misunderstanding over the duke of Burgundy and the threat from the local episcopate to Cluny's liberty. A clearing of the air by a meeting would go far to explain the return of cordiality by the winter of 1079-1080, when Cardinal Peter of Albano came to Cluny vindicated its liberty and Gregory made his synodal allocution in praise of Cluny. A successful meeting would also make credible Gregory's *animi concepta certitudo* about Hugh's concern for the integrity of the Roman church and about his zeal for righteousness in practice (*Reg.* 8.2), which led him, in his accompanying letter to the king of León-Castile, to say of himself and Abbot Hugh that *eadem enim via eodem sensu eodem spiritu ambulamus* (*Reg.* 8.3). While there is no definitive proof, a meeting between Gregory and Hugh in mid-1079 is strongly suggested by the evidence and is the likeliest explanation of the change in mutual relations which occurred at about that time.

As one would question Kohnle's treatment of particular episodes in actual relations between Cluny and Rome, so doubts arise about his presentation of the course of events. For him, there were three stages of Abbot Hugh's attitude to the reform papacy : up to 1073, close, energetic, and whole-hearted collaboration ; Gregory VII's pontificate, especially the years 1079-1080, as a turning-point when Hugh progressively withdrew from activity in church affairs while retaining pre-

Gregorian assumptions about the relations between *sacerdotium* and *regnum* ; the reigns of Urban II and Paschal II, when these features were accentuated. Kohnle claims that between Hugh and the Gregorian papacy there was a "Konflikt im Grundsätzlichen". It is salutary to compare this picture with such a case-study as that by Andreas Sohn on the Cluniac *abbatia* of Saint-Martial at Limoges under its first Cluniac abbot and Abbot Hugh's disciple Ademar (1063-1114) (Sohn, 1989). Particularly instructive is the virtual condominium in the diocese exercised in the late 1090s by the abbot and his former prior William, now bishop, in the wake of visits by the Cluniac pope Urban II and by Abbot Hugh. From such evidence it might well be concluded that, after 1073, the Cluniac diffusion of papal reforming intentions did not decline so much as change in character and manner of implementation. A pressing need in Cluniac studies is a comparison between the relations with Abbot Hugh of Gregory VII and Urban II — the non-Cluniac and the Cluniac pope. In Sohn's book especially, one gets a sense of the surer touch but cooler appraisal of Urban in dealing with one whom he knew and respected at first hand from their years of working together as abbot and prior of Cluny.

Kohnle has surprisingly little to say about Cluny's liberty and about how Gregory VII and Abbot Hugh regarded and defended it. Up to a point, this is understandable in a book about the person of Abbot Hugh rather than about Cluny as an institution. But it means that only one side of the problem of Cluny and the papacy is highlighted — that of the course of events as opposed to that of the ideas in men's minds. Preponderant emphasis on either side inevitably leads to distortion. The challenge before the next generation of historians of Cluny is to pay proportionate attention to both sides — to ideas like Cluny's liberty and to the course of events ; to take account of all the evidence, especially for relations between Gregory VII and Abbot Hugh ; and to give each item of evidence the close reading that it demands. No one has yet brought the problem of Cluny and Rome into full and true perspective, but the evidence is likely to prove sufficient for a satisfactory resolution in the not too distant future.

1. SOURCES

Reg. : *Gregorii VII Registrum*, ed. E. CASPAR. *Monumenta Germaniae Historica, Epistolae selectae*, 2, Berlin, 1920-1923.

QF : *Quellen und Forschungen zum Urkunden- und Kanzleiwesen Papst Gregors VII.* 1. Teil. *Quellen : Urkunden, Regesten, Facsimilia*, ed. L. SANTIFALLER, Vatican City, 1957 (Studi e testi, 190).

Epp. vag. : *The Epistolae vagantes of Pope Gregory VII*, ed. and trans. H. E. J. COWDREY, Oxford, 1972.

2. SECONDARY WORKS

H. E. J. COWDREY, *The Cluniacs and the Gregorian Reform*, Oxford, 1970.

ID., *The Age of Abbot Desiderius : Montecassino, the Papacy, and the Normans in the Eleventh and Early Twelfth Centuries*, Oxford, 1983.

ID., "St Hugh and Gregory VII", in *Le gouvernement d'Hugues de Semur à Cluny. Actes du Colloque scientifique international, Cluny, septembre 1988*, Cluny, 1990, pp. 173-190.

D. IOGNA-PRAT, "La geste des origines dans l'historiographie clunisienne des xie-xiie siècles", in *Revue bénédictine*, t. 102, 1992, pp. 135-191.

H. JAKOBS, "Die Cluniacenser und das Papsttum im 10. und 11. Jahrhundert. Bemerkungen zum Cluny-Bild eines neuen Buches", in *Francia*, t. 2, 1974, pp. 643-663.

A. KOHNLE, *Abt Hugo von Cluny (1049-1109)*, Sigmaringen, 1993 (Beihefte der Francia, 32).

X

265

A. Sohn, *Der Abbatiat Ademars von Saint-Martial de Limoges (1063-1114)*, Münster in W., 1989 (Beiträge zur Geschichte des alten Mönchtums und des Benediktinertums, 37).

B. Szabó-Bechstein, *Libertas Ecclesiae. Ein Schlusselbegriff des Investiturstreits und seine Vorgeschichte, 4.-11. Jahrhundert*, Rome, 1985 (*Studi Gregoriani*, 12).

COUNT SIMON OF CREPY'S MONASTIC CONVERSION

Between March and May 1077, Count Simon of Crépy (1048-81/2), a leading feudatory of the Capetian crown whose complex of lands lay mainly between the Rivers Seine and Somme, astounded his French contemporaries by withdrawing from the world and becoming a monk[1]. Medieval historians today are most familiar with this event from Guibert of Nogent's autobiography, written in 1114/15[2]. According to Guibert, Simon's conversion occurred with a suddenness reminiscent of St Paul's on the Damascus road. It happened thus : his powerful father, Count Ralph IV (1055-74) had been buried in a town, Montdidier (Somme), which he had seized and not inherited ; Simon decided to transfer his remains to a town of his inheritance, Crépy-en-Valois, where he had him buried at the abbey of Saint-Arnoul ; the sight of his father's corrupted body turned his thoughts to the misery of the human condition, and he now began to feel a distaste for his earthly glory. So he fled beyond the boundaries of France (as Guibert understood them), entering the Burgundian monastery of Saint-Oyend (later known as Saint-Claude) in the Jura, while his fiancée (Judith, daughter of Count Robert II of Auvergne) became a nun. A similar story of Simon's sudden conversion was told in France by Latin and vernacular writers from the twelfth to the fourteenth centuries[3].

---

1. The range of possible dates is securely indicated by two charters : (i) Simon's charter of 31 Mar. 1077 for Saint-Arnoul at Crépy, in : *Recueil des actes de Philippe Ier, roi de France (1059-1108)*, éd. M. PROU (Paris, 1908) (hereafter PROU) pp. 229-30, n° 88 ; (ii) Philip I's charter of before 23 May 1077 in confirmation of all Simon of Crépy's gifts to Cluny, in : PROU, pp. 230-2, n° 89, = *Recueil des chartes de l'abbaye de Cluny*, éd. A. BERNARD and A. BRUEL, 6 vols. (Paris, 1876-1903) (hereafter BRUEL), 4, p. 613-14, n° 3 499. PROU accurately dates these charters.

2. G. DE NOGENT, *Autobiographie*, 1.10, éd. E. R. LABANDE Paris, 1981, pp. 58-65.

3. In Latin, *Anecdotes historiques, légendes et apologues tirés du recueil inédit d'Etienne de Bourbon, dominicain du XIIIe siècle*, éd. A. LECOY DE LA MARCHE (Société de l'histoire de

However, a diametrically different construction of Simon's spiritual Odyssey is to be found in a *Vita Simonis* which was almost certainly written by a monk of Saint-Oyend[4] ; he claimed to rely upon the living testimony of companions who took the habit with Simon (1223A). Their lifespan provides the *terminus ante quem* of the *Vita*. Since it refers to Abbot Hugh of Cluny as being dead (1219A), it must have been written after 29 April 1109. Whereas Guibert reiterated that Simon's conversion was sudden, the *Vita* presents his development as a gradual and protracted matter of «how he brought the intention of faith to the fruition of activity» (1211B). In effect, his life was marked by four ascending stages. The first was his life in the world, and his monastic future was early presaged. In early youth his exasperation after an unsuccessful day's hawking led to perverse and foul thoughts. A reference to a comparable experience of St Benedict foreshadows the future[5] ; the dispelling of his thoughts by the Holy Spirit thus marked the start of a holy way of life (*conversatio*) the demands of which he kept in mind even when immersed in worldly affairs (1211BC). For the *Vita*, the re-burial of his father's remains was undertaken at the instigation of Pope Gregory VII to make amends for his father's seizure of Montdidier. It did not immediately lead to his becoming a monk, although it moved him to contempt of the world and to vigils, fasting, and almsgiving, and to wearing a hair shirt (1212B-1213B). A pause in his warfare against King Philip I of France allowed him to make a pilgrimage to Rome where he sought penance from Pope Gregory VII (1213C). But although he remembered Christ's precept : «Whoever does not renounce all that he has cannot be my disciple» (Luke 14 : 33), Gregory gave him penance and intimated that he should return to his warfare until peace was secured (1213CD). The time to be a monk was not yet.

France, Paris, 1877), pp. 66-7. In French, *Les Vers de Thibaud de Marly*, éd. H. K. STONE (Paris, 1932), pp. 107, 112 (written c. 1182/5) ; *Dou conte Symon and Histoire du filz du conte de Crespi*, poems respectively of the first half of the thirteenth century and of the fourteenth, in E. WALBERG, *Deux Anciens Poèmes inédits sur Saint Simon de Crépy* (Lund, 1909), pp. 45-54, 63-80.

4. *Vita beati Simonis comitis Crespeiensis auctore synchrono*, in : J.-P. MIGNE, *Patrologia Latina* (hereafter *PL*) 156.1211-24 (references are made in the text by column numbers). Excerpts from the *Vita* occur, in a lightly paraphrased form, in ALBERIC OF TROIS-FONTAINES, *Chronicon*, *Monumenta Germaniae Historica* (hereafter *MGH*), *Scriptores*, 23.674-950, at pp. 793, 797-9 ; Alberic wrote c.1250. For Saint-Oyend, and for a still-useful commentary on the *Vita*, see P. BENOIT, *Histoire de l'abbaye et de la terre de Saint-Claude*, 2 vols. Montreuil-sur-Mer, 1890, esp. 1.449-86. Further sources which do not ascribe Simon's monastic conversion to his seeing his dead father are : HARIULF, *Vita sancti Arnulfi episcopi Suessonensis*, 1.25, PL 174.1396 (written after c.1114) : the *Chronicon Besuense* (Bèze, Côte d'Or), of early twelfth-century date : *Joannis monachi Chronicon Besuense*, a.1088, PL 162.941A : HUGH OF FLEURY, *Liber qui modernorum regum Francorum continet actus*, MGH Scriptores, 9.390, early twelfth-century.

5. A loose citation of *Dialogues*, 2.1 : GREGOIRE LE GRAND, *Dialogues*, éd. A. DE VOGÜE and P. ANTIN, «Sources Chrétiennes», 251, 260, 265 (Paris, 1978-80), 1.136.

His progress to monasticism was the next stage. It began with his betrothal to and separation from Judith of Auvergne ; his marriage to her had been arranged, evidently by his magnates anxious for the continuance of his father's principality. Gradualness again prevailed : although Simon suggested that both should renounce the world (1214C) only Judith as yet entered a monastery (1214CD). The *Vita* does, indeed, compare Simon to St. Alexis, the fourth-century patrician's son who left his bride on their wedding night for a life of poverty and pilgrimage (1215AB)[6]. Yet its final comment concerned, not Simon's becoming a monk, but how by preaching chastity to his betrothed he shunned his father's myriad carnal sins (1215B). There followed another marriage negotiation with William, king of England, who offered him his daughter (1215B-1216A). Simon continued publicly to dissemble his purpose of celibacy and raised difficulties about consanguinity with the queen. The king agreed to his proposal that he should seek the counsel of Pope Gregory VII at Rome (1216AB). Instead he subsequently decided to become a monk at Saint-Oyend (1216B). The *Vita* offers no explanation of this change of course, which may have been partly occasioned by difficulties created by King Henry IV of Germany for those crossing the Alps[7]. It does, however, record a vision that Simon had experienced some time ago : the patron saints of the monasteries with which he was most closely associated, St. Arnulf and St. Oyend, had appeared to him with a third, nameless saint and charged him to become a monk at Saint-Oyend (1216CD). There he led a monastic life of exceptional austerity (1217A-D), although the *Vita* records a gradual progress in monastic virtues (1217D).

In due course Simon advanced to a third stage, of an eremitical life in the forest (1217D-1219A, 1220B), still progressing in his observances until he replaced his hair shirt with an iron corselet (1218D-1219A). Gregory VII eventually summoned him to Rome, choosing for him and his companions a hermitage near the church of St. Thecla on the Ostian Way ; life was so hard that all but two of his companions died of plague and only one of the survivors, Robert, stayed with him to the end (1220B-D, 1222B). Simon himself asked Gregory's leave to return to the Jura but died in St. Peter's basilica during a vigil of prayer that the pope imposed on him to seek the apostle's will (1221BC).

---

6. For the legends of Alexis, see *Acta Sanctorum*, Iul. 4 (Antwerp, 1725), pp. 238-70.

7. *Cf.* the experience of William of Warenne, future earl of Surrey, and his wife Gundrada as related in the foundation charter of the Cluniac priory of Lewes (1077) : W. DUGDALE, *Monasticon Anglicanum*, 6 vols. (new edn. by J. CALEY, H. ELLIS, and B. BANDINEL, London, 1817-30), 5.12, = BRUEL, 4, p. 689-96, n° 3561.

The final stage of the *Vita*'s account was the glory into which he was received. By Gregory's command he was buried in St. Peter's amongst the papal tombs (*inter apostolicos*). For the *Vita* it was the climax of his story : «because he sought to follow the apostolic life (*vitam apostolicam*), he rightly received the supreme honour» (1221D). A posthumous vision of his companion Robert confirmed that he indeed won a throne of glory among the apostles (1222C). For the *Vita*, Simon's life was a long and gradual ascent towards such final blessedness ; no single incident stands out in the climacteric way that the sight of his father's decaying corpse was to stand out for Guibert of Nogent.

Read by themselves, the accounts of Simon's conversion in Guibert of Nogent and in the *Vita* seem to offer contrasting traditions which were being concurrently narrated in monastic circles some thirty years after he died. It would *prima facie* be tempting to prefer the account in the *Vita* : it is fuller and more circumstantial, it reflects the traditions of Simon's own monastery of Saint-Oyend ; Guibert wrote with a more sharply focused, and perhaps more distorting, didactic purpose. Yet since he wrote at Nogent which is only some 34 km. from Crépy, Guibert's account is not to be dismissed out of hand. In fact, other and often earlier evidence that can be gleaned from charters, letters, and chronicles suggests that there is a measure of truth in both accounts, while neither should be exclusively followed.

Simon himself left a record of the transfer of his father's body in a most instructive charter of 1077[8]. Its significance is both political and religious. From a religious point of view it confirms the motive of filial piety upon which the *Vita* insists and which, in answer to his inquiry, Gregory VII had urged upon him (1212BC). Such piety must attend to both body and soul. Simon accordingly had his father brought from Montdidier, where he had rested for three years after the dissolution of his body, to the church of Saint-Arnoul. This church, the charter continues, was established according to a noble plan (*honorifico scemate*) by Ralph and his ancestors in their castle of Crépy, and there Ralph had been baptized. After the custom of his forebears Simon had him placed there and laid in a double tomb (*in spelunca duplici*) next Simon's mother and his own wife. It reads as a touching vignette of family piety in a society where agnatic relationships within families whose lordships were becoming increasingly centred upon their castles and their churches called for strict order and linear solidarity.

---

8. PROU, pp. 229-30, n° 88.

Other documents, however, disclose how much more there was to Ralph's reburial than that. Adela, Simon's mother, was but the first of three wives. After her death in 1054, Ralph had taken a second, Eleanor, heiress of Montdidier and Péronne, who had the unkind nickname Haquenez. It was by making this marriage that he had been able to seize Montdidier. But this did not satisfy his aspirations. When King Henry I of France died in 1060, he made the further coup of marrying, probably in 1061, his widow, Anne of Kiev, the mother of the eight-year-old King Philip I[9]. Ralph was related to the dead king, so the marriage was doubly flawed. Eleanor was not prepared to acquiesce in being put away. She appealed to Pope Alexander II at Rome, taking with her a letter from Archbishop Gervase of Reims in which he reported the disturbance of the realm and the boy-king's grief at his mother's remarriage. Gervase regretted that the plight of the kingdom prevented his coming to Rome in person ; but he commented upon how Eleanor had been wrongly set aside by her husband, though his plea on her behalf is lost through the incomplete preservation of the letter[10] . Alexander's reply, addressed to Gervase and his suffragans and to the archbishop of Sens, Richer, and his, shows that Eleanor was well able to speak for herself : Count Ralph had robbed her of all that she possessed (no doubt the reference is to his retention of Montdidier and Péronne), and he had put her away upon a false accusation of her unchastity. Archbishop Gervase was to investigate. If her story were true, he was to restore her possessions and to make Ralph take her back as his wife. Should Ralph refuse, Gervase was to pass canonical sentence upon him, and the pope would in due course confirm it[11]. A chronicler at Sens noted that Ralph had married Anne *contra ius et fas* (apart from putting away Eleanor, Ralph and Anne were related within the prohibited degrees), and that he was indeed excommunicated[12].

Whether or not he died an excommunicate[13], it can be understood that the sight of the bodily corruption of so sinful a father may have moved Simon as deeply as Guibert of Nogent suggested. One senses a deeper meaning even than family piety when Simon laid his father to rest at

---

9. For Anne, see R.-H. BAUTIER, «Anne de Kiev, reine de France, et de la politique royale au XIe siècle», *Revue des études slaves*, 57 (1975), 539-64.

10. *Recueil des historiens des Gaules et de la France*, éd. M. BOUQUET and others, 24 vols. (Paris, 1738-1904) (hereafter *RHF*), 11.499 : the probable date is mid-Nov 1061 : BAUTIER (as n. 9), p. 556. See also Gervase's earlier letter to Pope Nicholas II (died ? 22 July 1061) : *RHF* 11.498-9.

11. *RHF* 14.539, = Alexander II, Ep. 41, *PL* 146.1319-20 ; the date is after mid-1062 : BAUTIER (as n. 9), p. 557.

12. *Chronique de Saint-Pierre-le-Vif de Sens, dite de Clarius*, éd. R.-H. BAUTIER and M. GILLES (Paris, 1979), a.1060, p. 126.

13. BAUTIER (as n. 9), p. 558.

Crépy, rather than Montdidier, *in spelunca duplici* with his first wife. On earth, it was as though the carnal lusts and worldly ambition that had led Ralph to wrong Eleanor and to incur excommunication by taking Anne of Kiev had never prompted him[14]. In heaven, there was a hope that Ralph would receive remission of sins and stand renewed, if the duties of religion were duly performed for his soul though this was not a case for half measures.

And so, as his charter for Saint-Arnoul declares, Simon also took due thought for his father's soul. More than either the *Vita* or Guibert of Nogent makes clear, he took the sovereign remedy of turning to the monastic order for the benefit to his father of its prayers and alms. He particularly turned to Cluny, to which he had already, upon becoming count, assigned tithes at Mantes as well as founding a Cluniac house[15]. During his last year as count he went further, and assigned the monastery of Saint-Arnoul at Crépy to Abbot Hugh of Cluny so that it should be wholly subject to him under an abbot chosen from his monks. The gift of his family monastery was in several respects remarkable : 1076/7 was a very early date for Abbot Hugh to accept a dependency north of the River Loire ; the gift was evidently a by-product of Pope Gregory VII's direction that, in seeking peace with King Philip I of France, Simon should be guided by the papal legate Bishop Hugh of Die and by Abbot Hugh (1213D-1214A) ; and Simon described himself as the abbot's *servulus* who held him in outstanding love[16]. After entering Saint-Oyend, Simon secured from the king a confirmation of all his gifts to Cluny[17]. Simon did well for his father's soul no less than for his body. He procured for him the intercession of the Cluniacs, and at Crépy itself, his charter providing for his father's reburial ended by making gifts to Saint-Arnoul to ensure his local remembrance[18].

But what of Simon himself ? The *Vita* may have been correct in emphasizing that his main thought was for his father : it was for his welfare that he sought Gregory VII's advice (1212C) ; in due course his renunciation of the carnal delights of marriage was made in expiation of his father's sins (1215B). Except for Guibert of Nogent, no early source suggests that it was through his father's reburial that Simon's thoughts were

---

14. Nothing whatever is known of Anne after this point : BAUTIER (as n. 9), pp. 560-3.

15. BRUEL, 4.585-6, n° 3477.

16. PROU, pp. 268-9, n° 105, = BRUEL, 4, p. 608, n° 3493. For the date, see P. FEUCHERE, «Une tentative manquée de concentration territoriale entre Somme et Seine : la principauté d'Amiens-Valois au XIe siècle», *Le Moyen Age*, 60 (1954), 1-37, at p. 37.

17. PROU, pp. 230-2, n° 89, = BRUEL, 4, p. 613-14, n° 3499.

18. PROU, pp. 229-30, n° 88.

consciously directed towards his own monastic conversion ; his charter, perhaps drafted by a monk of Saint-Arnoul, tells only of Simon's recognition that the day of this life is as nothing in comparison to the life to come, and of his fixing his mind so far as he was able upon the contemplation of eternity[19]. When the *Vita* takes up this thought, it does not develop and intensify it beyond the pattern of an exemplary pious layman (1213AB). Nevertheless the *Vita* does indicate by the story of his vision (1216C) that a vocation to monasticism had in another way been forming in his mind[20]. If its depiction of Simon's spiritual development as gradual rather than sudden is probably basically true, it may still not do justice to the intensity of his response to his father's reburial which made him turn to Pope Gregory VII and to Cluny for help with his father's commemoration, or to the profound spiritual experience which led him to take the habit at Saint-Oyend. Guibert of Nogent may be correct at least to insist upon the depth of his spiritual reactions, even though he oversimplified and misconstrued them.

One thing seems certain : there is no need to postulate a clash in his loyalties or purposes as between Cluny and Saint-Oyend. He looked to the one for his father's posthumous commemoration, and to the other for his own monastic home. As a monk he still enjoyed good relations with Abbot Hugh whom he served well in a visit to the king's court (1219A), while his admirer and imitator, the saintly Stephen, later abbot of Bèze, was to move happily and profitably from Saint-Oyend to Cluny and back again[21]. It is not clear why Simon chose to be a monk of Saint-Oyend rather than of Cluny, but it is possible that the eremitical and austere manner of life which, according to the *Vita*, he increasingly adopted was more readily available at Saint-Oyend. It is quite conceivable that, discerning his spiritual bent, Abbot Hugh may have advised him accordingly.

If Simon of Crépy's monastic conversion raises questions about the process by which he formed and implemented his intention, it also provides evidence, especially through the *Vita*, for the ideas and actions of major ecclesiastical and secular rulers of his time, especially Pope Gregory VII, the Capetian King Philip I, and the Anglo-Norman King-duke

---

19. *Ibid*.

20. The suggestion that Simon's departure for Saint-Oyend was not a matter of sudden impulse but that it was deliberated for some time is confirmed by the statement of the *Chronicon Besuense* that he sent ahead of him two of his companions : a.1088, *PL* 162, 941A ; also by the *Vita*'s hints in his dealings of 1075 with Gregory VII (1213CD) and in his reaction to the arrangement of his marriage in 1077 (1214B : *ut bonum quod in se latebat penitus operiret*).

21. *PL* 162, 941B. For Stephen, see S. DE MONTENAY, *L'Abbaye bénédictine Saint-Pierre de Bèze, 630-1790*, Dijon, 1960, pp. 76-96.

XI

William I, with all of whom he had prolonged dealings. Three subjects may particularly be selected for discussion.

The first is Gregory VII's attitude to the monastic conversion of greater and lesser lay rulers. In one famous case at least, that of Abbot Hugh's admission to his abbey of Duke Hugh I of Burgundy (1075-8), Gregory quickly sent Hugh a letter of sharp reproof for admitting to the shelter of the cloister one of the few princes of his time who was a genuinely Christian ruler and for thus leaving countless Christian people with no protector :

> Behold ! those who seem to fear or love God flee from Christ's battle, put aside their brothers' safety, and seek rest as though loving only themselves. The shepherds flee as do the dogs, the defenders of the flock ; wolves and robbers attack Christ's sheep while no one resists. You have taken or received the duke into rest at Cluny, and brought it about that a hundred thousand Christians lack a guardian.

Gregory further drew Abbot Hugh's attention both to St. Benedict's prescription of a year of novitiate, and to Pope Gregory the Great's stipulation that a knight should not become a monk before three years had elapsed[22]. The question arises why Gregory should have condemned so roundly in the case of Hugh of Burgundy the monastic conversion that he appears to have welcomed, if not positively encouraged, in Simon of Crépy (1220B-D, 1221B-D) and that Pope Urban II treated with approval in the epitaph that he is said to have composed for Simon's tomb in St. Peter's (1223A-1224A). Not only does Gregory seem to have raised no difficulties based on the writings of St. Benedict or St. Gregory, but there is no suggestion that he did not approve of Simon's actions at every stage. This is particularly surprising for two reasons. One is that Simon's final decision to become a monk was his own, taken without consulting Gregory to whom, for whatever reason[23], he did not travel before entering Saint-Oyend (1214B, 1216BC). The second is that he was repeatedly the cause of other laymen, both great and small, leaving their stations in the world and becoming monks. Most remarkably, according to the *Vita* it was Simon's entering Saint-Oyend that prompted Duke Hugh of Burgundy to leave the world, as well as Count Guy of Mâcon and ma-

---

22. GREGORY VII, *Registrum*, 6.17, 2 Jan. 1079, in : *Das Register Gregors VII.*, éd. E. CASPAR, *MGH Epistolae selectae*, 2 (Berlin, 1920-3) (hereafter Reg.), pp. 423-4.

23. See above, p. 259.

ny others, great and small (1216D)[24]. When Simon's fiancée Judith took the veil at La Chaise-Dieu two of her kinsmen became monks there ; they were Adelbert who eventually became abbot of Bourg-Dieu at Déols (1087-92) and archbishop of Bourges (1092-7), and Garnier of Montmorillon who remained for some forty years as an exemplary monk (1214CD)[25]. When Simon himself entered Saint-Oyend, he took with him 'certain outstanding men of his own household » (1216BC) ; the *Chronicon Besuense* names Ralph and Franco whom he sent ahead, and Robert, Arnulf, and Warner who made their professions with him ; another nobleman, Stephen, later abbot of Bèze, followed them[26]. In 1080, as he returned to Rome from negotiations with Robert Guiscard, duke of Apulia, his preaching led almost sixty knights to take the habit in various monasteries (1221AB). Simon's conversion to monasticism was and remained infectious among the very classes whose members Gregory, when dealing with Duke Hugh of Burgundy, seems concerned to leave in the world. Why did he reprove Hugh's conversion but accept Simon's ?

The answer suggested by the evidence of the *Vita* is that Simon's conversion was, from Gregory's point of view, well prepared in political respects ; Hugh's had been impulsive and had «brought it about that a hundred thousand Christians lacked a guardian». Under Gregory's guidance, Simon had done all that was needed to establish *pax et concordia* in and around his lands. He had brought his father's body from burial in a place Montdidier that he had seized unjustly (1212C). On his penitential pilgrimage to Rome in 1076 he had received Gregory's direction that, while doing penance for his sins in the early part of his war with King Philip I, he should resume the governance of his lands under the guidance of Hugh of Die and Hugh of Cluny «until he had renewed peace with the king». He prosecuted his feud against the king until it was victoriously concluded and an assembly of magnates from both sides had established what rightfully belonged to Simon's inheritance. Thus «peace was restored and all things were set in order that had been in disorder during the long period of warfare» (1213C-1214B). That done, Gregory was happy for Simon to enter the monastic order. Gregory's chagrin that Duke Hugh had not taken similar thought for the peace and well being of his lands may have been the greater because Abbot Hugh who admitted him to the cloister had been the pope's agent in duly settling Simon's affairs.

---

24. For Count Guy of Mâcon, see BRUEL, 4, p. 650-1, 770-1, n° 3528, 3610.

25. They are referred to in *The Ecclesiastical History of Orderic Vitalis*, 8.27, éd. M. CHIBNALL, 6 vols., Oxford, 1969-80 (hereafter OV), 4.326-8.

26. A.1088, *PL* 162, 940A-942A, 960D-962B.

While in the world Simon promoted peace and concord by reburying his father in a place that had been rightly his, by ordering his own inheritance, and by winning through to agreement with his king. The pursuit of peace and concord was a prime religious and political aspiration of Gregory and of his contemporaries[27]. A second subject that deserves consideration is how the consequences of Simon's monastic conversion tended to give it political effect. For he became not only a monk and hermit, but a «holy man» from whom everyone, from the pope down to even humble people who everywhere turned to him (at Saint-Oyend : 1217D-1218A ; as a hermit : 1218B-D ; at Compiègne : 1219AB ; upon his former inheritance : 1219C-1220A ; in South Italy : 1221A ; at his funeral in Rome : 1221D), derived benefit. Gregory VII's employment of him to promote peace features in the *Vita*'s presentation of his journey from Rome in 1080 to Robert Guiscard, duke of Apulia. It refers to the pope's long discordance from the duke ; in fact, Roger had been three times excommunicated and Norman depredations upon the lands of St. Peter were a long-standing problem. Without referring either to the context of Gregory's second excommunication of Henry IV of Germany and consequent need to rehabilitate the treaty of Melfi (1059) or to the sequel in the Norman sack of Rome in 1084, the *Vita* exhibits Gregory as dispatching Simon from fear that Rome would suffer from a warfare that was not further defined ; he acted simply to make peace (*pacandi gratia*). Simon's successful negotiations with the duke are similarly regarded (*pacem reformans, omnibus illuc pacificatis*) ; upon returning to Rome Simon informed Gregory about what he had done for the sake of peace (*quidquid egerat de pace*) (1220D-1221B). For the *Vita*, the effect of Simon's journey was to bring about the peace with the Normans that the pope desired. The terms of Robert Guiscard's oath and investiture at Ceprano in June 1080, with their careful stipulation of matters settled and still left open, may well reflect the peace that Simon negotiated[28].

The *Vita* records Simon's dealings with William I of Normandy and England after his monastic conversion in a similar light. While still a hermit in the Jura, he journeyed in Northern France and Normandy, where he found William's eldest son Robert Curthose at war with his father, against whom he had been in rebellion since 1077. Simon contributed to the reconciliation of father and son which occurred by Easter 1080.

---

27. For some remarks on its importance for Gregory's relations with Byzantium, see H.E.J. COWDREY, «The Gregorian Papacy, Byzantium, and the First Crusade», in : *Byzantium and the West c.850-c.1200*, éd. J.D. HOWARD-JOHNSTON, Amsterdam, 1988, pp. 145-69, esp. pp. 153-60. I plan to discuss its significance in the West in my forthcoming study of Gregory.

28. *Reg.* 8.la, b, pp. 514-6, esp. pp. 514/24-515/10, 516/5-10.

The effect of Simon's mediation was, once again, to renew peace and to deliver a province from disorder : *utrique compassus, pace reformata pestilentiae malum a regione fugavit* (1219B-D). While the *Vita* makes no reference to this, Gregory VII himself urgently sought the reconciliation of William and Robert, and warmly applauded its achievement[29].

Simon sought in other ways to resolve French conflicts and feuds. The purpose which led him to France in 1079-80 was a request from Abbot Hugh of Cluny to the abbot of Saint-Oyend that he might go to Philip I's court to reprove the king for having taken away some of his possessions. Simon met the king at Compiègne, where his plea for their restoration was readily granted (1219AB). While Simon was staying at la Ferté, a castle of his sometime inheritance, he successfully obtained the pardon from a penalty of mutilation of a robber who had waylaid one of his former friends and explained his act of forgiveness (1220AB).

The *Vita* also sheds light on how his dealings with Simon both before and after his conversion helped Gregory to maintain the authority at Rome that he was remarkably successful in preserving until 1084, as well as to provide for leading supporters from outside Rome. When Count Simon made his penitential pilgrimage in 1075, his penance was evidently commuted for money or other valuables ; it yielded resources both for Gregory's own purposes and for the maintenance of two unnamed *religiosissimi viri* who were currently in Rome (1213D). Simon's death, which probably fell in the late September of 1081 or 1082, at a time when Rome was increasingly threatened by Henry IV (1221C)[30], provided the occa-

---

29. *Reg.* 7.25-7, pp. 505-8. For further discussion, see H.E.J. COWDREY, «The Gregorian Reform in the Anglo-Norman Lands and in Scandinavia», *Studi Gregoriani*, 13 (1989), 321-52, esp. pp. 336-7. For an act of restitution made by Simon while still count in 1075 to the archbishop of Rouen, see D.R. BATES, «The origins of the Justiciarship», *Proceedings of the Battle Abbey Conference on Anglo-Norman Studies*, 4 (1981), 1-12, at p. 7 and n. 57.

30. Simon's death must have occured before that of Queen Matilda of England (2 Nov. 1083) since the Vita records her sending to Rome the gold and silver to pay for his tomb (1222A) ; in Oct.-Nov. 1083 the situation at Rome would not have permitted his impressive funeral (1221D-1222A, cf. *Reg.* 9.35a, pp. 627-8). 1080 is not impossible, but (i) it would allow Simon only some three months after his return from France and Apulia to re-establish himself in Rome ; (ii) Gregory twice declined his request to return to Saint-Oyend (1221B) ; (iii) according to the Vita the Romans failed for some time duly to value him (1221D). The case for 1081 is stronger than has been appreciated : (i) the Vita places Simon's request to return to the Jura and so the vigil in St. Peter's during which he fell mortally ill not long after his return from Apulia (1221B) ; (ii) the monk who brought safely to Rome Queen Matilda of England's gold and silver for Simon's tomb (1222A) did well whether Simon died in 1081 or 1082. The monk is unlikely to have got to Rome before, at earliest, the Christmas after Simon's death. Henry IV was in the vicinity of Rome from early in 1083 ; though not impossible then, the monk's journey would have been easier a year earlier. Nevertheless, 1082 remains a possibility for Simon's death : (i) the *Vita* was compiled some thirty years afterwards, so that its *nec multo post* (1221B) can conceivably represent two years ; (ii) Simon's death in 1081 would reduce his stay at Rome after his journeys to a brief year and a quarter ; a further year would help to explain the impression that he left as well

sion both for a demonstration of Roman solidarity at his funeral and for a lavish papal distribution of alms to the Roman poor (1221D-1222A). This is excellent evidence for Gregory's methods of financial and social control at Rome.

Gregory's insistence upon the abbot of Saint-Oyend's sending a reluctant Simon to his side at Rome on pain of interdict upon himself and his monks (1220B-D), and his underlying acceptance of Simon's monastic conversion, are the more explicable in the light of Simon's character and services as a «holy man» to himself, to churchmen like Abbot Hugh of Cluny, and to friendly rulers like King William I of England.

A third subject deserving consideration is the effect of Simon's conversion upon the secular politics of his time. Historians have often indicated the course and results of the accumulation and dissolution of the lands of the counts of Crépy-Valois[31]. Although the family could claim Carolingian descent, it was only towards the end of Count Ralph IV's lifetime that his essentially personal agglomeration of power came to comprise seven counties that he held (Amiens, Vexin, Valois, Tardenois, Montdidier, Vitry, and Bar-sur-Aube), seven more from which he received homage (Corbie, Vermandois, Péronne, Meulan, Montfort, Dammartin, and Soissons), and five large advocacies (Saint-Denis, Jumièges, Saint-Wandrille, Saint-Père at Chartres, and Saint-Arnoul at Crépy). The clamp which this set upon the northern part of the Capetian demesne is clear. It is not surprising that, on Ralph's death, King Philip I who was newly married to Bertha of Frisia should have invaded the northern part of Simon's inheritance. By 1077 Simon had wrested back the whole of it and restored relations with the king. But since he left no male heirs, the effect of his monastic conversion was the rapid dispersal of his lands: three of his brothers-in-law were major beneficiaries Count Theobald I of Champagne secured Vitry and Bar, Bartholomew Bardoul and then his son Hugh the southern Barrois, and Count Herbert IV of Vermandois Valois and Montdidier; Philip I acquired the Vexin with the advocacy of Saint-Denis and Corbie; while the bishop of Amiens gained comital rights[32]. A prime political beneficiary was the king, especially by his ac-

---

as the monk Robert's long association (*diu conversatus*) (1222B). 1081 and 1082 are best regarded as equally possible. The *Vita* gives 30 Sept. as the day and month (1221C).

31. Among them, A. FLICHE, *Le Règne de Philippe Ier, roi de France (1060-1108)* (Paris, 1912); FEUCHERE (as n. 16); CHIBNALL, OV 4.xxx-xxxiv; M. BUR, *La formation du comté de Champagne vers 950-vers 1150* (Nancy, 1977), pp. 216-17; BAUTIER (as n. 9).

32. FEUCHERE (as n. 16), pp. 13-15. Simon's apparent lack of concern for the future of his inheritance finds an illuminating parallel in the case of St. Adelelme of La Chaise-Dieu and Burgos: *Vita Adelelmi auctore Rodulfo monacho Casae Dei*, cap. 2, *España Sagrada*, éd. H. FLOREZ, Madrid, 1747, 27.842-4.

quisition of the Vexin, the buffer county that bestrode the River Seine between Normandy and the Capetian demesne. Against the background of this dispersal, some political repercussions of Simon's conversion may be noticed.

As Simon pursued his monastic career, it reinforced his long-standing connections with both King Philip I of France and King William I of England. It is at first sight surprising that the *Vita* should introduce Simon as *regis Francorum primipilus* (1211B). But as his attestations of royal charters make clear, his father had been close to his Capetian suzerain[33]. Philip I quickly restored him to favour after his marriage to Anne of Kiev. From an early age he took Simon to the king's court where he witnessed charters in his father's company[34]. If Philip used Simon's accession to invade the Vexin and to encourage Simon's relative Hugh Bardoul to seize Bar-sur-Aube and Vitry, Simon was able within two years to recapture and pacify all his lands. Simon's monastic conversion took place in an atmosphere of reconciliation and amity that Pope Gregory VII encouraged (1213CD)[35]. As a monk Simon was listened to obediently at the Capetian court when he demanded the righting of the king's wrongs to Abbot Hugh of Cluny (1219AC)[36]. His presence and standing at the Capetian court, which were attested from his boyhood, were thus confirmed after he became a monk.

His connection with the Norman court at Rouen was no less close. It began early in the 1060s, perhaps just before 1063 when Duke William invaded Maine and Count Ralph acquired Amiens and the Vexin. These events brought the two men together, and Ralph sent Simon to be brought up at William's court[37]. The *Vita* several times refers to Simon's time there as a *nutritus*, as well as to his kinship with Duchess Matilda

---

33. For a list of charters in which Ralph is named, see FEUCHERE (as n. 16), p. 37.

34. PROU, p. 7, n° 2 (1060), p. 12, n° 3 (1060), p. 63, n° 22 (1065), p. 66, n° 23 (1065), p. 173, n° 66 (1074).

35. PROU, pp. 229-34, n° 88-90, pp. 268-9, n° 105.

36. According to the *Vita* Simon met the king in his palace at Compiègne, on the River Oise at the northern tip of the royal demesne. Simon had gone to Compiègne incognito to be present at the translation of a prominent relic, Christ's burial shroud, in the church of Saint-Corneille, but was recognized (1219AB). Further light on the occasion is shed by Philip I's charter of 1092 for Saint-Corneille which, evidently looking back to this translation, gives the history of the relic and notes that Queen Matilda of England paid for the costly new reliquary : PROU, pp. 318-21, n° 126.

37. The gap between 1060 and 1065 in Simon's attested presence at the Capetian court (above, n. 34) probably indicates the range of dates within which Simon's period with the duke of Normandy must be set, but it is likely to have begun in the context of the political events in Maine in 1062-3. Count Ralph attended the duke's court at Fécamp at Easter 1067 : OV 4, ed. CHIBNALL, 2.196-9.

(1215BC, 1215D, 1219C, 1222A) ; since Matilda gave lavishly to adorn his tomb, there was manifestly a life-long bond. It is not surprising that, in 1077, William, now king of England, wished to counter Philip I's gathering hostility by making Simon his son-in-law (1215C-1216B)[38]. As a monk, Simon was occasionally active at the Norman court as at the Capetian. His work in reconciling Robert Curthose to his father won the effusive gratitude of the king and queen (1219C-1220A).

To this extent, the monk Simon's continuing prestige at the Capetian and Norman courts served politically Gregory's purpose of promoting peace and concord by fostering just and strong dynasties. It may, however, be doubted whether Gregory understood the political implications of the dissolution of the lands of the counts of Crépy which was the inevitable consequence of the monastic conversion of the childless Simon. The passing of the Vexin to the Capetian king, in particular, contributed to the discord and warfare between him and William I that led to the latter's death in 1087 from an injury sustained during an attack upon Mantes, the capital of the Vexin. But it was not to such political consequences that those who encouraged or approved of Simon's withdrawal from the world primarily looked.

---

38. The difficulties attaching to the marriage negotiations to which the *Vita* refers (1215B-1216A) have been pointed out by F. BARLOW, *William Rufus* (London, 1983), pp. 443-4. It may be added that negociations that the *Vita* may have misdated would be plausible after the death of King Alphonso VI of León-Castille's first wife, Agnes of Aquitaine, on 6 June 1078 : for Alphonso's marriages, see P. DAVID, *Etudes historiques sur la Galice et le Portugal du VIe au XIIe siècle* (Lisbon, 1947), pp. 386-90. Robert Guiscard may have sought a wife for a member of his family rather than for himself.

XII

Pope Gregory VII and La Chaise-Dieu

The history of La Chaise-Dieu (dioc. Clermont) and its monastic congregation began with the foundation of the mother house in 1043 by Robert of Turlande and with its establishment soon after as a Benedictine abbey dedicated to Saint-Vital et Saint-Agricol ; this history was unbroken until the dissolution of the abbey in 1790. In his two studies, Professor Pierre-Roger Gaussin has provided an authoritative and full account of it[1]. The purpose of the present note is to comment upon the significance of La Chaise-Dieu for the late eleventh-century reform papacy particularly under Pope Gregory VII (1073-85), and upon the respects in which the abbey and the papacy impinged upon each other.

La Chaise-Dieu was an early example of the crossing to the north of the Alps of an austere and eremitical style of monasticism which had grown up in Italy under such figures as St Nilus and St Romuald. It was represented in Rome at an early date by such houses as the joint Latin and Greek abbey of SS. Bonifacio e Alessio. Before Gregory became pope, his long career as Hildebrand, a clerk and (since 1058) archdeacon of the Roman church, as well as his own early monastic experience, served to equip him with knowledge of it and to elicit his approval. Two examples are his long association at the Lateran with Peter Damiani, the hermit of Fonte Avellana who from 1057 to 1072 was cardinal-bishop of Ostia, and his admiration for the monks of Vallombrosa. One of his earliest letters as pope was one of condolence to them on the death of their founder, John Gualbertus, whom he had always held in great affection and

---

1 - *L'Abbaye de la Chaise-Dieu (1043-1518)* (Paris, 1962) ; *Huit Siècles d'histoire : l'abbaye de la Chaise-Dieu, 1043-1790* (Brioude, 1967).

whose zeal he urged them to continue. Hildebrand admired Vallombrosa the more because of an incident of 1068 when its monk Peter, later cardinal-bishop of Albano and a staunch Gregorian, exposed the simony of Peter Mezzabarba, bishop of Florence, through an ordeal by fire[2]. Such monasticism was praiseworthy in itself, and for its benefits to a church which was seeking to purge itself from its corruptions.

The early history of La Chaise-Dieu includes a number of occasions when its monks and affairs became conspicious at the Rome of Hildebrand the clerk and archdeacon. The lives of the first and third abbots, Robert of Turlande (1050-67) and Adelelme (1078) provide the principal evidence[3]. Robert's connection was a long one. After a brief stay at Cluny but before founding La Chaise-Dieu, he went to Rome and secured approval «to withdraw from the company of men and build in seclusion a monastery where, wearing the religious habit, he could live the canonical life with one or two others, being professed to God alone»[4]. In May 1052 Bishop Renco of Clermont secured from Pope Leo IX a privilege placing the new abbey under papal protection (*tuitio*) ; according to Robert's biographer, the pope knew of Robert's sanctity and insisted upon his being abbot. Pope Alexander II (1061-73) also issued a privilege for the abbey[5]. While

---

2 - *The Epistolae vagantes of Pope Gregory VII*, ed. and trans. H.E.J. Cowdrey (Oxford, 1972), pp. 4-8, no. 2 ; Andrew of Strumi, *Vita s. Iohannis Gualberti*, caps 61, 74-5, 85, ed. F. Baethgen, *Monumenta Germaniae Historica* [hereafter *MGH*], *Scriptores*, 30/2. 1092, 1095-9, 1102, = *Bibliotheca hagiographica latina*, edd. Socii Bollandiani (2 vols., Brussels, 1898-1901) [hereafter BHL], no. 4397.

3 - The earliest Life of Robert, written soon after his death by Gerard of Laveigne, is lost. It was replaced during the abbacy of Seguin (1078-1094) by a clearer and simpler Life and Miracles composed by Marbod of Rennes: *Acta sanctorum quotquot toto orbe coluntur* (Antwerp, Brussels, and Tongerloo, 1643-) [hereafter *AA.SS.*], Apr. 3.317-26, = *BHL* 7261-2 ; in 1160 a monk of la Chaise-Dieu named Bernard (*recte*: not Bertrand) wrote a new Life and Miracles: *AA.SS.* Apr. 3.326-33, = *BHL* no. 7263. (These Lives are hereafter referred to as Marbod and Bernard respectively.) The principal Life of Adelelme is an early twelfth-cent. work by a monk of la Chaise-Dieu named Ralph: *España Sagrada*, ed. H. Flórez (Madrid, 1747-), 27.841-66, = *BHL* no. 71 ; there is an abbreviation of it: ibid. 27.832-41, = *BHL* no. 72. (These Lives are hereafter referred to as Ralph and Abb. Ralph respectively.)

4 - Marbod, 1.6-7, p. 318DE.

5 - For Leo's privilege, Leo IX, *Ep.* 67, J.P. Migne, *Patrologia latina* [hereafter *PL*], 143.686-7, and for Marbod's account, 4.19, p. 321EF. In Sept. 1052, Abbot Robert secured from King Henry I of France a charter constituting la Chaise-Dieu an abbey and making it spiritually subject to the bishops of Clermont: see *Recueil des actes des ducs de Normandie (911-1066)*, ed. M. Fauroux (Caen, 1961), pp. 297-9, no. <127>. For Alexander II's confirmation, see J. von Pflugk-Harttung, *Iter italicum*

Robert was still abbot, Adelelme made a pilgrimage to Rome which was accompanied by extreme austerities. Meeting Robert on the way at Issoire (Puy-de-Dôme) he declined his suggestion that he should enter La Chaise-Dieu forthwith and first completed his pilgrimage. His fervour is unlikely to have passed unnoticed at Rome[6]. The most momentous happening, although the most problematical for the historian, is reported to have occurred at Rome in 1070 before Pope Alexander II and a company of cardinals ; Hildebrand's presence is not attested but is likely. Robert's chaplain, Gerard of Laveigne, read an account of the abbot's life and miracles ; in response the pope is said to have risen from his seat, blessed France on Robert's account, and declared that he should be commemorated annually among the confessors. Henceforth, Robert's commemoration was made at La Chaise-Dieu, in its houses, and beyond. Whether or not Alexander's words may be regarded as canonization, the main dedication of La Chaise-Dieu became to St Robert, and Popes Gregory VII and Urban II both referred to him with due honour[7]. The seal of liturgical commemoration and papal approval was set on his work. The three abbots who held office during Gregory VII's pontificate had only occasional direct contact with Rome, although all of them acted publicly in ways that were consonant with Gregory's purposes and materially assisted them. They particularly resisted simony. In the

---

(Stuttgart, 1881), p. 195, no. 151 ; A.-C. Chaix de Lavarène, *Monumenta pontificia Arverniae decurrentibus ix°, x°, xi° sœculis* (Clermont-Ferrand, 1880), p. 46, no. 25.

6 - Ralph, cap. 3, pp. 844-7.

7 - Marbod surprisingly does not refer to this happening, although it is recorded by Bernard, 2.5, p. 329C. Bernard's account is to be preferred to the excerpt from a *Chronicon Casae Dei* which is printed in Chaix de Lavarène (as n. 5), p. 46, no. 26, whence E.W. Kemp, *Canonization and Authority in the Western Church* (London, 1948), p. 65 ; the excerpt is from a late seventeenth-cent. history written by Dom C. Estiennot, and is correctly to be found in Paris, Bibliothèque nationale, MS lat. 12745, fo. 9. Unlike Estiennot, Bernard makes no reference to a papal document. Bernard's reference to Alexander's enjoining the observation of Robert's *transitus*, or death, which occurred on 17 Apr., presents a difficulty, for all medieval evidence places his commemoration, as does Estiennot, on 24 Apr., the day of his burial: for these dates, see J. van der Straeten, «Saint Robert de la Chaise-Dieu: sa canonisation, sa date de fête», *Analecta Bollandiana*, 82 (1964), 37-56 ; M. Huglo, «Les livres liturgiques de la Chaise-Dieu», *Revue bénédictine*, 87 (1977), 62-96, 289-348. Van der Straeten questions the appropriateness of speaking of a canonization before 1351 when the sometime monk of la Chaise-Dieu, Pope Clement VI, consecrated a new abbey church. Nevertheless, the cult of St Robert developed immediately and spread rapidly. In 1080 Gregory VII's privilege for la Chaise-Dieu referred to it as the *monasterium sancti Roberti*, and in 1095 Urban II referred to Robert as a source of merits : *Quellen und Forschungen zum Urkunden- und Kanzleiwesen Papst Gregors VII.*, 1: *Quellen: Urkunden. Regesten. Facsimilia*, ed. L. Santifaller, Studi e Testi, 190 (Vatican City, 1957) [hereafter *QF*], pp. 210-12, no. 181 ; Urban II, *Ep.* 149, *PL* 151.424-5.

early 1070s, the see of Clermont fell into the hands of two simoniacal bishops, Stephen V of Polignac (dates unknown) and William of Chamalières (1073-6) ; in 1077 Gregory was belatedly concerned that his legate Bishop Hugh of Die (later archbishop of Lyons) and Abbot Hugh of Cluny should settle its affairs[8]. Hugh of Die had in fact declared the deposition of the two simoniacs in a council at Clermont in the previous year. Abbot Durand of La Chaise-Dieu (1067-78) was chosen to fill the see under coercion by the clergy of Clermont[9]. He retained his abbacy for two years, and ruled as bishop according to the pattern of the reformers until 1095. He died after receiving Pope Urban II to his council at Clermont, and was buried by the pope in the presence of several of his own former monks[10].

The next abbot, Adelelme, ruled only briefly in 1078, but his very important Life shows that, both before and after this date, he, too, lived and acted in ways that were consonant with papal aspirations. A model monk of extreme austerity who attracted many by the fame of his miracles, he was made subdeacon and deacon reluctantly upon Abbot Durand's orders. He quickly learnt that the ordaining bishop, William of Clermont, had, according to his biographer, been interdicted by the pope for his simony. He therefore refused to exercise his orders until Durand made them good after becoming bishop as well as ordaining him priest[11]. Adelelme had already engaged in public preaching at Clermont and had effected the healing and conversion of a clerk who had strongly resisted him ; he had insisted upon his duty of preaching against clerical evils with the claim, «Sinner though I am, I am none the less a minister and preacher of Christ and the apostles»[12]. Adelelme was also novice-master at La Chaise-Dieu[13] ; upon election as abbot in 1078, according to his Life he was diligent in the duties of his office and in almsgiving but he refused its trappings and prestige. Desiring to return to the contemplative life,

---

8 - Hugh of Flavigny, *Chronicon*, 2, ed. G. Pertz, *MGH Scriptores*, 8.417 [hereafter Hugh of Flavigny] ; *Gregorii VII Registrum*, 4.22, ed. E. Caspar, *MGH Epistolae selectae*, 2 (Berlin, 1920-3) [hereafter *Reg.*], p. 333.

9 - Ralph, cap. 8, pp. 852-4.

10 - For Durand in 1095, see A. Becker, *Papst Urban II. 2: Der Papst, die griechische Christenheit und der Kreuzzug*, Schriften der MGH, 19/2 (Stuttgart, 1988), pp. 440-1 ; for Urban's visit to la Chaise-Dieu in the previous Apr., see *ibid.* p. 436.

11 - Ralph, caps 6,8, pp. 850, 852-4.

12 - *Ibid.* cap. 7, pp. 851-2.

13 - Abb. Ralph, cap. 6, p. 835.

he persuaded his monks to accept his resignation[14]. Thereafter, his fame spread far and wide, and particularly to two queens-consort who were concerned to promote religion in their lands. The queen of England to whom Adelelme's Life refers was clearly Matilda, wife of William the Conqueror. She sought healing of her lethargy (*letargia*) through the sending of either a crumb from Adelelme's table or water in which he had washed his hands. He generously sent, not a crumb, but a quarter of a loaf, which served to heal the queen and many in her realm. He thus encouraged a queen whom Gregory VII also regarded highly[15]. The other queen was Constance of Burgundy, niece of Abbot Hugh of Cluny, who in 1079 became the second wife of King Alphonso VI of León-Castile. She sent Adelelme a long letter in which she referred to the diversity of rites in Spain which it was also Gregory's purpose to end, imploring Adelelme to come to Spain and instruct the church. He secured the permission of his abbot, Seguin of Escotay (1078-94), to go to Spain, where his sanctity and miracles led King Alphonso by 1085 to give him the chapel and the abbey of San Juan at Burgos[16]. At the king's capture of Toledo from the Moslems in 1085, Adelelme was reputed, like Moses at the Red Sea, to have given heart to a reluctant Spanish army by leading it upon an ass dryshod across the River Tagus and so ensuring victory[17]. His reputed part in the Reconquest, like his championing of the Latin against the Hispanic rite, furthered Gregory VII's purposes in Spain.

Of Abbot Seguin's active commitment to causes that were shared by the reformed papacy there can be no doubt. He demonstrated this before becoming abbot by his approach, made in concert with a sometime monk of La Chaise-Dieu, Abbot Reginald of Saint-Cyprien, Poitiers, to Archbishop Lanfranc of Canterbury about the eucharistic teachings of Berengar of Tours[18]. Soon after he became abbot, Pope Gregory VII gave him the oversight of the monastery of Frassinoro

14 - Ralph, cap. 9, pp. 854-5.

15 - *Ibid.* cap. 11, pp. 856-7. The queen's resources and the reference to many being healed in her realms point strongly to Matilda.

16 - *Ibid.* caps 12-13, pp. 857-60 ; see also F. Fita, «El concilio nacional de Burgos en 1080. Nuevas ilustraciones», *Boletín de la Real Academia de la Historia*, 49 (1906), 337-84, esp. pp. 375-8, no. 12.

17 - Ralph, caps 13-14, pp. 859-61.

18 - *The Letters of Lanfranc, Archbishop of Canterbury*, edd. and trans. H. Clover and M. Gibson (Oxford, 1979), pp. 142-51, no. 46 ; for Abbot Reginald, see p. 142. In 1080, Gregory gave a charter to Saint-Cyprien, Poitiers, on the same day as his charter for la Chaise-Dieu: *QF* pp. 208-12, nos. 180-1.

(Modena), a foundation of Countess Matilda of Tuscany which she had given to the pope in 1077. According to Hugh of Flavigny, it was under Seguin that an abbot named Pontius was appointed (*ordinatus est*) abbot of Frassinoro by Gregory ; however, in the early 1080s pressure from King Henry IV of Germany made him wish to resign his office. Hugh of Flavigny gives the text of a letter from Gregory's standing legate in North Italy, Bishop Anselm II of Lucca, probably written in 1085/6, chiding Pontius for his lack of fortitude and expressing concern for his salvation, but from charity allowing him to resign. Anselm regarded Pontius as owing his position to the abbot and congregation of La Chaise-Dieu and to Archbishop Hugh of Lyons, and as having Gregory's blessing. He thus implied that all three parties joined in his appointment, and that Gregory had entrusted Frassinoro to La Chaise-Dieu, perhaps during a visit by Abbot Seguin to Rome in 1080 when Gregory issued his charter for La Chaise-Dieu. Anselm of Lucca's concluding injunction to Pontius that he should urge Archbishop Hugh of Lyons to come to the help of Rome, evidently in the dire crisis that followed Gregory's death on 25 May 1085, implies that Pontius would return to Burgundy and thence to the monastery, perhaps La Chaise-Dieu, to which he belonged[19].

Seguin's prolonged association with Hugh of Die/Lyons and other French reforming figures is further attested by his presence at the council that Hugh and Bishop Amatus of Oloron held at Saintes in January 1081. After the council, a charter by which Duke William VI of Aquitaine granted to Abbot Hugh of Cluny, who was also present, the church of Saint-Eutrope at Saintes records Seguin's attendance, as well as that of Abbot Reginald of Saint-Cyprien at Poitiers and of the monk Guy of La Chaise-Dieu, brother of Count William I of Nevers. The papal clerk Teuzo is also named[20].

_____

19 - Hugh of Flavigny, 2, pp. 443-4, cf. *QF* pp. 131-5, no. 130. For the history of Frassinoro and for comment on Anselm of Lucca's letter, see A. Mercati, «Intorno alla storia di Frassinoro», in: *Saggi di storia e letteratura*, 1 (Rome, 1951), pp. 379-402, esp. pp. 382-5. Pope Paschal II's bull of 1107 for la Chaise-Dieu promised its abbot that «in the monastery of Fossinoro which was built by the excellent Countess Matilda and her family and offered to St Peter, the abbot shall always be appointed (*ordinatur*) by your care» : Chaix de Lavarène (as n. 5), p. 128, no. 70. Hugh of Flavigny's use of the same verb in connection with Gregory VII's dealings with Pontius leaves la Chaise-Dieu's rights at Frossinoro c.1080 uncertain in detail.

20 - *Recueil des chartes de l'abbaye de Cluny*, edd. A. Bernard and A. Bruel, 6 vols. (Paris, 1876-1903), 4.715-16, no. 3580.

Apart from its abbots, a number of other figures illustrate ways in which La Chaise-Dieu came to Gregory VII's notice. Perhaps the greatest is Jarento who, having been brought up under Hugh of Cluny's careful eye, became a monk of La Chaise-Dieu (c.1074). In 1075, Hugh of Die conferred upon him the seven grades of holy orders. He quickly rose to be a *magister* and, for three years, prior, until in September 1077 he attended Hugh of Die's council at Autun. He was there designated to be abbot of Saint-Bénigne at Dijon ; after consultation with Abbot Hugh of Cluny, he restored it to the monastic standards of the abbacies of William of Volpiano (989/90-1031) and Halinard (1031-46). He earned from the chronicler Hugh of Flavigny the comment that he was *domno papae per omnia fidelissimus*. At the end of Gregory VII's life he twice served as his legate : in 1084 to Robert Guiscard, duke of Apulia, and later in the year he was a bearer of Gregory's last encyclical from Salerno – nominally to Portugal, though in fact he travelled to Saint-Gilles and Dijon[21].

A second significant figure is Hugh, bishop of Grenoble (1080-1132), whose Life, written by Prior Guigo I of La Grande Chartreuse, is a primary source for the long-term implementation of Gregory VII's reforming purposes in Dauphiné[22]. In February 1080, at a council held by Hugh of Die in Avignon, the canons of Grenoble requested and obtained the choice of the twenty-seven-year-old Hugh to be their bishop (765C-766B). According to Guigo, Hugh refused consecration at the hands of his metropolitan, Archbishop Warmund of Vienne, on account of his simony[23]; he travelled to Rome for consecration by Gregory VII. After his arrival, he was assailed by severe personal temptations and received the pope's careful and close personal advice (766C-767C). In due course, Gregory consecrated him and continued his personal favour, while Countess Matilda of Tuscany gave him his pastoral staff (767D-

---

21 - Hugh of Flavigny, 2, pp. 413, 415-17, 462-5, the citation is from p. 462 ; *Annales sancti Benigni Divionensis*, a. 1077, ed. G. Waitz, *MGH Scriptores*, 5.42.

22 - Guigo, *Vita sancti Hugonis Gratianopolitani episcopi*, PL 153.761-784, = *BHL* no. 4015. (References in the text of this and the next paragraphs are to columns in *PL*.) For Hugh of Grenoble, see H.E.J. Cowdrey, «Hugh of Avalon, Carthusian and Bishop», in: *De Cella in Seculum. Religious and Secular Life and Devotion in Late Medieval England*, ed. M.G. Sargent (Cambridge, 1989), pp. 41-57, esp. pp. 48-9.

23 - The allegation of simony is improbable: see N. Huyghebaert, «Un légat de Grégoire VII en Flandre, Warmond de Vienne», *Revue d'histoire ecclésiastique*, 40 (1944-5), 187-200.

768A). Upon returning to Grenoble, Hugh found the clergy and people riddled with abuses in the eyes of Gregorian reformers, especially clerical marriage, simony, and the wasting of church goods ; his endeavours at redress proved ineffectual (768A-C). Less than two years after being consecrated, he became a monk at La Chaise-Dieu and completed his year's noviciate. Under command by Gregory VII, he then returned to his diocese where for forty years he maintained the zealous and effective rule that, in Guigo's view, made him a model bishop (768D-769B) to whom Countess Matilda continued to look for counsel and intercession (768A). Apart from the command to return to his diocese, there is no indication of Gregory's reaction to Hugh's year-long retreat into the cloister at La Chaise-Dieu. But the record of his early temptations and of his future stature as a bishop and saint make it probable that Gregory would have seen it as a salutary experience which, since his command to return to Grenoble was obeyed, reflected well on La Chaise-Dieu.

La Chaise-Dieu also has its small place in the Life of Count Simon of Crépy which, in general, offers revealing parallels with the careers of figures at La Chaise-Dieu and especially St Adelelme[24]. Simon's progress from being a powerful and militarily successful lay prince to being an austere monk and hermit had Gregory's approval, for he summoned him to practise the eremitical life at Rome. His monastery was another strict community, that of Saint-Oyend (Jura). But when, before entering it, he and Judith, daughter of Count Robert II of Auvergne, to whom he had been betrothed, agreed to renounce marriage, she and two of her family took vows at La Chaise-Dieu (1214CD). Her male companions, Adalbert who later became abbot of Bourg-Dieu at Déols and archbishop of Bourges, and the exemplary monk Garnier of Montmorillon, remained at La Chaise-Dieu while Judith entered its house for women at Comps (later Lavaudieu) which Robert of Turlande had founded. Gregory's close knowledge of Simon's career and approval of his monastic conversion may well have extended to his sometime betrothed and her profession at La Chaise-Dieu.

---

24 - *Vita beati Simonis comitis Crespeiensis auctore synchrono*, PL 156.1211-24, = *BHL* 7757 ; on Simon, see H.E.J. Cowdrey, «Count Simon of Crépy's Monastic Conversion», forthcoming.

The character of the monasticism of La Chaise-Dieu, the reforming zeal which it radiated, and the place of its abbots and monks,
both present and erstwhile, in the network of friends and agents of
Gregory VII like Hugh of Die/Lyons, Amatus of Oloron, Hugh of
Cluny, and Matilda of Tuscany, are all considerations that may have
disposed Gregory VII in its favour.

So far as Gregory's own privileges and letters are concerned, his
three references to La Chaise-Dieu date from the early 1080s and
therefore from the time of Abbot Seguin. They indicate something of
the nature and limitations of Gregory's awareness of it. His charter of
27 March 1080 largely followed lines which, especially so far as its
arenga is concerned, often recur throughout his pontificate[25]; to this
extent, it does not indicate that he had a special view of or regard for
it. Nevertheless, the text shows two significant peculiarities. One is
that Gregory expressly confirmed La Chaise-Dieu's possession of the
abbeys of Saint-Michel at Gaillac (dioc. Albi) and Saint-Théodard at
Montauriol (dioc. Cahors). These abbeys had been given to it in 1079
by Counts William of Toulouse and Raymond of Saint-Gilles. The
phrase *confirmamus praefato monasterio vestro* strongly suggests
that Abbot Seguin was present at Rome. Gregory's confirmation of
these abbeys also suggests that he valued the advance of La Chaise-
Dieu to greater consequence in the region of the Rivers Lot and Tarn.
The second peculiarity concerns the special provision that Gregory
made for the defence of La Chaise-Dieu itself against outside interference. He particularly noticed the claims of the clergy of Clermont to
take part in abbatial elections as well as to a place and society with the
monks in their choir and dormitory at certain festivals. Such claims
may have gathered during Seguin's two-year simultaneous tenure of
the abbacy of La Chaise-Dieu and the see of Clermont (1076-8). They
may have been grounded in the phrase of King Henry I's charter of
1052, if correctly transmitted, that La Chaise-Dieu was subject to the
church of Clermont (*ecclesieque Arvernensi subdidimus*)[26]. In any
case, Gregory made no reference to or borrowing from the papal and
royal charters of 1052. He absolutely prohibited such interference as
the clergy of Clermont had engaged in, and provided that La Chaise-
Dieu should enjoy the security and peace that he and his predecessors

---

25 - *QF* pp. 210-12, no. 181, see *Liber diurnus. Studien und Forschungen von Leo
Santifaller*, ed. H. Zimmermann, Päpste und Papsttum, 10 (Stuttgart, 1976), p. 138,
cf. pp. 136-7.

26 - Fauroux, *Recueil* (as n. 5), p. 298.

had granted in their privileges for Cluny and other observant monasteries. Gregory's charter of 1080 followed hard upon his eulogy of Cluny's liberty at his Lent council of that year[27]. By this yardstick, the significance of the reference to Cluny should not be exaggerated. Gregory gave La Chaise-Dieu no such liberty as Cluny enjoyed, nor did he seek to reproduce Cluny's status as he sought at about this time to do in the cases of Saint-Victor at Marseilles, Allerheiligen at Schaffhausen, and Santos Facundo y Primitivo at Sahagún[28]. Nevertheless, at a time when Gregory was pressing Cluny's liberty, his reference to it suggests that he regarded La Chaise-Dieu as having special distinction as a monastic community for the example that it set to surrounding churches, and for services that it could render to him and to the apostolic see.

This finds some confirmation in his reference to it in a letter to Archbishop Manasses of Reims dated 17 April 1080. Gregory offered Manasses a final chance of purging his offences upon terms which included his temporary withdrawal from his see either to Cluny or La Chaise-Dieu, where he was to live devoutly at his own expense with only one clerical and two lay attendants[29]. Gregory evidently regarded the two abbeys as being equally suitable for the archbishop's penitential exile and retreat. A letter of 1082/3, however, makes clear the limitations of his horizons so far as La Chaise-Dieu was concerned. Writing to his standing legate Archbishop Hugh of Lyons, he raised the case of an unnamed abbot whom Hugh had placed under interdict for his failure to appear before him when summoned for the settlement of a dispute with Abbot Seguin. The abbot had gone to Rome and had claimed that the disorder of local society had prevented him from coming. Gregory wrote that because he lacked knowledge of the case and would not pass judgement in the absence of either party, he remitted the case for Hugh's decision. At the same time, he pressed for mercy towards the unnamed abbot and also for the raising of the interdict[30]. The letter is significant as evidence for Archbishop Hugh's actions in support of La Chaise-Dieu, but also for the pope's lack of detailed knowledge about the abbey and its affairs.

---

27 - Cowdrey, *Epistolae vagantes* (as n. 2), pp. 96-9 ; for Gregory's privilege, *QF* pp. 95-100, no. 107.

28 - Saint-Victor : *Reg.* 7.8, 2 Nov. 1079, pp. 469-70 ; Schaffhausen: *Reg.* 7.24, 8 May 1080, pp. 502-5 ; Sahagún: *QF* pp. 243-6, no. 208, 1083.

29 - *Reg.* 7.20, pp. 495-6.

30 - *Reg.* 9.19, p. 599.

The sources for an appreciation of Gregory VII's attitude to and dealings with La Chaise-Dieu are thus meagre. They must be interpreted in the light of its exemplary if very austere practice of the monastic life, of its strong and outward-looking zeal for reform in other monasteries and in the secular churches where its houses were to be found, and its active collaboration with several of Gregory's leading friends and agents. He seems to have appreciated its character, and his charter of 1080 marked his approval. It was to hand and serviceable. Yet Gregory's knowledge of it and its region was limited. As was not infrequently the case, he did not bring to La Chaise-Dieu a cut-and-dried programme to which he secured the obedience and collaboration of a well-informed monastic body. Rather, a strongly self-motivated and upwards thrusting centre of monastic reform answered to Gregory's own zeal and aspirations in so far as they percolated to it. Gregory used it as and when he could, to his considerable advantage. What he knew of it he seems warmly to have approved, and the services that he gained he seems strongly to have valued.

XIII

Legal Problems Raised by Agreements of Confraternity *)

Agreements of confraternity survive in great numbers from the medieval centuries. They were usually concluded between two religious communities, although on occasion they were settled by a group of religious superiors who bound their houses by them [1]; and others were made between religious communities and individual persons [2]. In each case they provided written guarantees of benefits, spiritual and/or material. Their long history was foreshadowed in the age of Bede, but it is from Carolingian times that the earliest surviving agreements come [3]. Their apogee was from the late eleventh

---

*) I am most grateful to Mr. Karl Leyser for drawing my attention to the material regarding Osnabrück and Reading which is discussed in this paper, and to Dr. Pierre Chaplais for allowing me to consult him about papal documents. Dr. Henry Mayr–Harting read and commented upon a draft of the whole paper; I warmly acknowledge his great kindness.

[1] Agreements of confraternity, many of them unpublished, are to be found with especial frequency on vacant folios of necrologies, e.g. of Saint–Remy, Reims, now Reims, Bibl. Mun. ms. 346, a few examples being printed by JEAN LECLERCQ, Documents sur la mort des moines (Revue Mabillon 45, 1955, pp. 165–180; 46, 1956, pp. 65–81) 46, pp. 66–70; and of Saint–Bénigne, Dijon, now Dijon, Bibl. Mun. ms. 634, and Troyes, Bibl. Mun. ms. 210. Some examples of agreements among abbots and bishops are: Attigny (762): MGH Conc. 2,1, no. 13, pp. 72f.; see KARL SCHMID – OTTO GERHARD OEXLE, Voraussetzungen und Wirkung des Gebetsbundes von Attigny (Francia 2, 1974, pp. 71–122); Dingolfing (c.770): MGH Conc. 2,1, no. 15B, pp. 96f., followed by another Bavarian agreement in 805: ibid. no. 31, p. 233; Regensburg (932): GIOVANNI DOMENICO MANSI, Sacrorum conciliorum nova et amplissima collectio, 31 vols., Florence–Venice 1759–1798, 18, cols. 365f.; Dortmund (1005), naming only bishops: MGH Const. 1, no. 28, p. 58; an English agreement of c.1010–20: Liber vitae. Register and Martyrology of New Minster and Hyde Abbey, Winchester, ed. WALTER DE GRAY BIRCH (Hampshire Record Society 1892) n. 1, p. 47, ROBERT BROTANEK, Texte und Untersuchungen zur altenglischen Literatur und Kirchengeschichte, Halle an der Saale 1913, pp. 27f., 36, 128–134, and MAX FÖRSTER, Die altenglischen Texte der Pariser Natio-nalbibliothek (Englische Studien 62, 1926/27, pp. 112–131) pp. 123ff.; Bishop Wulfstan of Worcester, six abbots, and the dean (i.e. prior) of Worcester (1077): BENJAMIN THORPE, Diplomatarium anglicum aevi Saxonici, London 1865, pp. 615ff., and Historia et cartularium monasterii sancti Petri Gloucestriae, 3 vols., ed. WILLIAM HENRY HART (Rolls Series, London 1863–1867) 3, pp. XVIIIff.; Reims (1131): AUGUSTE MOLINIER, Les Obituaires français au moyen âge, Paris 1890, no. 2, pp. 288f.,; URSMER BERLIÈRE, Les chapitres généraux de l'ordre de S. Benoît avant le IVe concile du Latran (1215) (Revue Bénédictine 8, 1891, pp. 255–264) pp. 260f.

[2] For reasons of space I have not commented, save exceptionally, on agreements with individuals. For a recent discussion, see HEINRICH DORMEIER, Montecassino und die Laien im 11. und 12. Jahrhundert (Schriften der MGH 27) Stuttgart 1979, pp. 107–198.

[3] For Bede see the Prologue to his Vita Cuthberti, ed. BERTRAM COLGRAVE, Two Lives of St. Cuthbert, Cambridge 1940, pp. 146, 342, and Historia abbatum, cap. 7, ed. CHARLES PLUMMER, Venerabilis Baedae opera historica, 2 vols., Oxford 1896, 1, p. 370. Early Carolingian agreements are to be found in the correspondence of Boniface, Lul, and Alcuin: MGH Epp. sel. 1, and MGH Epp. 2; the relevant items are listed by KARL SCHMID – JOACHIM WOLLASCH, Die Gemeinschaft der Lebenden und Verstorbenen in Zeugnissen des Mittelalters (Früh-

until the thirteenth centuries. Especially as between communities and individuals they continued to be made throughout the middle ages; but a number of factors, including their multiplication, led to their decline[4]. The earliest agreements conferred purely spiritual benefits, guaranteeing intercessory support in life and after death. St. Boniface gave classic statement to their ultimate object in a letter of 750/54 to Abbot Optatus of Montecassino: it was the establishment of a unity of faith and good works (*ut una sit inter nos et fides mentium et pietas actionum*), through which the bond of brotherly love (*familiaritas fraternae caritatis*) should prevail. To promote it there should be an exchange of prayers for the living, and for the departed prayers and masses initiated by the communication, when appropriate, of names[5].

As such exchanges multiplied, monasteries compiled books in which names were permanently recorded. Although the distinction is not absolute, these books were of two kinds: Libri vitae (Libri memoriales, Libri confraternitatum) in which were inscribed often in groups the names of living and/or dead, and which were placed upon the altar during mass; and Necrologies, in which names were individually entered according to the day of the year, and which were read in chapter[6]. Necrologies commonly formed part of a codex which included the Martyrology and the Rule of St. Benedict; such codices were sometimes referred to as a whole by these names (Martyrologia, Regulae). From St. Boniface's day Mortuary Rolls circulated to ensure that entries were duly made in Libri vitae and Necrologies. They informed other houses of the death of monks for whom their monasteries desired prayers, whether or not agreements of confraternity were in existence[7].

Such agreements are to be studied in the light of all the sources which illustrate the working of monastic confraternity. So, too, the institution of confraternity itself, as a participation in the community of the living and the dead which built upon the monastic round of prayers and alms, must be set in the context of the many other institutions which resembled it and exchanged characteristics with it[8]. Most nearly related were the religious confraternities of a more structured kind, having their own meetings, statutes, and ob-

---

mittelalterliche Studien 1, 1967, pp. 365–405) pp. 370f. For a discussion of Carolingian evidence see ADALBERT EBNER, Die klösterlichen Gebets–Verbrüderungen bis zum Ausgange des karolingischen Zeitalters, Regensburg 1890, pp. 35–82; see also JEAN MABILLON, Acta sanctorum ordinis sancti Benedicti saec. 3, pars 1, Paris 1672, pp. LXXVI–LXXX, and PHILIBERT SCHMITZ, Histoire de l'ordre de saint Benoît, 7 vols., 2nd ed. of 1–2, Maredsous 1948–1956, 1, pp. 323–328.

[4] MOLINIER (as n. 1) pp. 133–150.

[5] MGH Epp. sel. 1, no. 106, pp. 231f.

[6] The model edition of a Liber vitae is that of Remiremont, edd. EDUARD HLAWITSCHKA – KARL SCHMID – GERD TELLENBACH (MGH Libri mem. 1) Dublin – Zürich 1970. For other German examples see MGH Libri confr., and for Necrologies MGH Necr. Germ. 1–5. The surviving English Libri vitae are Liber vitae ecclesiae Dunelmensis, ed. JOSEPH STEVENSON (Surtees Society 13, 1841), facsimile edn. by ALEXANDER HAMILTON THOMPSON, 1 (ibid. 136, 1923), and Liber vitae. Register and Martyrology of New Minster and Hyde Abbey, Winchester (as n. 1).

[7] LECLERCQ (as n. 1) pp. 173–180, and LÉOPOLD DELISLE, Rouleaux des morts du IXᵉ au XVᵉ siècle (Société de l'histoire de France) Paris 1866. For a formulary from St. Boniface's time see MGH Eppl. sel. 1, no. 150, pp. 288f.

[8] The point is importantly made by SCHMID (as n. 1) pp. 80ff.; also by JOACHIM WOLLASCH, Gemeinschaftsbewußtsein und soziale Leistung im Mittelalter (Frühmittelalterliche Studien 9, 1975, pp. 268–286).

servances both pious and social, which sometimes centred upon monasteries [9]. Such confraternities in their turn resemble the protective and trade guilds which everywhere proliferated, and which often added a religious dimension to their secular purpose. Ecclesiastical councils and synods like that of Regensburg (932) which were the occasion of agreements of confraternity sometimes drew them up following agenda of legislation and of the appeasement of local strife [10]. Such manifestations of *fraternae caritatis amor* had much in common with the Peace and Truce of God whose assemblies bound men together, often under the auspices of such monasteries as Saint–Martial, Limoges, in seeking the welfare of Christian society [11]. These institutions extended far outside the cloister; within it the liturgical Clamor is a reminder that monasteries exercised a power to curse their enemies which was the counterpart of the confraternity through which they blessed their friends [12]. On the other hand, the *caritas*–Lieder with such refrains as *Ubi caritas est vera, Deus ibi est* led men's minds from the thought of *caritas* to those of order and social harmony:

Nam ut caritas coniungit et absentes,
Sic discordia seiungit et praesentes.
Unum omnes indivise sentiamus,
Ne et simul congregati dividamur [13].

A strong impulse led from *caritas* as the bond of Christian society towards the formation of a variety of institutions of which monastic confraternity was only one.

The purpose of this paper is to define and to discuss the legal problems raised by agreements of confraternity up to the high point of their development in the early thirteenth century [14]. Evidence must be mainly drawn

---

[9] See especially GILLES GÉRARD MEERSSEMAN, Ordo fraternitatis. Confraternite e pietà dei laici nel medioevo (Italia sacra 24–26) Rome 1977, pp. 13ff., 68–94. For the association with Saint–Évroul of *quaedam fraternitatis que vulgo dicitur frarria* see JEAN LAPORTE, Tableau des services obituaires assurés par les abbayes de Saint–Évroul et de Jumièges (XIIᵉ et XIVᵉ siècles) (Revue Mabillon 46, 1956, pp. 141–155, 169–188) p. 181.

[10] As above n. 1.

[11] HERBERT EDWARD JOHN COWDREY, The Peace and the Truce of God (Past and Present 46, 1970, pp. 42–67).

[12] LESTER K. LITTLE, La morphologie des malédictions monastiques (Annales 34, 1979, pp. 43–60).

[13] BERNHARD BISCHOFF, Caritas–Lieder (DERS., Mittelalterliche Studien, 2 vols., Stuttgart 1967, 2, pp. 56–77). For the citations see MGH Poetae latini aevi Carolini 4, no. 27, pp. 526–529.

[14] For confraternity and related matters see especially ACHILLE LUCHAIRE, Manuel des institutions françaises: période des capétiens directs, Paris 1892, pp. 98f., 116; DAVID KNOWLES, The Monastic Order in England, 2nd edn., Cambridge 1963, pp. 472–479; GERD TELLENBACH, Liturgische Gedenkbücher als historische Quellen (Mélanges Eugène Tisserant, vol. 5 [Studi e testi 235] Vatican City 1964, pp. 389–399); KARL SCHMID – JOACHIM WOLLASCH (as. n. 3); JOACHIM WOLLASCH, Mönchtum des Mittelalters zwischen Kirche und Welt (Münstersche Mittelalter–Schriften 7) Munich 1973; KARL SCHMID – JOACHIM WOLLASCH, Societas et Fraternitas. Begründung eines kommentierten Quellenwerkes zur Erforschung der Personen und Personengruppen des Mittelalters (Frühmittelalterliche Studien 9, 1975, pp. 1–48); JOACHIM WOLLASCH (as n. 8); OTTO GERHARD OEXLE, Memoria und Memorialüberlieferung im früheren Mittelalter (Frühmittelalterliche Studien 10, 1976, pp. 70–95); JOCHIM WOLLASCH, Les obituaires, témoins de la vie clunisienne (Cahiers de civilisation médiévale 22, 1979, pp. 139–171); The principal discussions of legal problems are URSMER BERLIÈRE, Les fraternités monastiques et leur rôle juridique (Académie royale de Belgique, Classe des lettres, Mémoires, 2ᵉ sér., 11, 1926, pp. 1–20), and RAPHAEL MOLITOR, Aus der Rechtsgeschichte benediktinischer Verbände, 3 vols., Münster 1928–1933, 1. pp. 55–58.

XIII

from the texts of such agreements themselves; for although other sources set them in their context, they seldom shed light upon their working. For example, although some sets of monastic Customs have sections on confraternity, they say little about formal agreements of confraternity as distinct from the manner in which individual monks, secular clergy, and laity were admitted to confraternity in chapter [15].

Agreements of confraternity were guarantees of brotherly aid. The earliest, and perhaps a majority, of them provided exclusively for spiritual benefits; these represent what is usually called their pure form. An example is this twelfth–century agreement between Saint–Remy, Reims, and Gorze:

> ‚This is the association (*societas*) between the church of Saint–Remy and the monastery of Gorze which their two abbots – namely Odo and Wigric – have established by common consent in the chapter of Saint–Remy. When the death of brothers of either place becomes known by Mortuary Roll or messenger, three offices shall be publicly performed for them in turn by each community, and they shall thereafter be sharers in all offices which are performed for the salvation of the souls of the faithful. When an abbot of either house departs this present life his name shall be noted in the Martyrology of either church, and in the same way a trental shall be appointed for him. The brothers of these churches are and will be sharers by faithful devotion in all the benefits that they perform for each other.‘ [16].

The problem arises whether the contractual form of such agreements indicates that they should be understood to have given rise to obligations having any degree of legal force. It is doubtful whether they did. For by origin they had the character of an exchange of gifts [17]. This point was made in the preamble to an agreement of 838 between the monasteries of Saint–Remy and Saint–Denis [18]. It declared that secular men showed mutual regard by the exchange of material gifts. Being vowed to poverty monks could make no such gifts; but they could exchange *potiora et precelsiora caritatis munera* – the service of mutual intercession. They proved thereby that they were disciples of Christ who said that *in hoc cognoscent omnes, quia mei discipuli estis, si dilectionem ad invicem habueritis* (John 13:35). It would be inappropriate for spiritual even more than for temporal gifts to be subject to legal sanction or to be deemed to create legal obligations. Therefore formularies reiterated that their basis was *consuetudo* [19]. Similarly, in England the *Regularis concordia* regarded a monastery having confraternity with another as being, in the sense of the Rule of St. Benedict, cap. 61, well known

---

[15] The evidence in Custumals is summarized by SCHMID – WOLLASCH (as n. 14) p. 6, n. 15.

[16] Reims, Bibl. Mun. ms. 346, fol. 197r; LECLERQ (as n. 1) pp. 69f. Odo was abbot of Saint–Remy from 1118 to 1151; Wigric was abbot of Gorze from c.1132 to c.1150.

[17] BERLIÈRE (as n. 14) p. 11 regarded agreements of confraternity up to the twelfth century as based on ‚un acte de charité réciproque‘.

[18] MOLINIER (as n. 1) no. 1, pp. 285–288. Cf. how in 908 the monks of St. Gall repaid the material gifts of Bishop Adalbero of Augsburg by promising liturgical commemorations of himself and his successors: MGH Libri confr., no. (6), pp. 137f.; there are similar exchanges in several of the agreements on pp. 136–142: see nos. (5), (8), (9), (11). For the significance of prayers as gifts see OEXLE (as n. 14) pp. 87–95.

[19] Formulae Salicae Merkelianae, no. 60, Formulae Alsaticae, no. 7, Formulae Augienses, no. 21, Formulae extravagantes, nos. 34f. (MGH Formulae, pp. 261, 331, 347, 571).

(*notus*) to it [20]: the houses were bound by a degree of confidence which rendered legal sanctions irrelevant.

That there was an ever present danger of the lapse of agreements of spiritual confraternity through carelessness or through time and distance is at once a consequence and a confirmation of their basis in brotherly love and not in law [21]. Some did lapse and had to be re-negotiated [22]; while a conscientious abbot might journey to a confederate house in order to renew their agreement [23]. The reforming abbots of late eleventh–century Germany were particularly zealous to ensure by every device of confirmation that agreements should be made permanently secure [24]. In the twelfth century other means were employed to keep them in mind. At Saint–Remy, Reims, provision was occasionally made for the reciprocal keeping of patronal festivals [25]. The exchange of relics was also negotiated to ensure perpetual remembrance [26]. It was by such means, and not by legal sanctions, that the permanence of confraternity was sought.

By the twelfth century the maintenance of agreements cannot have been made easier by the variety of spiritual benefits that was often prescribed in different houses [27], or by the practice whereby public offices performed by a community upon hearing of an obituary were supplemented by the private masses of priest-monks and by the recitation of psalms by individual lay

[20] Regularis concordia Anglicae nationis monachorum sanctimonialiumque, cap. 68, ed. THOMAS SYMONS, London, etc. 1953, p. 67, cf. p. 6.

[21] Thus an early ninth–century Reichenau formula requested the regular sending of names by a negligent partner; MGH Formulae, no. 2, p. 365.

[22] Like that between Prüm and Stavelot, renewed in 1187: Recueil des chartes de l'abbaye de Stavelot-Malmédy, edd. JOSEPH HALKIN – C.-G. ROLAND, 2 vols., Académie royale de Belgique 1909–1930, 1, no. 274, pp. 515f. The arrival of a Mortuary Roll might serve as a reminder, as did the coming to Westminster in 1122 of Abbot Vitalis of Savigny's: JOSEPH ARMITAGE ROBINSON, Gilbert Crispin Abbot of Westminster, Cambridge 1911, p. 27.

[23] Thus in 1155 the abbot of Reichenau travelled to St. Gall *pro renovanda fraternitate et pro cogitanda utriusque loci utilitate*: MGH Libri confr., no. (15), pp. 142f.

[24] See especially the agreements between Hirsau, St. Blasien, and Muri (1086/91), Hirsau and All Saints', Schaffhausen (1083/91) and Cluny and St. Blasien (1093/4): JOACHIM WOLLASCH, Muri und St. Blasien. Perspektiven schwäbischen Mönchtums in der Reform (Deutsches Archiv 17, 1961, pp. 420–446) pp. 444ff.; and those between All Saints' Schaffhausen and Petershausen (1086/93), and Reichenau and St. Blasien (late eleventh cent.): DIETER GEUENICH, Verbrüderungsverträge als Zeugnisse der monastischen Reform des 11. Jahrhunderts in Schwaben (Zeitschrift für die Geschichte des Oberrheins 123, 1975, pp. 17–30) pp. 18, 23.

[25] With Worcester it agreed upon the mutual commemoration of St. Remigius and St. Oswald: record of an agreement of 1118/24, The Cartulary of Worcester Cathedral Priory (Register I), ed. REGINALD R. DARLINGTON (Pipe Roll Society, New Series 38) London 1968 for 1962/63, no. 302, p. 159; and with Montierender of St. Remigius and St. Bercarius: Reims, Bibl. Mun. ms. 346, fol. 211v (from the time of Abbot Guy of Saint-Remy [?1206–12] and Abbot Aucherius of Montierender [c.1203–c.1208]).

[26] As in the agreement of 1177/1203 between Michaelsberg, Bamberg and Melk: IGNAZ F. KEIBLINGER, Geschichte des Benediktiner-Stiftes Melk, 2 vols., Vienna 1867–1869, 1, pp. 1136f., cited by WOLLASCH (as n. 14) p. 120, n. 363, and in that of 1208 between Saint-Remy, Reims and Saint-Remy, Sens (Reims, Bibl. Mun. ms 346, fol. 211v): *Et ne processu temporis societas ista dissolvi valeat, in memoriam et monimentum mutui federis partem reliquiarum nostrarum abbati et sociis eius qui huius rei causa venerant liberaliter contulimus – digitum videlicet beati Remigii prope beati Hilarii cum aliis reliquiis*.

[27] Some particularly full examples are Rochester Cathedral Priory: Textus Roffensis, cap. 214, ed. THOMAS HEARNE, Oxford 1720, pp. 231–234, and ed. PETER H. SAWYER, 2 vols., Copenhagen 1962, fols. 222r–223v; and Saint-Évroul: LAPORTE (as n. 9) pp. 169–187.

brothers. At St. Swithun's, Winchester (the cathedral priory) steps were taken to reduce the complexity and burden of corporate and individual observance, and to guarantee the performance of offices for very distant monasteries. A division was made between benefits for monasteries *infra Angliam* which were performed promptly upon the reading in chapter of a deceased *confrater*'s Mortuary Roll, and for monasteries *extra Angliam* which were performed for all the departed in the first weeks of Advent and Lent while only bishops and abbots were recorded individually in Necrologies [28]. Such general commemorations were not infrequent between distant houses [29]. They illustrate how agreements of confraternity were managed by practical adjustment in the light of convenience and not by legal means.

The agreements of confraternity which have hitherto been considered have mainly been ‚pure' agreements promising only spiritual benefits. But there were also many ‚mixed' agreements which also named some or others of a wide range of temporal benefits; while a small number exchanged these alone [30]. The principal terms of temporal benefit may be classified as follows: [31]:

    I. Many of the most important and frequent were concerned with the relief of internal conflict within monasteries.

        1. Individual monks had a right of recourse to an associated house, if for some transgression they were expelled from their own [32] or if they

---

[28] Details are set out in the priory's cartulary, London, Brit. Libr. ms. Addit. 29436, fols. 44v–45r, partly printed in Register and Martyrology of New Minster (as n. 1) p. 47, no. 1; cf. the Christ Church, Canterbury, observances in London, Brit. Libr. ms. Cotton Claudius C VI, fols. 171r–172v, and those of St. Mary's Abbey, York, in London, Brit. Libr. ms. Addit. 38816, fols. 37r–39r, printed by JANET BURTON, A Confraternity List from St. Mary's Abbey, York (Revue Bénédictine 89, 1979, pp. 325–333) pp. 330–333.

[29] Thus because of hazards of communication (*quia vero difficile brevia hinc inde transire possunt*) Saint–Remy, Reims, and Saint–Gilles mutually commemorated their departed on the day after the octave of All Saints: Reims, Bibl. Mun. ms. 346, fol. 190r, LECLERQ (as. n. 1) pp. 67f. (1151/62). CLuny and Mont–Saint–Michel agreed to do likewise at Michaelmas, following a visit to the latter in 1172 by Abbot Stephan I. of Cluny: Chronique de Robert de Torigni, ed. LÉOPOLD DELISLE (Société de l'histoire de Normandie) 2 vols., 1872–1873, 2, pp. 294f., no. 30. For Saint–Bénigne, Dijon, see Dijon, Bibl. Mun. ms. 634, fol. 124v, and Troyes, Bibl. Mun. ms. 210, fol. 116v.

[30] E.g. the agreement of 1070 between the canons of Pibrac and of Brioude, which was nevertheless concluded *ut ipsi communicata fraternitate in Christo unanimes essent, et Deus esset omnia in omnibus*: Gallia Christiania 2, instr., no. 5, cols. 131f.; and that of 1161 between the abbey of Tréport and the canons regular of Eu: Cartulaire de l'abbaye de Saint–Michel de Tréport, ed. PIERRE-PAUL LAFFLEUR DE KERMAINGANT, Paris 1880, no. 27, pp. 57ff.

[31] Cf. BERLIÈRE (as n. 14) pp. 17–26, and MOLITOR (as n. 14) 1, pp. 56f.; Berlière, however, includes material from the later middle ages and shows the increasing complexity of later agreements. It should be remembered that in practice the benefits were sometimes less clearly distinguished from each other than an analysis may suggest.

[32] *Demum almificam dilectionem vestram petimus, ut si quislibet nostrorum vitio suo lapsus abiectusve fuerit, a vobis recipiatur, nec aliorsum eat, quousque satisfactione acta, spreto vitio, aut recipiatur aut certe iudicio vestro quid agendum sit decernatur*: agreement between Flavigny and Saint–Martin, Autun (894): CHARLES DU CANGE, Glossarium mediae et infimae Latinitatis, new edn. by LÉOPOLD FAVRE, 10 vols. Niort/London 1884–1887, 3, p. 598, s.v. 3. Fraternitatis; *... si, quod absit et nonnumquam accidere solet, frater ab altero locorum istorum pro re qualibet remotus fuerit, ad alterum in tali casu transmigrare possit ac ianuam patentem, locum, prebendam et omnem humanitatem fraternitatis in vinculo pacis paratum inveniat, remoto omni scrupulo contradictionis; quod si dilectionis et societatis causa illuc morari in loco venerit et rogaverit, non negabitur ipsi, per quantum tempus voluerit*: agreement between Stavelot and Cornelimünster (1174/92), Recueil des chartes de l'abbaye de Stavelot-Malmédy (as n. 22) 1, n. 278, p. 521.

fled without licence [33]. Exceptions were made against those guilty of the gravest offences [34]. But in cases of lesser faults monks were to be well received; they were assured food and clothing, and a place in chapter and at community offices [35]. They might be called upon to express and carry out an intention of amendment [36]. The term of their stay was variously defined: for as long as they wished, or until they repented, or until they were reconciled, or in one case for eight days only [37].

2. Superiors might send monks to another monastery for custody or residence [38].

3. When a monk fled to another house its abbot might have a duty to

---

[33] In the 980s the Old and New Minsters at Winchester agreed, following a monk's illicit pilgrimage, that ,if any priest should misconduct himself in either minster, he would go no whither but would seek his neighbours and they would mediate for him': Register and Martyrology of New Minster (as n. 1) pp. 96–100; *Et si forte aliquis instinctu diabolico et propriae voluntatis arbitrio absque licentia domum propriam egressus fuerit, in altera refugium habebit; et si ibi condigna satisfactione poenituerit, per abbatem illius ecclesiae domui suae reconciliari, et loco proprio debet restitui, nisi talis fuerit culpa, pro qua debeat utraque privari* : agreement between Malmesbury and Evesham (1190/1208; Evesham had similar agreements with Whitby, St. Mary's, York, and Odense), WILLIAM DUGDALE, Monasticon Anglicanum, new edn. by JOHN CALEY – HENRY ELLIS – BULKELEY BANDINEL, 6 vols. in 8, London 1817–1830, 2, no. 16, p. 19

[34] Agreement between Malmesbury and Evesham (as n. 33) (an offence deserving expulsion); between St. Benet's, Holme, and Bury St. Edmunds (1020), Memorials of St. Edmund's Abbey, ed. THOMAS ARNOLD, 3 vols. (Rolls Series, London 1890–1896) 3, pp. 2f. (betrayal of his monastery and abbot); between St. Augustine's, Canterbury, and Bury St. Edmunds (1200), WILLIAM THORNE, De rebus gestis abbatum sancti Augustini Cantuariae, 16.9 (ROGER TWYSDEN, Historiae Anglicanae scriptores decem, London 1652) p. 1843 (*flagitium reatus horribilis*); between Saint–Michel en Thiérache and Saint–Nicholas de Ribemont (no date), and Hautmont (1203), Cartulaire de l'abbaye de Saint–Michel en Thiérache, ed. AMÉDÉE PIETTE, Vervins 1883, nos. 277ff., pp. 156ff. (theft and ill repute); between Vendôme and Saint–Pierre, Bourgueil (1188/1200), Cartulaire de l'abbaye cardinale de la Trinité, Vendôme, ed. CHARLES MÉTAIS, 4 vols., Paris 1892–1900, 2, no. 631, pp. 510f., (a crime meriting expulsion or excommunication); between Silos and San Millan de la Cogolla (1190), Recueil des chartes de l'abbaye de Silos, ed. MARIUS FÉROTIN, Paris 1897, no. 74, pp. 112ff. (for just cause).

[35] ... *in altero monasterio tanquam unus fratrum loci illius collocetur* : agreement of St. Benet's, Holme, and Bury St. Edmunds (as n. 34); ... *usque ad reconciliationem suam ab alterutra ecclesia materne confoveatur et conservetur* : agreement between Corbie and Stavelot (1147/8), Recueil des chartes de l'abbaye de Stavelot-Malmédy (as n. 22) 1, no. 187, pp. 187f.; for food and clothing: agreement of Saint–Germer-de-Fly and Saint–Maur–des–Fossés (1214), MIGNE, PL 156, no. 24, cols. 1098f.; for a place in chapter: agreement of Saint–Michel en Thiérache and Hautmont (as n. 34).

[36] Agreement of St. Gall and Reichenau (as n. 23).

[37] Agreements between Stavelot and Cornelimünster, and Flavigny and Saint–Martin, Autun (as n. 32); *Si cuiuslibet praefatae ecclesiae frater abbatis suae offensam incurrerit, quod absit, tamdiu cum conventu alterius ecclesiae morabitur, usque dum in pristinam restituatur gratiam* : agreements between Saint–Germain–des–Prés and Saint–Denis (1186/92): JACQUES BOUILL-ART, Histoire de l'abbaye royale de Saint–Germain–des–Prés, Paris 1724, p. 107, n.a ; *Si [quis] monachus vel canonicus harum ecclesiarum aliqua ductus infirmitate de ecclesia sua exierit, ad quamlibet harum fugerit, sine [offen]sione pro octo dies recipiatur. Quod si infra prescriptum tempus sue [ecclesie recon]ciliari non possit, deinceps non retineatur, sed eat quo voluerit* : agreement between Tréport and Eu (as n. 30).

[38] In 1131 the abbots of the province of Reims agreed that: *Liceat abbati, si necessitas vel ratio ingruerit, fratrem suam ad quemlibet abbatum mittere, tamen ei in vestitu provideat. Si vero paupertas exiguerit, abbas ad quem frater ille missus fuerit vestitum ei prebeat* (as n. 1); *Si vero contigerit aliquem fratrum alterutrius ecclesiae ob aliquem excessum ad alteram directum fuisse, nulla nisi generali debet custodia coartari* : agreeement between Malmesbury and Evesham (as n. 33).

adjudicate in his case, whether by determining what should be done or by way of mediation [39].

II. Another frequent benefit was the right for monks in good standing to enjoy hospitality in all or some aspects of monastic life.

1. It was a common practice to make overall grants of hospitality with few if any qualifications [40].

2. It might be stipulated that monks enjoying hospitality should be placed according to their seniority by profession, and that they should celebrate the conventual mass in their turn [41].

3. Some agreements named only the right of admission to chapter. There might be a caution about the confidentiality of chapter proceedings [42].

---

[39] Agreements of St. Gall and Reichenau, and Malmesbury and Evesham (as nn. 23, 33); cf. that between Saint–Remy, Reims, and Saint–Remy, Sens(1135/45) (Reims, Bibl. Mun. ms. 346, fol. 192r-v): *Quod si forte aliquis fratrum ex his cenobiis aliquomodo discors a suo capitulo fuerit, per abbatem et preces communis conventus utriusque partis in reconciliatonem et pacem merebitur recipi*.

[40] Thus in 942 the monasteries of Fleury, Saint–Martial, Limoges, and Solignac entered into confraternity *ita ut ab ea die in reliquum aevum nulla esset differentia inter monachos ... sed utrique, dum ad se invicem transirent, communis agnosceretur in omnibus conversatio et quasi una haberetur congregatio*: JEAN MABILLON, Annales ordinis sancti Benedicti, 6 vols., Paris 1703–1739, 3, p. 459; *Fratrem scilicet ab alterutro venientem quasi proprium recipi preter hoc quod capitulum non ingredietur quilibet fratrum absque licentia*: agreement between Worcester and Gloucester (1072/95), Cartulary of Worcester Cathedral Priory (as n. 25) no. 305, p. 161 (Worcester had similar agreements with Malmesbury, Evesham, Winchcombe, Tewkesbury, and Pershore); *in omnibus habeant fratres alterutrum hinc et inde locum*: agreement between Worcester and Ramsey (1077/80), ibid. no. 304, pp. 180f.; *Igitur si de alterutro monasteriorum fratres ad alterum venerint, sicut eiusdem loci monachi suscipientur et in ordine erunt, si moram ibi seu voluntate seu necessite aliquandiu sunt facturi*: agreement between Mont–Saint–Michel and Cluny (as n. 29); *Inter vivos talis est institucio, ut communia sunt (sic) nobis omnia, hoc est claustrum, monasterium, capitulum et cetere officine, victusque et vestibus, itus et reditus; sicut in abbacia, ita per omnia monasteria nostra forinseca hec communio servetur. Et ut breviur summam complectamur, per omnia unum sumus, solo nomine discrepat*: agreement between Saint–Oyend de Joux and Tournus (? c.1175/c.1183), Recueil des historiens de la France 5,1: Obituaires de la province de Lyon 1 (hereafter RHF Obit.), edd. GEORGES GUIGUE – JACQUES LAURENT, Paris 1933, p. 328. St. Mary's, York in the late twelfth century granted monks of Holy Trinity, York, *plenarium monachatum ecclesie nostre*: BURTON (as n. 28) p. 331.

[41] *Ut utrumque monasterium utrique conventui commune sit et unum; fratres quoque alterutri, qualibet necessitate pulsati, in altero locorum oportunum refugium habeant et subsidium, et loca sua utrimque tam in monasterio quam in capitulo vel refectorio consequantur, secundum conversionis suae tempus*: agreement between Peterborough and Ramsey (1177/93), DUGDALE (as n. 33) 1, no. 46, p. 395; agreement of Saint–Évroul and Jumièges (1223), cited in translation by JULIEN LOTH, Histoire de l'abbaye royale de Saint-Pierre de Jumièges, 3 vols. (Société de l'histoire de Normandie) Rouen 1882–1885, 1, p. 354.

[42] *Noveritis ergo nos ei eiusque fratribus per omnia loca nostra concessisse capitulum*: agreement between Cluny and Rebais (c.1133/45) (Ep. 16, MIGNE, PL 189, col. 477); similarly Saint–Oyend de Joux and Cluny (1122/47) (RHF Obit. 5, 1, p. 330). At Saint–Bénigne, Dijon, such phrases recur as *capitulum utrimque commune habemus, capitulum commune est, ut utrumque habeant communia capitula*, and *capitulum unum sit*: Dijon, Bibl. Mun. ms. 634, fols. 123v–125v; Troyes, Bibl. Mun. ms. 210, fols. 115r–118v. Rights might be restricted to a visiting abbot and his immediate retinue: *De capitulo hanc habemus societatem, ut si abbas eorum ad nos venerit vel noster ad illos, fratres qui cum illis venerint capitulum intrabunt, alias minime*: agreement with Tonnerre (Dijon, Bibl. Mun. ms. 634, fol. 124r; Troyes, Bibl. Mun. ms. 210, fol. 116r). As regards confidentiality, the agreement of Peterborough and Ramsey (as n. 41) laid down that *utriuslibet autem loci fratres sub interminatione anathematis capituli alterius tanquam sui secreta celanda meminerint*.

4. Others referred to hospitality in terms of board and lodging, by conferring a right of indefinite residence or of paying repeated visits. A right to hospitality during very short visits might be excluded [43].

5. Some such grants of hospitality were so broadly drafted as to constitute in effect permission to transfer indefinitely from one monastery to another (*transitus*) [44].

6. The duty of a monk to seek from his abbot the letter of commendation (*literae commendatitiae*) required by the Rule of St. Benedict, cap. 61, was sometimes expressed and was probably generally fulfilled when a monk in good standing with his own monastery sought hospitality [45].

7. It might also be provided that a monk keep his rights even after he went to another monastery [46].

III. Agreements sometimes stipulated mutual help in case of material distress or calamity.

1. Specific contingencies might be named, as when St. Benet's, Holme, and Bury St. Edmunds arranged that, in the event of damage by fire, war, or other calamity, half the convent of the stricken house might, by agreement of the two abbots and convents, migrate to the other until restoration was complete [47].

2. But it was more usual for help to be stipulated in any necessity [48].

IV. Sometimes agreements of confraternity gave special rights to the abbots of allied houses.

1. These usually concerned their place in chapter and refectory. In c.1107 Abbot Hugh of Cluny granted Abbot Godfrey of Vendôme the right, if he came to Cluny in its abbot's absence, to preside in chapter and refectory; and Peter the Venerable gave similar rights to the abbots of Rebais and of Saint–Remy, Reims [49].

---

[43] ... *quamdiu illuc habitare voluerit* : agreement of Saint–Remy, Reims, and Worcester (as n. 25); ... *et quanto tempore morari voluerint, vel ab abbate suo permissi fuerint, in omnibus necessariis congruam accipient humanitatem* : agreement between Saint–Pierre–le–Vif, Sens, and Hautvilliers (1155), ed. MAXIMILIEN QUANTIN, Cartulaire générale de l'Yonne, 2 vols., Auxerre 1854, 1, no. 371, pp. 531f.; agreement between Saint–Germain–des–Prés and Saint–Denis (as n. 37).

[44] Saint–Remy, Reims, agreed with Peter, a monk of Moutier–la–Celle (Troyes) (1162/81), *ut, quando voluerit et sibi placuerit, ut monachus noster venire et morari nobiscum poterit* : Reims, Bibl. Mun. ms. 346, fol. 191v, LECLERCQ (as n. 1) 46, p. 68; cf. Saint–Bénigne, Dijon's agreement with Saint–Seine (Dijon, Bibl. Mun. ms. 634, fol. 124v, Troyes, Bibl. Mun. ms. 210, fol. 117v); *Si quis de fratribus vestris ad nos transire voluerit, cum litteris abbatis et ecclesie veniat et tamquam filius recipietur* : agreement between Stavelot and Saint–Hubert en Ardennes, Recueil des chartes de l'abbaye de Stavelot–Malmédy (as n. 22) 2, no. 295, pp. 7f.

[45] Ibid.

[46] Agreement of Saint–Michel en Thiérache and Hautmont (as n. 34).

[47] Agreement of St. Benet's, Holme, and Bury St. Edmunds (as n. 34).

[48] *In qualibet necessitate* : agreements of Worcester with Great Malvern and Ramsey, Cartulary of Worcester Cathedral Priory (as n. 25) nos. 300, 304, pp. 158, 160f., *quacumque occasione vel necessitate* : Saint–Pierre–le–Vif, Sens, and Hautvillers (as n. 43); *Placuit eciam ut sibi ad auxilium necessitate concurrant et provida sagacitate indempnitati suae prospiciant* : St. Augustine's, Canterbury, and Bury St. Edmunds (as n. 34).

[49] Vendôme: Cartulaire (as n. 34) 2, no. 416, pp. 179f.; Rebais (as n. 42); Saint–Remy, Reims: Peter granted to Abbot Odo (1118–51) that *capitulum teneat in Cluniaco et in nostris locis quemadmodum abbates nobis professi* : Reims, Bibl. Mun. ms. 346, fol. 198v, CHARLES H. TALBOT, Odo of Saint–Remy, a Friend of Peter the Venerable (Studia Anselmiana 40, 1956, pp. 21–37) pp. 21f., corrected.

2. Provision might be made for the solemn reception of a visiting abbot [50].

3. There might be specific reference to presidency over the chapter of faults [51].

4. Disputes between two monasteries might first be discussed between their abbots, before recourse was had to an external authority [52].

V. In some instances the rights of intervention by the respective abbots were so largely defined as to constitute virtual powers of visitation [53].

VI. The rights of monks in confederate houses might extend so far as to participation in the election of an abbot.

1. This might take the form of the presence and counsel of both communities in the process of election [54].

2. If a suitable candidate were not forthcoming from the house having the vacancy, it might have recourse to the other for a candidate [55].

VII. Meetings of religious superiors sometimes included in group agreements of confraternity clauses which were of wider political or disciplinary effect.

1. The English abbots who met in 1077 under the presidency of the monk–bishop Wulfstan II of Worcester included a declaration of loyalty to the king – the Norman conqueror William I – and his queen [56].

2. At Reims in 1131 the assembled abbots drew up rules for the reverent conduct of services, on fasting, and on claustral discipline [57].

It is not difficult to suggest reasons why such temporal benefits of confraternity should often have been mixed with its spiritual provisions. First, the *societas* which confraternity created was the expression of an *amicitia* which prompted benevolence in material as well as spiritual forms [58]. Put differently, since prayers were seen as the gifts which were exchanged by members of religious communities allowing corporate but not individual possessions [59], they pointed the way to the corporate exchange of other, temporal gifts. For

---

[50] Agreement between St. Benet's, Holme, and Bury St. Edmunds (as n. 34).

[51] Agreement between Saint–Josse–sur–Mer and Blagny (1218) (Gallia Christiana 10, instr., no. 63, p. 339).

[52] *Item si discordia inter abbates et conventus duarum ecclesiarum, quod absit, oborta fuerit, ad maiorum non vocent personam, donec abbates duarum ecclesiarum inter se pacem redintegrent, si fieri possit* : agreement between Vendôme and Saint–Pierre de Borgueil (as n. 34).

[53] Saint–Pierre–le–Vif, Sens, and Hautvillers agreed that if either abbot visited the other house *et quoslibet ex fratribus in graviori culpa, aut in aliqua sententia positos invenerit, sive praesente sive absente abbate capitulum tenebit, de ordine et disciplina ut voluerit loquetur et in sententia positos absolvet. Adolescentes de scola, si ei visum fuerit, eiiciet. Simultates et discordias, si inter abbates et conventum invenerit, potens erit sedare* : (as n. 43); see also the agreements between Saint–Évroul and Jumièges, Saint–Michel en Thiérache and Hautmont, and Saint–Bénigne, Dijon, and Montierender (as nn. 34, 41 and Troyes, Bibl. Mun. ms. 210, fol. 116v).

[54] *Et cum abbas eligendus fuerit e diverso, fratres hinc inde conveniant ut communi consilio canonica celebretur electio* : agreement between St. Augustine's, Canterbury, and Bury St. Edmunds (as n. 34).

[55] *Et si dignus inventus fuerit in ecclesia cui praeficiendus est assumatur; si aliqua causa obviaverit recurratur ad aliam* : ibid.

[56] As n. 1.

[57] Ibid.

[58] See e.g. the agreement between Ferrières and York (c.849): MGH Epp. 6, no. 61, pp. 61f.

[59] See above p. 236.

example, it was right that wealthy houses should relieve their poorer neighbours [60]. Secondly, such monastic confraternities as are the subject of this study existed alongside an abundance of other confraternities, both religious and secular, which unlike them were organic bodies whose members assembled regularly to promote their common purposes. *Ubi societas ibi lex*: such bodies – in French ,confrairies' as opposed to ,confraternités' – had their statutes, prescribing for their members not only prayers but a variety of caritative duties and benefits [61]. Sometimes associated with such monasteries as Fulda and Saint-Martial, Limoges, they provided an obvious model for extending the scope of confraternity from spiritual to temporal benefits. Thirdly, and most important, the characteristics of Benedictine monasticism itself created the need for the building up of a network of external relationships amongst monasteries [62]. The Rule spoke only of the individual monastery in which monks were vowed to *stabilitas loci* under the fatherly and final authority of the abbot. There was thus no provision for appeal beyond its walls, and so the individual monk needed some recourse if he found himself at odds with his abbot or community. In any case, monks did not always remain literally in one place but often expressed their detachment from the world by *peregrinatio*, or a life with no abiding location. They nevertheless needed a framework within which their commitment to stability might be lived in terms of stability to their profession rather than in a single place [63]. They needed a means of belonging in houses which they might visit. Again, abbots required ways of regulating mutual hospitality, of dealing with turbulent or disaffected monks, and of surmounting such catastrophes as fire, famine, and warfare. In due course such monastic structures as the Cluniac, and still more the emergence with the Cistercians of the organized religious order, would go far to satisfy the need for overarching authority in those sectors of the monastic world [64]. In the twelfth century, too, black–monk abbots occasionally found it useful to assemble for the discussion of common interests and problems [65]; but it was only with the Fourth Lateran Council (1215) that papal legislation provided for general chapters [66]. In the meantime there was an urgent need, especially amongst black–monk houses, for mutual self–help such as that expressed in mixed agreements of confraternity in providing piecemeal for such temporal contingencies as have been set out.

---

[60] Thus in 1020 St. Benet's, Holme, and Bury St. Edmunds declared that *quaecumque harum ecclesiarum maiori rerum copia videretur abundare, opulentior inferiorem relevaret*: (as n. 34).
[61] MEERSSEMAN (as n. 9).
[62] The point is well made by BERLIÈRE (as n. 14) pp. 4f.
[63] See GILES CONSTABLE, Monachisme et pèlerinage au moyen âge (Revue historique 258, 1977, pp. 3–27); reprint in: ID., Religious Life and Thought (11th–12th Centuries), London 1979, no. 3.
[64] See WOLLASCH (as n. 14) pp. 136–186.
[65] Besides the Reims assembly of 1131 (as n. 14), see St. Bernard, Ep. 91 (1130), edd. JEAN-LECLERCQ – HENRI M. ROCHAIS, Sancti Berardi Opera, 8 vols. so far, Rome 1957ff., 7, pp. 239ff.; Gesta abbatum Lobbiensium, cap. 22, ed. WILHELM ARNDT (MGH SS 21, pp. 324f.); Innocent II, Ep. 202 (1135/6), MIGNE, PL 179, cols. 253f.; Peter the Venerable, Ep. 79 (1131/43), ed. GILES CONSTABLE, The Letters of Peter the Venerable, 2 vols., Cambridge/Mass. 1967, 1, pp. 213f., and 2, pp. 151f.; letters of the chapter of Reims to Popes Hadrian IV (c.1155) and Alexander III (soon after 1159), PL 182, cols. 713–716, nos. 493f. On this material see BERLIÈRE (as n. 1).
[66] Canon 12, MANSI (as n. 1) 22, cols. 999–1002.

The problem, therefore, arises of whether such agreements were legally binding in a sense that came increasingly to distinguish them from purely spiritual agreements with their basis in mutual charity. Dom Ursmer Berlière and Dom Raphael Molitor suggested that, at least from the late twelfth century, this was so [67]. Some considerations admittedly support such a view. First and foremost, the range, detail, and precision of temporal benefits suggest the development of careful draftsmanship directed towards the undertaking of effective and legally binding commitments. Consistently with this, re-negotiated agreements were carefully revised [68]. Secondly, mid–twelfth century papal bulls settling disputes between monasteries occasionally embodied provisions characteristic of agreements of confraternity, perhaps indicating that in the view of the papal curia such agreements had or could be given legal force [69]. Thirdly, at the Fourth Lateran Council Pope Innocent III legislated to reform an aspect of monastic confraternity, when he forbade any monk to have a place in several monasteries [70]. His purpose was made clear some ten years later by the Evesham chronicler Thomas of Marleberge. Writing about the election in 1214 of Abbot Randulf who had been both prior of Worcester and a monk of Evesham, he explained that it had then (i.e. before the Council) been permissible for a monk to have a place in two chapters and a stall in two choirs [71]. Innocent may have regarded agreements of confraternity as having established a legal rule which demanded a legal reform. Finally, another canon of the Council which may shed some light is that which required a triennial general chapter of black–monk abbots and ruling priors to be held in each kingdom or province; it was to be backed up

---

[67] BERLIÈRE (as n. 14) pp. 11f.; MOLITOR (as n. 14) 1, pp. 56f.

[68] E.g. the agreement between Stavelot and Cornelimünster (as n. 32).

[69] Thus, in 1138 Innocent II confirmed the spiritual confraternity between the black–monk house of Pierremont (dioc. Metz) and the Premonstratensian house of Saint–Nicholas de Troisfontaines (dioc. Langres), but forbade the reception of each other's members without their superior's knowledge: Ep. 340, MIGNE, PL 179, cols. 391ff.; cf. Ep. 202 (as n. 65).

[70] Illud etiam prohibemus, ne quis in diversis monasteriis locum monachi habere praesumat, nec unus abbas pluribus monasteriis praesidere: canon 13, MANSI (as n. 1) 22, cols. 1002f. The background of this canon is legislation of French councils, Paris (1212/13) canon 8, Rouen (1213) canon 9, and Montpellier (1214) canon 25, MANSI (as n. 1) 22, cols. 827, 907, 945.

[71] Chronicon abbatiae de Evesham, ed. WILLIAM D. MACRAY (Rolls Series, London 1863) p. 255: ... quod tunc temporis bene licuit, videlicet quod monachus in pluribus monasteriis haberet locum in capitulo et stallum in choro. A further item of English evidence appears to establish, in contradiction of this Evesham view, that such a plurality was already uncanonical under Pope Alexander III. It is a bull, ostensibly of 1179/81, preserved by the St. Augustine's, Canterbury, chronicler Thomas of Elmham. A pope ordered the archbishop and the archdeacon of Canterbury to investigate an agreement of confraternity between St. Augustine's and St. Swithun's, Winchester. He declared that the former was an exempt monastery depending upon the Roman church nullo medio; he had been informed that of its own will (motu proprio) it had entered into the agreement, but he declared it to be against canonical sanctions that monks should be reciprocally received ut monachi et confratres, having et stallum in choro et locum in capitulo ut in proprio monasterio: Thomas of Elmham, Historia monasterii S. Augustini Cantuariensis, ed. CHARLES HARDWICK (Rolls Series, London 1858) no. 77, pp. 447f. (at p. 448 line 12 the text should read appellatione postposita), cf. no. 76, pp. 446f. There are no grounds for regarding the item as a forgery, but it may be from the reign of Pope Alexander IV (1254–61) rather than Alexander III. 1. Thomas wrote as late as c.1413. 2. Unlike most letters of Alexander III which Thomas cites this is not dated. 3. There is no record of a canonical sanction in or before Alexander III's reign though canon 13 of the Fourth Lateran Council would apply.

by a system of episcopal and regular visitation to oversee observance and discipline [72]. This canon was stated to be indebted to Cistercian arrangements. But it was also the first attempt of papal legislation to fulfil universally the needs of black-monk monasteries that agreements of confraternity and occasional meetings of abbots had for long catered for in a haphazard and occasional way [73], especially by attempts to provide for visitation [74]. In England, where it was quickly and energetically applied [75], general chapters saw such exchanges of spiritual benefits as agreements of confraternity established and they announced a similar bond of love [76]. The chapters of both the northern and the southern provinces legislated about visitation [77]. The first chapter of the Canterbury province (1219) made a strict ruling about fugitive monks which may have beend intended to temper the freedom which agreements of confraternity gave [78]. The additions of 1225 enjoined monasteries to provide for the relief of a house which fell upon poverty through fire or other mischance [79]. To this extent the early English general chapters acknowledged the caritative bond of spiritual confraternity and also legislated about some of its temporal concomitants. They suggest that by 1215 some features of agreements of confraternity were of at least a quasi-legal character.

Yet this evidence that agreements ever approached or acquired legal force is slight, and many considerations indicate that they did not. First, the argument that from the late twelfth century mixed agreements acquired a heightened juridical force exaggerated the change that then took place. Berlière himself recognized that monasteries began to exchange temporal benefits as early as 894 [80]. In fact, by c.1100 many of those benefits which have been listed are attested in France and England, and others appear between 1100 and 1150 [81]; mixed agreements, therefore, developed gradually

---

[72] As n. 66.

[73] As above p. 243.

[74] As above p. 242.

[75] KNOWLES (as n. 14) pp. 372ff., 653.

[76] *Et in eodem capitulo devote petentes fraternitatem capituli, in societatem beneficiorum monasteriorum per participationem admittantur, ad quod defuncti, amicis eorum pro ipsis humiliter intervenientibus, recipiantur. In fine vero capituli, simul omnibus in unum congregatis, fiat communis confessio, et tam presentium quam absentium, vivorum ac defunctorum fiat fratrum capituli absolutio; et data est accepta benedictione, cum pace corporaliter ab invicem discedant, per caritatem semper in Christo manentes coniuncti*: Documents Illustrating the Activities of the General and Provincial Chapters of the English Black Monks, 1215–1540, ed. WILLIAM ABEL PANTIN [1] (Camden Society, 3rd Series 45) London 1931, p. 20.

[77] Ibid. pp. 8, 13, 19, 21, 241ff.

[78] Ibid. p. 13.

[79] Ibid. p. 19.

[80] (As n. 14) pp. 5, 11ff.; see the agreement between Flavigny and Saint-Martin, Autun (as n. 32).

[81] By 1100, see I 1, II 1, III 1, VI 1, and VII 1,2, and between 1100 and 1150 also I 3, II 3,4, IV 1 (above pp. 238–242). Mixed agreements developed in Germany only from the mid-twelfth century. The stronger structure of the Ottonian and Salian ‚Reichskirche' left less scope or need for such self-help, while the reformed monasteries of the late eleventh century continued to form exclusively spiritual agreements; see above n. 24, and the material from St. Blasien in MGH Necr. Germ. 1, pp. 327ff. For the confraternities of St. Peter's, Salzburg, see K. FRIEDRICH HERMANN, Confraternitatis Sanpetrensis. Die Geschichte der Gebetsverbrüderungen in St. Peter zu Salzburg (Studien und Mitteilungen zur Geschichte des Benediktiner-Ordens und seiner Zweige 79, 1968, pp. 26–53); and for the early twelfth-century confraternities of Deutz (dioc. Cologne) see BRUNO ALBERS, Das Verbrüderungsbuch der Abtei Deutz (Studien und Mitteilungen aus den Benediktiner- und Cistercienser-Orden 16, 1895, pp.

and from an early date. There is no discernible change of character in the more legally-minded late twelfth century. This being so, it is probable that, like purely spiritual agreements, they always had a caritative and not a juridical sanction. Secondly, it is open to question how far they were intended to be regularly and literally put into effect, or how far they simply gave particularized and graphic expression to the underlying bond of mutual charity. Even thirteenth-century agreements were sometimes so drafted as to suggest that moral enthusiasm, not legal definition, was the determining factor [82]. Thirdly, although it is prima facie probable that, if spiritual benefits of confraternity were normally effective so too were temporal benefits, as a guide to what actually happened the detail of mixed agreements may be misleading. Doubts have been expressed as to how far the rights which they stipulated were ever exercised [83]. Very occasionally an abbot may be seen presiding over the chapter of another monastery when an agreement of confraternity was made or confirmed [84]; or a casual mention points to an actual exchange of hospitality [85]. But whenever instances occur of monasteries helping each other or an individual monk, it is rarely if ever possible to establish that an agreement of confraternity was a warrant for the help [86]. Instead, houses known to have had agreements seem in practice to have made such arrangements as were convenient without regard to them [87]. Finally, the

---

96–104). The earliest text of a German mixed agreement seems to be that of 1145 between St. Gall and Reichenau (as n. 23), although it is a renegotiation. Somewhat older mixed agreements may underlie the references to *plenam fraternitatem; tam in temporalibus quam in spiritualibus* established with Maria Laach, Affligem, and St. Eucharius in the St. Maximin, Trier, confraternity records of Trier, Stadtbibliothek, ms. 1634/394, fols. 80v–85r: see DIETER GEUENICH, Eine unveröffentlichte Verbrüderungsliste des 12. Jahrhundert aus St. Maximin/Trier (Rheinische Vierteljahresblätter 41, 1977, pp. 26–53) p. 181.

[82] See the final clause of the agreement between Stavelot and Saint-Hubert en Ardennes (as n. 44): ... *et si quis est artior nodus mutue karitatis, vos in litteris vestris exprimatis, et nos nichilominus litteris nostris inseremus. Iden enim velle et idem nolle, ut ait quidam sapiens* (Sallust, Catilina 20,4) *firma amicitia est*.

[83] KNOWLES (as n. 14) pp. 474f. I do not know upon what evidence he states that ,all such engagements are symptomatic of what may be called the democratic movement among the black monks of the time, by which the chapters, isolated from the abbot, were claiming to act as a body with definite rights'; at all times and places abbots and chapters appear to have acted in concert.

[84] *H[ec]est societas inter ecclesiam beati Remigii cenobii et illam quae est constructa in honore ipsius sancti apud Senonas, quam venerabilis Girardus Senonensis abbas presidens in capitulo iam dicti confessoris Remis cum ipso confirmavit :* (as n. 39).

[85] For an expression of gratitude, see the agreement between Saint-Remy, Reims, and Worcester (as n. 25); for a comment that the abbot of St. Benet's, Holme, came more often to Bury St. Edmunds than vice versa, see the statement regarding the solemn reception of abbots in the Bury Chronicle (as n. 34) pp. 2f.

[86] Thus, the instances of fire and other disaster listed by BERLIÈRE (as n. 14) p. 12, n. 1, yield no clear proof.

[87] The twelfth- and thirteenth-century transferences of monks in the Gesta abbatum sancti Albani, ed. HENRY T. RILEY, 3 vols. (Rolls Series, London 1867–1869) 1, pp. 108, 109f., 111, 260, seem in no case demonstrably to have as their background an agreement of confraternity; see however, KNOWLES (as n. 14) p. 475. There is also no reference in the stories of how Abbot Hugh of Bury St. Edmunds (1157–1180) sent monks into exile: The Chronicle of Jocelin of Brakelond, ed. HAROLD E. BUTLER, London, etc. 1949, p. 4; or in Peter of Celle's letters about fugitive monks written while he was abbot of Saint-Remy, Reims: Epp. 140–143, MIGNE, PL 202, cols. 583–587. Nor is it certain that an agreement underlies the letter of Ulrich, provost of the Premonstratensian house of Steinfeld (c.1153–1170) to Abbot Rether of Prüm (c.1157–c.1174): ALPHONS ZÁK, Aus dem Codex von Arnstein (Studien und Mitteilungen aus den Benediktiner- und Cistercienser-Orden 23, 1902, pp. 439–451, p. 441. Even when no agreement

Fourth Lateran Council does not seem to have succeeded in stemming the tide of confraternity which allowed monks to have a place in several monasteries, for agreements continued to confer it [88]; new legal rulings did not inhibit traditional expressions of charity. The conclusion to which the evidence points is that at all times mixed agreements of confraternity, no less than pure ones, expressed fraternal aspirations of charity. They did not establish a law for detailed and continual observance in a literal sense. When they did take effect, there is little if any reason to conclude that their sanction was more than fraternal custom. Only exceptionally, as when papal warrant was added, did they acquire anything approaching juridical force.

All the agreements of confraternity amongst monasteries and other religious houses which have so far been discussed treated the houses concerned as equal partners. However, from the late eleventh century there are examples which reflect a difference in standing. The earliest is of 1088 between the Saxon monastery of Iburg – the recent foundation of Bishop Benno II of Osnabrück – and the church of Osnabrück itself. Benno's death in the same year gave rise to a short but sharp dispute, which the monks won, regarding the place of his burial. Abbot Nortbert sought to perpetuate the monks' advantage by proposing a bond of confraternity in which the church would be mother and mistress to the monastery not by power but by love (*non tam potestate quam caritate mater esset et domina*): the sons of both would be associates in counsel, aid, goodwill and prayer [89]. Secondly, in the next decade a relationship as between mother and daughter was expressed in an agreement between the abbey of Evesham and its Danish dependency of Odense [90]. No document of the 1090s survives. The earliest evidence of their confraternity is a letter of 1138/39 from Bishop Riculf of Odense (1138–63) to Evesham referring to the relationship *inter matrem et filiam* and to the very full terms of confraternity which included Evesham's right to confirm the election of the prior [91]. In 1174 King Waldemar of Denmark renewed the confraternity which – he stated – Odense had enjoyed with Evesham since its foundation, and a new prior was elected at Evesham [92]. It is apparent that

---

of confraternity is known to have existed, a visiting abbot might claim (and be refused) precedence in chapter and in a procession on Sunday: see the account of the visit to Bury St. Edmunds in 1200 of Abbot Hugh V of Cluny (1199–1207), The Chronicle of Jocelin of Brakelond, p. 124; cf. The Customary of the Benedictine Abbey of Bury St. Edmunds in Suffolk, ed. ANTONIA GRANSDEN (Henry Bradshaw Society 99) London 1973 for 1966, pp. 20f.

[88] Even in England, despite the early introduction of general chapters: see e.g. the agreements between Worcester and Notley Priory (1216/22), and between Worcester and Westminster (1232): DARLINGTON (as n. 25) nos. 306f., pp. 161f.

[89] Vita Bennonis II episcopi Osnabrugensis auctore Nortberto abbate Iburgensi, cap. 28, ed. HARRY BRESSLAU (MGH SS. rer. Germ., Hannover und Leipzig 1902, p. 39). The Vita was written between 1090 and 1100.

[90] Odense was established at the request of King Eric of Denmark (1095–1103) by the dispatch of twelve Evesham monks. For Evesham and Odense, see Chronicon monasterii de Evesham (as n. 71) pp. XLIIIff., 325, and cf. KNOWLES (as n. 14) pp. 163f., 475.

[91] The evidence for the confraternity survives in the Evesham Cartulary, London, Brit. Libr. ms. Cotton Vespasian B.XXIV; it is discussed and edited by WALTHER HOLTZMANN, Urkunden zur Geschichte des Domklosters von Odense (Schriften des Vereins für Schleswig–Holsteinische Kirchengeschichte 9, 1929, pp. 59–65). The letter of 1138/9, which occurs in slightly differing forms on fols. 22r–v and 48v, is printed as no. 1, pp. 61f.; also in: DUGDALE (as n. 33) 2, no. 30, p. 26.

[92] Waldemar's letter is on fol. 19r–v of the ms.; printed by HOLTZMANN (as n. 91) no. 3, pp. 63f., and DUGDALE (as n. 33) 2, no. 29, p. 25.

whatever its vicissitudes, Evesham's relation with its oversea dependency was expressed in terms of confraternity, and that much of the impetus came from the Danish side[93]. Thirdly, in 1144 Pope Celestine II resolved the long controversy between Camaldoli and its cell at Vivo (dioc. Chiusi), *ut vinculum charitatis inter vos conservetur*, by means of an agreement of confraternity; again the relationship of a dependent house to its superior was thus confirmed[94].

Such agreements raise the legal problem of whether they made any contribution to the constitutional structures which developed at the same time within western monasticism, especially the Cluniac and the Cistercian. By this time the Cluniac constitution was formed. The Cluniacs had for long admitted to their confraternity both non–Cluniac houses and individual persons. They offered participation in the prayers and alms not only of Cluny itself but also of the whole ecclesia Cluniacensis, granting both spiritual and temporal benefits[95]. They also exchanged confraternity with whole orders, notably the Carthusians and the Premonstratensians[96]. Thus, although surprisingly few Cluniac agreements of confraternity survive, there can be no doubt of the number and variety of its associations[97]. A little evidence exists to suggest that in the twelfth century they might serve as a quasi–juridical bond between Cluny and a house at the fringe of its connection which, although not constitutionally its subject, wished to follow its Customs and have its guidance. The critical case is Reading, an abbey founded in 1121 by King Henry I of England but fully established only in 1123[98]. Its relationship with Cluny was defined by an agreement of confraternity in a letter from Peter the Venerable to Reading's first abbot, Hugh of Amiens. It made stipulations both spiritual and temporal; they included the provision, *in signum tante unitatis et ad maiorem Cluniacensis ordinis in domo Radingensi stabilitatem*, that future abbots if not monks of Reading should be elected only from Cluniac houses, save that the prior of Cluny should never be elected[99]. Reading was at pains to continue and intensify this bond[100]. Thus, Peter the Venerable wrote to its

---

[93] See also the fragment of a letter from Bishop Riculf to Evesham (c.1138/49) on fol. 19v of the ms.; printed by HOLTZMANN (as n. 91) no. 2, pp. 62f.

[94] Ep. 39, MIGNE, PL 179, cols. 806f.

[95] See the examples in nn. 42, 49, 50.

[96] Carthusians: Epp. 18f., MIGNE, PL 189, cols. 478f. Premonstratensians: JOANNES LE PAIGE, Bibliotheca Praemonstratensis ordinis, Paris 1633, pp. 321f.

[97] Cluny's own Necrology has also not survived, but its scale is to be judged from the Marcigny codex Paris, Bibl. Nat. ms. nouv. acq. l. 348, edited by GUSTAV SCHNÜRER, Das Necrologium des Cluniacenser–Priorates Münchenwiler (Villar–les–Moines), (Collectanea Friburgensia, n.s. 10, 1906); see JOACHIM WOLLASCH, Ein cluniacensisches Totenbuch as der Zeit Abt Hugos von Cluny (Frühmittelalterliche Studien 1, 1967, pp. 406–443). The range of Cluny's confraternity arrangements by the end of the middle ages, many being by then very old, is apparent from the roll drawn up under its first secular abbot, John IV, cardinal of Lorraine (1529–50), printed in: RHF Obit. 6,2, edd. JACQUES LAURENT – PIERRE GRAS, pp. 472–481.

[98] For the founding of Reading see KNOWLES (as n. 14) pp. 281f.; KARL LEYSER, Frederick Barbarossa, Henry II and the Hand of St. James (English Historical Review 90, 1975, pp. 481–506) pp. 491–495.

[99] London, Brit. Libr. ms. Egerton 3031, fol. 48v. The Reading documents here discussed are mainly from this source which is of thirteenth–century compilation. Dr. B.R. Kemp is preparing an edition.

[100] A rubric in the Cartulary following Peter the Venerable's letter makes it clear that a second, lost agreement followed.

second abbot, Ansger (1130–35), acceding to his request that the names of
deceased Reading monks should be inscribed in Cluny's Necrology among
Cluny's own monks, not apart from them as was the custom with Cluny's
abbatiae [101]. Under Abbot Reginald (1154–58) Reading secured from Pope
Hadrian IV a papal confirmation of its confraternity with Cluny [102]. Hadrian
declared that caritative agreements of religious men should be permanent and
that they deserved papal reinforcement [103]. He accordingly confirmed for ever
the *societatis vinculum et unitatem fraternitatis* between Reading and
Cluny [104]. The vigour of this agreement is apparent in a letter of 1186 from
Abbot Hugh IV of Cluny to the newly elected Abbot Hugh of Reading. At
Reading's request the confraternity (*mutue societatis iura*) was renewed upon
terms including the right of Reading monks to be recorded in Cluny's
Necrology among departed Cluniacs [105]. The case of Reading shows how, by
papal sanction, an agreement of confraternity might assume a markedly
juridical character, defining the bond between one abbey and another to
which it looked for its Customs and for its abbots [106]. But it is not certain that
Cluny elsewhere used confraternity in a comparable way [107]. Reading brings
out the constitutional and juridical potential of an agreement of confraternity.
But Cluniac monasticism yields little evidence that the potential was often
developed.

In all essential respects Cluniac monasticism was mature before it was

---

101 *Tum quia vos precipuo affectu diligimus, tum quia petitiones vestras mutue inter nos karitati
augende et societati artius connectende in perpetuum non mediocriter valere perpendimus,
eapropter ... quod petitis libenter annuimus, et ut vestra defunctorum nomina cum nostris professis
mixtim scribantur precipimus, quamvis proprias abbatias nostras hanc nobiscum communionem
non habere minime ignoremus*: (as n. 99) fols. 48v–49r. The original agreement was that
Reading monks should *inter fratres nostros scribi in regula capituli annuatim recitandos*: fol.
48v. For Cluny's *abbatiae*, see HERBERT EDWARD JOHN COWDREY, Abbot Pontius of Cluny
(1109–22/6) (Studi Gregoriani 11, 1978, pp. 177–277) pp. 206–216, 249–253. A full examination of Cluniac Necrologies in the light of this statement is called for. In that of
Saint–Gilles – London, Brit. Libr. ms. Addit. 16979, written in 1227 – Abbot Pontius was
entered, not with its own monks, and popes and other magnates, but in the column marked *F*
(for *[con]fratres*): fol. 21r.

102 London, Brit. Libr. ms. Egerton 3031, fol. 67v, printed by WALTHER HOLTZMANN, Papsturkunden in England 3 (Abhandlungen der Akademie der Wissenschaften in Göttingen,
Philologisch–Historische Klasse, dritte Folge 33) Göttingen 1952, no. 127, p. 271.

103 *Ea, que inter viros religiosos caritative statuta et confirmata esse noscuntur, in sua debent
stabilitate consistere et, ne quandoque a suo statu debeant ulla ratione mutari, apostolice sedis
munimine convenit roborari*.

104 *... societatis vinculum et unitatem fraternitatis, que inter monasterium Radingense et Cluniacense
statuta et scripto atque sigillo Cluniacensis abbatis firmata esse dinoscitur, sicut in eodem scripto
continetur, nos auctoritate apostolica confirmamus et presentium litterarum patrocinio com-
munimus*.

105 London, Brit. Libr. ms. Egerton 3031, fol. 49r: *Pro defunctis etiam eorum in domibus nostris
cum breve perlatum fuerit, fiat eis quantum nostris professis et in regula scribentur cum nostris
annuatim recitandis*.

106 Reading drew its early abbots from the English Cluniac priory of Lewes. Abbot Hugh
(1186–99), to whom the last letter cited was addressed, became abbot of Cluny itself
(1199–1207).

107 But a similar arrangement may have arisen from the confraternity which Cluny had under
Peter the Venerable with Mount Tabor in the Holy Land; Bibliotheca Cluniacensis, ed.
MARTIN MARRIER, Paris 1614, col. 600D; cf. The Letters of Peter the Venerable Ep. 80, ed.
CONSTABLE (as n. 65) 1, pp. 214–217 and 2, p. 152, also Ep. 31, CONSTABLE, 1, pp. 105f. and 2,
pp. 121f.

250

likely that agreements of confraternity could contribute even in details to its constitutional forms. The Cistercian order was more open to be coloured by them. By black–monk standards, it is true, its liturgical commemoration of the departed and so the institutions of confraternity were always on a limited scale [108]. There is little direct evidence until the general chapters began to legislate about confraternity in 1183 [109]. It is in the surviving thirteenth-century Necrologies, including that of Cîteaux itself, that the extent of Cistercian commemorations emerges [110]. The Necrologies are brief, and most memorials fell on two days: on 20 November, at Cîteaux, those of all Cistercian departed, of parents, brothers, and sisters, and of monks of orders and houses with which Cîteaux had confraternity; and on 11 January those of all Cistercian departed, of all abbots of Cîteaux by name, of all departed bishops and abbots of the Cistercian order, and of a few favoured individuals together with founders and benefactors [111]. Although such Necrologies raise legal problems about the control of the general chapters over Cistercian observances [112], the dearth of Cistercian agreements of confraternity makes such sources of limited value for determining the legal arrangements of Cistercian monasticism.

It may be more fruitful to inquire how far black–monk confraternity shaped the ethos and constitutional structure of the Cistercian order itself. What is now generally agreed to have been the gradual character of Cistercian development makes its significance the more plausible [113]. By the 1090s – the decade which saw the foundation of Cîteaux by Robert of Molesme – an agreement of confraternity could, in the case of Iburg and Osnabrück, prescribe that the one should be related to the other as mother and daughter, not by power but by love [114]. With Evesham and Odense a founding house

---

[108] For Cistercian commemoration of the departed see JACQUES LAURENT, La prière pour les défunts et les obituaires dans l'ordre de Cîteaux (Mélanges Saint Bernard, Dijon 1954, pp. 383–396); CHARLES H. TALBOT, Associations of Clairvaux, Clairmarais and Ter Doest (Cîteaux in de Nederlanden 5, 1954, pp. 233–245); and JOACHIM WOLLASCH, Neue Quellen zur Geschichte der Cistercienser (Zeitschrift für Kirchengeschichte 84, 1973, pp. 188–232).

[109] Statuta capitulorum generalium ordinis Cisterciensis ab anno 1116 ad annum 1786, ed. JOSEPH-MARIA CANIVEZ, 8 vols., Louvain 1933–1941, 1, pp. 91–95, caps. 19,21. However, Stephen Harding could make an agreement of confraternity with another monastery, see the spiritual agreement between Cîteaux and Saint–Vaast, Arras (1124), referred to in: JEAN MARILIER, Chartes et documents concernant l'abbaye de Cîteaux, 1098–1182, Rome 1961, nos. 74f., pp. 83f. St. Bernard granted confraternity by letter to Archbishop Malachy of Armagh and King Dermot II of Ireland: Sancti Bernardi Opera, edd. LECLERCQ – ROCHAIS (as n. 65) 8, nos. 545f., pp. 512ff. In 1142 the Cistercian and Premonstratensian orders made a mixed agreememt of confraternity: J.B. VALVEKENS, Actus Confraternitatis inter Ordinem Praemonstratensem et Ordinem Cisterciensem (Analecta Praemonstratensia 42, 1966, pp. 326–330) text on pp. 329f., cf. Statuta, ed. CANIVEZ, 1, pp. 35ff.; the general chapter of 1191 called for its strict observance: Statuta, cap. 6, ed. CANIVEZ, 1, p. 135; cf. 1239, cap. 17, p. 206. For references to disputes see 1194, cap. 12, 1198, cap. 42, and 1207, cap. 54, IBID. pp. 173, 230, 344. References to the Cluniacs begin in 1184, cap. 21, p. 98; for the Carthusians see 1192, cap. 10, 1195, cap. 41, and 1210, cap. 1, pp. 148, 187f., 368f.

[110] For Cîteaux see RHF Obit. 6,2, pp. 608–662, and the articles by TALBOT and WOLLASCH (as n. 108), esp. WOLLASCH pp. 230f.

[111] RHF Obit. 6,2, pp. 612, 619f.

[112] WOLLASCH (as n. 108) pp. 196f., 204–207, 222f., 227.

[113] See esp. JEAN–BAPTISTE VAN DAMME, La constitution cistercienne de 1165 (Analecta sacri ordinis Cisterciensis 19, 1963, pp. 51–104) esp. pp. 53f.

[114] Above p. 247.

could be in a like relationship to its dependency [115]. During the past century
agreements of religious superiors had insisted upon the bonds of love and
like-mindedness. Nowhere were such bonds more insisted upon than in
England, the homeland of Stephen Harding, monk of Molesme and abbot of
Cîteaux [116]. When they became the basis of monastic agreements between
mother and daughter houses, and when spiritual and temporal benefits
followed as expressions of them, there was at least a foreshadowing of the
Carta caritatis and of the new relationship of Cistercian houses to one
another.

It would exceed the purpose of this paper to discuss Cistercian origins; in
any case the criticism and reassessment of the primitive Cistercian documents
is still far from complete. But two areas may be selected for discussion. The
first is the relation of Molesme in the years 1097 and 1110 to its daughter
house of Aulps; for this relationship anticipated the early developments at
Cîteaux itself [117]. In 1097 Aulps, hitherto *per omnia subditus ut cellam* to
Molesme, requested and received the status of an abbey. In 1110 in chapter
there Robert of Molesme established *pax et concordia* between the abbey of
Aulps and its own foundation of Baleine by making Baleine too, an abbey. In
either case many of the arrangements were similar in spirit and letter to those
of black-monk agreements of confraternity. Such agreements gave abbots the
right to preside in other chapters: in the arrangements of 1097, when the abbot
of Molesme came to Aulps he was to be accepted with reverence in the
abbot's chair [118]; so in the Concordia Molesmensis of 1110 was the abbot of
Aulps at Baleine. Black-monk agreements provided for adjudication in
disputes between abbots and their monks: in 1097 if there were dispute at
Aulps the abbot of Molesme should be called in [119]; in 1110 the abbot of
Baleine was answerable at Aulps if he transgressed the Rule, he might appeal
to the abbot and church of Molesme [120], and *propter ecclesie disciplinam vel
necessitatem* he might seek to borrow monks from Aulps. At Odense the prior
was to be confirmed in office by the abbot of Evesham: in 1097 the abbot of
Aulps was to be chosen from Molesme and instituted by its abbot.
Black-monk agreements provided for the transfer of monks: in 1097 and 1110
it was more strictly ruled that monks could be received only with their own

---

[115] Above pp. 247–248.

[116] Thus, the Regularis concordia, cap. 4 (as n. 20) pp. 2f. opened with a royal injunction that, to avoid dissention, all should be of one mind in monastic usage. Of the agreements referred to above n. 1, that of c.1010–20 bade bishops and abbots to be in unity and love towards God and the world, and as it were *cor unum et anima una* (Acts 4:32). The same aspiration was twice expressed in the Worcester agreement of 1077, which provided that ‚we will all be in unity as if all seven monasteries were one monastery, and be *quasi cor unum et anima una*. Stephen Harding kept in touch with his original English monastery of Sherborne: MARILIER (as n. 109) no. 88, p. 91.

[117] For the documents see JACQUES LAURENT, Cartulaire de l'abbaye de Molesme, 2 vols., Paris 1907–1911, 2, nos. 4, 158, pp. 7f., 150f.; JEAN–BAPTISTE VAN DAMME (Ed.), Documenta pro Cisterciensis ordinis historiae ac iuris studio, Collecta A, Westmalle 1959, pp. 3ff. See also ID., Formation de la constitution cistercienne (Studia monastica 4, 1962, pp. 111–137) pp. 128–131.

[118] ... *omnis ei reverentia tam in sede quam in iusticiis regulariter tamen peragendis exhibebitur*.

[119] ... *ad hoc examinandum vel pacificandum noster abbas* (i.e. of Molesme), *non alia quelibet persona, advocabitur*.

[120] The latter phrase anticipates Cistercian terminology: see WOLLASCH (as n. 14) pp. 180f.

abbot's leave. And like agreements of confraternity these arrangements had the sanction not of law but of love. Here, however, the similarity ends; for the limits of agreements of confraternity were exceeded. There was an unprecedented sense of the nearness between the elder and the younger houses which was expressed in a provision of 1110 that remarkably anticipated the Carta caritatis: the elder house would levy no material exaction *nisi quod ex caritate sibi utrimque servient* [121]. An altogether fresh clarity and inventiveness distinguish the documents of Aulps and Baleine from black–monk agreements.

A second area of inquiry is a comparison with the earliest documents of Cîteaux itself [122]. The keynote of these documents was that the sole guide to monastic legislation should be charity and the benefit of souls in matters divine and human [123]. Sometimes, as with the reception of fugitive monks, the Cistercians imposed restrictions that were uncharacteristic, and perhaps deliberately so, of black–monk agreements of confraternity [124]. But in others they seem to have adapted some of their caritative provisions. Thus, in what seems to have been a very early formulation, Cîteaux and its daughters extended mutual hospitality to each others' monks [125]. Later on, fugitives from incorrigibly errant houses might always come *ad suam matrem videlicet novum monasterium* (i.e. Cîteaux) *ad habitandum ... sicut filius ecclesie monachus* [126]. Further, provisions of agreements of confraternity regarding visiting abbots seem to have prepared the way for the detailed Cistercian legislation about the visits of the abbot of Cîteaux to daughter abbeys, of their abbots to Cîteaux, and of the abbots of Cistercian houses to each other [127]. Above all, the early

---

[121] Cf. the Carta caritatis cum sua approbatione (1119), cap. 1, VAN DAMME, Documenta (as n. 117) p. 16.

[122] It is not possible here to discuss the still unresolved problems concerning Cîteaux's origins. I have taken account of the following contributions: JEAN A. LEFÈVRE, whose articles are listed by DAVID KNOWLES, Great Historical Enterprises. Problems in Monastic History, London etc. 1963, p. 198 as a preface to his own discussion pp. 137f., 198–222 ('The Primitive Cistercian Documents'); VAN DAMME (as n. 117); ID., Autour des origines cisterciennes (Collectanea ordinis Cisterciensium reformatorum 20, 1958, pp. 37–60, 153–168, 374–390; 21, 1959, pp. 70–86, 137–156), reprinted together Westmalle 1959; ID., Genèse des *Instituta Generalis Capituli* (Cîteaux 12, 1961, pp. 28–60); ID., Saint Étienne Harding mieux connu (Cîteaux 14, 1963, pp. 307–313); ID., Vir Dei Alberici (Analecta sacri ordinis Cisterciensis 20, 1964, pp. 153–164); ID., Autour des origines cisterciennes. Quelques à-propos (Analecta Cisterciensia 21, 1965, pp. 128–137); ID., Les pouvoirs de l'Abbé de Cîteaux aux XIIe et au XIIIe siècle (Analecta Cisterciensia 24, 1968, pp. 47–85); CHARLES DEREINE, La fondation de Cîteaux d'après l'*Exordium Cistercii* et l'*Exordium parvum* (Cîteaux 10, 1959, pp. 125–139); EDITH PÁSZTOR, Le origini dell'Ordine Cisterciense e la riforma monastica (Analecta Cisterciensia 21, 1965, pp. 112–127); POLYCARP ZAKAR, Die Anfänge des Zisterzienserordens. Kurze Bemerkungen zu den Studien der letzten zehn Jahre (Analecta sacri ordinis Cisterciensis 20, 1964, pp. 101–138); ID., Réponse aux *Quelques à-propos* du Père Van Damme sur les origines cisterciennes. Quelques conclusions (Analecta Cisterciensia 21, 1965, pp. 138–166).

[123] *Hoc etiam decretum kartam caritatis vocari censebant quia eius statutum omnis exactionis gravamen propulsans solam caritatem et animarum utilitatem in divinis et humanis exsequitur*: Carta caritatis (1119), Pref., VAN DAMME, Documenta (as n. 117) p. 16.

[124] Ibid. cap. 9, p. 19, lines 5–10.

[125] *Et quia omnes monachos ipsorum ad nos venientes in claustro nostro recipimus, et ipsi similiter nostros in claustris suis recipiant* ...: ibid. cap. 3, p. 17. For the development of the Carta caritatis see VAN DAMME, Documenta (as n. 117) esp. pp. 102f.

[126] Cap. 9, VAN DAMME, Documenta (as n. 117) p. 18, line 42 – p. 19, line 5.

[127] Caps. 4, 6, 10, ibid. pp. 17,20.

development of Cistercian general chapters, which took place by the addition of the abbots of daughter houses to meetings of the abbot and community of Cîteaux, may have been helped by black–monk agreements of confraternity which allowed monks of associated houses to be present at chapter meetings [128].

Yet – as at Aulps and Baleine – whatever such agreements may have contributed in detail to Cistercian institutions, they did not touch their core and centre. The earliest form of the Carta caritatis, which was drawn up by 1114 [129], stated the principle, present in the Concordia Molismensis of 1110 but unknown in agreements of confraternity, that the mother house should renounce all material exactions from its daughters; Cîteaux was to exercise cure of souls through charity (*gratia caritatis*), and was carefully to recall a daughter abbey which deviated from the Rule [130]. The Carta caritatis of 1119 expressed more fully still the principles upon which the ordo Cisterciensis would develop: the regular visitation of daughter houses by the mother; the holding of annual general chapters [131]; and the extension to all founding abbeys in relation to their daughters of the relationship between Cîteaux and its own daughters [132]. All this far outran black–monk arrangements. For the first time in monastic history, and with utter freshness, the structure of a religious order came into being. Its aim was to follow in strictness the Rule of St. Benedict: *in arta et angusta via quam regula demonstrat* [133]. Papal sanction set the seal upon this development [134].

It must be concluded that, when compared with the Cistercian achievement, black–monk agreements of confraternity at no time transcended the limitations set by their early character as gift–exchanges. For all their variety and detail it cannot be shown that they had legal force. Apart from their spiritual provisions it is not even apparent that they were normally observed in practice. They remained in the tradition of Carolingian times, and they were never adapted to the legal age represented by Stephen Harding, Gratian of Bologna, and Pope Innocent III. However the terms in which they were drafted disclosed a need for constitutional developments in black monasticism which the Fourth Lateran Council sought to meet by the institution of general chapters. By insisting upon charity and concord as the basis of monastic association they prepared the way for the early Cistercian le-

---

[128] See esp. VAN DAMME, Genèse (as n. 122) pp. 54ff.; cf. KNOWLES (as n. 122) pp. 206ff.

[129] It is referred to as the *Carta ... caritatis et unanimitatis inter novum monasterium et abbatias ab eo propagatas* in the foundation charter of Pontigny (1114): TIBURTIUS HÜMPFNER, Exordium Cistercii cum summa cartae caritatis et fundatio primarum quattuor filiarum Cistercii, Kapisztrán Nyomda, Vác 1932, pp. 19–21, no. 3, p. 19.

[130] Cap. I, VAN DAMME, Documenta (as n. 117) p. 16.

[131] *... ibique de salute animarum suarum suorumque tractent, in observatione sancte regule vel ordinis si quid est emendandum vel augendum ordinent, bonum pacis et caritatis inter se reforment* : cap. 7, ibid. p. 17.

[132] *Cum vero aliqua ecclesiarum nostrarum Dei gratia adeo creverit ut aliud cenobium construere possit illam diffinitionem quam nos inter nostros confratres tenemus, et ipsi inter se teneant* : cap. 8, ibid. p. 18.

[133] Exordium parvum, Epistola, ibid. p. 5.

[134] For the bulls of Paschal II (1119), Eugenius III (1152), Anastasius IV (1153), and Alexander III (1163 and 1165) see ibid. pp. 20f.; JOSEPH TURK, Cistercii statuta antiqua (Analecta Cisterciensia 4, 1948, pp. 114–129); JEAN-A. LEFÈVRE, Une bulle inconnue d'Alexandre III dans le ms. Dijon 87 (Cistercienser Chronik 62, 1965, pp. 1–7).

gislation, which in some aspects owed a debt to them. But in its essential features the ordo Cisterciensis was new, and opened vistas which were not those of traditional black–monk arrangements.

"QUIDAM FRATER STEPHANUS NOMINE, ANGLICUS NATIONE"

THE ENGLISH BACKGROUND OF STEPHEN HARDING *

'A certain brother, Stephen by name, English by nation': thus a perhaps late passage of the EP (17.2) referred to the man whom modern historians call Stephen Harding. The debate that for the past forty years has gathered about Cistercian origins has done nothing to reduce his stature as a leader of the early Cistercians. He was one of the group of twenty-one under Abbot Robert of Molesme who in 1098 left that abbey for Cîteaux; during the abbacy of Alberic (1099-1108) he was prior of Cîteaux, and he was abbot from 1108 until failing health compelled his resignation in 1133, the year before his death. The latest appraisal of Stephen's work, by J.B. Auberger, has emphasized the distinctiveness of his rule at Cîteaux as compared with St Bernard's at Clairvaux. Auberger's hypothesis of two traditions in early Cistercian monasticism is an arresting one which, if open to debate and reconsideration, suggests many lines of further inquiry. The purpose of this

---

* Bibliography and Abbreviations. — The earliest Cistercian documents are best studied in *Les plus anciens textes de Cîteaux*, edd. J. de la C. BOUTON and J.B. VAN DAMME (Achel, 1985); they are abbreviated as follows: EP: *Exordium Cisterciensis Coenobii* (*Exordium Parvum*); CCP: *Carta Caritatis Prior*, followed by the *Privilegium Calixti*; EC: *Exordium Cistercii, Summa Cartae Caritatis* (SCC), *et Capitula*. To them are added: Stat(s): The *Statuta* 'of 1134', in: *Statuta capitulorum generalium Ordinis Cisterciensis*, ed. J.-M. CANIVEZ, 8 vols. (Louvain, 1933-41), 1, 12-32; EM: *Exordium Magnum Cisterciense, sive Narratio de initio Cisterciensis Ordinis auctore Conrado*, ed. B. GRIESSER (Rome, 1961). — Bede's *Ecclesiastical History* and *History of the Abbots* are edited in *Baedae Historia Ecclesiastica gentis Anglorum*: *Venerabilis Bedae opera historica*, ed. C. PLUMMER, 2 vols. (Oxford, 1896); the *Eccles. Hist.* is also edited in *Bede's Ecclesiastical History of the English People*, edd. B. COLGRAVE and R.A.B. MYNORS (Oxford, 1969). — Other abbreviations used are: AUBERGER: J.B. AUBERGER, *L'unanimité cistercienne primitive: mythe ou réalité?* (Achel, 1986); LAURENT: *Cartulaire de Molesme (916-1250)*, ed. J. LAURENT, 2 vols. (Paris, 1907-11); MARILIER: *Chartes et documents concernant l'abbaye de Cîteaux (1098-1182)*, ed. J. MARILIER (Rome, 1961); PL: *Patrologia Latina*, ed. J.P. MIGNE; ZALUSKA: Y. ZALUSKA, *L'enluminure et le scriptorium de Cîteaux au XIIe siècle* (Cîteaux, 1989).
This paper was stimulated by my participation in the *Colloque Saint Bernard* at Lyons and Cîteaux, 5-9 June 1990. My special thanks are due to Frère Auberger and Mᵐᵉ Zaluska for their papers, and to Père Dominique Bertrand for his invitation to attend.

paper is to raise just one consequential question : is it possible that Stephen's monastic outlook and achievement may have owed more to his English background than has hitherto been appreciated ?

*
 *   *

Since Auberger's work is not well known amongst English historians, four of its leading conclusions may be indicated, all of which impress the present writer as being basically well founded. The first is that the early Cistercian documents provide evidence for two distinct traditions : an 'official' tradition maintained at Cîteaux which was intended to inform new recruits to the Cistercians about how the order had come to be as it was (EP Prol.), and an 'unofficial' record emanating from Clairvaux which was concerned not so much to inform as to educate and edify. In terms of the sources, Auberger departs from the conclusions of J.A. Lefèvre, for whom (in the simplest terms) the EP was late, tendentious, and unreliable, while the EC disclosed the mind of Stephen Harding. [1] Rather, so far as events up to 1134 are concerned, the 'official' record from Cîteaux is mainly to be found in (i) EP caps 1-10 and 14 ; (ii) CCP, of which caps 1-3 date from the foundation of its first 'daughter' at la Ferté (1112/13), and caps 4-11 were a gradual response to the foundations as well in 1114 and 1115 of Pontigny, Morimond, and Clairvaux, the whole being confirmed by Pope Calixtus II in his *privilegium* of 1119 ; and (iii) Statutes 1-27 of the Statutes 'of 1134'. The 'unofficial', Clairvaux record began to take shape at about the time of Bernard's *Apologia to Abbot William of Saint-Thierry*, dated to 1123/4 ; its documents are the EC with the accompanying SCC and Capitula.

Secondly, the difference between the 'official' and 'unofficial' records can be epitomized in two adverbs, *artius* and *altius* : should the Rule of St Benedict be followed 'more strictly', or is the keynote 'more highly' ? According to the Cîteaux tradition, at Molesme the Rule had been followed with culpable laxity — *tepide ac negligenter* ; henceforth it should be followed *artius ... atque perfectius*, and the

---

1. For a list and discussion of Lefèvre's articles, see D. KNOWLES. *Great Historical Enterprises. Problems in Monastic History* (London, etc., 1963), pp. 198-222. Subsequent work before Auberger's is discussed by K. HALLINGER, 'Die Anfänge von Cîteaux', in : *Aus Kirche und Reich : Studien zu Theologie, Politik und Recht im Mittelalter. Festschrift für Friedrich Kempf*, ed. H. MORDEK (Sigmaringen, 1983), pp. 225-35.

Lord should be served *salubrius atque quietius* (EP 2.3-4).   In the
Clairvaux tradition, on the other hand, the hardships of the reforming party at Molesme before 1098 (EP 9.39) had not been directly
experienced.   Molesme was a praiseworthy monastery — *fama cele-
berrium, religione conspicuum* ; but some of its members who aspired
more highly (*altius intelligentes*) and were lovers of virtues took
thought about how they could better themselves under a regime of
fertile poverty (*paupertas foecunda*) and serve the better as *milites
Christi* (EC 1).   For the one tradition, the change was from bad to
good, but for the other from good to better.

Thirdly, so far as Stephen was concerned, his association was,
therefore, with the aspiration to live *artius*.   Even so, as abbot of
Cîteaux his outlook and style of rule developed as the Cistercians
multiplied and diversified.   Initially, as ruler of only one house, his
concern was to foster in perpetuity a strict observance within his
own community there ; only with the multiplication of new foundations did he become concerned with authenticity and unanimity
throughout a Cistercian family.   His wider concern is first expressed in the foundation charter of Pontigny (1114), in the reference to
a *carta caritatis et unanimitatis* between Cîteaux and its daughters
(in the plural) which is generally accepted to be found in CCP caps.
1-3. [2]   As settled by *c.* 1119, the CCP was extended to make sophis-
ticated provision for visitations and general chapters.   Stephen's
constitution-making was a prolonged process which involved major
developments in response to the expansion of the order.

And fourthly, as scholars have for some time appreciated, the
earliest documents of Stephen's abbacy indicate that he at first
exercised strong personal, even monarchical authority — a veritable
paternalisme abbatial.   In his *Monitum* concerning the Bible (1109),
he could write that 'we prohibit by the authority of God and of our
congregation ...'.   In his encyclical letter on the chant, probably of
the same date and, significantly, addressed *successoribus suis*, he
declared that 'by God's authority and our own we enjoin that you
never presume by your levity to change or root out the integrity of
the holy regulation (*integritatem sanctae regulae*) which you see that
we have worked out and established in this matter by no small
labour'. [3]   It has long been recognized that CCP 1-3, the so-called

2. For the Pontigny charter, see Marilier, p. 66, no. 43.
3. Auberger, p. 327, no. I/1a, b ; Załuska, pp. 274-5.

325

'primitive' *Carta Caritatis*, is distinctively expressed in the first person plural as an expression of the abbot's authority. Even so late
as the CCP, some of the plural verbs, like *si aliquid constituerimus
aut permutaverimus* (8.4), still read like expressions of Stephen's own
authority. [4] Stephen's persistent, if diminishing, exercise of the
abbot's powers must be borne in mind, no less than his constitutio-
nalism.

What, then, may Stephen's English background have contributed
to his part in shaping Cistercian monasticism, especially if these
four points are borne in mind?

There is only a little evidence for Stephen's life in England and
elsewhere before he entered Molesme — though there is rather more
than historians seem currently to appreciate. To begin with what
is familiar, that master of digression, William of Malmesbury, made
a digression about the Cistercians which was prompted by the
approximate synchronism of their foundation in 1098 with the
death of King William II (1087-1100). [5] He gloried in Stephen's
English birth, and exaggerated his part in the separation of the
Cistercians from their confrères at Molesme: 'It redounds to the
glory of England, that it produced such a man who was both the
author and the promotor of this way of monastic life' (cap. 334, cf.
335). William wrote at an early date, for he referred to the archbishop of Vienne, Guy, whose papal name was Calixtus II (1119-24),
as the reigning pope when he wrote (cap. 335). It was not until
1128 that the first Cistercian house, Waverley (dioc. Winchester),
was founded in England; one suspects that William gained his
information through the foundation from Cîteaux in 1121 of Waverley's parent-house, l'Aumône (dioc. Chartres). Though William's
facts were not always full or correct he was remarkably well informed, although there is no evidence that he had seen the EP or the
CCP in any form. As regards Stephen's English background, only
William records that, until he adopted this name, he was called

---

4. *Ibid.* p. 31. For the abbot's authority, see L.J. LEKAI, *Histoire de l'Ordre
cistercien* (Paris, 1957), pp. 37-45 ; also the comments of L. MOULIN, 'Note sur les
particularités de l'Ordre cartusien', in *Historia et spiritualitas Cartusiensis : Collo-
quii quarti internationalis Acta*, ed. J. DE GRAUWE (Destelbergen, 1983), pp. 283-
8.

5. WILLIAM OF MALMESBURY, *De gestis regum Anglorum libri quinque*, iv. 334-
7, ed. W. STUBBS, 2 vols. (London : Rolls Series, 90, 1887-9), 2.380-5.

Harding (caps. 334, 335). Born to parents of middling social rank, he was a child oblate at the cathedral priory of Sherborne and was evidently professed there : he was *a puero monachus*, and at Molesme he easily resumed the elements of the religious life with which he had once been familiar. But he had tired of monastic life at Sherborne, and had wandered first to Scotland and then to France (cap. 334). Familiar English sources make it possible to say a little more about Sherborne. It is not known when Harding became an oblate there, but since he died an old man in 1134 it is likely to have been soon after the Norman Conquest of 1066 — probably in the 1070s or 1080s. Materially Sherborne was probably fairly prosperous, for the Domesday evidence suggests that it suffered little from the Norman Conquest. [6] Ecclesiastically, Sherborne had been made a cathedral priory *c.*993 by its then bishop, St Wulfsin (*c.* 993-1002). Bishop Alfwold (1045-58) had rebuilt the monastery and translated the relics of St Wulfsin and of the Cornish St Juthwara. The see and priory further benefited from the return to England in 1058 of Bishop Herman of Ramsbury, who from that date held the sees of Ramsbury and Sherborne and established himself at the latter place. He had recently himself become a monk of Saint-Bertin (dioc. Arras), whence he brought the monk and hagiographer Goscelin who seems to have spent some time as a monk at Sherborne. There, in 1077/8 Goscelin was to write a Life of St Wulfsin, [7] which incidentally shows the night office being faithfully performed (cap. 19) and St Wulfsin being vigilant to safeguard the bishop's rights against royal officials (cap. 20). All this points to there having been a fair standard of monastic observance and study in the Sherborne that Harding knew. But in 1075 the council of London decreed the transfer of Herman's see to Salisbury ; only in 1122 was the priory raised to the status of an abbey. Goscelin's Life of Wulfsin shows that it was ruled by priors of English name — Wulfric under Bishop Herman (d. 1078) (Pref.) and Aelfric under Bishop Osmund of Salisbury (1078-99) (cap. 21). The bishop-

---

6. *Domesday Book*, vol. i, fo. 77ab ; see M.M.C. CALTHROP, 'Sherborne', in : *Victoria County History of the County of Dorset*, ed. W. PAGE, 2 (London, 1908), p. 63.
7. C.H. TALBOT, 'The Life of St Wulfsin of Sherborne by Goscelin', *Revue Bénédictine*, 69 (1959), 68-85. For Goscelin, see also TALBOT, 'The *Liber confortatorius* of Goscelin of Saint Bertin', *Analecta Monastica, 3ᵉ sér.*, edd. M.M. LEBRETON, J. LECLERCQ, and C.H. TALBOT, Studia Anselmiana, 37 (Rome, 1955), 1-117, esp. pp. 1-22.

abbots' withdrawal and the sole rule of a prior may have had a permanently unsettling effect which might help to account for Harding's departure.

According to William of Malmesbury, when Harding reached France he spent some years studying the liberal arts before experiencing spiritual compunction. Then he journeyed to Rome with a clerk who had been a fellow-student; whatever the difficulties of the journey they persisted in the daily recitation of the whole Psalter. Upon his return to Burgundy, Harding became a monk at Molesme, 'a new and great monastery' (cap. 334). Important light is thrown upon these events by another, largely neglected source for Stephen's English connections which discloses who was Stephen's companion upon his journey to Rome. [8] He was another Englishman, named Peter, who died in 1136 two years after Stephen, and whose Life was written between *c.* 1160 and *c.* 1185 from a strongly Molesme standpoint. His career interlocked with Stephen's for many years. According to the Life, he was born in England of noble parents; in the course of a devout childhood he studied the liberal arts (1257B-58C). But, like Stephen, he left England for France (1258D-59A); one wonders how many more Englishmen may have reacted to the Norman Conquest in this way. In France, Peter determined to live *peregre*, that is, to live the wandering life of a stranger and pilgrim upon earth, 'like another Abraham', said his Life, 'travelling from his land and kindred, and from his father's house' (1258D). Peter's wanderings brought him to Burgundy, where he met Stephen, 'a man of most chaste life'; Stephen's religious amendment to which William of Malmesbury referred seems to have predated their meeting. Peter and Stephen became friends, and Peter's Life confirms William of Malmesbury's record by saying that they used daily to recite the whole Psalter, saying alternate verses (1259BC). In due course they journeyed to Rome, where they together spent a time of rigorous devotion and penance. Then they returned to Burgundy, and both of them became monks at Molesme (1259CD). The Life depicts Peter at Molesme as an exemplary monk. His friendship with Stephen continued, but since a monastic regime did

---

8. *Vita sancti Petri prioris Juliacensis puellarum monasterii et monachi Molismensis*, *PL* 185.1255-70; see G. MATHON, 'Pietro de Jully, beato', *Bibliotheca Sanctorum*, 10 (Rome, 1968), 704. William of Malmesbury's account of the journey to Rome is repeated by HERBERT OF CLAIRVAUX, writing *c.* 1178: *De miraculis libri tres*, 2.24, *PL* 185.1333D, whence EM 1.21.

not permit their continuing to say the Psalter together daily as they had been accustomed, they divided it between them and said half each (1259D-60A). It is to be observed that the Life always referred to Stephen by this name, with the implication that he adopted it long before his entry into Molesme. Peter's own name is an unlikely one for him to have received from his parents, since it was introduced into England by the Normans. The possibility must be entertained that both Peter and Stephen discarded their original names in favour of those of the prince of the apostles and of the New Testament protomartyr, as part of the dissociation from the past that went with the *vita peregrina.* [9]

The Life of Peter said nothing about him between his entry into Molesme and Stephen's election to be abbot of Cîteaux. However, his religious strictness and his friendship with Stephen raise the question whether he was not the Peter who was named in the EP in company with Stephen, Abbot Robert of Molesme, and four other monks in the text of the letter which the papal legate, Archbishop Hugh of Lyons, wrote in late 1097 to the monks of Molesme. Hugh confirmed the purpose of the abbot and his companions to follow the Benedictine Rule more strictly and perfectly elsewhere than at Molesme (2.5). If so, Peter must have been one of those who in 1099 returned with their abbot from Cîteaux to Molesme, for his future was wholly bound up with the latter abbey. The EP documented the steps whereby, through Archbishop Hugh's good offices, a *modus vivendi* was established between Molesme and Cîteaux so that the two abbeys henceforth lived in peace and in freedom from mutual claims (*in pace et libertate*) (7). It is remarkable that Peter could live as strictly at Molesme as Stephen did at Cîteaux, and that their spiritual friendship should have persisted, at least on Peter's side; there is no evidence of any kind on Stephen's.

At the time of Abbot Alberic of Cîteaux's death, Peter's abbot had sent him to one of Molesme's cells, at Useldingen in Luxemburg (1260A, cf. 1261A). [10] Possibly Molesme gave its more eremitically inclined members an opportunity to fulfill their aspirations by thus directing them to the solitude of its cells. Molesme's relations with

---

9. Although Peter took a continuing interest in English affairs; in his last illness he warned Count Theobald of Blois and Champagne that it was not God's will that he should seek the English crown: 1266AB.

10. For Useldingen, see LAURENT, 1.236-7, no. 47, and 2.175, no. 194.

Cîteaux seem to have been sympathetic. The Life referred to it kindly, as 'that new plantation of Cîteaux which fled the tumult of the peoples and the storms of the world, and sought in solitude to serve God alone' (1260A). [11] When Cîteaux lost its abbot, it sought the prayers of its mother (Molesme); upon the advice of godfearing men it elected Stephen as its abbot. Peter persisted in his bond of prayer with Stephen: knowing how busy an abbot must be, he now adopted the custom of reciting both halves of the Psalter daily on his own and Stephen's behalf (1260B). The spiritual friendship of the two expatriate Englishmen was, indeed, enduring and significant. It was possible for two equally rigorous monks, bound by lasting spiritual friendship, to be equally at home in Molesme and Cîteaux. The 'unofficial' Clairvaux presentation of Molesme as *religione conspicuus* (EC 1.2) was evidently not without foundation.

In the light of the Life of Peter, it was also explicable. For Peter was eventually sent to be claustral prior of its house for women, Jully-les-Nonnains (dioc. Langres), established there in 1113 (1263C-64C). The Cistercians were for long reluctant to make provision for women who wished, or who were under pressure, to become nuns, and it was Jully that two of Bernard of Clairvaux's closest female relatives entered — Elizabeth, the wife of his eldest brother Guy who became a monk of Clairvaux, and his younger sister Hombeline who, after a spectacular conversion from a worldly life, secured her husband's permission to enter religion. [12] Both women became prioresses of Jully. Given this link with Bernard, it is easy to understand why, if the EC is to be associated with Clairvaux, it should be characterized by a favourable view of Molesme.

The Life of Peter thus offers invaluable evidence to the student of early Cistercian history. For the question principally raised in this paper, whether Peter's friend Stephen's monastic outlook and achievement owed more to his English background than has been appreciated, it may be helpful to reflect further upon the *peregrina vita* that Peter embarked upon and shared with Stephen. It was, of

---

11. 'novella illa Cisterciensis plantatio, quae populorum tumultum et saeculi turbinem fugiens in solitudine soli Deo vacare contendebat'; for the vocabulary, cf. EC 1.7, 2.11.

12. For Jully, see LAURENT, 1.253-6. For Bernard's relatives, see WILLIAM OF SAINT-THIERRY, *Sancti Bernardi abbatis Clarae-Vallensis vita et res gestae* (*Vita prima*) 1.3.10, 6.30, *PL* 185.232-3, 244-5; *Secunda vita sancti Bernardi abbatis auctore Alano*, 3.9, *PL* 185.474; *Vita sancti Petri* (as n. 8), cap. 10, *PL* 185.1264D-5B.

course, anything but a novel commitment: ever since the Columba-
nian mission to the continent of Europe in the late sixth century,
the Celtic mission to England in the seventh, and the Anglo-Saxon
missions to the continent in the eighth, it was a familiar way of
religious self-devotion. It may be that the two men adopted it
simply as a well established custom of the Christianity in which
they had been brought up. Yet both were educated men; Stephen,
at least, had had access to a monastic library at Sherborne. Therefore they may have read of the *peregrina vita* in Bede's *Ecclesiastical
History*, where it was presented in memorable terms. One thinks
especially of Egbert, one of Bede's central characters, who lived in
exile in Ireland for the sake of Christ (3.4). There, he had as a
companion Ethelhun; both caught the plague, and Ethelhun's
death frustrated their hope that they might enter into eternal life
together. The survivor, Egbert, took a vow so to live as a pilgrim
(*peregrinus*) that he would never return to Britain, and in addition
to the canonical psalmody he would daily recite the whole Psalter to
the praise of God (3.27). Egbert had earlier lived a similar life with
Chad, the future bishop (4.3), and later had missionary companions; he thought of himself preaching to the heathen on the continent or of going as a pilgrim to Rome (5.9). However he ended his
life with a stay of thirteen years in the monastery of Iona which he
taught to observe the Catholic Easter (5.22). There is no positive
evidence that Peter and Stephen were moved by Egbert's example,
yet Bede's account of him could have put into their heads so many
features of their own life as *peregrini*. And if there is much in Bede
that may have inspired Stephen the *peregrinus*, it is worth asking
whether Bede may not also have inspired Stephen, the monk and
abbot.

In the late eleventh century Bede's *Ecclesiastical History* is
widely attested both in England and on the continent; in the
England of King William I it was keenly studied, not least in
connection with the revival of northern monasticism in Bedan sites,
including Bede's own monastery of Wearmouth-Jarrow.[13] In his
Life of St Wulfsin, Goscelin of Saint-Bertin cited the *Ecclesiastical*

---

13. For the manuscript tradition of the *Ecclesiastical History*, see the edition
of Colgrave and Mynors, pp. XLII-LXIV. For its influence in Stephen's lifetime,
see R.H.C. DAVIS, 'Bede after Bede', in: *Studies in Medieval History presented to
R. Allen Brown*, edd. C. HARPER-BILL, C.J. HOLDSWORTH, and J.L. NELSON
(Woodbridge/Wolfboro, 1989), pp. 103-16.

History, in all likelihood from a copy which he saw at Sherborne. [14]   If William of Malmesbury was right about Stephen's journey
to Rome, he was probably also right about his journey to Scotland.
This may have taken him to Durham, where the books which
Bishop William of St Carilef (1080-96) gave to the library of his
cathedral priory included Bede's *Ecclesiastical History*; early in the
twelfth century Bede's *History of the Abbots of Wearmouth and Jarrow* was added to the manuscript. [15]   Even at a time when *pueriles
ineptiae* were obscuring his true vocation, Stephen may have been
sufficiently interested in the revival of northern monasticism to read
the Bedan works that were available at places like Durham.   He is
certainly more likely to have gained any knowledge of them that he
may have had in England rather than on the continent; it is not
known whether Bede was included in the early libraries of Molesme
and Cîteaux, although later in the twelfth century Cîteaux possessed a copy of the *Ecclesiastical History* and *Life of St Cuthbert* wich
still survives. [16]

The earliest Cistercian documents, and especially those which,
upon Auberger's construction of them, are to be associated with
Cîteaux rather than with Clairvaux, are notoriously barren of indications, whether express or implicit, of sources from the past which
may have helped to shape them.   Simple and practical, they focused upon immediate and particular problems rather than upon general principles, and especially upon the Rule of St Benedict and how
it should be interpreted and lived.   Auberger has made clear that
there is no reason for thinking that, at the Cîteaux which Stephen
knew, anyone had in mind the monasticism of the Desert Fathers;
the Cistercian attraction to their writings was a mark just a little of
the early Bernard of Clairvaux, but mainly of later generations. [17]

---

14. (as n. 7), cap. 9.
15. For the manuscript tradition of Bede's *History of the Abbots*, see PLUM-
MER's edition of Bede, l. CXXXII-CXL, CXLIV.   For the DURHAM MS of Bede,
Cathedral Library, B.II.35, see R.A.B. MYNORS, *Durham Cathedral Manuscripts*
(Oxford, 1939), pp. 41-2, no. 47.
16. DIJON, *Bibliothèque Municipale*, MS 574; Załuska assigns a date in the
third quarter of the twelfth century: pp. 244-5, no. 54.   She also lists the following of Bede's works amongst Cîteaux's later twelfth-century MSS: *In librum
beati patris Tobiae, De tabernaculo, De templo Salomonis, Expositio in Evangelium
Lucae, Expositio in Epistolas catholicas*: pp. 232-3, 235, 237, 238-9, 246, nos. 29,
34, 38, 41, 59.
17. AUBERGER, pp. 123, 133, 159, 167, 173-4, 319, 323.

Nor is there evidence that in the early years of Cîteaux there was antagonism, express or implied, to Cluny. [18]   Not only did the Cluniac Pope Urban II seek to ease the tension between Molesme and Cîteaux by encouraging Abbot Robert to return to Molesme (EP 6), but at the subsequent successful negotiations over which Archbishop Hugh of Lyons presided at *Portus Ansillae*, the Cluniac papal chamberlain Peter was approvingly present (EP 7.12). [19]   Yet if the early Cistercians were neither inspired by the Desert Fathers nor in reaction against the Cluniacs but concerned with their own particular and immediate problems, they are not likely to have proceeded in a total vacuum.   There are three connections in which it may be worth posing the question whether seventh-century Northumbrian monasticism as exhibited by Bede may not have been in Stephen's mind, perhaps already as a monk at Molesme and more strongly as abbot of Cîteaux: the concept of a *carta caritatis et unanimitatis*; the role of the abbot of Cîteaux, especially in relation to the Rule of St Benedict; and Stephen's agenda as abbot of Cîteaux, especially in his early years.

First, the concept of a *carta caritatis et unanimitatis*. [20]   No one reading Bede's account of the double monastery of Wearmouth and Jarrow in his *History of the Abbots* with the Cistercian CCP in mind can fail to be struck by the comparability of the two situations. There was a similar need to maintain constitutional unity and monastic uniformity amongst related communities that were set at a distance from each other.   Wearmouth-Jarrow was not, of course, a blueprint that Stephen could have merely copied, if only because of the multiplication of Cistercian houses.   Yet Bede, who was himself a monk of Wearmouth-Jarrow from 679/80 until 735 under the abbots of whom he wrote, penetrated to the heart of how, in the earliest days of the Rule of St Benedict in England, [21] its

---

18. *Ibid.*, pp. 8, 59.
19. For Peter, see *Imprecatio beati Hugonis abbatis*, in: 'Memorials of Abbot Hugh of Cluny', ed. H.E.J. Cowdrey, *Studi Gregoriani*, 11 (1978), 174-5.
20. For the phrase, see the foundation charter of Pontigny, as n. 2.
21. It is unlikely that the Rule of St Benedict was the sole Rule of the early communities at Wearmouth-Jarrow, since Benedict Biscop spoke of the seventeen monasteries upon which he drew: *History of the Abbots*, 1.11.   But Bede laid emphasis upon the Rule of St Benedict: 1.11, 2.16, and was at pains to associate Benedict Biscop with Benedict of Nursia: 1.1.   Eleventh-century readers would certainly have regarded the communities as Benedictine.   For the problem of the Rule followed by them, see P. Wormald, 'Bede and Benedict Biscop', in: *Famulus Christi*, ed. G. Bonner (London, 1976), pp. 141-5.

earliest followers so applied it that plurality was balanced by unity, and unanimity was preserved. In this light, the *History of the Abbots* might almost be called a *Carta caritatis et unanimitatis.*

The early development of Wearmouth-Jarrow was as follows. In 674, Benedict Biscop founded Wearmouth, dedicating it to St Peter; in 681 he founded Jarrow, some ten kilometres to the north, dedicating it to St Paul, thus already invoking the heavenly unanimity of the martyred princes of the apostles. Benedict Biscop, abbot of both houses, soon afterwards departed upon his sixth journey to Rome, having appointed Ceolfrid to be abbot of Jarrow and Eosterwine of Wearmouth. As Bede pointed out, this produced the situation, which called for a defence, of one monastery with two abbots (1.7). Before Benedict Biscop returned, Eosterwine died; on arrival Benedict was glad to find that Eosterwine had been replaced by Sigfrid. However, in 689 and 690 respectively, both Benedict Biscop and Sigfrid died; Bede wrote a moving account of their fraternity during their last illnesses (1.11-13). Ceolfrid became abbot of both monasteries until he resigned through old age and infirmity in 716; he was then replaced by Hwaetbert.

Bede commented at length on the bonds between Wearmouth and Jarrow. At the beginning, Benedict Biscop established as the guiding principle (*ratio*)

> that between the two places a single peace and concord, the same familiarity and goodwill, should be perpetually observed; and that just as, for example, the body cannot be sundered from the head through which it breathes, and the head cannot forget the body through which it lives, so no one should seek by any device to divide from each other the two monasteries which are joined in the fraternal society of the chief apostles.

Bede rounded off his comments with the example of St Benedict of Nursia, who found it convenient to set twelve abbots over his disciples 'without detriment to charity — nay, to the increase of charity' (1.7). [22] A very similar thought concluded what is generally taken to be the primitive *Carta Caritatis*: there must be a single usage in customs, chant, and liturgical books, 'so that in what we do there may be no discord, but we live by one charity, one rule, and like

---

22. Bede referred to GREGORY THE GREAT, *Dialogues*, 2.3.13, edd. A. DE VOGÜÉ and P. ANTIN, 3 vols, Sources Chrétiennes, 251, 260, 265 (Paris, 1978-80), 2.148-51.

customs' (CCP 3.2 ; cf. Prol. 3-4, Stats. 2-4).   As dedication to St Peter and St Paul joined Wearmouth and Jarrow, because Molesme and Cîteaux were dedicated to the Blessed Virgin, all Cistercian houses were to be so dedicated (Stat. 18).   Perhaps a similar situation generated a similar response ; but perhaps when Stephen considered the specific problems of Cîteaux and her daughters, Bede's model was present in his mind.

The earliest evolution of the Cistercian general chapter further suggests that this cannot be excluded.   Both before and after the dying Benedict Biscop concluded that, after his death, it would conduce to peace, unity, and concord if a sole abbot ruled both houses (1.13), the collaboration of the two monastic chapters in abbatial elections provided a significant model.   When Eosterwine died in Benedict Biscop's absence, the Wearmouth chapter met with his co-abbot Ceolfrid of Jarrow to elect Sigfrid — in Benedict's retrospective opinion, an admirable step to have taken (1.10).   In due course, Hwaetbert was elected abbot of both monasteries by all the Wearmouth monks together with many of the seniors of Jarrow. 'Fit una concordia, eadem utrorumque sententia', Bede commented (2.18).   There is an interesting similarity to the earliest general chapters at Cîteaux under Stephen as reflected in the CCP, where abbots of other houses at first assembled with the conventual chapter of Cîteaux, only gradually reserving business to themselves (7.3, 8.2).   Perhaps again, Stephen was acting along lines which he recalled from Bede, until Cîteaux's distinctive arrangements became fully established.

A comparison with Molesme may serve to underline the special nature of the arrangements which developed at Cîteaux under Stephen's guiding hand as abbot.   In 1097, by a charter written by a Stephen who may have been the future abbot of Cîteaux, Abbot Robert of Molesme, assisted by his prior Alberic, constituted its dependent cell at Aulps (dioc. Geneva) an abbey with its own abbot. Aulps had been established early in the 1090s by monks from Molesme who, in a phrase anticipating the Cistercians, aspired to hold to the precepts of St Benedict *arcius*.   But in 1097, relations between the two abbeys remained largely within those familiar in monastic confraternity agreements.   In 1107, Aulps founded its own dependency of Balerne (dioc. Besançon).   A dispute quickly arose between Aulps and Balerne which Robert of Molesme settled in an adjudication of 1110 which sought to establish *pax et concordia* between them.   In a remarkable anticipation of the primitive Cistercian *Carta Caritatis* (CCP 1), neither Aulps nor Balerne was to make any material exaction from the other.   But, overall, Balerne was simply made subject to Aulps under Molesme's general superiority. [23]   On the one hand, the Molesme documents show that, after the composition with Cîteaux (EP 7) and with the good relations between Molesme and Cîteaux that seem to have prevailed when Stephen was elected abbot, [24]   Molesme anticipated a major Cistercian principle; yet, on the other hand, the development at Molesme seems to have been arrested there.   In the second decade of the twelfth century, it did not accompany Cîteaux down the path that led to general chapters as provided for in the CCP.   As abbot, Stephen seems to have had a powerful and individual vision of how mother and daughter abbeys might be bound together which his recollection of Bede could have induced.

Secondly, his recollection of Bede may have suggested to Stephen at least some features of his role as an abbot who sought himself to live strictly according to the Rule of St Benedict and to guide his monastic family in a common fidelity to it.   For there is much in Bede's depiction in his *History of the Abbots* of the abbots under whom he lived that can be paralleled in Stephen's government.   Thus, Bede commended abbots who attended sedulously to their true monastic business — Ceolfrid, with his peerless and unfailing diligence in prayer and psalmody (2.16), and Hwaetbert, who deserved election as abbot because from boyhood he had not only been

---

23. For the documents, see LAURENT, 2.7-8, 150-1, nos. 4, 158; reprinted with indication of parallels in CCP, by BOUTON and VAN DAMME, *Textes*, pp. 129-31.   For further comment, see H.E.J. COWDREY, 'Legal Problems Raised by Agreements of Confraternity', in : *Memoria.   Der geschichtliche Zeugniswert des liturgischen Gedenkens im Mittelalter*, edd. K. SCHMID and J. WOLLASCH (Munich, 1984), pp. 233-54, esp. pp. 250-4.

24. See above, p. 328-329.   Stephen's custom of referring to himself as the second, not the third, abbot of Cîteaux : see the encyclical letter on the chant (AUBERGER, p. 327, no. I/1b), EP 17.1, is perhaps best understood as a courteous and conciliatory gesture to Molesme.   The contrast between such good relations and the sharp criticism of Molesme in the EP (see above, p. 323-324) presents a difficulty.   However, there is a similar contrast in St Bernard's attitude to Cluny, with on the one hand his strictures as in the *Apologia ad Guillelmum abbatem* and, on the other, the mutually good relations that ultimately prevailed between him and Abbot Peter the Venerable — good relations that are surely more comprehensible if Peter were the 'reformer' and his predecessor Pontius the 'traditionalist' (H.E.J. COWDREY, 'Abbot Pontius of Cluny (1109-22/6)', *Studi Gregoriani*, 11 (1978), 177-268) than if, as Auberger suggests (pp. 276-7, 320), the roles were reversed.

brought up to the observance of regular discipline but had also been zealous in writing, singing, reading, and teaching (2.18); at Cîteaux, Stephen was *amator regulae et loci*, a model of observance and stability (EP 17.2). Bede's abbots shared in all the work of the monastery, particularly manual labour — Eosterwine was an especial exemplar (1.8); so at Cîteaux the abbot and monks shared in performing 'the ecclesiastical and all the precepts of the Rule' (EP 15.1-4), and a story in the EM displayed Stephen at manual labour with his monks (1.22, p. 80/35-81/3). Abbot Ceolfrid, who in so many respects suggests himself as a model for Stephen, was frugal in food and drink and wore coarse clothing, all to a degree which Bede noticed as being unusual among those in authority (2.16); at Cîteaux, Stephen would have nothing in the house of God that smacked of pride or superfluity, or that damaged poverty, the guardian of virtues (EP 17.5, cf. EM 1.21,27). Ceolfrid's decision to resign as abbot when extreme old age (*impedimentum suppraemae aetatis*) unfitted him for zealous leadership (2.16) remarkably resembles Stephen's resignation in 1133 when he was *longo senio confectus*, in spite of the presumption of the Rule of St Benedict that an abbot was appointed for life. [25] The example of the Ceolfrid as a very early Benedictine abbot may well have satisfied Stephen that resignation was a proper course to take.

Underlying such particular features of Stephen's abbacy, Bede's presentation of an abbot's duty in relation to the Rule of St Benedict also shows perhaps significant parallels. Bede wrote of Ceolfrid that he resigned 'after an abundant schooling in regular observance which, as a provident father, he brought to bear by the authority of his predecessors alike upon himself and upon those subject to him', and that 'he sought to exhibit a proper pattern of spiritual duty alike by his teaching and in his own life' (2.16). Stephen expressed himself remarkably similarly when, in the primitive *Carta Caritatis*, he required a like interpretation of the Rule in all Cistercian houses: as Ceolfrid appealed to the *priorum auctoritas*, probably meaning earlier abbots since St Benedict of Nursia of whom Bede regarded Benedict Biscop, founder of Wearmouth-Jarrow, with special honour (1.1), so Stephen instructed his subjects

---

25. CCP 9 already provided for the enforced resignation of an unworthy abbot. For Stephen's resignation, see HERBERT, *De miraculis*, 2.24, *PL* 185.1334A, whence EM 1.31.

337

everywhere to construe the Rule 'as our predecessors (*antecessores*), the holy fathers — I mean the monks of the New Monastery [Cîteaux] — understood and held it and as we ourselves today understand and hold it' (CCP 2.2-3). The common appeal to the *auctoritas* of those best qualified to judge in matters of the Rule amongst whom the founding fathers were pre-eminent, is complemented by a common appeal to critical thought. As the *History of the Abbots* gave a *ratio* of relations between associated houses (1.7) while Ceolfrid sought to exhibit 'a proper pattern of spiritual duty', so the EP recalled how at Molesme before 1098 there was earnest debate about the Rule and how it should rightly be kept (3.6). [26] Again, the example of Ceolfrid comes to the mind of the student of Stephen and the writings of his time as abbot.

Thirdly, several items of his agenda as abbot of Cîteaux may recall Bede's account of Wearmouth-Jarrow. This is particularly the case with Stephen's early years, when Cîteaux was in straitened circumstances, in terms both of the number of its monks and of the sufficiency of its resources to support them (EP 16.2-4, 19.9). One of the greatest achievements of Ceolfrid was the making of three copies of the 'new translation' (i.e. the Vulgate of Jerome) of the whole Bible, to be added to a copy of the 'old translation' which Ceolfrid had himself brought from Rome. Ceolfrid left a copy of the 'new translation' to each of his monasteries at Wearmouth and Jarrow ; he took the third — the *Codex Amiatinus*, now in the Laurenziana at Florence — on his last journey to Rome, intending it to be a present for Pope Gregory II (2.15). [27] Stephen's *Monitum* of

---

26. Auberger's hypothesis of a late date for EP 3.6 (pp. 73, 116) may be questioned in the light of William of Malmesbury's admittedly artificial reconstruction of debates at Molesme (cap. 334). For all the artificiality, writing as early as *c.* 1125 William could envisage debates in which Stephen was involved as turning upon how the Rule should be interpreted in the light of tradition and reason. There is no inherent anachronism in EP 3.6 as a résumé of the debates upon which William embroidered. For William's account, see esp. C. WADDELL, 'The Origin and Early Evolution of the Cistercian Antiphonary : Reflections on Two Cistercian Chant Reforms', in : *The Cistercian Spirit : a Symposium in Memory of Thomas Merton*, ed. M.B. PENNINGTON (Washington, DC, 1973), pp. 190-223, at pp. 202-4, and 'The Reform of the Liturgy from a Renaissance Perspective', in : *Renaissance and Renewal in the Twelfth Century*, edd. R.L. BENSON and G. CONSTABLE (Oxford, 1982), pp. 88-109, at pp. 104-5 ; G. CONSTABLE, 'Renewal and Reform in Religious Life : Concepts and Realities', in : *Renaissance and Renewal*, pp. 37-67, at pp. 61-2.

27. For the *Codex Amiatinus*, see R. LOEWE, 'The Medieval History of the Latin Vulgate', in : *The Cambridge History of the Bible*, 2 : *The West from the Fathers to the Reformation*, ed. G.W.H. LAMPE (Cambridge, 1969), pp. 116-18, 136.

1109 recorded his concern to establish a corrected biblical text. The so-called 'Bible of Stephen Harding', now Dijon, *Bibliothèque municipale*, MSS 12-15, embodies the result of his endeavours. [28] Again, Benedict Biscop had been greatly concerned to establish in his monasteries the order of chanting, psalmody, and conducting divine service which was current at Rome (1.6), and part of the experience in such matters that Hwaetbert brought to bear as abbot was acquired in Rome (2.18). Stephen looked to less than fortunate sources in his quest for authentic models — to Metz for the Roman chant and to Milan for hymns. [29] But what matters in the present connection is the fact of a comparable quest for authentic material, with an emphasis upon Roman models, at both Wearmouth-Jarrow and Cîteaux. There are points of contrast, as well: Bede made much of Benedict Biscop's bringing home from Rome pictures to adorn his churches (1.6,9), while for the early Cistercians, most decoration of churches was forbidden (CCP 17.6-8, Stats 13, 20); yet the earliest Cistercian manuscripts showed a variety and elaboration of illumination that probably owed much to Stephen's English past and familiarity with the Anglo-Saxon artistic tradition.[30]

In constitutional matters, the Cîteaux of Stephen from its foundation until his death had several features in common with the Wearmouth-Jarrow of Bede's early abbots. They had been anxious to receive the blessing of their local bishop at the time of their election; Benedict Biscop charged his monks always to summon the bishop to confirm an abbot-elect with the customary benediction (1.11); when Hwaetbert was elected, Bishop Acca of Hexham duly thus confirmed him in office (2.20). The early Cistercians took a similar view in theory and in practice (EP 4.1,7-8, CCP Prol. 2). Yet the protection of papal authority was no less important either for the abbots of Wearmouth-Jarrow (1.6,11, 2.15) or for the abbots of Cîteaux (EP 14, *Privilegium Calixti*). As regards lay donors, Bede's abbots secured sufficient endowments from them, whether from kings (1.4,7) or from lesser men (2.15); but they saw to it that excessive lay demands upon them did not develop in

---

28. Auberger, pp. 190-4; Załuska, pp. 64-111.
29. See the articles by Waddell cited in n. 26.
30. See Auberger, pp. 183-223. For English influences upon the 'first style' of Cistercian manuscript illustration, see Załuska, pp. 76, 78, 82, 90, 111.

339

return : Benedict Biscop insisted that temporal considerations should not affect the choice of an abbot (1.11), and Ceolfrid told his monks that he would never accept a gift without giving back as much as he received (2.17); then, no counterclaim could develop.   The early Cistercians had received land and material benefits both from local petty lords and from Duke Odo of Burgundy, though under Alberic no new gifts were received, perhaps on account of reduced numbers after Abbot Robert and his companions returned to Molesme.   Under Abbot Stephen, in due course gifts became substantial. [31]   But under his regime, the monks of Cîteaux forbade the duke of Burgundy or any other prince to hold court at Cîteaux during solemn festivals (EP 17.4). [32]   The balance between receiving lands or other gifts and avoiding inappropriate obligations was carefully struck in both the circles that are under consideration, so that it is reasonable to ask whether Stephen may not have reflected upon the practice that Bede put on record.

*
*   *

In conclusion, it cannot be demonstrated that Abbot Stephen of Cîteaux had in mind or drew inspiration and models from Bede's writings such as the *Ecclesiastical History* or the *History of the Abbots*.   Yet there is a likelihood that he knew them, at least during his years as a monk and then a traveller in his native England.   The sources upon which he drew at Cîteaux remain problematic, and it is unwarranted to read back into his mind or into the earliest Cistercian documents the outlook of St Bernard or later Cistercian leaders and thinkers.   It is appropriate to seek other mentors.   The similarities between Stephen's work at Cîteaux and the monastic world that Bede depicted are sufficient in number and strength to warrant the question whether Stephen did not owe a major debt to his English background, and whether he may not have been numbered with those Englishmen who found in the pages of Bede a great deal of guidance in renewing the monastic life of the late eleventh and early twelfth centuries.   Such guidance, if Stephen indeed sought it, did not take the form of direct copying.   It

---

31. See MARILIER, pp. 49-51, 52-3, 57-65, 67-77, 79-81, nos. 23, 26, 33-8, 39-41, 46-61, 66-7, and the discussion by AUBERGER, pp. 135-49.
32. MARILIER, pp. 52-3, no. 26, may illustrate the holding of the ducal court at Cîteaux.

was a matter of finding in abbots who were near to Benedict of Nursia in time and tradition the spiritual orientation and practical discernment with which to provide for the early Cistercian family as it began to multiply. One may conclude by asking which of all the sources of guidance that were available to Stephen would have been more useful and appropriate than the works of Bede?

XV

PETER, MONK OF MOLESME AND PRIOR OF JULLY

Amongst the figures who are of importance for the origin and early history of the Cistercian Order, Peter, monk of Molesme and prior of Jully, has been little studied. This is not surprising in view of the scantiness of the evidence about him. The principal source is his *Life*, written by an anonymous author some years after his death in 1136 and not before 1160.[1] In his Prologue, the author lamented the negligence and sloth of Peter's monastic confrères at Molesme in failing to record his good deeds and miracles; the author perforce depended on the scraps of information that survived among the nuns of Jully-les-Nonnains (dioc. Langres, dpt. Yonne), whose claustral prior he had become and amongst whom he was buried (1258AB). The distance at which the author set himself from the monks of Molesme suggests, but does not prove, that he was not of their number; but he knew the community well. His purposes in writing were to commemorate Peter and to edify a monastic audience. Because of its lateness and its purpose, the *Life* yields only a limited amount of evidence about Peter. The only other narrative source which contributes significantly to the evidence for Peter's activities is the account of the foundation of the Cistercian Order written before 1124 by William of Malmesbury in his *Gesta regum*.[2] Although William did not name Peter, he is undoubtedly the companion of the Englishman Harding, later known as Stephen, who from 1109 until 1133 was the third abbot of Cîteaux, upon a journey to Rome which preceded their together becoming monks at Molesme (dioc. Langres, dpt. Côte d'Or).

---

[1] *Vita sancti Petri prioris Juliacensis puellarum monasterii et monachi Molismensis*, J.P. Migne, *Patrologia Latina*, 185.1255-70 (four-figure references in the text of this paper refer to this edition); *Bibliotheca Hagiographica Latina*, 2 vols (Brussels, 1898-1901), no. 6715. See G. Mathon, 'Pietro di Jully, beato', *Bibliotheca Sanctorum*, 10 (1968): 704.

[2] William of Malmesbury, *De gestis regum Anglorum libri quinque*, 4.334, ed. W. Stubbs, 2 vols (London: Rolls Series, 90, 1887-9), 2.380-1. William's account was used by Herbert of Clairvaux, writing c. 1178: *De miraculis libri tres*, 2.24, *PL* 185.1333F-1334A, whence *Exordium magnum Cisterciense, sive Narratio de initio Cisterciensis ordinis auctore Conrado*, 1.21, ed. B. Griesser (Rome, 1961), p. 77.

60

Despite the paucity of information about him, Peter's career from his childhood in England, through his travels on the continent at first alone and then with Stephen, to his connection with Molesme and his death at Jully deserves consideration. First of all, it illustrates the fortunes of two Englishmen, Peter and Stephen, who independently of each other left their native land for ever at about the time of the Norman Conquest of 1066. As regards Peter's origins, his *Life* records only that he was a native of England and that, in the conventional terms of hagiography, his parents were *nobiles*. He had a sister and several brothers. There is no indication of even the approximate date of his birth; although, since he had passed through *pueritia* and *adolescentia* and had come to adult years (*ad virilem aetatem*) before leaving England and since he died an old man in 1136, his birth may safely be placed before the Norman Conquest. At an early age he began to study the liberal arts but also to experience an attraction to the monastic life which also led him to begin to study and follow the precepts of the Gospel (1257B-1259A, 1260D-1261A). According to the *Life*, it was in response to these precepts that Peter decided, like another Abraham, to leave his land and his kindred. He did so after his parents' deaths, and crossed to France as a stranger and sojourner (*peregrinus et hospes*). He thereafter led an itinerant life of visits to sanctuaries and monasteries and of constant religious exercises (1258C-1259B).

It was upon coming to Burgundy that Peter, whom William of Malmesbury described as a *clericus* and therefore as in at least minor orders, fell in with another Englishman, Stephen, who had left England for comparable motives. Conscious of similar purposes in life, the two of them entered upon a formal bond of religious association (*sanctae societatis...foedus*). This bond provides a striking anticipation of the secular brotherhood-in-arms of lay knights in the later Middle Ages,[3] but it also recalls the spiritual observances of Anglo-Saxon exiles for the sake of Christ (*peregrini*) in Bede's *Ecclesiastical History* so closely that there is a case for supposing deliberate imitation.[4] Their life of mutual encouragement and edification had its principal expression, noticed by

---

[3]M. Keen, 'Brotherhood in Arms', *History* 47 (1962): 1-17, esp. pp. 11-12.

[4]See H. E. J. Cowdrey, '*Quidam frater Stephanus nomine, anglicus natione*: The English Background of Stephen Harding', *Revue Bénédictine* 101 (1991): 322-40, at pp. 329-30.

William of Malmesbury as well as in the *Life*, in the daily joint recitation of the whole Psalter, with each man reciting alternate verses (1250BC). Perhaps from the beginning of their association they may have divested themselves of their English names and assumed those of the chief of the apostles and of the first Christian martyr.[5] When their association had persisted for some time, they undertook a pilgrimage to Rome (1259C). Upon returning to Burgundy, the two men decided to terminate their *eremitismo ambulante* by together entering the monastic life at Molesme, which William of Malmesbury described as a *novum et magnum monasterium*. If this description is to be taken literally, their entry is not likely to have occurred until some ten years at least after Molesme was founded c.1075, for only thereafter could its buildings, lands, and numbers be said to justify the adjective *magnum*.

At Molesme, the *Life* predictably depicts Peter as an exemplary monk in respect of both corporate and private devotions as well as of progress in the monastic virtues (1259D-1260A). It provides evidence that, at about the time of the foundation of Cîteaux from Molesme in 1098, Molesme afforded a spiritual nursery and home for a saintly monk. He was not, however, always resident there. Even while still a novice, he spent time at its cell of Useldingen (dioc. Trier; now in Luxemburg), where his contacts with the external world included his receiving a visit by the wife of a local official (*quemdam praefectum nequissimum*) who had been confronted by sudden death. When Peter acceded to his request for a home visit, the official confessed to having suspected Peter of undue familiarity with his wife, for which suspicion the official did penance before Peter gave him the viaticum (1261AB).[6] Another of Molesme's cells at which Peter spent considerable periods of time was la Maison-Dieu at la Ferté-Gaucher, which was named after its founder, Gaucher, who was lord of the place.[7] A series of miracle stories

---

[5] In the *Life*, Peter's companion is always referred to as Stephen, which may indicate that Harding changed his name to Stephen at this stage of his life. Since Peter is little attested as an English name, he also may have changed his name at the same time.

[6] For Useldingen, see *Cartulaire de Molesme (916-1250)*, ed. J. Laurent, 2 vols. (Paris, 1907-11), 1.236-7, no. 47, 2.175, no. 195.

[7] For its foundation, see *Cartulaire de Molesme*, 2.95, no. 89 (1089/90-1102), and for pancartes of Bishop Manasses I of Meaux confirming its possessions, *Ibid.* 2.455-6, no. 568 (1112), 2.185-6, no. 202 (1115). See also

62

associated with Peter's residence there attests to aspects of his sanctity. During his nocturnal recitation of matins of the feast of Pope Markus (7 October), an appearance of the devil singing by his side led to his seeing that another monk was stealing the monks' clothes from their dormitory; next morning, Peter identified the thief and made possible the recovery of the clothing (1261BC). By a similar miracle of perception at a distance, Peter identified a clerk who had stolen church plate and censers (1261D). Probably also at la Ferté-Gaucher, Peter proved himself immune from being scalded by boiling water, thus attesting that heat could not harm the flesh of a monk whose heart was pure (1261D-1262A). When the founder's son Helias had succeeded his father as lord of la Ferté-Gaucher and had gone on pilgrimage to Jerusalem, Peter was able by second sight to reveal to his anxious mother Elizabeth that her son was sick but would recover; he would return bearing gifts — an ivory comb for his mother and a fine cup for Peter (1262B-D).[8] Three further stories follow, all illustrating Peter's powers of second sight (1262D-1263C).[9] Such stories were calculated to establish Peter as a source of

Ibid. 1.217, no. 15. Laurent provides no evidence for his assertion that Peter was prior of either Useldingen or la Ferté-Gaucher. Another than Peter was prior of the latter in two miracle stories in the *Life* (1262C, 1263B). But one stay there was for more than a year (1262D), and a monk's addressing him as *pater* (1262D) may indicate that he was eventually prior. The story that, when returning to Molesme before his transfer to Jully, Peter saved his servant from drowning at les Riceys, near Bar-sur Seine, would be consistent with his coming from la Ferté-Gaucher, and his familiarity with Robert, lord of les Riceys, may be significant (1263D-1264A); for Robert's association with Molesme, see *Cartulaire de Molesme*, 2.148-9, no. 156 (1102-11) and 2.211, no. 227 (1107-25) .

[8]For Helias as the son of Gaucher and co-founder with him of la Ferté-Gaucher, see *Cartulaire de Molesme*, 2.453-4, no. 565 (1177-8).

[9]Their occurrence at la Ferté-Gaucher is indicated by the reference in the last story to *monasterium praedictum* (1263C, cf. 1261BC). This story, according to which Peter knew at a distance of the death of an *abbas Nigellae*, appears to refer to the death of an abbot of Nestle-la-Reposte (dioc. Troyes, dpt. Marne). Little is known about the succession of its abbots, although an Abbot Ralph I attested a charter of Bishop Atto of Troyes (1122-after 1145): *Gallia Christiana in provincias ecclesiasticas distributa*, 16 vols. (Paris, 1716-1865), 12.536, cf. 498-500. If the abbot in question was Ralph, Peter must still have been at la Ferté-Gaucher at a date after 1122.

discipline within a monastic community and of authority in the eyes of its lay patrons and neighbours.

It was while Peter was, at the behest of Abbot Robert of Molesme (c. 1075-1110), visiting one of its cells that his friend Stephen was, in 1109, chosen to be abbot of Cîteaux. Stephen had been one of the initial band of monks who, in 1098, had set out from Molesme to found Cîteaux. It is possible that Peter, too, was involved in the steps that led to its foundation. For in the Cistercian *Exordium parvum*, a Peter is named along with Abbot Robert, Stephen, and four other monks in the letter by which Pope Urban II's legate, Archbishop Hugh of Lyons, confirmed their purpose of following the Benedictine Rule more strictly and perfectly than had been the case at Molesme.[10] The most likely alternative identification is with Peter, the Cistercian monk who, from 1132 to 1140, was archbishop of Tarentaise. But it is uncertain when this Peter became a monk of Cîteaux, and the long friendship of the other Peter with Stephen may have drawn them to a common purpose.[11] But, if so, Peter must have returned to Molesme in 1099 with Abbot Robert; for his monastic future lay in Molesme and its dependencies, in which he continued to lead an exemplary life.

Despite the strictures which the Cistercian *Exordium parvum*, in particular, passed upon Molesme,[12] Peter's *Life* provides a remarkable amount of evidence, much of it centring upon Peter himself, for the persistence of contact and sympathy between Molesme and the new monastery at Cîteaux. The author of the *Life* wrote with approval of Cîteaux in 1109 as *novella ista Cisterciensis plantatio, quae populorum tumultum, et saeculi turbinem fugiens, in solitudine soli Deo vacare contendebat* (1260A). When Abbot Alberic of Cîteaux died, its bereaved monks had recourse to the kindly aid of Molesme, their mother house

---

[10]*Exordium parvum*, 2.5, *Les Plus Anciens Textes de Cîteaux*, ed. J. de la C. Bouton and J. B. Van Damme (Achel, 1985), p. 58.

[11]For Peter of Tarentaise, see M.A. Dimier, 'Saint Pierre 1er de Tarentaise,' *Cistercienser-Chronik*, 47 (1935): 1-7, and *Ibid*, 'Pietro I di Tarentaise, santo,' *Bibliotheca Sanctorum* 10 (1968): 772-4. Another possibility is Peter, the companion of St. Bruno, founder of la Grande Chartreuse, during his brief stay in the early 1080s at Molesme's dependency of la Sèche Fontaine: *Cartulaire de Molesme*, 2.134-6, no. 138; but nothing is known of Peter thereafter.

[12]e.g. 2.3-4, 3.6, *Les Plus Anciens Textes*, pp. 58, 60.

64

(*ad matris pia suffragia recurrens*), and by the advice of God-fearing men made Stephen their abbot. Before and after he became abbot, the bond between Peter and him was sustained. While both were together at Molesme, and by implication after Stephen moved to Cîteaux, their custom of daily reciting the Psalter continued; it was modified only in that, from deference to the monastic discouragement of particular friendships, each separately recited half of the Psalter (1260A). After Stephen became abbot, Peter not only prayed assiduously for him but, knowing that an abbot has many duties, he undertook to say daily Stephen's half of the Psalter as well as his own (1260AB). Upon an occasion when he found this obligation (*votivum debitum*) onerous, an angel assisted him to renew his zeal (1260B-D); he persisted in his custom almost until the end of his life (1260A). It is not known how Stephen regarded his friend's daily discharge of their common obligation, but he is not likely to have been unmindful of it. It should not be overlooked as a continuing bond between Molesme and Cîteaux during their early years.

Probably at a date in the mid-1120s, a new departure in Peter's monastic career occurred in circumstances which tended further to promote contacts and goodwill between Molesme and the Cistercians, if not necessarily with Cîteaux itself. From its inception, Molesme had attracted devout women who wished to have a part in its religious life. At first, they lived in a number of places near the monastery; but, in 1113, the nunnery of Jully-les-Nonnains was established.[13] It at once came under the influence of St. Bernard, who entered Cîteaux in that year and who from 1115 was abbot of Clairvaux. Jully afforded a haven for the wives of followers who entered Cîteaux with Bernard. His sister-in-law Elizabeth and, after she left c.1128 to become prioress of Larrey (dioc. Langres, dpt. Côte d'Or), his sister Hombeline became its first two prioresses. Bernard's influence on Jully's foundation charter of 1113/15 has recently been claimed.[14] Cistercian influence persisted, for at an

---

[13]For its foundation charter, see *Cartulaire de Molesme*, 2.225-6, no. 241, and for its early history, *Ibid.* 1.255-6.

[14]William of Saint-Thierry, *Sancti Bernardi abbatis Clarae-Vallensis vita et res gestae*, 1.3.10, 6.60, *PL* 185.232-3, 244-5; *Secunda vita sancti Bernardi abbatis auctore Alano*, 3.9, *PL* 185.474. Bernard's connection with the foundation charter of Jully is suggested by J. Leclercq, 'La paternité de S. Bernard et les débuts de l'Ordre cistercien,' *Revue Bénédictine* 103 (1993): 445-

unknown date between 1115 and 1132, Abbot Guy of Molesme (1111-32) acted upon consultation with Abbots Hugh of Pontigny and Bernard of Clairvaux and with the abbots of Morimond and Fontenay to formulate statutes about the nuns' enclosure and other matters.[15] There was no mention of the abbot of Cîteaux. Clairvaux's influence, in particular, was probably already registered at Jully when, upon the death of the monk who served as its claustral prior, the community requested Abbot Guy to appoint Peter in his stead. For reasons that do not emerge, the abbot was at first reluctant and wished to appoint someone else; but he was eventually persuaded after representations from Count Theobald of Blois and Champagne and from his seneschal, Andrew, lord of Baudement (dpt. Marne), to send Peter to Jully.[16] At the time of his appointment, which certainly occurred before 1128,[17] Peter was away from Molesme. After being summoned there, Guy dispatched him to Jully, where he spent the remainder of his life (1263C-1264C). There is no evidence for absences from it. Peter's long association with Jully during years when its prioresses were near relatives of St Bernard who also took a share in formulating its statutes helps to explain the relatively favourable estimate of Molesme as *religione conspicuus* in such documents as the *Exordium Cistercii* which seem to present the

---

81, esp. 460-3, 476-7.

[15]J. Leclercq, *Études sur Saint Bernard et le texte de ses écrits*, Analecta sacri ordinis Cisterciensis, 9 (Rome, 1953), pp. 192-4.

[16]Theobald was count of Blois (1102-52) and Champagne (1125-52). For Andrew, who was his seneschal from c.1111-c.1133, as a witness to a charter, see *Cartulaire de Molesme*, 2.321, no. 173B (1108); for his service of Theobald, see M. Bur, *La Formation du comté de Champagne, v.950-v.1150* (Nancy, 1977), pp. 431-2.

[17]The earliest datable reference to Peter as prior of Jully appears in a charter of 28 Mar. 1128 in which Aanolz, aunt of Bernard of Clairvaux and widow of Walter de la Roche, having become a nun at Jully, made a gift to Peter in chapter of an annual rent of ten pounds upon the fair of Bar-sur-Aube which her husband had held in fief of Count Theobald of Blois. The distinguished company present included Count Theobald, Bernard with three monks of Clairvaux named Godfrey, Gerard and Rainer, and three monks of Molesme named Robert, Guy and Odo. A monk of Jully, Guy, is also named: L'Abbé (J.-B.) Jobin, *Histoire du prieuré de Jully-les-Nonnains* (Paris, 1881), pièces justificatives, no. 3, pp. 208-10, see also pp. 98-107.

66

Clairvaux, rather than the Cîteaux, tradition about the origins of the Cistercian Order.[18]

It is harder to determine whether the foundation of the first Cistercian nunnery at Tart (dioc. Langres, dpt. Côte d'Or), which cannot be more precisely dated than c.1120-5, involved Peter and, if so, how.[19] The circumstances and consequences of its foundation show several points of contrast with Jully. Whereas Peter's friend Abbot Stephen of Cîteaux played no discernible part in the early history of Jully while Bernard of Clairvaux and other Cistercian abbots were influential, Stephen was a key figure in the establishment of Tart. His associates at its inception were Bishop Josceran of Langres (1112-25) and a prominent patroness of the early Cistercians, Elizabeth de Vergy. Tart was ruled by an abbess, unlike Jully with its prioress assisted by a male claustral prior. Tart's way of life was modelled upon Cîteaux, from which it was only 12 km. distant. Stephen's control was close; in the documents concerning its foundation, its lands were said to have been received *per manum domni Stephani abbatis Cisterciensis.*[20] Stephen's

---

[18]The hypothesis of a double tradition in early Cistercian sources is strongly argued by J.-F. Auberger, *L'Unanimité cistercienne primitive: mythe ou réalité?* (Achel, 1986), cf. the summary of his conclusions: *Ibid,* 'La législation cistercienne primitive et sa relecture cistercienne;' *Bernard de Clairvaux: histoire, mentalités, spiritualité,* Sources chrétiennes, 380 (Paris, 1992), pp. 181-208.

[19]For the foundation and early history of Tart, see B. Degler-Spengler, 'Die Zisterzierserinnen in der Schweiz: Einleitung,' *Die Zisterzienser und Zisterzienserinnen, die Reformierten Bernhardinerinnen, die Trappisten und Trappistinnen und die Wilhelmiten in der Schweiz,* Helvetia Sacra, 3/3 (Berne, 1982), 510-19, French version in *Eadem,* 'La filiation de Tart: l'organisation des premiers monastères de Cisterciennes.' *Naissance et fonctionnement des réseaux monastiques et canoniaux* (Saint-Étienne, 1991), pp. 53-60; *Les Moniales Cisterciennes,* Bk. 1: *Histoire externe,* Pt. 1: *Jusqu'à la fin du XVe siècle* (Aiguebelle, 1986), 37-45.

[20]For the foundation document as formulated in 1132, see *PL* 185.1409-11, no. 12; for the statement of Tart's constitutional position by Abbot Guy of Cîteaux (1194-1200), see *PL* 185.1413-14, no. 16. For the document of 1132 see also B. Hene, 'Einiges über die Cistercienserinnen,' *Cistercienser Chronik* 9 (1897): 48-57, 85-9, 110-18, at p. 88, n. 6. For Stephen, see *PL* 185.1410A, 1413CD.

rule there was, perhaps, tolerated rather than approved by other Cistercian abbots; for it is probably not coincidental that, in 1134, the year of his death, the Cistercian general chapter enacted a prohibition upon the blessing of a nun (*monacham benedicere*) by a Cistercian abbot or monk.[21]

It is commonly stated by historians that, when Tart was founded, its first abbess, Elizabeth de Vergy, daughter of Stephen's associate in its establishment, and a larger or smaller group of its nuns came from Jully.[22] The evidence that the first abbess of Tart came from Jully is restricted to a late, but probably reliable, tradition at Tart which was written down early in the eighteenth century from documentary evidence then its archives.[23] The tradition made no mention of a transfer of nuns, which however likely must be regarded as unproven.[24] It is in

---

[21]*Statuta capitulorum generalium Ordinis Cisterciensis, 1116-1786*, ed. J.-M. Canivez, 8 vols. (Louvain, 1933-41), 1.19, no. 29. Bernard of Clairvaux's understanding of this statute as binding only within the Order, as well as his continuing care for Jully, is illustrated by a document of 1142 in which Bishop Godfrey of Langres (1138/9-1162/3) told how, at the request of Andrew of Baudement (see above, p.66) and his son Guy, he and Bernard had visited Jully where they had admitted as nuns Andrew's daughters Mahault and Elwide: Jobin, *Histoire du prieuré de Jully-les-Nonnains*, pièces justificatives, no. 9, pp. 215-15, cf. pp. 115-16.

[22]For the two Elizabeth de Vergys, see J. de la C. Bouton, 'L'établissement des moniales cisterciennes,' *Mémoires de la société pour l'histoire du droit et des institutions des anciens pays bourguignons, comtois et romands* 15 (1953): 83-116, at pp. 90-6; *Les Moniales Cisterciennes*, 1/1, 44-5.

[23]᠎e Bouton, 'L'établissement,' pp. 90, 106. The tradition is recorded among the entries for 11 Oct. in *Journal des saints de l'ordre de Cîteaux à estre honoré chaque jour dans l'abaye de Notre Dame de Tart* (Dijon, 1706), pp. 530-3: 'Ce même jour la Bienheureuse ELISABETH première Abesse de Notre Dame de Tart, fille de Savaric Comte de Vergy et d'Elisabeth Comtesse de Chalon...; ils marièrent Elisabeth leur fille à Humbert de Mailly, seigneur de Fauvernay. Etant restée veuve fort jeune, elle se consecra à Dieu dans l'Abaye de Juilly de l'Ordre de s.Benoit; elle en fut tirée en 1120, par S. Estienne 3 Abé de Cîteaux, pour fonder l'Abaye de Notre Dame de Tart...'. (I am most grateful to Père Jean de la Croix Bouton for his great kindness in transcribing this and other material for me, as well as for other information and generous help.)

[24]See, for a cautious view, R. Locatelli, 'L'expansion de l'ordre cistercien,' *Bernard de Clairvaux: histoire, mentalités, spiritualité*, pp. 103-40, at pp. 136-7.

any case not clear whether Tart was founded before or after Peter moved to Jully as its claustral prior and impossible to say how he regarded the new foundation. The silence of the cartularies of Molesme and Jully about the origin and early history of Tart precludes inferences about how the new house was regarded. But Peter's long and strict custody of the community at Jully, which he undertook at its request (1236C), and St. Bernard's long and close concern for its affairs, tell against the likelihood that a body of nuns left Jully for Tart in reaction against Jully's laxity. Tart probably originated in Abbot Stephen's personal wish to have a house of nuns which would stand to Cîteaux much as Jully stood to Molesme. Whether or not Tart recruited from Jully, there are no grounds for supposing that the differences of constitution and custom between the two houses implied any censure upon or antagonism to Jully from the side of Tart.

So far as the friendship of Peter and Stephen is concerned, it may be concluded that, rooted as it was in their sworn brotherhood in prayer and good works during their long travels together, its significance lay in its lasting power to offset and to mitigate the contrasts in early Cistercian history by which the two men were surrounded — that between Molesme and Cîteaux as practising different standards in Benedictine life, that between Cîteaux and Clairvaux as expressing distinct interpretations of the Cistercian spirit, and that between Jully and Tart as promoting alternative styles of life for women religious. Their friendship tended to mitigate divisions which could have become wider.

It may also have made its own contribution to the Cistercian spirit. Both as it was itself phrased and as it was interpreted by the black monks including the Cluniacs, the Rule of St. Benedict set forth a pattern of cenobitic life which, although sufficient for the corporate and individual sanctification of most monks, was a 'little rule for beginners' pointing aspirants to greater perfection towards a more austere way of life which lay outside, beyond, and above itself: *non omnis iustitiae observatio in hac sit regula constituta* (cap. 73). After long testing and training as a monk, one might go on to be a hermit. In a very real sense, Peter and Stephen reversed this order of things: first they lived their austere lives as *peregrini*; only thereafter at Molesme did they place themselves under the Rule of St. Benedict. It is a paradox of Cistercian monasticism that, after Stephen moved to Cîteaux and to the yet stricter observance of the Rule *ad apicem literae*, he and his followers including

St. Bernard did not insist upon its statement that life in accordance with it could be propadeutic to a further stage of the religious life. According to the *Exordium parvum*, Cîteaux was itself set up *ut ... monachi heremum diligentes in pace consisterent* (5.3); its founders intended for its monks *ut ... in arta et angusta via quam regula demonstrat, usque ad exhalationem spiritus desudent* (Prol. 4-6). Like the personal spiritual growth of its third abbot, monastic life at Cîteaux culminated in the Rule and did not look beyond. The Cistercians did not find the place among themselves for the eremitical life that the Cluniacs reserved; the keeping of the Rule was enough. That so crucial a Cistercian figure as Stephen came to the Rule as the apex of his development is likely to have assisted this conclusion; that he was for long in close association with Peter may help to explain why Bernard thought well of Jully and why, through all vicissitudes, links persisted between the Cistercians and Jully's mother house of Molesme.

Peter's *Life* confirms his lasting zeal during his life at Jully. He combined the spiritual and material oversight of the nuns (1264B-D, 1264D-1265B, 1265C-1266A, 1266C-1267B) with provision for his own separate devotions in an oratory which he built for himself near the church (1246D) and with an extensive ministry to those who resorted to him from a wide area of Burgundy (1265B). Miracles were ascribed to him during his lifetime (1265CD). He remained in contact with Molesme; its prior, Hatto, came to him for the sake of his own healing during Peter's last illness and stayed to minister to Peter until his death (1266A-1267A). The monks of Molesme wished his body to be buried there, but it was secretly restored to Jully where his tomb became the site of many miracles (1267C-1268C). Throughout his years at Jully, Peter retained contact with Count Theobald of Blois and Champagne, upon whose plea he had been sent there (1263CD). When the count visited Jully with his pregnant wife, Peter predicted that she would bear the daughter, Adela, who in 1160 married King Louis VII of France and that Louis would thus make good his lordship over the kingdom (1265C).[25] Theobald sent a chaplain to Peter's deathbed, upon which

---

[25]The phrase in the *Life* is *dominium regni obtinuit*. Louis compensated for the diminution of royal power after his first wife, Eleanor of Aquitaine, married King Henry II of England by forming an alliance with the house of Champagne. Adela was Theobald's fifth child.

Peter predicted that, in a few years, the count would be at war with the French king, but that if he safeguarded churches and their property he would emerge victor (1266B).[26] Peter thus was a mentor of the most powerful prince in the eastern part of the French kingdom. Peter seems to have been concerned more often than Stephen with the affairs of great men of this world.

But a final matter which they had in common was that neither ever completely forgot his links with his native England. Peter retained a concern for his only sister; after praying specially about her, he had a vision of the tomb in which she had recently been buried and received an assurance of her salvation (1260D-1261A). During his terminal illness, he was instructed in a vision to send word to Count Theobald of Champagne, elder brother of Stephen of Blois who succeeded Henry I as king of England upon the latter's death on 1 December 1135, that he should not cross the sea to England in pursuit of its kingdom; God had not ordained that he should receive it (1266AB).[27] Stephen's mindfulness of his English roots emerges in a letter which he wrote towards the end of his years at Cîteaux, and so probably in the early 1130s, to the abbot — Thurstan, blessed as abbot in 1122 — and community of his original monastery of Sherborne.[28] In a language heavy with echoes of the Vulgate Bible,[29] Stephen spoke of the monks

---

[26]Bur, *La Formation*, pp. 290-2.

[27]For Theobald and the English crown, see *The Ecclesiastical History of Orderic Vitalis*, 13.20,44, ed. M. Chibnall, 6 vols. (Oxford, 1969-80), 6.454-5, 548-9; *Chronica Roberti de Torigneio, Chronicles of the Reigns of Stephen, Henry II, and Richard II*, ed. R. Howlett, 4 vols. (London: Rolls Series, 82, 1884-9), 4.128-9.

[28]For the best edition and an invaluable commentary to which I am much indebted, see C. Waddell, Notes Towards the Exegesis of a Letter by Stephen Harding, *Noble Piety and Reformed Monasticism*, Studies in Medieval Cistercian History, 7, ed. E. R. Elder (Kalamazoo, 1981), pp. 10-39. For the text, see p. 14; cf. the photograph which forms the frontispiece to the volume (one- and two-figure references in the text of this paper refer to Waddell's edition). Comparison with the photograph suggests that, in Waddell's text, besides the correction of the typing slip *decludunt* to *secludunt* (6), *sanctissima* should be *scientia* (11) (for the omission of *et*, cf. line 19).

[29]As indicated in Waddell's notes; in lines 6-7, the reference is more directly to Heb. 13: 22 than to 2 Cor. 11: 19.

as being of his bone and flesh (6). His letter made no reference to such foot-looseness or disenchantment on his part with the monastic life as William of Malmesbury gave as his reasons for leaving Sherborne.[30]

---

[30]'Cum adolescentem seculi urtica sollicitaret, pannos illos perosus, primo Scottiam, mox Franciam contendit': as n. 2. The evidence of Stephen's letter neither supports nor excludes the suggestion that Stephen may have left Sherborne for political purposes which is made by J. B. Van Damme, 'Saint Étienne Harding mieux connu,' *Cîteaux: Commentarii Cistercienses* 14 (1963): 307-15. Van Damme draws attention to references in Domesday Book to holdings ascribed to a man or men named Harding in the vicinity of Sherborne. A full list of such references is as follows:

Domesday Book fo.	County	Place(s)	Form of name	TRE or *modo*
67c	Wiltshire	Beechingstoke	Harding	TRE
68d	Wiltshire	Winterslow	Harding	TRE
69a	Wiltshire	Compton, Durrington, Winterslow, Ablington, Chitterne, Tytherington	Harding	TRE
74a	Wiltshire	Knighton, Figheldean, Ogbourne	Harding	TRE; *modo*
82c	Dorset	Bredy	Harding	TRE
90d	Somerset	Cranmore	Harding	TRE; *modo*
98d	Somerset	Lopen	Harding f. Alnod	*modo*
98d	Somerset	Bradon, Capland, Merriott, Buckland, Discove	Harding	*modo*

The name Harding also occurs in Leicestershire, Warwickshire, and Suffolk. Van Damme proposed that Stephen Harding may have been a grandson or nephew of the Alnoth whose son Harding held Lopen in 1086, and that Alnoth may be identified with Ednoth the Staller who, having held high office before the Norman Conquest, was recruited by William the Conqueror to put down west-country rebels and who was killed in 1068: William of Malmesbury, *Gesta regum*, 3.254, p. 313 (*Ednodus* is described as *domi belloque Anglorum temporibus iuxta insignis, pater Herdingi qui adhuc superest*); Anglo-Saxon Chronicle, D text, a. 1067 (where events of 1068 are included); Florence of Worcester, *Chronicon ex chronicis*, ed. B. Thorpe, 2 vols (London, 1848-9), 2.2-3 (where *Eadnothus* was *Haroldi regis stallarius*). The Harding son of Ednoth to whom William of Malmesbury refers may be the Domesday tenant of Lopen and a layman; Van Damme proposed that, as another kinsman of the

XV

72

He paid tribute to Sherborne's past in terms of its superior pedigree in respect of learning and family continuity (*vos qui meliores scientia parentela eratis*: 11-12); for its history began in the seventh century and thus in the time of St Aldhelm. He also referred to the good report of its present condition; no doubt he had in mind its being raised in 1122 to abbatial status. A spiritual bond between him and the monks of Sherborne persisted; for, he said, the Lord as the living fountain had filled him the empty vessel in order that they might be strong in their monastic profession and bold in the Lord (10-13).

A striking feature of Stephen's letter is the use of imagery derived from the stories of the patriarchs in the book of Genesis. The monks of Sherborne were *os nostrum et caro nostra* (6) — a phrase that Laban used to the returning patriarch Jacob (Gen. 29: 13-14). When Stephen left Sherborne and crossed the sea 'with nothing but a staff' (*in baculo meo mare transivi*: 8) he again emulated Jacob who said that *in baculo meo transivi Iordanem istum* (Gen. 32:10). As, in old age, Abraham recalled how the Lord had called him from the land of his ancestry (Gen. 24:7), so Stephen left his land alone and poor (*solus de terra mea et pauper egressus sum*: 13). As Jacob returned over the Jordan that he had once crossed *in baculo meo* with two companies of men (*cum duabus turmis*: Gen. 32:10), Stephen could face death gladly because he was now rich with forty companies (*cum quadraginta turbis*: 13-14) of monks. In his *Life*, Peter's departure from England was likewise expressed in imagery drawn from the patriarchs: 'like another Abraham, he determined to leave as a pilgrim his land and his kindred, and the house of his father' (1258D, cf. Gen. 12:1); like the patriarchs of old as commemorated in the book of Hebrews, Peter came to France a pilgrim and sojourner (*peregrinus et hospes*: 1259A, cf. Heb. 11:13). Stephen

---

quisling Ednoth, the monk Harding became *persona non grata* among the English monks of Sherborne and, under pressure, left the country, as Van Damme thought, after 1070 and perhaps in 1072. It may, however, be pointed out that Harding was a fairly common Old English name, and it is far from certain that the *Alnod* of Domesday can be identified with Ednoth the Staller. As Waddell pointed out (as above, n. 28, pp. 19-20), if the monk or oblate Harding was forced out of Sherborne for the reason that Van Damme proposed, it is surprising that he should have spent so long before entering another monastery. The evidence is insufficient to support a positive conclusion, although Van Damme's suggestion remains interesting.

and Peter evidently looked back over long lives in terms of a shared spiritual course which brought them separately to France, then together to Rome and Molesme, and finally separately again to Cîteaux and Jully, but which was never dislocated. The lasting bond of aspiration and experience between the two men should not be overlooked in the complex problem of relations between Molesme and the Cistercians during the early decades of the twelfth century.

XVI

THE CARTHUSIANS AND THEIR CONTEMPORARY WORLD:
THE EVIDENCE OF TWELFTH-CENTURY BISHOPS'
VITAE[x]

One of the most striking respects in which the Carthusians interacted with their contemporary world during the first century or so of their history was in their relations with the episcopate.   Amongst the sources for this interaction, especial importance attaches to the *Vitae* of three outstanding bishops who exemplified the pattern of episcopal life that the Carthusians formed and disseminated.   The earliest in date is that of Hugh I, bishop of Grenoble from 1080 to 1132. [1] Hugh was not himself professed as a Carthusian but at la Chaise-Dieu (dioc. Clermont), although in 1084 St Bruno founded la Grande Chartreuse in his diocese, and he was a visitor, adviser, and protector in the vicissitudes of its

----

[x] ABBREVIATIONS.   The following abbreviations are used:

BHL — *Bibliotheca Hagiographica Latina Antiquae et Mediae Aetatis ediderunt Socii Bollandiani* (2 vols., Brussels, 1898–1901);   ibid., *Supplementi Editio Altera Auctior* (Brussels, 1911);   ibid., *Novum Supplementum*, ed. H. Fros (Brussels, 1986)

Coutumes — *Guigues 1er, Coutumes de Chartreuse*, ed. by a Carthusian, *SC* 313 (Paris, 1984)

DDFI — *Monumenta Germaniae Historica, Diplomata regum et imperatorum Germaniae*, 10|1–5: *Frederici I. Diplomata* (Hanover, 1975–90)

Lettres — *Les Lettres des premiers Chartreux, 1: St Bruno, Guigues, St Anthelme* (2nd edn), 2: *Les moines de Portes*, ed. by a Carthusian, *SC* 88, 274 (Paris, 1980–8)

Mansi — *Sacrorum conciliorum nova et amplissima collectio*, ed. J.D. Mansi (31 vols, Florence and Venice, 1759–1798)

MVSH — *The Life of St Hugh of Lincoln*, edd. D.L. Douie and H. Farmer (2 vols, London, etc., 1961–2;   repr. with corrections, Oxford, 1985)

PL — *Patrologia Latina*

Recueil — *Recueil des plus anciens actes de la Grande-Chartreuse (1086–1196)*, ed. B. Bligny (Grenoble, 1958)

SC — *Sources Chrétiennes*

VSA — *Vie de Saint Antelme, evêque de Belley, chartreux, par son chapelin Guillaume, chartreux de Portes*, ed. J. Picard (Belley, 1978)

VSH — Guigo I, *Vita sancti Hugonis Gratianopolitani*, PL 153.761–84

[1] *VSH*;   BHL 4016.   See H.E.J. Cowdrey, 'Hugh of Avalon, Carthusian and Bishop', in: *De cella in seculum: Religious Life and Secular Life and Devotion in Late Medieval England*, ed. M.G. Sargent (Cambridge, 1989), pp. 41–57, at pp. 48–9.

early years.[2]   He was imbued with its spirituality and aspirations. Two years after he died, Pope Innocent II (1130-43) charged Guigo I, fifth prior of Chartreuse (1109-36) and compiler of its Customs,[3] to write his Life.   The Life provides a model for the spiritual and pastoral work of a bishop as Guigo envisaged it.   The second *Vita* is   that   of   Anthelme, bishop of Belley, in Bugey, from 1163 to 1178, who had for most of his earlier life been an exemplary Carthusian monk and prior.[4]   His *Vita* is anonymous, but it was probably written before 1200 by his chaplain, William, who had himself been a Carthusian at Portes.[5]   Thirdly, there is the *Magna vita* of Hugh of Lincoln, monk of Chartreuse, prior of Witham (dioc. Bath and Wells), and bishop of Lincoln from 1186 to 1200.[6] It was written before 1214, not by a Carthusian, but by Adam of Eynsham, a Benedictine monk of Eynsham abbey (dioc. Lincoln), who knew Hugh well since he was his chaplain during the final three years of his episcopate.

Since the *Vita* of Anthelme is the least well-known of the three although it is of prime historical interest, and since its subject and, in all probability, its author were alike Carthusians, this paper will concentrate upon the evidence that it provides.   But illustrations will be taken from the other two in order to indicate common features in their depiction of how the Carthusians interacted with their contemporary world.

Since the course of Anthelme's rather complex monastic career may not be generally familiar, it may be helpful briefly to summarize it.[7]   Having received a sound education in theology and canon law, and having served as a secular clerk in the churches of Geneva and Belley, he took the habit in 1135|6 at the Charterhouse of Portes (dioc. Belley).[8] But before a year had passed, at the prompting of the Carthusian,

----

[2] For Hugh's profession, see *VSH* 3.10, cols 768D-769A;   for his relations with Chartreuse, see especially *Recueil*, nos 1-19, pp. 1-50.

[3] *Coutumes.*

[4] *VSA; BHL* 560.

[5] For the problem of authorship, see *VSA* pp. 72ˣ-74ˣ.

[6] *MVSH; BHL* 4018.   For Hugh, see esp. the relevant essays in *St Hugh of Lincoln*, ed. H. Mayr-Harting (Oxford, 1987), and *De cella in seculum* (as n. 1).

[7] The principal source is *VSA* caps 2-21, pp. 3-20;   I follow Picard's reconstruction of Anthelme's life: pp. 17ˣ-31ˣ, 57ˣ-59ˣ, 64ˣ-67ˣ, 41-5.

[8] For the early history of Portes, see *Lettres*, 2.7-10, 17-24.

Bishop Hugh II of Grenoble (1132-48), he was sent while still a novice to Chartreuse; the avalanche that had devastated Chartreuse on 30 January 1132, killing in all seven of its monks and a novice, and destroying most of its buildings, had left it somewhat demoralized and in need of recruits. It was, therefore, at Chartreuse that Anthelme made his profession. Between 1136|7 and 1139, he held there the office of *procurator*, with oversight of the lower house of the lay brothers;[9] from 1139 to 1151, he was prior, that is superior, of Chartreuse. He was active in building, in extending the limits *(termini)* of Chartreuse, and in supplementing the Customs as written down by Prior Guigo I; it was from his priorate that general chapters of the Carthusians began to be held.[10] According to his *Vita*, he laid down his office, having provided for his own replacement by another who was, in fact, the diligent and statesmanlike Basil of Burgundy, prior from 1151 to 1174, because he sought the quiet of the cell.[11] Other evidence makes it plain that his standing down followed a crisis in the Carthusian Order. The crisis arose from a disputed episcopal election at Grenoble when Bishop Hugh II was translated to be archbishop of Vienne.[12] St Bernard of Clairvaux recorded that Pope Eugenius III (1145-53) refused to confirm the election by the chapter of Grenoble of Noël, a Carthusian of Portes. Bernard indicated that the objections to him arose from the recentness of his conversion to

----

[9] For the duties of the *procurator*, see *Coutumes*, caps 16, 18, 46. 1-2, 60.1, 62-3, 66, pp. 200-5, 254-7, 270-5.

[10] For Anthelme's Customs, which were mostly about liturgical matters, see J. Hogg, 'Die ältesten Consuetudines der Kartäuser', *Analecta Cartusiana*, 1 (1970), 104-16. For his two recorded general chapters, see (i) ibid. pp. 117-21, = *Recueil*, no. 21, pp. 53-8; (ii) pp. 122-5. For his rule in general, see *VSA* caps 6-8, pp. 7-12.

[11] *VSA* cap. 9|1-15, p. 12.

[12] The details of the Grenoble election and its consequences are difficult to determine. The problems raised at Chartreuse are referred to only obliquely in *VSA* cap. 6|27-33, p. 8. The principal sources are: St Bernard, abbot of Clairvaux, *Epp.* 250.1-2 (to Prior Bernard of Portes and his community, 1150|1), 270.1-2 (to Pope Eugenius III, 1151), 389 (to Abbot Peter the Venerable of Cluny, 1149), in: *Sancti Bernardi Opera*, edd. J. Leclercq and H. Rochais (8 vols, Rome, 1957-77), 8.145-6, 178-80, 356-7; Peter the Venerable, *Epp.* 149 (to Bernard of Clairvaux, 1149), 158 (to Pope Eugenius III (1150|1), in: *The Letters of Peter the Venerable*, ed. G. Constable (2 vols, Cambridge, Mass., 1967), 1.363-6, 377-9.

the religious life and from real or alleged moral and personal shortcomings while still in the world.[13]   Other Carthusians, probably but not demonstrably from Chartreuse itself, quickly succeeded to the see—first the transient Othmar, and then Geoffrey who was bishop from ?1151 until 1163.[14]   Within the Carthusian Order, a twofold crisis arose from Noël's election.   First, its houses were sharply divided between those which, like Chartreuse, Ecouges, and Durbon, opposed Noël, and those which, like Portes, Meyriat, Silve-Bénite, and Arvières, held that it was not for hermits to become involved in litigation outside their houses.[15] Secondly, according to St Bernard, a number of Carthusians, some if not all of whom were from Chartreuse and who were led by a pertinacious modern Achitophel, had gone to Pope Eugenius.   Deceived by their story, he had absolved them from penances that Prior Anthelme had imposed—ostensibly, though not demonstrably, for transgressions arising from the election at Grenoble.   Both their headstrong exodus from the cell and their restoration even by the pope without due process within their priory contravened the Customs of Prior Guigo I.[16]   According to Bernard's information, Anthelme felt that his authority had been undermined, and he had ceased to be prior.   In concert with Peter the Venerable, abbot of Cluny, Bernard was his strong and pertinacious champion;   he urged Eugenius to acknowledge that he had been deceived and to bring about Anthelme's reinstatement as prior.[17]

There is nothing to suggest that Anthelme was reinstated, however briefly.   Everything points to the events which Bernard described

----

[13] *Ep.* 250, pp. 145|22-146|12.

[14] An early date for Othmar's election is indicated by Bernard, *Ep.* 389, p. 357|10-11.

[15] Peter the Venerable, *Ep.* 158, pp. 388|27-379|16.

[16] *Coutumes,* 31.1, 71, pp. 230-3, 282-5.

[17] *Ep.* 270;   for Bernard's statements that Anthelme had ceased to be prior, see pp. 179|9-12, 180|1-3.   The letter provides no evidence that Eugenius had recognized Noël as bishop.   The latest reference to Anthelme as prior is in the foundation charter of the priory of le Reposoir (dioc. Annecy), dated 22 Jan. 1151: C. le Couteulx, *Annales ordinis Cartusiensis ab anno 1084 ad annum 1429* (8 vols, Montreuil-sur-Mer, 1887-91), 2.118-20.

as having been the occasion for his handing over his office to Basil and reverting to the life of the cell at Chartreuse. The *Vita* indicates that he gave strong support to the new prior,[18] who, for his part, sought healing and concord. The carefully drafted record of his general chapter of 1155 established the general chapter as an annual event, provided the transfer to it of the corrective jurisdiction of the local bishop save that he, jointly with it, should excommunicate houses that were minded to secede and monks who individually or collectively disobeyed the general chapter, and required every Carthusian priory to promise obedience to the general chapter.[19] By such means, Basil reinforced the constitutional unity of the Order and effectively excluded the irregular acts of would-be Achitophels. But it remained to compose feelings and loyalties within particular priories, and especially Portes.[20] It was probably in a bid to restore peace and concord at Portes and to heal its relations with Chartreuse that, in 1156|7, and so after his attendance at Basil's general chapter of 1155, the aged Prior Bernard of Ambronay, when he resolved finally to retire, named Anthelme as his successor. According to Anthelme's *Vita*, the need for peace to be restored combined with the constraint of religious obedience to compel his return to his former priory.[21] His moderation, energy, and skill served to heal the wounds of the past.[22] After two years, he felt able to go back to Chartreuse as a simple monk. Such he remained until 1163 when, after a disputed election in the see of Belley, he obeyed the command of Pope Alexander III (1159–81) that he become its bishop.

The interaction between twelfth-century Carthusian priories and the neighbouring episcopate which Anthelme's experiences serve to illustrate makes it unsurprising that the Carthusian episcopal *Vitae* should all testify to a generally close bond between the Carthusian cell and the

----

[18] *VSA* cap. 9|5–12, p. 12.

[19] As n. 10.

[20] That the question of appeals to Rome, whether to the curia or to the pope in person, which had become acute in the crisis of 1149–51, remained troublesome is indicated by Prior Basil's rigorous legislation against such appeals in the second record of his general chapters: caps 4, 7–8 (as n. 10), pp. 38–40.

[21] *VSA* cap. 15|3–4, p. 16.

[22] *VSA* caps 12–13, pp. 13–16.

bishop and his household, both in spirit and in everyday actuality. The Customs of Prior Guigo I envisaged that guests would come to Chartreuse, especially bishops, abbots, and other religious; but he sounded a note of caution lest resources be strained or observances diluted.[23]   Anthelme's biographer's account of his years at Chartreuse and Portes shows no such reservations about the reception of guests.   There were practical reasons for entertaining them.   The superabundance of production in the developing economies of priories allayed fears about pressure upon resources;[24]   suitable novices could best be recruited if young men were allowed to visit in some numbers so that some, at least, might discover vocations there as monks.[25] In addition, many people, great and small, lay and clerical, came to Carthusian houses, including Chartreuse while Anthelme was prior, for their spiritual benefit;   those whom he corrected included negligent, avaricious, and simoniacal bishops and lax abbots.[26]   Senior clergy came for encouragement, as well: Archbishop Heraclius of Lyons (1153–63) and other dignitaries from a distance were accustomed to seek counsel about major matters from Anthelme while he was at Portes.[27]

Since Carthusian priories thus welcomed and directed episcopal visitors, it comes as no surprise that, according to their *Vitae*, Carthusians who became bishops continued to participate in the life of the cell. While bishop of Belley, Anthelme always retained a cell at Chartreuse;   he remained so much a member of the community that he was reckoned among the thirteen, or at most fourteen, to which Prior Guigo I restricted the monks of the upper house.[28]   Accordingly, he often came to Chartreuse for the spiritual recreation which was the proper solace of a bishop:

> When wearied by temporal affairs, spiritual man that he was he resided there in order that he might be renewed by exhibiting not the majesty of a bishop but the subordination of

____

[23] *Coutumes*, caps 10, 18–20, 36, 79.1, pp. 184–5, 202–11, 238–9, 284–7.

[24] *VSA* caps 8|2–9, 13–21, 12|5–13|5, pp. 11, 13–15.

[25] *VSA* cap. 3|1–28, pp. 4–5; cf. *MVSH* 1.7–8, vol. 1.22–7.

[26] *VSA* cap. 7|1–22, pp. 10–11.   Visitors to Chartreuse included King Louis VII of France (1137–80): Anthelme, *Ep. 2*, *Lettres*, 1.238–9, cf. 233–4.

[27] *VSA* cap. 14|4–7, p. 15. Heraclius was a brother of Peter the Venerable.

[28] *Coutumes*, cap. 78, pp. 284–5.

a humble monk. He was renewed, I say, not by delicate food but by fastings and prayers, not by sleep or inactivity but by vigils and exercises, not by gossip or stories or songs upon musical instruments but by sacred meditation and divine contemplation such as fills the mind with true joy, not by empty delight which ends in grief but by the sorrow which ends in everlasting joy. By such nourishment, God's servant was refreshed and strengthened, being fortified by the hope of eternal glory.[29]

Following a similar pattern of episcopal life, Bishop Hugh I of Grenoble had regularly withdrawn to the community at Chartreuse under Prior Guigo I; he was with the monks 'not as their lord or bishop, but as their fellow and most humble brother'. Guigo had to urge him to return to his see and care for his flock, discharging his duty towards them.[30] Bishop Hugh of Lincoln's *Vita* confirms that Chartreuse was open to bishops for such periods of spiritual retreat; while he was a youthful monk there, he was deputed to attend upon Peter, the saintly Cistercian who was archbishop of Tarentaise (1142-74), during his frequent and prolonged visits.[31] While bishop of Lincoln, Hugh used himself to withdraw to his sometime priory of Witham once or twice in almost every year.[32] Both Hugh of Grenoble and Anthelme of Belley took refuge at Chartreuse in times of political harassment.[33] Conversely, while bishop, Anthelme was accompanied by Carthusian monks as permanent or temporary members of his household.[34]

The two Carthusian bishops were more than periodic guests at their priories; they continued to exercise a measure of authority in them and in other houses even though they were outside their dioceses. While bishop of Belley, Anthelme's oversight of them was active and comprehensive:

He gave no less care than before to the standard of the religious life. He watched the more carefully lest anywhere in

----

[29] *VSA* cap. 30|7-18, p. 27.

[30] *VSH,* cap. 3.12, col. 770AB.

[31] *MVSH* 1.13, vol. 1.38-40. Peter's *Vita* and Miracles may be found in *Acta sanctorum quotquot toto orbe coluntur: Maius 2* (Antwerp, 1680), pp. 320-48; *BHL* 6772-7. They may be compared with *VSA*.

[32] *MVSH* 4.9-14, vol. 2.44-71.

[33] *VSH* cap. 4.17, col. 774A; *VSA* cap. 27|22-6, cf. cap. 30|9-11, pp. 25-6, 27.

[34] *VSA* Prol. 26|4, cap. 37|22-5, pp. 2-3, 30-1.

the Carthusian Order the rigour of its Customs might be relaxed and the fervour cooled. Priors kept their eyes fixed upon his nod of command, and the disposal of sacred business was in his hands.[35]

In addition, he sought to have confraternity at all Carthusian houses.[36] Similarly, while bishop of Lincoln, Hugh retained a positive, if perhaps undefined, authority over affairs at Witham; for example, he refused pardon and readmission to the monk Alexander who had left to become a Cluniac.[37] In such personal respects, relations between Carthusian priories and individual bishops, especially if they had themselves been Carthusian monks, were close and sustained.

The Carthusians formed a clear vision of the attitudes and qualities that were expected of a bishop, especially a monk-bishop, in the course of his life and duties. A monk should accede to the episcopate only with reluctance and under the sanction of obedience. Anthelme's election was depicted as immediately the providential work of Christ himself. When a *sanior pars* of the divided chapter at Belley successfully promoted his candidature, its members knew that he could not be torn from his *eremus* without much force. They therefore appealed to Pope Alexander III, who wrote to him commanding him by apostolic authority to accept, and to the prior and whole community at Chartreuse who were to release him and, if necessary, compel him to leave under obedience. Even so, it was only after prolonged resistance and a visit to the pope at Bourges that Anthelme agreed.[38] As, in 1080, Hugh of Grenoble was ordained bishop by Pope Gregory VII so, in 1163, Anthelme was ordained by Pope Alexander III; both bishops spent a considerable period with the pope.[39] Hugh of Lincoln would accept election to his see, even after the due canonical process upon which he insisted, only upon the command of Prior Jancelin of Chartreuse (1180-

----

[35] *VSA* cap. 30|2-6, p. 27.

[36] *VSA* cap. 31|15-17, p. 28.

[37] *MVSH* cap. 2.11, vol. 1.82-3. According to the Witham Chronicle, in 1191 Hugh summoned to his presence Prior Albert, examined his alleged shortcomings, and deposed him: A. Wilmart, 'Maître Adam chanoine Prémontré devenu Chartreux à Witham', *Analecta Praemonstratensia*, 9 (1933), 209-32, at p. 231; J. Hogg, 'The Pre-Reformation Priors of the *Provincia Angliae, Analecta Cartusiana,* NS 1 (1989), 25-58, at pp. 35-6 n. 22.

[38] *VSA* caps 17-20, pp. 17-20.

[39] *VSH* cap. 2.6-8, cols 766C-767D; *VSA* cap. 21, p. 20.

1233).   'Short of the order of our prior', he told the messengers of the chapter of Lincoln, 'no one shall lay upon my shoulders so great a burden.'[40]

Once the burden of the episcopate was shouldered under the sanction of religious obedience, the monk-bishop, as has been described, maintained his link with his priory and Order.   According to the bishops' *Vitae*, he exhibited throughout his episcopal life, for the welfare of his diocese and of the church at large, the qualities that flowed from his religious vocation.   The primary *speculum episcopi* which   the Carthusians offered to themselves and to others was Prior Guigo I's *Vita* of Hugh of Grenoble.   It is known to have circulated and to have left its mark upon other bishops.   Together with the *Vita sancti Antelmi* and the *Magna vita* of Hugh of Lincoln, it figures in the fifteenth-century manuscript of the Charterhouse of Bois-Saint-Martin (dioc. Cambrai), now Brussels, Bibliothèque royale, MS 298-306.[41]   Hugh of Lincoln himself took both Hugh of Grenoble and Anthelme as models of exemplary sanctity, especially when giving conferences to the monks of Chartreuse.[42] The virtues of a monk-bishop as Prior Guigo settled and disseminated them were partly personal and partly official.   As regards his personal conduct, Bishop Hugh of Grenoble was an exemplary custodian of his five senses and of his tongue.   Above all, he maintained a custody of the eyes which was needful in one who must often converse respectfully and affably with powerful men and noble women.   Eye-contact with men all too readily communicated anger, ill-humour, and lust.   As for women, many of whom came to him from his diocese and beyond for confession and counsel, only once in his years as a bishop did he look upon a woman's face;   she, Guigo assured his readers, was of little beauty *(parum quidem formosa)*. He insisted that clergy must learn from the outset of their ministry to discipline their lusts by controlling their senses of sight and touch: 'Let them ponder and imitate these things if they can', wrote Guigo;   'if not, let them wonder and stand in awe.'[43]

---

[40] *MVSH* 3.2-4, vol. 1.95-101;   citation at p. 98.

[41] *VSA* pp. 76-77.

[42] *MVSH* 4.9, 12, vol. 2.43-4, 55-61, cf. 3. Prol., vol. 1.90. *VSH* is included in the hagiographical material in Lincoln Cathedral MS 107 (A.4.15), which may have belonged to Hugh: R.M. Thomson, *Catalogue of the Manuscripts of Lincoln Cathedral Chapter Library* (Cambridge, 1989), pp. 80-1.

[43] *VSH* cap. 4.15, 18, cols 772A-773B.

To illustrate Hugh's custody of his tongue, Guigo dwelt upon his dealings with a long-term lay opponent, a count also named Guigo. Hugh won the count's high esteem for his unfailing truthfulness, while Hugh's own charity and humility led him to pray unceasingly for his persecutor. Hostility exhibited by a lay and worldly person was never to be soured by episcopal animosity.[44]

By highlighting these personal virtues, Prior Guigo was rein-forcing two of the ideals of the ecclesiastical reforms of the period of Pope Gregory VII: to secure the celibacy of the clergy in body and spirit, and to seek the obedience and service of lay rulers through the pursuit of peace and concord. His choice of official virtues was simi-larly formed. The bishop's household and lifestyle were to embody apostolic poverty and simplicity, and so to facilitate prayer, fasting, and (an especial obligation) almsgiving.[45] In a church riddled with practices that reformers deemed simoniacal, Bishop Hugh avoided every contagion of money, gifts, or respect of persons.[46] In a litigious and war-torn world, he promoted peace, especially for churches and for the poor.[47] He was an indefatigable preacher and dispenser of penance,[48] and he guided and guarded both his clergy and laity, and the monas-teries and religious communities within his sphere of influence.[49]

The *Vitae* of Anthelme and Hugh of Lincoln follow suit in estab-lishing the virtues of a monk-bishop, thus confirming the outward-looking and active pastoral and political role that the Carthusian tradition promoted. Although neither of them was presented as rivalling Hugh of Grenoble in the strictness of his custody of his five senses and especial-ly of the eyes, Anthelme shared his austerity in tasting food and drink and in finding recreation by fasting and vigils; while Hugh of Lincoln was similarly abstemious at table, restraining all his exterior senses. Both Hugh of Grenoble and Hugh of Lincoln became immune to sexual temptation; the latter thus became the better able as bishop to minister

----

[44] *VSH* cap. 4.16-17, cols 773B-774C. The identity of the count is uncertain; he may have been Count Guigo II of Forez and the Lyon-nais (*c*. 1109-37), or Count Guigo VIII of Albon (1079-?1133).

[45] *VSH* cap. 5.19, col. 775B-D.

[46] *VSH* cap. 5.20, cols 775D-776C.

[47] *VSH* cap. 5.21, cols 776C-777A.

[48] *VSH* cap. 5.22, col. 777A-D.

[49] *VSH* cap. 5.23, col. 778B.

wisely and safely to women.[50]   Both bishops emulated Hugh of Grenoble's prudent control over his tongue, likewise to the advantage of their ministrations to lay magnates.   Anthelme was subject to incessant vexation by Count Humbert III of Savoy (1148–89).   He countered his hatred and threats by a judicious blend of strictness and amiability;   on his deathbed, he blessed the still troublesome count, including in his blessing a prophecy that soon came to pass that he would at last have a son.   Hugh of Lincoln's ability to return the soft answer that turns away wrath was likewise an asset in his dealings with the Angevin kings of England;   one needs only to instance his humouring of King Henry II, when angered by his refusal to prefer a royal servant to a prebend, by jesting about the king's family connection with a tanner's daughter at Falaise.[51]   Hugh's love of truthfulness mirrored that of Hugh of Grenoble and won him similar lay respect.[52]

The bishop as seen through Carthusian eyes had a particular duty to promote peace.   Anthelme was solicitous to safeguard the vulnerable--clergy, widows, and the poor, as well as to promote unity and concord among the clergy;   Hugh of Lincoln was 'the especial refuge of the oppressed and the unvanquished champion of justice'.   All three bishops resisted the excesses of officials--Hugh of Grenoble those of a duly penitent officer of Count Amadeus III of Savoy (1103–48), Anthelme those of the *prévôt* of Count Humbert III, and Hugh of Lincoln those of royal foresters.[53]   The bishops were resolute when necessary in imposing excommunication and penance, thereby making clear the authority of their office.[54]   They were also assiduous almsgivers.[55]   They cared for religious houses in their dioceses--Hugh of Grenoble for the charterhouses of Chartreuse and Ecouges and the abbey of Chalais, as well as for houses

----
[50] *VSA* cap. 30|11–18, cf. *VSH* cap. 4.18, cols 774C–775A;   *MVSH* 2.2, 3.13, 4.9, vols 1.49–52, 49–59, 125–7, 2.47–8.

[51] *VSA* caps 29, 37|34–40, cf. 41.17–26, pp. 26, 31, 34.   For Count Humbert III, see C.W. Previté Orton, *The Early History of the House of Savoy (1000–1233)*, (Cambridge, 1912), pp. 316–52.

[52] *MVSH* 4.9, vol. 2.48, cf. *VSH* cap. 4.16, cols 773C–774A.

[53] *VSH* cap. 6.29, col. 781BC;   *VSA* caps 24|8–14, 25|1–4, 37|41–2, pp. 22, 23, 30;   *MVSH* 3.9–10, 4.6, vols 1.113–14, 118–19, 2.27–8, 32–3.

[54] *VSA* caps 26, 33, pp. 23–5, 28;   *MVSH* 4.4–6, vol. 2.15–33.

[55] *VSH* cap. 5.19, col. 775B–D;   *VSA* caps 34, 36, pp. 28–30;   *MVSH* 4.3, vol. 2.15.

of regular canons at Miseray (dioc. Bourges) and Saint–Georges (dioc. Angers), Anthelme especially for the nuns of Bons and the leper hospital at Entresaxe, and Hugh of Lincoln for his biographer's abbey of Eynsham.[56]

The specific objectives of the bishops' reforming zeal followed those of the reformers, including the popes, of the late eleventh century and after. This is not surprising, for Bishop Hugh I of Grenoble's ordination by Pope Gregory VII provided a direct link with the apostolic see and its aspirations.[57] Prior Guigo's arraignment of the state of the diocese of Grenoble as Hugh found it begins with a catalogue of the principal abuses that the reformers were concerned to extirpate: first, the matrimony of all grades of the clergy up to the priesthood; secondly, the buying and selling of holy things; and thirdly, the lay possession of churches, oblations, tithes, and cemeteries with the concomitant subjection of priests, churches, and sacraments to lay jurisdiction and control. There was a total lack of discipline which Hugh was untiring in his efforts to remedy.[58] The model of personal chastity in thought and deed which the three bishops' *Vitae* offered was itself a weapon against the endemic and, indeed, ineradicable problem of clerical incontinence. The problem was an especial concern of Anthelme. Positively, he sought to promote the honour and reputation of worthy ministers of holy orders, and especially priests, while castigating clerical concubinage and adultery. Anthelme's biographer recorded at length a synod held in his first year as bishop in which he addressed his clergy about the appropriateness of strict celebacy. In the following year, he punished the minority which had shown itself to be utterly incorrigible.[59] He also encouraged his married lay friends in conjugal fidelity and true love.[60]

----

[56] *VSH* cap. 5.23, col. 798B; *VSA* caps 35–6, pp. 29–30; *MVSH* 4.8, vol. 2.39–42. For Hugh of Lincoln's concern for lepers, see *MVSH* 4.3, vol. 2.12–15.

[57] *VSH* cap. 2.6–8, cols 766C–767D.

[58] *VSH* cap. 2.9, col. 768A–C.

[59] *VSA* caps 22|12–24|8, pp. 21–2.

[60] *VSA* cap. 44, p. 35. Anthelme knew how to lighten marital counselling by a jest. When staying with a family in Geneva, a husband told him that his wife was barren. He made the sign of the cross upon her forehead and as if jesting said to her, 'In the Lord's name, make *for me* a son'. She forthwith conceived by her husband.

Bishop Hugh of Lincoln was similarly concerned to urge chastity, along with truthfulness and charity, upon all sorts and conditions of people-- monks, clergy, and laity, according to their state of life.[61]

The problem of simony was not, as such, emphatically addressed in any of the *Vitae;*[62] but the freedom of holy persons and holy things from lay predation, dominance, and control was a prime concern of both Anthelme and Hugh of Lincoln. Anthelme sedulously safeguarded his own and the church's lands, men, cemeteries, and other possessions.[63] His *Vita* gives prominence to how he vindicated the church against laymen who he thought were transgressing its rights. He was doing so already in 1157|8 as prior of Portes. In November 1157, the Emperor Frederick Barbarossa granted to Archbishop Heraclius of Lyons his so-called 'golden bull', in which he invested the archbishop and his successors with the city of Lyons and all regalian rights throughout his archdiocese. This grant provoked an attack upon the city by Count Guigo III of Forez and the Lyonnais (1137-c. 1199). During it, Anthelme gave the arch- bishop and his clergy a refuge at Portes until they were restored to their rightful possession of the city.[64]

As bishop of Belley, Anthelme fought a long battle to vindicate the freedom of his church from the pressures of Count Humbert III of Savoy. Although Thomas Becket, the archbishop of Canterbury who was martyred in his cathedral on 29 December 1170, is not named, Anthelme's Carthusian biographer almost certainly had him in mind when describing his resistance to the lay power; since in 1168 Anthelme is known from other sources to have visited King Henry II in France, together with Prior Basil of Chartreuse, in connection with the Becket dispute,[65] it is

----

[61] *MVSH* 4.6,9, vol. 2.31-2, 43-8.

[62] But see above, p . **37.**

[63] *VSA* cap. 24|8-10, p. 22.

[64] *VSA* cap. 14, pp. 15-16. For the 'golden bull', see DDFI no. 192, and for Barbarossa's intervention in Burgundy, *Ottonis episcopi Frisingensis et Rahewini Gesta Frederici seu rectius Cronica,* 3.14(12), edd. G. Waitz and B. von Simson, revised by F.-J. Schmale, *Ausgewählte Quellen zur deutschen Geschichte des Mittelalters,* 17 (Darmstadt, 1965), pp. 420-3. It is discussed in H. Simonsfeld, *Jahrbücher des deutschen Reiches unter Friedrich I.,* 1: *1152-8* (Leipzig, 1908), pp. 580-2.

[65] *Materials for the History of Thomas Becket,* edd. J.C. Robertson and J.B. Sheppard (7 vols, London: Rolls Series, 67, 1875-85), 6, nos 404, 424, pp. 394-6, 438-40; for Carthusian involvement in relations between king and archbishop, see also no. 289, pp. 165-6.

likely that Anthelme himself took Becket as a model.   According to the *Vita*, while he always resisted those who acted wrongfully in respect of what he himself was obliged to defend, he was especially resolute when there was a danger of his martyrdom;   when resisting Count Humbert, 'he would have rejoiced exceedingly to have been worthy of such grace as to merit the palm and the glory of martyrdom for righteousness' sake'.[66] Anthelme would brook no lay assaults upon his clergy.   When Humbert had a priest arrested, he demanded his release.   He dispatched Bishop William II of Maurienne (?1160–?) who freed him in spite of the protests of Humbert's *prévôt*.   When, fearing re-arrest, the priest afterwards fled and was killed by the *prévôt*'s servants, Anthelme required Humbert to submit to a penance which he at last accepted at Anthelme's deathbed.[67]

More gravely still, Anthelme was confronted with Count Humbert's claims to regalian rights over the possessions of his church.   He successfully fought them off during his lifetime, though only with difficulty and by invoking the sanction of excommunication.   The count claimed to be in possession of a papal privilege which exempted him from excommunication, but Anthelme excommunicated him in his presence.   Just as, while prior of Chartreuse, Anthelme had stood firm against Pope Eugenius III when he released his subjects from their penances,[68] he now stood firm when Humbert successfully appealed to Pope Alexander III. The pope commissioned Archbishop Peter of Tarentaise and another bishop to persuade Anthelme to absolve Humbert or, if he refused, to do so themselves.   Anthelme remained adamant unless Humbert first made satisfaction for his transgressions.   When the two prelates deferred further action and Alexander himself absolved the count, Anthelme withdrew to Chartreuse.   He returned to Belley only when his clergy had secured from the pope a letter urging him to return;   thereafter, Anthelme continued to treat the count as an excommunicate.   Even upon his deathbed, Anthelme withheld absolution from the count until he had shown due contrition.   Notwithstanding, a miracle on Anthelme's part was necessary before Humbert desisted from his claims to *spolia* after the bishop's death.[69]

----

[66] *VSA* caps 24|14–15, 26|17–19, pp. 22, 24.

[67] *VSA* caps 25, 37|17–34, pp. 23, 30–1.

[68] See above, p. **29**.

[69] *VSA* caps 26–9, 37|16–40, 41|17–26, pp. 23–6, 30–1, 34.

Anthelme's invincible determination to preserve the clergy and the property of his church from lay depredation and exactions, even under colour of such claims as those of *regalia* and *spolia,* was matched by Hugh of Lincoln's care for the liberty of the church. 'God forbid', he once declared, 'that the decree of any lay person should infringe the privileges that belong to the church's liberty.' He rebuked King Henry II for what he saw as his abuse of royal powers, which his predecessors had usurped, in the appointment of bishops and abbots; he demanded free election in conformity with canon law. He insisted that his own election should be freely and canonically made in the chapter house at Lincoln. He excommunicated the king's chief forester whose maltreatment of other people defied the liberties of the church, and he refused to give a prebend at Lincoln to a courtier, requiring that ecclesiastical benefices should not be conferred upon royal officials but upon bona fide churchmen, who would not serve at the king's treasury or exchequer but at the altar. He would not allow royal officials to make improper or excessive financial demands upon his church; he said that he would rather submit himself to perpetual indigence than tolerate the least danger to the liberty of the church. In a similar spirit, he recovered from the crown his patronage of the abbey of Eynsham.[70] The curbing of lay power over churches and churchmen was a common feature of the Carthusian image of a bishop.

A final aspect of the Carthusian presentation of a bishop's office that calls for notice, in the case of Hugh I of Grenoble and Anthelme of Belley, is the fidelity that he owed to the papacy, especially when the papacy was itself under pressure from the imperial power. It is no surprise that such a fidelity should be inculcated by Prior Guigo I of Chartreuse, for he was himself a strong supporter of Pope Innocent II in the Anacletan schism of 1130-8.[71] He wrote his *Vita* of Hugh at Innocent's request after Hugh's canonization in 1134.[72] Hugh himself owed

----

[70] *MVSH* 2.7, 3.1-2, 9, 4.7-8, vols 1.70-2, 92-6, 113-15, 2.33-7, 39-41.

[71] See his *Epp.* 3 (to Pope Innocent II), 4 (to Duke William X of Aquitaine), and 5 (to the papal chancellor Cardinal Haimeric), *Lettres,* 1.163-95. Guigo's censures in the last of these letters upon the papal curia may be compared with the opinion of Bishop Hugh of Lincoln: *MVSH* 3.12, vol. 1.122.

[72] *VSH, Epistola Innocentii II papae, Prol.*, cols 761A-763B.

the papacy a debt for his ordination by Pope Gregory VII and for Gregory's pastoral care of him.[73]   He made it clear after the events of 1111 in Rome, when the Emperor Henry V (1106-25) imprisoned Pope Paschal II (1099-1118) and secured from him a papal privilege conceding to him lay investiture.   In September 1112, Hugh played a leading part in securing Henry's excommunication by the council of Vienne which Archbishop Guy of Vienne (1088-1119), afterwards Pope Calixtus II (1119-24), convened.[74]   Despite the goodwill and services that Hugh received from the Roman family of Pierleone, in 1130 he was not deflected to support one of its members who was elected as rival pope to Innocent II under the name of Anacletus II.   Despite his advanced age and debility, Hugh hastened to a council at le Puy which excommunicated Anacletus as a schismatic.   In 1132, when Innocent was in France, Hugh met him at Valence.[75]

        During and after the disputed papal election of 1159, Anthelme was no less firm in his support of Pope Alexander III.   The election occurred soon after Anthelme had returned to his cell at Chartreuse from his two years as prior of Portes.   When a group of cardinals proclaimed a supporter of the Emperor Frederick Barbarossa, named Cardinal Octavian, pope under the name of Victor IV, Anthelme emerged as Victor's strenuous opponent.   He did do partly because of his concern for catholic unity and of his horror of schism, but more because Victor's success would have delivered the church into the lay power of the emperor.   Together with another monk of Chartreuse named Geoffrey, who had been the founder and first prior of the Carthusian house of Mont-Dieu (dioc. Reims) (1136- c. 1145), Anthelme rallied the whole Carthusian Order to Alexander's support, as well as many others not of the Order.   As a result, Anthelme incurred, at least temporarily, the ill-will of the emperor.[76]   The *Vita* noted that, as bishop of Belley, he was held in respect even at the Roman curia.[77]

----

[73] See above, p. **33**.

[74] *VSH* cap. 5.25, col. 779AB.   For the events of 1111-12, see G. Meyer von Knonau, *Jahrbücher des deutschen Reiches unter Heinrich IV. und Heinrich V.* (7 vols, Leipzig, 1890-1907), 6.154-65, 240-4.   For the council of Vienne, see Mansi, 21.73-8.

[75] *VSH* cap. 5.25, cols 778D-779C.   For the council of le Puy, see Mansi, 21.435-8.

[76] *VSA* cap. 16, pp. 16-17.

[77] *VSA* cap. 32|3-4, p. 28.

It should be added to the account in the *Vita* that   he   was in due course restored to Barbarossa's favour.   On 26 March 1175, after the emperor's fifth Italian expedition of 1174 but before his defeat by the Lombard League at the battle of Legnano in May 1176 and his preliminary peace with Alexander III at Anagni in the following November, Anthelme received from the emperor a diploma which granted him imperial protection, confirmed him in the possession of regalian rights and judicial immunity in his see, and gave him a licence to fortify the city of Belley.[78] The diploma is, perhaps, best regarded as a reminder of how considerably Anthelme's outlook was determined by his need to secure the local rights and interests of his see, for Barbarossa's grants protected him from the claims of the counts of Savoy.   In 1159, he had evidently welcomed Barbarossa's 'golden bull' by which the archbishop of Lyons had secured regalian rights throughout his see.[79]   Similarly, in 1175, he was prepared to secure comparable rights for his own see even from an excommunicate emperor.   The freedom of his own see of Belley from lay power was an overriding consideration.

The silence of the *Vita* about Barbarossa's diploma of 1175 is a reminder that due regard must be given to the purpose of an episcopal *Vita*.   It was to provide, not a balanced and rounded account of a man and his life as seen in everyday reality, but an image of sanctity for admiration and imitation.   The Carthusian author of the *Vita Antelmi* drew an illuminating comparison.   In his Prologue, he recalled that, in pagan antiquity, it was customary to set up statues or portraits of one's natural ancestors, so that their posterity might be incited to seek the fame of valour and public spirit by contemplating the examples of strong men.   Christian worshippers of the true God did far better by commending to future generations for imitation and celebration, not mere statues and paintings, but the very lives of unconquered martyrs or (more usually) valiant confessors who overcame the world by striving against spiritual enemies for the reward of an eternal kingdom.   Rich in virtues and miracles, such men were examples, patrons, and intercessors before God;   it was as such that Anthelme was commemorated in his *Vita*.[80]

----

[78] *DDFI* no. 637;   see Previtè Orton (as n. 51), pp. 342-3, 426.
[79] See above, p. **38**.
[80] *VSA* cap. 1|1-26, p. 2.

Such being the purposes of hagiographical literature, the common features of the *Vitae* of twelfth-century monk-bishops which were written in Carthusian circles disclose the image of the bishop's office that the early Carthusians envisaged. Far from being mutually exclusive, the lives of the Carthusian monk and of the bishop complemented each other. They were mutually supporting aspects of the Carthusian vocation in a church and world which called for the renewal that the eleventh-century reformers had initiated.[81] In his cell, the Carthusian monk, and especially the Carthusian prior, was never to be unmindful of the work of the bishop but was to support and reinforce it; in his household and diocese, the monk-bishop was to maintain his link with the cell, to which he did well to return regularly for spiritual refreshment. The monk-bishop's virtues, especially chastity and truthfulness, were those which promoted the Gregorian ideal that the church should 'return to her true glory and stand free, chaste, and catholic';[82] a clergy deserving of respect should enjoy the willing obedience of a laity which was won over by episcopal strictness and amiability. A monk-bishop must adapt his ministry and message to suit all sorts and conditions of men and women. It was the especial duty of a monk-bishop to promote the freedom of the church from lay proprietorship and control, above all in his own diocese but also in the papacy itself. The bishop must never neglect his diocese, but it was his duty to be available for service in a wider sphere.

Alike in its integration of the monastic and the episcopal vocations in the life of the individual monk-bishop and in its programme for his activity in his diocese and beyond, the Carthusian model for the monk-bishop was amongst the most authentic, effective, and attractive expressions of the aspirations for reform which multiplied in the Latin church of the late eleventh and twelfth centuries.

----

[81] For reflections upon the relation between the reform papacy and monasticism, see H.E.J. Cowdrey, 'The Gregorian Papacy and Monasticism', forthcoming Proceedings of the conference on 'Bruno di Colonia e la Certosa', Serra San Bruno and Squillace, 1991.

[82] *The Epistolae vagantes of Pope Gregory VII*, ed. and trans. H.E.J. Cowdrey (Oxford, 1972), Ep. 54, p. 132|31-2.

XVII

HUGH OF AVALON, CARTHUSIAN AND BISHOP

In May 1186, and so just eight hundred years ago, Hugh of Avalon was elected bishop of Lincoln, and on 21 September he received consecration.[*] He occupied the see until his death on 16 November 1200, as the last of the truly great and saintly foreigners who, in the wake of the Norman Conquest of 1066, ruled medieval English dioceses. Hugh was not only a foreigner, born at Avalon in Burgundy not far from the frontier with Savoy, but also a Carthusian monk and so a member of the strictest and most withdrawn monastic family of the twelfth-century western church. The purpose of this paper is to inquire how a Carthusian, born not far from Chartreuse, could become a diocesan bishop in far-distant England, and do so in a manner that, in his own eyes as well as those of contemporaries, fulfilled rather than contradicted his Carthusian vocation.

I

The Carthusians had been founded in 1084 by St Bruno, and between 1121 and 1128 Prior Guigo I had written down the Customs that governed their life.[1] Many features of the Carthusian order made it prima facie

[*] The following abbreviations are used:

Colloque	La Naissance des Chartreuses. VIe Colloque Internationale d'Histoire et de Spiritualité Cartusiennes, 1984 (Grenoble, 1986)
Coutumes	Guigues Ier, Coutumes de Chartreuse, ed. by a Carthusian, SC 313 (Paris, 1984)
Lettres	Les Lettres des premiers Chartreux, 1: St Bruno, Guigues, St Anthelme, 2: Les Moines de Portes, ed. by a Carthusian, SC 88, 274 (Paris, 1962-80)
Magna vita s. Hugonis	The Life of St Hugh of Lincoln, edd. D. L. Douie and H. Farmer (2 vols., London, etc., 1961-2; repr. with corrections, Oxford, 1985)
PL	Patrologia Latina
Recueil	Recueil des plus anciens actes de la Grande-Chartreuse (1086-1196), ed. B. Bligny (Grenoble, 1958)
SC	Sources chrétiennes
Vita s. Hugonis	Guigo I, Vita sancti Hugonis Gratianopolitani, PL 153. 761-84

[1] Coutumes. Bruno's own conception of the eremitical life is stated in his letters

unlikely that it would develop into what it quite rapidly became – a nursery of outstanding diocesan bishops. It was founded and grew up in the context of the *crise du monachisme* to which, at the end of the eleventh and the beginning of the twelfth centuries, proximity to the world had brought the black monks, including the Cluniacs. A number of new foundations, including the Carthusians' younger sister-order the Cistercians, removed themselves from the habitations of men to a distant *eremus*, or desert place; but the Cistercians, for example, acquired extensive lands and far-flung granges. The Carthusians, by contrast, carried the search for seclusion to its practicable limit. In a memorable phrase, Dom David Knowles commented upon their 'logical formality and uncompromising strength', in which he saw a quintessential expression of the French genius.[2] The Carthusian *eremus* was to be as complete and as uncompromising as human resourcefulness could make it.

It would be wrong to envisage the *spaciosa heremus* which Prior Bruno established in the high mountains behind Grenoble,[3] as if it were a piece of the Sahara incongruously transported into France, or a mere hankering after the fourth-century Egyptian desert of St Antony. It was a solitude which here and now could provide all the spiritual and material necessities of a small and austere community of men who were single-mindedly dedicated to penitence and meditative prayer. Chartreuse, and in principle its first five dependent Charterhouses which were founded under Guigo I – in 1115 Portes, and in 1116 Les Écouges, Durbon, la Sylve-Bénite, and Meyriat – are each set in a high mountain valley which forms a natural cul-de-sac. The sole, easily controlled entry leads first to a lower house of the *conversi* or lay brothers, and only then to an upper house of the monks themselves. From the very beginning the Carthusians were anxious to set strict boundaries (*termini*) to the patrimony of their houses. Those of Chartreuse itself were established by stages between 1084 and 1129.[4] Within their *termini* – here, Knowles's 'logical formality' is particularly evident – the Carthusians possessed everything; outside them they were to possess nothing. As nearly as possible the *termini* were to be impervious

to Ralph *le Verd* (1096/1101) and to the Carthusian community (1099/1100): *Lettres*, 1.66-89.

[2] D. Knowles, *The Monastic Order in England*, 2nd edn (Cambridge, 1963), pp. 375-391, at p. 380. I have also particularly used the following: B. Bligny, *L'Église et les ordres religieux dans le royaume de Bourgogne aux xie et xiie siècles* (Paris, 1960); *ibid.*, 'Les chartreux dans la société occidentale du xiie siècle', in *Aspects de la vie conventuelle aux xie-xiie siècles* (Lyons, etc., 1975), pp. 29-58. A Carthusian and J. Dubois, 'Certosini', in *Dizionario degli Istituti di Perfezione*, 2 (Rome, 1975), cols. 782-821. J. Dubois, *Histoire monastique en France au xiie siècle* (London, 1982), nos. VII-X; *ibid.*, 'Le désert, cadre de vie des chartreux au Moyen-Age', *Colloque*, pp. 15-35.

[3] *Recueil*, no. 1, pp. 1:8; see also Guibert of Nogent, *De vita sua*, 1.11, Guibert de Nogent, *Histoire de sa vie*, ed. G. Bourgin (Paris, 1907), pp. 32-6, and Peter the Venerable, *De miraculis*, 2.28, PL 189. 943-5, esp. col. 944BC.

[4] i. 1084: *Recueil*, no. 1, pp. 1-8. ii. Before 1103: *ibid.*, no. 8, pp. 22-4. iii. 1103: *ibid.*, no. 9, pp. 24-7. iv. 1107/9: nos. 10-11, pp. 27-30. v. c. 1112: *ibid.*, nos. 12-14, pp. 30-4. 1129: *ibid.*, nos. 15-17, pp. 35-45.

Hugh of Avalon, Carthusian and Bishop

in both directions. They were to contain no habitations save those of the monks and the *conversi*. Women and armed men were strenuously excluded from entry, as were hunters, fishers, and graziers. When some iron miners tried to resume their operations at Chartreuse, a former land-owner who had given them leave to do so was speedily made to repent and to affirm that henceforth he would grant no more concessions, even if not just an iron mine but a gold mine were discovered there![5] In his Customs, Guigo prescribed the complement to this so far as the monks were concerned: 'To exclude so far as possible every occasion of greed, we order that those who dwell in this place shall possess absolutely nothing outside the boundaries of their desert (*extra suae terminos heremi*) – no fields, no vines, no gardens, no churches, cemeteries, oblations, tithes, or anything of that kind.'[6]

To ensure physical sustenance in the high mountains even for a manner of life marked by *vilitas et asperitas*,[7] the Carthusians strictly limited numbers within their houses: Guigo allowed only thirteen or fourteen monks and, normally, sixteen *conversi*.[8] Guests were bluntly warned to expect no provender for their horses; above all, Guigo ruled out the monastic almsgiving that elsewhere was a universal obligation. He explained himself with further Gallic directness: 'We did not flee to the solitude of this desert in order to undertake the material care of other men's bodies; we did so to seek the eternal salvation of our own souls. Therefore let no one marvel if we offer greater friendship and solace to those who come here rather for the good of their souls than of their bodies. Were it otherwise, we would have done better from the start to have established ourselves somewhere by a public highway, not in a savage, remote, and well-nigh inaccessible place.' For, as Guigo insisted, the Carthusians followed the way of Mary, not that of Martha.[9]

Indeed, they took the way of Mary almost, but not quite, to the extreme, practising a form of eremitical life tempered by a little common life.[10] The ideal of the Carthusians was the *vita solitaria*; the place of its habitual conduct, whether in prayer, work, or recreation, was the individual cell. Of the daily offices, only Matins and Vespers were recited in community; the remainder were said in the cell. In the early decades there was not even a daily mass. Social recreation and conversation were allowed only occasionally. Except on Sundays and greater festivals, meals were taken alone in the cell, though here as so often Carthusian austerity was applied with good sense; on the day when a Carthusian was buried, his brethren were not bound to keep to their cells, but to provide solace (*consolationis gratia*), unless it were a major fast they twice ate together.[11] Thus, occasional meetings for prayer, meals, or recreation punctuated the prevailing

[5]   *Ibid.*, nos. 6, 18, pp. 16-20, 45-7.
[6]   *Coutumes*, cap. 41.1, p. 244.
[7]   *Ibid.*, cap. 22.1, p. 212.
[8]   *Ibid.*, caps. 78-9, pp. 284-6.
[9]   *Ibid.*, caps. 19-20, pp. 204-10.
[10] Cf. *Lettres*, p. 20.
[11] *Coutumes*, cap. 14.2, p. 194.

solitude. But the strongest bond of common life was the vow of stability and obedience that bound the Carthusian to the direction of his prior, as the head of Chartreuse was called.[12] Guigo prescribed for the novice that from the time of his profession 'he should consider himself so alien from all things of the world, that without the prior's leave he has power over nothing whatever, not even his own self. Although [Guigo commented] obedience should be maintained with great zeal by all who have undertaken to live under a monastic rule, it should be practised the more devotedly and carefully by those who have embraced a stricter and more severe vocation.'[13]

One might think that a final commitment to a life of solitude and seclusion, lived under obedience within the carefully drawn boundaries of a Charterhouse, could not be more categorically stated, nor could a progression to the episcopate be more categorically debarred. But there was another side to the Carthusian monasticism into which Hugh of Avalon was admitted c.1163. From its very beginning and increasingly as time went on, Chartreuse inevitably interacted with the surrounding church and world much as did other parts of western monasticism. It owed an incalculable debt to succeeding bishops of Grenoble – Hugh I (1080-1132), Hugh II (1132-48), and then, after the transient Othmar, Geoffrey (1151-63) and John I of Sassenage (1163-1220). Their advice and protection were essential for the establishment and protection of Chartreuse's *eremus*, which lay entirely within their diocese. In his Life of Hugh I, Prior Guigo recalled how the bishop had helped Bruno with the foundation of his house.[14] The early Carthusian *acta* document the continuing debt. Thus, in 1086 at a diocesan synod, Hugh confirmed the gift of the original *spaciosa heremus* by a number of local lords and by Abbot Seguin of la Chaise-Dieu, one of whose priories, Saint-Robert-du-Mont-Cornillon, had certain rights there. In 1090, after Bruno's departure to Italy had led to the dispersal of the community and the return of its lands to Seguin, Pope Urban II charged Archbishop Hugh of Lyons and Bishop Hugh of Grenoble to reinstate them. It was Bishop Hugh who, some ten years later, by a mandate to the clergy and laity of his diocese, prohibited the circulation within Chartreuse's *termini* of women and of armed men.[15] Again, it was Bishop Hugh who warded off the intrusion of iron miners and haymakers.[16] As the *termini* were gradually extended between 1099 and 1129, almost every stage took place through donations made in the bishop's presence and fortified by his confirmation.[17] Even a matter so domestic to the order as the emergence of the Carthusian general chapter took place under close episcopal guidance. In 1141, when Prior Anthelme convened the first true general chapter of himself and five other priors besides himself, he did so upon Bishop Hugh II's advice; the bishop

[12]   *Ibid.*, cap. 23.1, p.214; cf. *Magna vita s. Hugonis*, 1.7, 10, vol. 1.22-4, 31-4.
[13]   *Coutumes*, cap. 25.2, p.218.
[14]   *Vita s. Hugonis*, 2.11, cf. 5.23, PL 153.769-70, 778.
[15]   *Recueil*, nos.1, 3, 4, 6, pp.1-8, 11-14, 16-20.
[16]   *Ibid.*, nos.18-19, pp.45-50.
[17]   As n.4; the exception is nos.10-11.

Hugh of Avalon, Carthusian and Bishop

was present and himself received the priors' promise of obedience to the chapter. In 1155 under Prior Basil, when general chapters assumed settled form and became regular occasions, Bishop Geoffrey fulfilled a similar role as guardian of the Carthusian order.[18] As late as 1196, Bishop John of Sassenage could allude to the 'good customs' which by agreement had admitted himself and his predecessors to a place in Carthusian affairs; only if a bishop of Grenoble were persistently to transgress these customs should the Carthusians' papally conferred exemption be invoked against him.[19]

For during the first hundred years of Carthusian history the papacy, too, had become deeply concerned and reinforced Chartreuse's liberty. Its involvement began as early as with Pope Urban II, who in 1090 remedied the problems that Bruno's departure had occasioned by persuading Abbot Seguin of la Chaise-Dieu to restore Chartreuse to its returning monks so that it might remain *in libertate pristina*; in 1091 he took it under papal protection and approved the election of Landuin, the second prior whom Bruno had designated.[20] In 1133 Pope Innocent II followed (as he said) the example not only of Urban II but also of his successors Paschal II, Calixtus II, and Honorius II, by approving Carthusian constitutions and customs as well as by giving papal protection to all Carthusian possessions both present and future; his bull included a detailed description and guarantee of the *termini* of Chartreuse, with the observation that the *sacer ordo eremeticus Cartusiensis ... ad honorem sacrosanctae Romanae ecclesiae ... omnino devotus est.*[21] It was particularly after 1163, when Bishop Geoffrey of Grenoble was deposed for having adhered to the Emperor Frederick Barbarossa and his antipope – an episode by which the Carthusians themselves were not directly compromised – that the popes frequently and comprehensively protected the Carthusians and their interests. Their acts protected the Carthusians' lands and privacy, developed their exemption, and confirmed the statutes of their general chapters.[22] The papacy became more important than the bishops in giving the Carthusians the protection that they needed; inevitably they themselves reciprocated by sharing papal aspirations and by being drawn into papal service and papal affairs.

They began to be so involved from very early days. Bruno, the first prior, had formerly been *scholasticus* of the cathedral of Reims where Odo of Châtillon, the future Pope Urban II, had been his pupil. Urban remem-

---

[18]   *Ibid.*, nos. 21-2, pp. 53-64.
[19]   *Ibid.*, no. 67, pp. 180-1. The bishop of Grenoble's part in Carthusian deliberations is illustrated by the discussions that preceded Hugh of Avalon's departure for Witham: *Magna vita s. Hugonis*, 2.3-4, vol. 1.53-9.
[20]   *Recueil*, nos. 2-5, pp. 9-16.
[21]   *Ibid.*, no. 20, pp. 50-3. No *acta* of Paschal II, Calixtus II, or Honorius II survive, but for a reference to a lost papal letter, see *Magna vita s. Hugonis*, 1.10, vol. 1.33.
[22]   Alexander III: *Recueil*, nos. 25 (1164), 29-30 (1173/6), 31 (1176), 32 (1177), pp. 70-2, 83-94. Lucius III: *ibid.* nos. 37-9 (1184), 40-2 (1185), pp. 103-20. Urban III: *ibid.*, nos. 44-5 (1186/7), pp. 126-8. Clement III: *ibid.*, nos. 46-7 (1188), 51-2 (1190), pp. 129-36, 144-7. Celestine III: *ibid.*, 53-7 (1192), 58 (1193), pp. 147-64.

XVII

bered his master and c.1090 he called him to the service of the apostolic see; although Bruno, having refused the pope's offer of the archbishopric of Reggio/Calabria, quickly withdrew to found a new eremitical community at La Torre. There, in 1100, his successor at Chartreuse, Landuin, came to consult him; on his return journey he died while a captive of the antipope Clement III's partisans.[23] A generation later, like Bernard of Clairvaux, Prior Guigo I of Chartreuse became deeply committed to Pope Innocent II and his cause in the Anacletan Schism of 1130-9. As early as 1131 he wrote to Innocent and exhorted him to steadfastness in the afflictions of the Roman church. He strongly condemned the leader of the French Anacletans, Bishop Gerard of Angoulême, and he pleaded with Duke William X of Aquitaine to abandon his support of Bishop Gerard. Most important was his cordial contact with the papal chancellor, Cardinal Haimeric, to whom he wrote after the cardinal had recently visited Chartreuse. Guigo deplored the *cruenta scissio* which rent the Roman church. He traced its spiritual origins to pride in the mind and indulgence in the body (*elatio in mente et voluptas in corpore*); the consequence had been the arming of Christian against Christian. Guigo proceeded to his most considerable discussion that survives of how Christians should interact with the rulers of this world. With an allusion to the dangers that lurked in the notion of a bishop's *regalia* to which the concordat of Worms (1122) had given prominence, he urged that it was better that churches should give laws to kings' palaces than that palaces should give laws to churches. Kings should receive sackcloth from churchmen, rather than churchmen receive the purple from kings. 'It better serves them,' Guigo commented, 'to borrow our poverty, fasts, and humility, than it serves us to borrow their greed, delicacy, and pride.'[24] Guigo's letters make it clear that Chartreuse had its spiritual and moral message for transmission to churchmen and to kings.

After the Anacletan schism had thus served to extend Chartreuse's horizons of concern far beyond its own *eremus*, the process of dialogue with those outside developed in three especial ways. First, loyalties engendered during the schism led to the Carthusians' maintaining close spiritual and personal contacts, especially through letter-writing and confraternity, with other monastic families – notably the Cluny of Peter the Venerable and the Clairvaux of St Bernard.[25] In 1128 Guigo wrote to Hugh of Payns, grand master of the Templars, exhorting him to spiritual

[23] For the lives of the early priors of Chartreuse, see A. Wilmart, 'La chronique des premiers chartreux', *Revue Mabillon*, 16 (1926), 77-142. For the letter that Landuin was bringing back, *Lettres*, no. 2, vol. 1.82-8.
[24] *Lettres*, nos. 3-5, vol. 1.166-95. The special greeting at the end of no. 5 for Cardinals Matthew of Albano and John of Ostia is further evidence for Guigo's contact with the papal curia.
[25] Peter the Venerable: *Recueil*, nos. 23-4, pp. 64-9; *The Letters of Peter the Venerable*, ed. G. Constable (2 vols., Cambridge, Mass., 1967), nos. 24, 48, 132, vol. 1.44-7, 146-8, 333-4. St Bernard: *S. Bernardi Opera*, 7-8, *Epistolae*, edd. J. Leclercq and H. Rochais (Rome, 1974-7), nos. 11-12, 153-4, 250, vol. 1.52-62, 359-61, vol. 2.145-7.

46

Hugh of Avalon, Carthusian and Bishop

rather than military valour, but also calling down upon him divine aid *in spiritualibus quam etiam in corporalibus praeliis*.[26] Secondly, the expansion and development of the Carthusian order, which by 1200 numbered some thirty-nine foundations, also fostered its interaction with the world outside. It did so in many ways. When a new house was established at a distance, the goodwill of the local bishop might need to be secured.[27] When monks were dispatched to institute new houses, they might come up against and feel bound to contend for the church's wider needs. Thus, when the Carthusian monk Einhard, who set up many Charterhouses, once heard of the Albigensian heretics' brazen blasphemy (as Adam of Eynsham described it) against all the sacraments of the church, he did not stand idly by. 'White-hot with zeal against such godless men,' Adam wrote, 'he went to the nearest Catholic magnates and aroused them to take up arms against the heretics, slaying many of them, and a preacher of so damnable a heresy never again appeared in the neighbourhood.'[28] Besides the foundation of new houses, the regular holding of general chapters of all Carthusian priors involved Chartreuse in larger expenditure than its infertile *eremus* could sustain. Therefore the Carthusians came to welcome grants of fiscal privileges, rights of pasture, and other benefits from magnates and kings. In 1192 Pope Celestine III vindicated against local 'tyrants' their right to receive testamentary bequests; it is noteworthy that the pope appealed, not to Carthusian traditions and customs, but to natural human justice and the norms of canon and civil law.[29] As a result of such contacts with magnates and kings, Carthusian values were impressed upon kings, as when the future Carthusian *conversus*, Count Gerard of Nevers, shamed the idleness of the French royal court under King Louis VII and showed the Carthusian life to be a better route to Jerusalem than the Second Crusade upon which the king was about to embark.[30] In 1133 Prior Guigo I heard of an attack on the reforming bishop of Paris, Stephen of Senlis, and joined the ageing Bishop Hugh I of Grenoble to write a letter urging the council of Jouarre to deprive perpetually of their benefices the clerks who had been involved.[31] Thirdly, if Chartreuse had its windows to the world, outsiders came to Chartreuse and stayed with its monks. For although it discouraged visits from those seeking merely material alms, it was always welcoming to those who came for their spiritual benefit. Bishops were especially admitted to benefit from, and also contribute to, life at Chartreuse; this is well illustrated by the frequent spiritual retreats there of the Cistercian Archbishop Peter of Tarentaise (1142-75), during which he also instructed Hugh of Avalon when a young monk.[32]

[26] *Lettres*, no.2, vol.1.154-61.
[27] *Lettres*, no.9, to Archbishop Reynald of Reims (1136), vol.1.224-5.
[28] *Magna vita s. Hugonis*, 4.13, vol.2.62-9, esp. 65-6.
[29] Fiscal privileges: *Recueil*, nos.33-5, 61-2, 65-6, pp.94-100, 169-71, 175-9. Gifts: *ibid.*, nos.34, 36, 50, 59, 60, pp.96-8, 100-2, 142-4, 164-9. Celestine III's bull: *ibid.*, no.53, pp.147-9.
[30] *Magna vita s. Hugonis*, 4.12, vol.2.55-8.
[31] *Lettres*, no.6, vol.1.201-2.
[32] Visitors might come on a surprisingly large scale, as during Hugh of Avalon's

In view of Chartreuse's long history of interacting in such ways as these with the world outside, it is not surprising that, from an early date, its priors and monks did not regard the episcopal office as being alien to the Carthusian vocation. On the one hand, bishops who were not themselves Carthusians might so behave as to reflect and propagate Carthusian principles; on the other, a Carthusian vocation might itself lead on to the episcopate.

The figure of Bishop Hugh I of Grenoble was of the utmost importance in leading the Carthusians to adopt this view. Two years after he died in 1132, Pope Innocent II canonised him and imposed upon Prior Guigo I the task of writing his Life. Innocent's stated reasons were that God should be honoured in his saint, and that the clergy who read and the laity who heard his Life might give God glory and have the benefit of Hugh's intercessions.[33] Since Hugh was already canonised, Guigo had no need to rehearse his miracles. He could present him as an exemplary monk-bishop according to a pattern that the Carthusians understood and approved: he was torn between his desire for the monastic or eremitical life at its most demanding, and his zeal for the well-being of his diocese and its people as required by contemporary reforming aspirations and by pastoral necessities. Guigo set out Hugh's Life in six chapters. The first concerned his parents, education, and years as a canon of Valence. It featured Hugh's father, Odo of Châteauroux, a knight of virtuous life who upon his second wife's death entered Chartreuse and became an exemplary Carthusian. At Valence, Hugh attracted the notice of Pope Gregory VII's standing legate in France, Hugh, then bishop of Die and later archbishop of Lyons. Hugh of Die enlisted the young man as his helper against the prime targets in France of the papal reform – laymen who held churches, tithes, and cemeteries; married priests; and simoniacs. Secondly, Guigo described how, in 1080, Hugh became bishop of Grenoble at the age of twenty-seven: at Hugh of Die's council of Avignon, the clergy of Grenoble requested him as its bishop; he refused episcopal consecration from his metropolitan, Archbishop Warmund of Vienne, on grounds of his simony, and received it instead at Rome from Gregory VII himself. Guigo dwelt upon Gregory's pastoral care of the young man when he encountered severe temptation, and upon the continuing favour that he showed him. He described the parlous state of the new bishop's diocese, which arose from its married clergy, the prevalence of simony, the churches, tithes, and cemeteries in lay hands and so subject to secular jurisdiction, and the wasting of church property. Thirdly, Guigo showed how, after becoming a bishop, Hugh experienced a deep longing for the monastic life. In 1082 he completed a noviciate and made his profession at la Chaise-Dieu which he admired for its *paupertas* and *humilitas*; but Gregory VII himself intervened and ordered him to resume his pastoral care. In 1084 when Chartreuse was founded, Hugh was Bruno's adviser and helper, and he

last journey: *Magna vita s. Hugonis*, 5.14, vol. 2.164-6. For Peter of Tarentaise, *ibid.*, 1.13, vol. 1.38-40.
[33] *Vita s. Hugonis*, *PL* 153.761-2.

Hugh of Avalon, Carthusian and Bishop

always maintained familiarity with the Carthusians. 'He was with them not as lord and bishop,' Guigo wrote, 'but as one of themselves and as a most humble brother.' When he stayed with them, Bruno sometimes had to drive him back to his flock and counsel him to moderate his austerities. Fourthly, Guigo exhibited Hugh as a model in respect of custody of the senses and of the tongue. His fifth chapter concerned his external actions as bishop – his almsgiving, his refusal of gifts for himself and his other virtues, his zeal as peacemaker and preacher, and his services to the papacy in 1111 when the German Emperor Henry V descended upon Rome as well as during the Anacletan schism. Guigo concluded with an account of Hugh's last sickness, death, and burial. Overall he provided the Carthusian model of a saintly bishop, to whom Chartreuse owed a great debt, who aspired to the monastic life and lived by its standards, but who also measured up to the spiritual, moral, and political demands of Gregory VII, his agents, and successors, no less than to the standards of the Carthusians.

Because the Carthusians had so clear a model of the episcopal life and office, it is not surprising that Chartreuse and other Carthusian priories became an important source of bishops for the provinces that lay in their vicinity.[34] At Grenoble, Guigo's Life of Bishop Hugh I relates that, in his declining years, a monk of Chartreuse became his coadjutor, and in due course succeeded to the see as Bishop Hugh II.[35] The remaining twelfth-century bishops of Grenoble – Othmar, Geoffrey, and John of Sassenage – were all Carthusians.[36] In 1148, Pope Eugenius III translated Hugh II to the archbishopric of Vienne, although after a troubled period he withdrew in 1155 to the Charterhouse of Portes. It was the Charterhouse of Meyriat which, in 1121, had provided the first Carthusian bishop in Pons II of Belley; this see for most of the remainder of the twelfth century had Carthusian bishops, chief among whom was the subsequently canonised Anthelme (1164-78) who had been prior of Chartreuse itself (1139-51) and then of Portes. Between 1130 and 1200 the see of Maurienne had three Carthusian bishops, as did Die; Geneva and Valence each had one. There were also archbishops: Arles received a Carthusian in 1137, Tarentaise in 1174, and Embrun in 1194.

Thus, by 1186 when Hugh of Avalon became bishop of Lincoln, the Carthusian bishop was a familiar figure in the provinces of the church that were adjacent to Chartreuse. One may doubt whether there was any derogation of *Cartusia nunquam reformata quia nunquam deformata*.[37] Without abandoning its original vision, Chartreuse found its place, as new developments in western monasticism have usually done, in the wider context of the church and of society. From the first, Bruno, the friend of

---

[34] The following details of Carthusian bishops are taken from Bligny, *L'Église*, pp. 310-15, and 'Les Chartreux', pp. 45-6.

[35] *Vita s. Hugonis*, 5.33, *PL* 153.784A.

[36] Upon Hugh II's departure in 1148, Noel, a Carthusian from Portes, was rejected as a candidate for the see of Grenoble on account of objections from Chartreuse itself.

[37] But cf. Bligny's opinion: 'Les Chartreux', p. 38. The Latin citation is, of course, of much later origin.

Pope Urban II, began the process tentatively and somewhat clumsily; especially when the Anacletan schism called so many in the newer orders of monks and canons to the support of Pope Innocent II, Prior Guigo I made it definitive and fruitful. In ideal through Guigo's Life of Bishop Hugh of Grenoble and in practice when Carthusian monks themselves accepted the episcopal office, the monk-bishop became a frequent and characteristic means of Carthusian influence.

II

Hugh of Avalon's own progress from the community of Chartreuse to the see of Lincoln was thus well prepared within the development of the Carthusian order. Hugh's novice-master's prediction that 'now you will become a priest and afterwards, in God's good time, a bishop', and Adam of Eynsham's observation that by his austerities at Chartreuse 'he was being prepared by God for the highest grade of priesthood [that is, the episcopate]', have the ring of *ex eventu* wisdom; yet they are not incongruous with the outlook at Chartreuse.[38] His eventual monastic office of procurator, with charge of the lower house of the *conversi* and consequent administrative duties that led Guigo I to describe the procurator as the Martha of the Carthusian community, was also a preparation for a more active life.[39]

Hugh's coming to England was facilitated politically by England's place in the Angevin Empire of King Henry II (1154-89), to whose cousin Henry of Blois, bishop of Winchester (1129-71) Chartreuse accorded exceptional liturgical benefits.[40] Henry II's Empire extended so far to the south-east as the county of Auvergne, and in 1172-3 he was negotiating an abortive marriage settlement for his youngest son John with Count Humbert of Maurienne. His interests thus embraced Burgundy and its vicinity. In the 1160s, his quarrel with Archbishop Thomas Becket brought about contacts between the Carthusians and adherents of both parties. They included the dispatch from Chartreuse in 1167 of a reproving letter to the king, and in 1168 Prior Basil of Chartreuse and his predecessor in office Anthelme, now bishop of Belley, visited Henry in France as bearers of a papal letter.[41] According to an unconfirmed Carthusian tradition, Henry's foundation c.1178/9 of the first English Charterhouse at Witham (Somerset) was part of his commutation of a vow of pilgrimage to the

[38] *Magna vita s. Hugonis*, 1.11-12, cf. 2.3-4, vol.1.36-7, 54-7.
[39] *Ibid.*, 1.14, vol.1.41-4. For the procurator's duties, *Coutumes*, caps. 16, 18, pp.200-5.
[40] *Recueil*, no.24, pp.67-9; cf. the decree of the Carthusian general chapter of 1156: PL 153.1128D-1129A.
[41] *Materials for the History of Thomas Becket*, edd. J.C.Robertson and J.B. Sheppard (7 vols., London: Rolls Series, 67, 1875-85), 6, nos.289, 404, 424, pp.165-6, 394-6, 438-40. See also H.E.J.Cowdrey, 'The Carthusians in England', *Colloque*, pp.345-56.

Hugh of Avalon, Carthusian and Bishop

Holy Land that he made after Becket's murder.[42]

The king himself brought about Hugh's coming to England after the first two priors had proved themselves unequal to the task of setting up the new priory. Henry, who crossed to the continent in mid-1180, there questioned an unnamed *nobilis* from Maurienne about the Carthusians, and received the advice that their procurator Hugh was the only man for the task. He thereupon sent to Chartreuse an embassy headed by Reginald, bishop of Bath, in whose diocese Witham was situated; with Bishop John of Grenoble's strong support he procured Hugh's dispatch.[43] During the next six years or so, Hugh, whom Adam of Eynsham described as Witham's *fundator et institutor*,[44] resolved successfully the problem that had defeated his two predecessors, by establishing Witham's exclusive patrimony within inviolable boundaries. Backed by the king's authority, he offered the peasantry who must be displaced the alternative of receiving lands and habitations comparable with those that they must vacate upon royal manors of their choice, or of emancipation from villeinage; they also received from the king financial compensation for the loss of their homes. The contact with Hugh that was involved in establishing Witham led Henry to adopt him as his especial spiritual counsellor. A belief that Hugh's intercessions saved him from shipwreck reputedly made Henry determined to endeavour to make him a bishop.[45]

Thus Hugh came to the English episcopate. His work as bishop of Lincoln is most fully set out by Adam, monk of Eynsham, who was his chaplain and companion during the last three years of his life. Adam referred to Bishop Hugh I of Grenoble as Hugh of Lincoln's model only once, when he spoke of him as 'the inheritor alike of [Hugh of Grenoble's] name and of his sanctity'.[46] But his principal model was his patron St Martin (c.316-97), whose Life by Sulpicius Severus depicted an ecclesiastical cursus from life as a solitary monk to being abbot of Ligugé and eventually bishop of Tours. St Martin was one of the most powerful influences upon French monasticism during the middle ages and upon conceptions of the monk's place in the episcopate; Hugh of Lincoln saw in him, above all others, a pattern to adopt and imitate.[47]

But literary models were less important for Hugh of Avalon as Adam of Eynsham presents him than the traditions of Chartreuse. His own

---

[42] C. le Couteulx, *Annales ordinis Cartusiensis ab anno 1084 ad annum 1429*, 2 (Montreuil-sur-Mer, 1888), 449-52.

[43] *Magna vita s. Hugonis*, 2.1-4, vol.1.46-60. Bishop Reynald of Bath had been consecrated in 1174 at Maurienne by Archbishops Richard of Canterbury and Peter of Tarentaise.

[44] *Ibid.*, 1, Prol., vol.1.3.

[45] Hugh's years as prior of Witham are the subject of Adam of Eynsham's second book: *ibid.*, vol.1.45-89.

[46] *Ibid.*, 4.9, vol.2.43-4; but for Hugh's own use of Guigo's Life, see 4.12, vol.2.55.

[47] For references to St Martin, see *ibid.*, 1.7, 4.9, 5.17, 19, vol.1.24, vol.2.43, 199-206, 217, 219, 223-4. The Lives of Martin and Hugh of Grenoble appear together in Lincoln Cathedral MS 107 which may be associated with Hugh of Lincoln: R. M. Woolley, *Catalogue of the Manuscripts of Lincoln Cathedral Chapter Library* (Oxford, 1927), pp. 70-1.

commitment to Chartreuse was always strong. He accepted the see of Lincoln only under obedience from its prior, Jancelin;[48] he never ceased to wish to return there, and in 1200 he paid a final, memorable visit.[49] Whenever possible he returned to Witham once or twice a year and shared its life to the full; indeed, he seems to have retained formal authority over it until the end of his life.[50] In his everyday conduct he is reminiscent of Guigo I's admonition to Cardinal Haimeric that churchmen should not borrow kings' greed, delicacy, and pride, for he maintained a Carthusian life-style so far as he could; like Bishop Hugh of Grenoble he kept careful custody of his senses.[51]

By his references to Bishop Hugh of Grenoble's travels with Hugh of Die and to his favour with Pope Gregory VII, Guigo I had established the freeing of churches from lay lordship and jurisdiction as a due part of a bishop's activities. In his dealings with the Angevin kings of England, Hugh of Lincoln strongly asserted it. In 1186 he would not accept the see of Lincoln otherwise than by free election. Throughout his episcopate he championed the freedom of the church in all its forms: 'God forbid,' he once exclaimed, 'that ecclesiastical liberties and privileges should be infringed by decree of any layman!'[52]

Like Hugh of Grenoble, Hugh of Lincoln was also conspicuous for his performance of external good works, for which his duties as procurator at Chartreuse had in some measure prepared him.[53] Adam of Eynsham made much of his assiduousness in ministering to children and in performing confirmations and burials, and he took especial care for lepers and for the sick.[54] He was deeply concerned for the reform of clerical morals and for the edification and instruction of his clergy, both in his cathedral and throughout his diocese.[55] He defended the vulnerable against the rapacity of his own archdeacons and rural deans no less than that of the king's foresters.[56] He was a distinguished papal judge-delegate;[57] yet, just as Guigo I in his letter to Cardinal Haimeric was deeply critical of standards in the papal entourage, so Hugh warned Archbishop Baldwin of Canterbury against recourse to Rome: 'You will be exposed to the pride and aggravation of the Roman curia,' he said, 'and to the host of high and mighty

[48] *Magna vita s. Hugonis*, 3.3-5, vol. 1.98-102.
[49] *Ibid.*, 4.5, 5.13, 14, vol. 2.99, 149, 164-7.
[50] *Ibid.*, 4.9, 10-14, vol. 2.44-5, 49-73. See also A. Wilmart, 'Maître Adam, chanoine Prémontré devenu Chartreux à Witham', *Analecta Praemonstratensia*, 9 (1933), fasc. 3-4, 209-32, at p. 231.
[51] *Magna vita s. Hugonis*, 3.5, 13, 5.16, vol. 1.102-3, 125-7, vol. 2, 195-7.
[52] Lincoln: *ibid.*, 3.1-3, vol. 1.92-8. Freedom of the church: *ibid.*, 2.7, 3.9, 4.7-8, vol. 1.71-2, 114-15, vol. 2.34-7, 39-41.
[53] *Ibid.*, 1.14, vol. 1.41-4.
[54] Children: *ibid.*, 3.14, vol. 1.129-33. Confirmations: *ibid.*, 1.13, vol. 1.127-8. Burials: *ibid.*, 5.1-2, vol. 2.75-85. Lepers and the sick: *ibid.*, 4.3, vol. 2.11-15.
[55] *Ibid.*, 3.11, 5.5, vol. 1.119-21, vol. 2.95-8.
[56] Archdeacons and rural deans: *ibid.*, 4.7, vol. 2.37-8. Foresters: *ibid.*, 3.9, 4.5-6, vol. 1.114, vol. 2.26-8.
[57] *Ibid.*, 3.12, 5.13, vol. 1.121-3, vol. 2.149-52.

men who are to be found there.'[58] Deeply though Hugh venerated Thomas Becket as a martyr, he deprecated his practice during his lifetime of taking monetary fines from spiritual offenders.[59] He reserved his sharpest criticisms for the Angevin kings and their ministers, earning himself the sobriquet 'hammer of kings (*regum malleus*)'.[60] While still prior of Witham he admonished Henry II about the conduct of episcopal and abbatial elections. Throughout his episcopate he spared no words in rebuking Henry's sons Richard I and John, as well as their ministers, amongst whom he especially took to task Archbishop Hubert Walter who was for long the royal justiciar. Hugh was particularly insistent in refusing to provide Richard I with military service beyond the shores of England from the resources of the see of Lincoln.[61] One recalls the strictures of the future Carthusian, Count Gerard of Nevers, upon the court and the Crusading plans of King Louis VII of France. Overall, Hugh's manner of life and his public attitudes and activities as bishop of Lincoln were well grounded in the Carthusian tradition and ran true to it.

Yet Hugh was a bishop of such stature that, in the episcopal office, he was not constrained by that tradition, but was very much his own man. In this respect it would be wrong to eulogise him uncritically. There are sides to his episcopal activity that do not immediately commend themselves to the modern observer. Two examples are his use of his powers of anathema and his conduct as a collector of relics. Adam of Eynsham gloried in how many men and women 'he gave over to a wretched death by the power of his excommunication alone', and how, by contrast with the sanctions deployed by less saintly bishops, the mere threat deterred royal officers from seizing his goods because they dreaded it as quite literally a death sentence. But it was not only the over-mighty whom it struck down. Even an adulterous Oxford girl of burgess origins suffered death for her disobedience:

'As you have refused my blessing and have preferred my curse [said Hugh to her], lo! my curse will seize you.' She went home still defiant, and during the few days that God allowed her for coming to a better mind, her heart became more hardened and impenitent. She was smothered by the devil, and suddenly exchanged her illicit and perishable delights for eternal and just torments.[62]

If Hugh's use of his anathema may seem excessive and vindictive, his zeal in collecting relics was greedy and even deceitful. Thus, when he visited the abbey of Fécamp which possessed a relic of St Mary Magdalen's armbone, he was not allowed to see the relic itself. So he took a knife from one of his notaries, cut the thread that bound it, and himself undid its wrappings. After contemplating it and kissing it he tried to prise a piece

[58] *Ibid.*, 3.12, vol.1.122.
[59] *Ibid.*, 4.7, vol.2.38.
[60] *Ibid.*, 2.4, 5.20, vol.1.56, vol.2.231-2.
[61] Henry II: *ibid.*, 2.7-8, 3.9-10, vol.1.68-74, 114-19. Richard I: *ibid.*, 5.1, 5-6, vol.2.78-9, 98-106. John: *ibid.*, 5.11, 16, 19, vol.2.137-44, 188, 225. Hubert Walter: *ibid.*, 3.12, 5.5, 7, 16, vol.1.123, vol.2.98-100, 110-14, 188-9.
[62] *Ibid.*, 4.4-6, vol.2.19-33.

off for himself with his fingers, but unsuccessfully. So he bit it, first with his front teeth and then with his back ones, breaking off two fragments which he handed to Adam of Eynsham. The abbot and monks were beside themselves: 'What an outrage!' they exclaimed; 'we supposed that the bishop asked to see this relic out of devotion, but look! he has gnawed it with his teeth like a dog!' To calm them, Hugh observed that he had not long before handled the body of the Lord of the saints with his fingers and bitten it with his teeth; for his welfare, why should he not similarly treat the bones of the saints and, when he had a chance, acquire them?[63] In such respects, Hugh was, perhaps, all too much a child of his day and age.

But not in other, far more important respects, in which he rose far above them. He did so because he understood with exceptional clarity that to different men and women, different modes of the Christian life are appropriate. Hermits and monks, clergy and laity, have their several and very different callings. The very austerity of Hugh's Carthusian background, which he well knew that only rare individuals could support, made him aware of this truth, as St Bernard, for example, seems never to have understood it. An elderly Carthusian had put the point of the Carthusians' exceptional vocation to him in unforgettable words when, still a young regular canon, he had first sought admission to Chartreuse. 'My dear boy,' he had said, 'how can you ever think of coming here? The men you see inhabiting these rocks are harder than any stones; they take pity neither upon themselves nor upon those who live with them. This place is dreadful to look at, but our way of life is harder by far. ... The rigour of our discipline would crush the bones of one so tender as you seem.'[64] Hugh never forgot that the Carthusian life is for the very few who are personally fitted to receive it, and that it is not a model even for most monks to copy. Thus, when an abbot went beyond the Rule of St Benedict in compelling his monks to abstain from meat, Hugh was far from praising his zeal; instead, he warned him of the danger of hypocrisy and scrupulosity, saying,

> I do not eat meat, not because of my own judgement, but because that is the decree of the order to which long ago I made myself subject. It has so very few members, because it was not designed for a lot of people, all of them made differently. You, however, have been set over a large community; as your Founder decreed you must take account of many different sorts of men and condescend to many kinds of weakness and human need.[65]

Because Hugh knew exactly where he himself stood as a Carthusian, he could perceive clearly the roles and duties of other kinds of people, and point them out with firmness and charity.

Hugh's perceptiveness, and the maturity and confidence to which it conduced, enabled him, in sharp contrast to Thomas Becket, resolutely to

---

[63] Hugh and relics: *ibid.*, 5.13, 14, vol. 2.153-4, 167-73.
[64] *Ibid.*, 1.7, vol. 1.23-4.
[65] *Ibid.*, 5.16, vol. 2.196-7; cf. Rule of St Benedict, cap. 2.

Hugh of Avalon, Carthusian and Bishop

defend what contemporary reformers understood by the liberty of the church, and to act as a *regum malleus* in reproving kings, without ever sacrificing his personal relationship with them – even so difficult a line as the Angevins of his time. His sureness of pastoral touch was early manifest in his handling of Henry II, when the king was offended by his refusal, couched in terms reminiscent of Prior Guigo I's letter to Cardinal Haimeric, to collate a royal nominee to a prebend of Lincoln cathedral. 'Ecclesiastical benefices,' Hugh said, 'should not be conferred upon courtiers but upon ecclesiastics, and their holders should not serve the court (*palatium*) or treasury or exchequer but, as Scripture teaches, the altar.' When the king sulked publicly and called for a needle and thread to play at repairing a finger-stall that he was wearing, Hugh impudently mocked him: 'How like you are to your Falaise cousins!' Henry himself explained to his courtiers Hugh's allusion to his own great grandfather William the Conqueror's being the bastard of a supposedly leather-working family at Falaise. Relishing the joke, he came round to Hugh's point of view.[66] Again, Hugh shrewdly made use of the kiss of peace at mass to be reconciled to Richard I after his refusal of overseas military service.[67] Although Hugh fruitlessly drew attention to the sculpture of the Last Judgement over the porch at the abbey of Fontevraud to warn John of his sins, John visited him on his deathbed and at his funeral carried his coffin.[58] Hugh was exceptional in maintaining the highest standards of the episcopal office under such kings, and yet in preserving his friendship with them.

He rose no less far above the generality of his contemporaries in his attitude to women. He differed even from Carthusian tradition. Not only were women rigorously excluded from the *termini* of Chartreuse but, in his Customs, Guigo I drew upon many Old Testament examples to drive home how hard it was to escape their flatteries and deceits. His exemplary bishop, Hugh of Grenoble, always ministered faithfully to them, but only once did he allow his eyes to settle upon a woman's face, and then for an urgent pastoral reason.[69] Hugh, on the other hand, had a profound regard and care for women. He did not hesitate to follow the general custom of bishops by occasionally admitting matrons and widows to eat at his table. His regard for women was based upon his understanding of Christ's Incarnation. 'Almighty God,' he used to say to them, 'well deserves to have women love him, for he did not disdain to be born of a woman. He thereby conferred a splendid and truly fitting privilege upon all women. For to no man was it granted to be, or to be called, the father of God; but a woman was allowed to become the mother of God.'[70]

Above all, Hugh exhibited his personal stature and uniqueness by the

---

[66] *Magna vita s. Hugonis*, 3.9-10, vol. 1.114-19. Cf. E. M. C. van Houts, 'The Origins of Herleva, Mother of William the Conqueror', *English Historical Review*, 101 (1986), 399-404.

[67] *Magna vita s. Hugonis*, 5.5, vol. 2.100-02.

[68] *Ibid.*, 5.11, 16, 19, vol. 2.138-44, 188, 225.

[69] *Coutumes*, cap. 21.1-2, p. 210; *Vita s. Hugonis*, 4.15, *PL* 153.772-3.

[70] *Magna vita s. Hugonis*, 4.9, vol. 2.48.

high value that he set upon the life and witness of ordinary lay Christians. He was far from holding the conventional view, that only a few would be saved, and most of them would be monks. When lay persons praised his own Carthusian style of life and conventionally deplored the hindrances of life in the world, so long as he knew them to have no calling to the monastic life he would assure them of the sufficiency for salvation of their own state:

> Monks, not to mention hermits and anchorites [he used to say to them] will not be the only ones to inherit the kingdom of God. When God comes in judgement upon every man, he will upbraid no one for not being a hermit or a monk; but he will dismiss from himself those who have not been true Christians. Three things are required of every Christian; if one of them is lacking when he meets his judgement, the mere name of Christian will not help him. No, rather, the name without the practice will do him harm, because falsehood is all the more blameworthy in one who makes profession of the truth. A man must bear Christ's blessed name both in fact and in truth; therefore the true Christian carries love in his heart, truth on his lips, and chastity in his body.

And so married people, even though they never changed their state for a single life, had the virtue of chastity and would share an equal heavenly reward with virgins and celibates. In recording this teaching, Adam of Eynsham added that Hugh was no less adept in explaining the Christian life to simple folk than to the learned.[71]

Hugh of Avalon was one of those rare individuals whose personal qualities raise them above whatever background or environment, however admirable, that they may have had. Nevertheless, the foundation of his episcopate was always his Carthusian life and training, and he manifested and built upon its best characteristics of spiritual and human wisdom. For the historian, his significance is, perhaps, threefold. First, he is the supreme example in Angevin England of a model diocesan bishop, ruling his diocese, shepherding all its people, and discharging a bishop's national role resolutely but acceptably to kings and magnates even when he most strenuously reproved them. Secondly, his conduct as a bishop warrants the conclusion that the relationship which the Carthusians from the first began to form with the wider church and world did not contradict or detract from their primary call to the eremitical life; it was a proper and authentic complement to it. Thirdly, Hugh of Avalon, as champion of the liberty of the church and of its moral reform, must be understood within the long sequence of Carthusian links with the episcopate which began with the paradigm figure of Bishop Hugh I of Grenoble, who was himself the favoured disciple of Pope Gregory VII. Tangible links between Gregory and the twelfth century are remarkably few and difficult to observe. Hugh of Avalon, Carthusian and bishop, stands within a living

---

[71]   *Ibid.*, 4.9, vol. 2.46-7.

Hugh of Avalon, Carthusian and Bishop

tradition of episcopal spirituality and activity that Gregory was concerned to foster. He continued it until Pope Innocent III, the most effective of all the medieval reforming popes, had ascended the papal throne.

XVIII

In numerical terms, the Carthusian settlement in Angevin England was small. Only one house, Witham (dioc. Bath), was established; its impact upon English life was largely owing to one man, Hugh of Avalon, who came from la Grande Chartreuse probably in 1180 to be its third prior and who was bishop of Lincoln from 1186 until his death in 1200.[1] However, King Henry II's part in the foundation of Witham and in determining Hugh's career was a considerable one.[2] This paper will be concerned with two topics. The first is the hundred years and more of association between the Norman and Angevin royal families and strict and eremitical forms of the religious life which made Henry II's sponsorship of the Carthusians a natural development. The second is the factors, apart from the personal stature of Hugh of Avalon, which enabled the Carthusians to find a larger place in Angevin England than their small numbers might lead one to expect.

In a broad sense, the coming of the Carthusians was well prepared. The Rule of St Benedict itself which formed the basis of all western monastic life declared that it was only 'a little rule for beginners' (*hanc minimam inchoationis regulam*: 73.8). St Benedict's second sort of monks were the anchorites or hermits who, after long proving in a monastery, advanced to the single combat of the desert and fought alone against the vices of the flesh and of the mind (1.3-5). In the tenth and eleventh centuries, a tide of strict, eremitical monasticism, which began in Italy, spread ever more widely in Western Europe; in it, the Carthusians had their place after 1084, when St Bruno founded la Grande Chartreuse. It should be noticed that the tide in general left its mark upon Rome, for example, at an early stage in the mixed monastic community of Greek and Latin monks on the Aventine which from the early 980s was jointly dedicated to St Boniface and St Alexius; half a century or so later, the prior of the hermit community at Fonteavellana (dioc. Gubbio), Peter Damiani, was also from 1057 to 1072 cardinal-bishop of Ostia and a mentor of the reform papacy. The foundation

---

[1]H.E.J. Cowdrey, 'The Carthusians in England', in: *La Naissance des Chartreuses. Actes du VI° Colloque International d'Histoire et de Spiritualité Cartusiennes (Grenoble, 12-15 Septembre 1984)*, edd. B. Bligny and G. Chaix (Grenoble, 1986), pp. 345-56, 'Hugh of Avalon, Carthusian and Bishop', in: *De Cella in Seculum: Religious and Secular Life and Devotion in Late Medieval England,* ed. M.G. Sargent (Cambridge, 1989), pp. 41-57.

[2]Cowdrey, 'The Carthusians' (as n. 1), p. 348.

XVIII

of Camaldoli and, still more, Vallombrosa, reinforced the links between eremitism and reform. Pope Gregory VII's admiration for St John Gualbertus of Vallombrosa, both for the quality of his monastic life and for its good effect upon the surrounding churches, was such as to make eremitical monasticism one of the inspirations of the reform that goes by Gregory's name.[3]

During the eleventh century, such forms of monasticism had been well established north of the Alps. In the light of the esteem that the Rule of St Benedict accords to eremitism, it is not surprising that even a Benedictine house like Cluny had its dependent hermits who lived in the woods nearby or further afield.[4] Other ancient houses, like Saint-Oyend (dioc. Lyons), which was itself originally a hermit community, directed their members more regularly to the eremitical life. As the Lives of its early abbots show, la Chaise-Dieu (dioc. Clermont) which Robert of Turlande founded in 1043 was from the start deeply imbued with eremitical aspirations. Cîteaux (dioc. Chalon-sur-Saône), founded in 1098 by Robert of Molesme, is the culminating example of an abbey and head of a monastic family which, according to the *Exordium parvum*, thought that its remoteness made it 'the more suited to the religious way that they had for long had in mind ... as it was more contemptible and inaccessible in worldly eyes.'[5]

The Cistercians were somewhat slow to impinge upon the Anglo-Norman lands until the foundation close to Normandy in 1121 of l'Aumône (dioc. Chartres), from which Waverley (dioc. Winchester) was founded seven years later. But other centres of stricter monasticism were founded upon lands subject to King Henry I. Tiron (dioc. Chartres) grew into an abbey *c.*1109/14 from a hermit community set up by Bernard of Abbeville; by the end of Henry I's reign it had seven houses in England and Wales. Savigny (dioc. Avranches) was established in 1112 by the hermit Vitalis in the forest of Craon; it came to have a dozen English daughter houses.

Given the diffusion and strength of eremitical life in its many forms, it is not surprising that its impact upon the Norman and Angevin royal families was considerable. Not only were they its friends and patrons, but they were also willing to heed, and even to welcome, the admonitions of monks and hermits

[3]*The Epistolae vagantes of Pope Gregory VII*, ed. and trans. H.E.J. Cowdrey (Oxford, 1972), pp. 4-7, no. 2.

[4]e.g. the hermit Anastasius: H.E.J. Cowdrey, 'Two Studies in Cluniac History', *Studi Gregoriani*, 11 (1978), p. 145, no. 3.

[5]*Les Plus Anciens Textes de Cîteaux*, edd. J. de la C. Bouton and J.B. van Damme (Achel, 1985), p. 60.

in their capacity as 'holy men'.[6]

King William II's reign apart, this was especially true of the Normans. King William I does not seem to have had significant dealings with hermits, but he was spectacularly deferential to holy men of monastic background. Archbishop Lanfranc of Canterbury once figured in this role. At a banquet after a crown-wearing when the king sat regally adorned with Lanfranc at his side, a jester ironically exclaimed of him, 'Behold, I see God! Behold, I see God!' Not only did William obey Lanfranc's injunction that he have the jester thrashed for his blasphemy, but Lanfranc chastened the king by recalling the fate of King Herod Agrippa who, while listening to a conquered people as they shouted of him, 'The voice of a god and not a man!' was smitten by an angel, and he was eaten of worms, and died (Acts 12:20-23).[7] Whatever the truth behind Orderic Vitalis's story of Guitmund, monk of la-Croix-Saint-Leufroi, who, when offered high ecclesiastical office, rebuked William mercilessly for his plundering the church, it further illustrates the king's reputation for docility when subject to correction by holy men.[8]

His queen, Matilda, held eremitical figures in high repute, as three examples will illustrate. First, there is her attachment to Count Simon of Crêpy who, having been a valiant warrior, in 1077 became a monk of Saint-Oyend; he quickly moved out from the monastery to lead an eremitical life in the nearby Juran forest, only to be summoned by Pope Gregory VII to continue such a life at Rome.[9] A kinsman of Matilda, Simon had been brought up in the ducal court at Rouen (5,11,14); according to his Life, while a hermit he restored peace to Normandy by reconciling their rebellious son Robert Curthose to the king and queen(11). Upon Simon's death at Rome, probably in 1082, Matilda sent gold and silver to pay for his marble tomb in St Peter's (14). Matilda seems especially

---

[6]The term 'holy man' is used according to the usage established by P. Brown, 'The Rise and Function of the Holy Man in Late Antiquity', *Journal of Roman Studies*, 61 (1971), 80-101, repr. *Society and the Holy in Late Antiquity* (London, 1982), pp. 103-52. For Hugh of Avalon as a 'holy man', see K.J. Leyser, 'The Angevin Kings and the Holy Man', in: *St Hugh of Lincoln*, ed. H. Mayr-Harting (Oxford, 1987), pp. 49-73.

[7]Milo Crispin, *Vita Lanfranci*, cap. 7, J.P. Migne, *Patrologia Latina* [hereafter *PL*] 150.53-4. I am grateful to Dr Margaret Gibson for pointing out the full force of this story.

[8]*The Ecclesiastical History of Orderic Vitalis*, 4, ed. M. Chibnall, 6 vols. (Oxford, 1969-80), 2.270-81.

[9]*Vita beati Simonis comitis Crespeiensis auctore synchrono*, *PL* 156.1211-24. Numbers in the text of this and following paragraphs refer to books and chapters of the sources referred to. For Simon, see H.E.J. Cowdrey, 'Count Simon of Crêpy's Monastic Conversion', in: *Mélanges Marcel Pacaut*, forthcoming.

to have valued the services of hermits as regards family stresses, for, secondly, Orderic Vitalis has a story of her consulting a German hermit with the gift of prophecy about the futures of the king and Robert Curthose.   She received auguries both good and bad about the future of their lands.[10]   Thirdly, there is a story that Matilda owed St Adelelme, third abbot of la Chaise-Dieu, a debt for his therapeutic powers.[11]   His Life relates how she sought relief from her lethargy *(letargia)* through his sending her either a crumb from his table or some water in which he had washed his hands.   He generously sent a quarter of a loaf, which served to heal both her and others in her realm (11).[12]   All three stories spoke of the queen's generous gifts to these men.

The Conqueror's half-brothers, Bishop Odo of Bayeux and Robert of Mortain, also had contacts with eremitical monasticism.   Odo was, perhaps, an early patron of Vitalis of Savigny (1.4).[13]   Vitalis was for long the highly regarded chaplain of Robert (1.5).   He used his position boldly to correct the count's faults.   Thus, in face of his ill-treatment of the countess, Vitalis threatened to leave the court if it continued, whereupon Robert submitted to severe corporal chastisement (1.6-7).

King Henry I was an active patron of Vitalis and his successor Geoffrey as abbots of Savigny.   Geoffrey's biographer observed that 'he won such familiarity with King Henry that he both called him father and regarded him more highly than all other men; whatever the abbot asked the king he secured without difficulty'.   It was because of such familiarity that Savigny was able to establish twenty-nine abbeys upon Henry's lands (12).   In Normandy, Henry conferred upon Vitalis a series of benefits.   As early as 1112 he freed him and his companions from tolls and customs; in 1113 he confirmed the grant by the founder, Ralph, lord of Fougères, of the forest of Savigny; in 1118 he made a concord between Vitalis and the abbot of Saint-Étienne at Caen about a disputed gift to Savigny, in 1119 he granted a church to Savigny, and in 1117/19 he confirmed a further grant.[14]   Monastic foundations apart, Vitalis's favoured

---

[10] *Eccles. Hist.* 5.10, ed. Chibnall, 3.102-9.

[11] *Vita sancti Adelelmi auctore Rodolfo monachi Casae Dei,* in: *España Sagrada,* ed. H. Flórez (Madrid, 1747-), 27.832-41.

[12] For a tradition, mainly liturgical, at la Chaise-Dieu that Edith, an English queen who must be the widow of Harold Godwinson, was cured of leprosy by St Adelelme and built a dormitory at la Chaise-Dieu, see P.-R. Gaussin, *L'Abbaye de la Chaise-Dieu (1043-1518)* (Paris, 1962), pp. 126-7.

[13] For the Lives of Vitalis and Geoffrey of Savigny, see E.P. Sauvage, *'Vitae BB. Vitalis et Gaufridi primi et secundi abbatum Savigniacensium',* *Analecta Bollandiana,* 1 (1882), 355-410.

[14] *Regesta regum Anglo-Normannorum, 1066-1154,* 2: *Regesta Henrici Primi,* edd. C. Johnson and H.A. Cronne (Oxford, 1956), nos. 1003, 1015, 1183, 1212, 1215.

position enabled him to play an active role in England.   He was an assiduous
preacher whose eloquence leapt the barrier of language;   probably at the council
of Westminster (1102) his zeal led to an attempt upon his life, but he finally
converted his assailant (1.2,4,5,11).   He also brought to mutual peace citizens
of London who were at odds (1.11), and saved criminals from hanging (2.5).
Under Henry I, Savigny came to form a significant bond between eremitical
monasticism and the Anglo-Norman king and his lands and people on both sides of
the Channel.

Glimpses of Henry I's dealings with a native English anchorite, as well,
are afforded by the Life of Wulfric, who lived in the Somerset village of Haselbury Plucknett.[15]   One of Henry's *curiales*, Drogo de Munci, was so rash as to
suggest that the king should send to Wulfric's cell and seize his money, whereupon he was struck down by fits--an eventuality that convinced bystanders of
Wulfric's sanctity.   They informed the queen, Adela, who urged Henry not to ag-
grieve so great a man of God whose prayers and merits brought blessing to the
king and to the realm.   Henry soon afterwards visited Wulfric and, at the queen's
prompting, successfully asked for Drogo, whom they had brought, to be healed.
The king left Haselbury spiritually fortified and delighted (46).   Later,
Wulfric correctly prophesied that Henry's crossing of the Channel in 1133 would
be the last that he would make alive and entire;   he confirmed the prophecy to an
understandably anxious king.   Nevertheless, upon learning that his prophecy had
come true, Wulfric declared that Henry would find mercy with the Lord, 'because
in this life he had striven for peace and justice, and he had built the Lord's
house at Reading with regal magnificence' (90).   To such as Wulfric, kings knew
their need to listen and to defer.   Their sanctions were to be feared and their
blessings sought, while their good opinion carried weight with the king's own
subjects.

Stephen and his kindred were like-minded with King Henry and Queen Adela.
As count of Boulogne, Stephen facilitated the coming of the Savignacs to England
by giving land at Tulket, near Preston, for their first foundation there;   in
1127, it was transferred to his forest of Furness.[16]   The Life of Wulfric of
Haselbury shows how, as king, he was well aware of the role of an anchorite and
holy man.   Before his accession, he and his brother Henry, bishop of Winchester,
had visited Wulfric who prophetically hailed him as king, admonishing him to

[15]*Wulfric of Haselbury, by John, Abbot of Ford*, ed. M. Bell, Somerset
Record Society, 47 (1932).   Wulfric is well discussed by H. Mayr-Harting,
'Functions of a Twelfth-Century Recluse', *History*, 60 (1975), 337-52.

[16]W. Dugdale, *Monasticon Anglicanum* (new edn. by J. Caley, H. Ellis, and
B. Bandinel, 6 vols. in 8 parts, London, 1817-30), 5.246-7.

promote peace and equity and to protect and honour the church. But Wulfric
also foretold the disturbance that would follow a disputed succession. In due
course he foresaw Stephen's captivity at Lincoln in 1141 and his rival, Earl
Robert of Gloucester's suffering a like fate. Towards the end of his reign,
Stephen paid a final visit to Wulfric. He received many reproofs and exhortations, but also the comforting promise that he would reign for as long as he
lived. Wulfric also warned the king of a grave sin that he knew him to have
committed, telling him that until he repented his throne would not be safe or
his affairs in peace. Stephen repented by making full and tearful confession
(91).

Wulfric censured the queen, Matilda, no less effectively when she came
to Haselbury. At court, she had snubbed the wife of the lord of Haselbury,
William FitzWalter. Wulfric treated the queen with a prophet's loftiness (in
magnificentia prophetali). He warned her that one day she would have to defer
to the lowest in the land--as happened when she pleaded for Stephen's release
from captivity (81). A holy man was unsparing even to royalty who nevertheless
felt the need to resort to him. Further, and perhaps surprising, testimony to
the links between Stephen's family and eremitical monasticism is provided by
Bishop Henry of Winchester's admission to spiritual benefits at la Grande
Chartreuse itself.[17]

Like his two royal predecessors, King Henry II finds a place in Wulfric's
Life. As a sixteen-year-old boy he had led a raid into England in 1149 which
had not left happy memories: in general (according to the Life) his followers
had been guilty of the sacrilege, plunder, and universal licentiousness that
characterized foreign mercenaries, and more particularly they had robbed Wulfric's hermitage. Wulfric afterwards sent Henry a bill for twelve shillings in
respect of his losses; he also complemented his prophecy to Stephen by foretell-
ing that Henry would not reign during Stephen's natural life. It was an added
bonus for Wulfric that, as he had prophesied, his predators, who had stolen his
horse, as they left the country suffered at the Lord's hands the penalty of the
biblical Song of Moses: 'The horse and its rider he has hurled into the sea'
(Ex. 15:4)(76). There were less baleful contacts. Stephen of Fougères, the
biographer of Vitalis and Geoffrey of Savigny, served in Henry's household.[18]
During the late 1160s, the Becket controversy brought the king into occasional
contact with the Carthusians.[19] The Pipe Rolls record numerous payments that

[17] *Recueil des plus anciens actes de la Grande-Chartreuse (1086-1196)*,
ed. B. Bligny (Grenoble, 1958), pp. 67-9, no. 24.
[18] As above, n. 13.
[19] Cowdrey, 'Hugh of Avalon' (as n. 1), p. 50.

the king made to hermits.   His particular, and life-long, predilection for the Grandmontines led him to acts of especial generosity.[20]

By the time of the foundation of Witham, contacts between English royalty and various forms of eremitical life were well established and formalized.   For royalty as for other grades of society, those who followed them often possessed a kind of holiness that made them expedient to consult and to foster.   When necessary, such persons were to be sought out, and it was their prerogative to use great boldness of speech when admonishing even kings and rulers.   Their friendship and their reproof were alike salutary.   Their role was fulfilled to perfection with regard to the Angevin kings by Hugh of Avalon, who thus earned himself the epitaph *regum malleus*--'the hammer of kings'.[21]   He stood in a familiar tradition, and was exceptional only for the finesse and balance which he brought to bear.   By the 1180s the order to which he belonged, the Carthusians, had become by virtue of their standard of life and observance the group that was best able to meet the expectations that kings and their subjects had formed during a century and a half of increasing familiarity with the eremitical style of life.

The extent to which the Carthusians, and particularly Hugh of Avalon, fulfilled such expectations largely accounts for their impact upon Angevin England.   Other reasons may also be suggested.   First, in 1147 the monastic family of Savigny secured from the Cistercian general chapter of that year its aggregation into the Cistercian order, a step which caused malaise in Savigny's English houses, especially Furness.[22]   By the middle years of Henry II's reign, the Cistercians themselves had lost much of their spiritual impetus in England. The rate of new foundations had risen gently between the foundation of Waverley and *c.*1143.   The next five years or so had witnessed a rapid acceleration of their number, but from 1149 until the end of Stephen's reign there was already a sharp falling off.   With the death of Abbot Aelred of Rievaulx in 1167, the great age of the Cistercians in England may be said to have ended.   In the western church at large as in England, a tide of criticism mounted.   Especially

---

[20]See especially E. M. Hallam, 'Henry II, Richard I and the Order of Grandmont', *Journal of Medieval History*, 1 (1975), 165-86; C. A. Hutchison, *The Hermit Monks of Grandmont* (Kalamazoo, 1989), pp. 57-64.

[21]*The Life of St Hugh of Lincoln*, 2.4, 5.20, edd. D.L. Douie and H. Farmer (2 vols., London, etc., 1961-2, repr. with corrections, Oxford, 1985), 1.56, 2.231-2; see Cowdrey, 'Hugh of Avalon' (as n.1), p. 53, and for a contrasting view, Leyser (as n.6), pp. 71-3.   The image of the hammer may allude to the prophet Jeremiah (Jer. 23:29) and to his relationship with King Zedekiah of Judah.

[22]B.D. Hill, *English Cistercian Monasteries and their Patrons in the Twelfth Century* (Urbana/Chicago/London, 1968), pp. 80-115.

in letters of 1159 and 1169, Pope Alexander III expressed his unease at the Cistercians' economic dealings.[23]   In England, even the Cistercian author of the Life of Wulfric of Haselbury tempered his praise with similar reservations.[24] Walter Map's savage satire is familiar,[25] and it found an echo upon royal lips: when in 1198 the Crusading preacher Fulk of Neuilly exhorted Richard I to abandon his 'daughters'--his pride, his avarice, and his lust, the king replied that his pride he would abandon to the Templars, his avarice to the Cistercians, and his lust to the bishops.[26]   In Angevin England, there was room for another religious order which would embody people's highest expectations of monasticism.

   This room the Carthusians, despite their small numbers, did much to fill. The connections and zeal of the early monks are a second reason for their impact. Of the seven priors who held authority at Witham up to the death of King John in 1216, the first three-- Narbert, Hamo, and Hugh of Avalon-- and the fifth-- Bovo-- were professed of la Grande Chartreuse, and the fourth-- Albert-- at the Charter-house of Portes (dioc. Lyons); thus, links with continental Charterhouses were sustained.   The sixth and seventh priors, Robert FitzHenry, sometime prior of the cathedral priory of St Swithun at Winchester, and Robert Caveford, were of English birth and profession; the former is said to have been 'mild in spirit and of gentle disposition'.[27]   Two at least of the early Witham Carthusians, Einard and Gerard, were, by contrast, men of proven fire and zeal.[28]   Bishop Hugh of Lincoln's regular visits and continuing watchfulness must have served to sustain the life of Witham.[29]   The stay there of another prelate, Archbishop Hubert Walter of Canterbury is described in a surviving fragment of the Witham Chronicle; since it is revealing of the way in which the early English Car-thusians interacted with English magnates, it deserves to be retailed at length.

_____

[23]J. Leclercq, 'Passage supprimé dans une épitre d'Alexandre III', and 'Épitres d'Alexandre III sur les Cisterciens', *Revue Bénédictine*, 62 (1952), 149-51, 64 (1954), 68-82.

[24](As n.15), p. 66, cap. 48.

[25]Walter Map, *De nugis curialium*, 1.25, ed. and trans. M.R. James, revised by C.N.L. Brooke and R.A.B. Mynors (Oxford, 1983), pp. 84-113.

[26]*Chronica Rogeri de Houedene*, 2, ed. W. Stubbs, 4 vols. (London: Rolls Series, 51, 1868-71), 4.76-7.

[27]For the priors, see J. Hogg, 'The Pre-Reformation Priors of the *Provincia Angliae*', *Analecta Cartusiana*, NS 1 (1989), 25-29, at pp. 26, 35-8. For sources, see, besides the *Life of St Hugh* (as n.21), A. Wilmart, 'Maître Adam chanoine Prémontré devenu Chartreux à Witham', *Analecta Praemonstratensia*, 9 (1933), 209-32, with fragments of the Witham Chronicle.

[28]*Life of St Hugh*, 2.6, 4.13, (as n.21), 1.65-6, 2.62-9.

[29]*Life of St Hugh*, 4.9,10-14, 5.13, 14 (as n.21), 2.44-5, 49-73, 99, 149, 164-7; Wilmart, 'Maître Adam' (as n.27), p. 231, no. 4.

Hubert came to Witham by chance when at the height of his power as Richard I's chief justiciar (1193-8); he was on his way to Glastonbury, and held Witham in such enmity *(exosam habuit)* that he would not look kindly upon any Carthusian. For his mind had been prejudiced by allegations of the king's foresters who bitterly challenged the Carthusians' claim to a certain pasture. However, Prior Robert FitzHenry and the brethren invited him to Witham, where he and his entourage were at first welcomed to the lower house of the *conversi*. In response, Hubert became more friendly; Ralph, the *procurator* in charge of the lower house, satisfied him that the foresters' allegations were groundless, so that he reproved himself for listening to them. From such mundane trifles, the Chronicle continues, Ralph directed the conversation to the discussion of the Carthusian life that the foresters had arraigned. Hubert was gently led further. Some of his clerks had heard from Bishop Hugh of Lincoln about the spiritual reputation and scholarly learning of Adam of Dryburgh, the erstwhile Premonstratensian canon who was now a monk of Witham. So Hubert's wish that he might hear mass in the upper house of the monks and converse with Adam was granted. When, on the second day of his visit, Hubert assisted at a mass celebrated by the prior he was at first shocked by the simplicity of his vestments and gave him a precious chasuble from his own chapel which the prior prudently put on. Yet Hubert came quickly to appreciate the simplicity of the Carthusian rite. After mass, Hubert caused Adam to give a conference to himself and his clerks; his words moved them deeply. Thereafter Hubert returned privately to Adam's cell where he made confession with abundant tears; removing his garments 'like a little child of Christ', he received discipline by the rod, and he asked Adam to compose for him a tract on the Lord's Prayer. Before leaving Witham, Hubert was granted confraternity. He promised that for the rest of his days the Carthusian order should be his special care, and he gave the prior what nowadays would be called a 'hot line' to him if he should need his help. Hubert honoured his promise by thereafter always according special honour to the prior of Witham. When need arose, he had the prior's horses stabled with his own. When Hubert's crossing the English Channel on royal business coincided with the prior's visits to Carthusian general chapters, Hubert not only conveyed the prior in his own ship, but in common peril he joined him for private prayers and mutual edification. The Chronicle comments that the story of Hubert's conversion from enmity towards the Carthusians to such special friendship was passed round by the English bishops and other magnates, who thus were also drawn towards Witham and its monastic life.[30]

---

[30] Wilmart, 'Maître Adam' (as n. 27), pp. 224-8, cap. 12; cf. p. 224, cap. 11, for the frequent recourse to Adam at Witham of bishops and magnates.

Thirdly, the Carthusians had the benefit of a generally favourable reputation with those who wrote about them. In his *Courtiers' Trifles*, which was mostly written in 1181-2, Walter Map, who had a good word for few monks, spared the Carthusians his satirical wit and wrote with respect. In his review of monastic orders, he had nothing but praise for la Grande Chartreuse itself; if he could not resist retailing the story of an unidentified apostate dependency, he referred in it to the salutary endeavours of the prior of la Grande Chartreuse and ascribed its apostasy to its longing for a mother like itself in the shape of Cîteaux![31] At about the end of John's reign, two biographies of St Hugh of Lincoln were written. The first, by Gerald of Wales, was probably requested by the canons of Lincoln; Gerald's professed concern was to show how, in the protracted medieval conflict of *sacerdotium* and *regnum*, Hugh was the bright lily of Lincoln as compared with the martyred Thomas Becket, who was the red rose of Kent.[32] Gerald's Life was almost immediately used by Adam of Eynsham, who was Bishop Hugh's major biographer.[33] Adam was a Benedictine monk who had been Hugh's chaplain during the last three years of his life; he had thereafter been sub-prior and abbot of Eynsham (dioc. Lincoln). He wrote at the request of the Carthusians of Witham, and dedicated his *Magna Vita* to Prior Robert of Caveford and his holy brethren there. His main concern was to praise Hugh's spiritual qualities; in so doing, he displayed a deep understanding of and regard for the history and qualities of Carthusian life. He had observed it at first hand, for he accompanied his bishop to la Grande Chartreuse upon his final visit there in 1200. Adam's Life is redolent of the high and informed regard in which a black-monk author held Carthusian traditions, both as exemplified in the subject of his biography and in their own right.

Black-monk comment upon the Carthusians was not always so favourable, and a word must be said about the chronicler Richard of Devizes. Richard was a monk of St Swithun's, Winchester, who between 1192 and 1198 recorded the first four years of Richard I's reign.[34] His work was dedicated to Robert FitzHenry, the former prior of St Swithun's who in 1191 became a monk at Witham (1). He adopted a tone of satire which, as a later annotation confirms (26),[35] expresses

---

[31] 1.16, 28 (as n. 25), pp. 50-3, 117-18.

[32] *Giraldi Cambrensis opera*, edd. J.S. Brewer, J.F. Dimock, and G.F. Warner, 8 vols. (London: Rolls Series, 21, 1861-91), 7.83-147 (citation at p. 87); the *Legenda*, pp. 172-92, were written a little later. For the Life, see A. Gransden, *Historical Writing in England, c.550-c.1307* (London, 1974), pp. 310-13.

[33] As n. 21; see Gransden (as n. 32), pp. 312-17.

[34] *The Chronicle of Richard of Devizes of the Time of King Richard I*, ed. J.T. Appleby (London, etc., 1963) (references in the text are to the pages of this edition); see also Gransden (as n. 32), pp. 247-52.

[35] According to the note, Robert abandoned his priorate and set aside his

his rancour that Robert should have thus departed; other matters may have rankled as well, such as that of King Henry II and the illuminated bible from Winchester that he had presented to Witham.[36]   Richard claimed to have for long harboured a thought of following his prior, but during a visit to Witham with two companions he was disenchanted by what he saw (1).   He indicated three gravamina.   He mocked a life that was centred upon the cell (1)-- showing no openness to the eremitical life to which St Benedict pointed in the Rule and to the theology of the cell as developed in twelfth-century devotional literature. He carped at the Carthusians' disregard of hospitality and almsgiving (2)-- showing ignorance, whether real or studied, of Prior Guigo I's comments on the subject in the Customs of la Grande Chartreuse.[37]   And he noticed how, despite their more-than-Pythagorean rule of silence, the Carthusians were plied with all the world's gossip (2)-- showing no insight into the interaction with the wider church and world that the Carthusians had maintained since their inception.[38] To fuel such gossip, Richard concluded, he had written his Chronicle, so here it was (2-3)!   Dom David Knowles was surely right to comment that Richard's preface was 'of studied irony', and if sent to Witham-- and there is no reason for thinking that it was not-- that it 'can only have been sent in a spirit of cold and bitter hostility'.[39]   The rancour was too blatant, and the critique of the Carthusians was too blind and uninformed, for Richard's words to stand as more than the outburst of a soured individual.

Nevertheless, such outbursts were repeated in cases of others who temporarily transferred to Witham.   Richard of Devizes also referred to Prior Walter of Bath, who *c*.1190 anticipated Robert FitzHenry 'through a like fervour-- or madness; but once he had extricated himself, nothing seemed farther from his mind than returning' (27).   Walter's obituary in the Annals of Winchester, which Richard of Devizes may have penned, recalled that he had once been sub-prior of Hyde Abbey at Winchester; he had left Bath 'preferring to look after himself than to govern others'.   A Hyde monk who visited him at Witham saw him who once had been intent on the salvation of souls now intent upon cooking pots and

──────
    35 (cont'd)profession; at Witham, through grief-- or was it devotion?-- he had cast himself down into the sect of the Charterhouse.

    36For the incident of the bible, see *Life of St Hugh*, 2.13 (as n. 21, 1.84-8; see W. Oakeshott, *The Two Winchester Bibles* (Oxford, 1981), pp. 33-4.

    37*Coutumes de Chartreuse*, caps. 19-20, ed. un Chartreux, Sources Chrétiennes, 313 (Paris, 1984), pp. 204-10.

    38Cowdrey, 'Hugh of Avalon' (as n. 1), pp. 44-50.

    39D. Knowles, *The Monastic Order in England*, 2nd edn. (Cambridge, 1963), p. 387.

vegetables. The monk resorted to mockery: 'What you are doing is *kere*! What you are performing is *Kirewiwere*!' (The mocking words have never been explained.) However, 'when he came to himself'-- the Annals evoke the Prodigal Son (Luke 15.17)!-- he quickly returned to be prior of Bath again.[40] Two other monks who transferred to Witham did not persist and were sharp in their criticism. They were Andrew, formerly monk and sacrist at Muchelney, and Alexander of Lewes, a former secular canon.[41] At Witham, they complained bitterly of the tedium of an eremitical as opposed to a claustral manner of life. The letters of Peter of Blois, archdeacon of Bath, include a letter of vigorous reproof to Alexander, whose complaints had included the lack of daily mass (264B). Peter urged him to persist: if there were anything harsh or burdensome in the Carthusian order, charity would temper it; *nihil difficile est amanti* (272A).[42] Like Richard of Devizes, Andrew and Alexander appear as disaffected individuals who no doubt spoke for some others, but there is no reason to consider them representative of general opinion.

For, as a fourth feature of the Carthusian impact upon Angevin England, the Carthusian way of life was widely apprehended as an ultimate in religious commitment to which an aspirant to perfection might aspire. The Witham Chronicle recorded how, despite Prior Albert's ultimate failure to measure up to the high standards for which St Hugh of Lincoln looked, his priorate saw the arrival of four men, three of them from other orders, who were regarded as outstanding recruits: Abbot Adam of Dryburgh, Prior Robert of Winchester, Prior Walter of Bath, and a lay youth named Theodore.[43] It is tempting to suggest baldly that, with the early charisma of the Cistercians in England now settled into routine and worldliness, the Carthusians after *c*.1180 stood out as the order to which the *âmes d'élite* of monasticism might aspire. Peter of Blois's writings suggest that this would be over-simplified, for his esteem for the Cistercians remained high. He told the monk Alexander, who was minded to transfer from Witham to the Cluniacs, that he could bear more readily with his wish if his destination were the Cistercians, whom he warmly praised, than the Cluniacs with their endless musical repetitiveness (270AB). In a subsequent emollient letter to Abbot Adam of Evesham, himself an erstwhile Cluniac of la Charité and Bermondsey, Peter begged the abbot not to be aggrieved by his com-

---

[40] *Annales monasterii de Wintonia, 519-1277*, a.1198, in: *Annales monastici*, ed. H. Luard (5 vols., London: Rolls Series, 36, 1864-9), 2.68.

[41] *Life of St Hugh*, 2.11 (as n. 21), 1.80-4.

[42] *Ep.* 86, *PL* 207.262-72. For Peter, see J. Armitage Robinson, *Somerset Historical Essays* (London, 1921), pp. 100-40.

[43] Wilmart, 'Maître Adam' (as n. 27), pp. 231-2, nos. 3,4.

mendation of the Carthusians and Cistercians, for he applauded all monks; indeed, he had reproved Alexander for looking down on the orders that he had left.[44]   But if Peter praised the Cistercians, he had particular regard for the Carthusians.   He highly praised Witham which it is clear from his *Compendium in Job* that he had visited; he wondered at the all-night vigils of the monk Gerard whom he went there to see, and at the prevailing unworldliness.[45] Peter impressed upon the wavering Alexander the high and holy repute of the Carthusians (*sanctum et gloriosae opinionis ordinem Carthusiensem* (264AB)); in its rocky remoteness, la Grande Chartreuse itself was the habitation of angels rather than of men (268A).

To this extent, there was a vision of the Carthusians as the *ne plus ultra* of the religious life, and so they attracted men who felt drawn to it. There were those who stayed, like Robert FitzHenry of Winchester or, apparently, his companion Ralph, formerly sacrist of Winchester.[46]   By far the most notable was Adam, sometime abbot of the Premonstratensian house of Dryburgh in the Scottish borders.[47]   Besides his admiration of Hugh of Lincoln, Adam was drawn by his observation of Carthusian life in France.   He visited the Charterhouse of Val Saint-Pierre (dioc. Lyons), and he followed the example of an English friend and former Premonstratensian abbot named Roger who had become a Carthusian at Val Dieu (dioc. le Mans).   (Can he have been the Roger who, from 1152 to 1177, was the first abbot of Dryburgh?)   Adam entered Witham with the commendation of Hugh of Lincoln, who also helped to appease Premonstratensian objections to his migration.   The Witham Chronicle listed his writings, and confirm that he completed the tract on the Lord's Prayer which he promised Archbishop Hubert Walter.[48]   His most influential work was his *De quadripartito exercitio cellae*, probably written in the early 1190s.[49]   Warm and detailed in his praise of the Carthusian life which manifestly suited his aspirations, Adam explored its several aspects-- reading, prayer, and manual labour; but above all he expounded the stages of contemplative prayer.   The work is a sustained praise and justification of the solitary life that Richard of Devizes had summarily dismissed.   Its circulation in England and beyond during and after the

[44]*Ep.* 97, *PL* 207.304-6; cf. *Life of St Hugh*, 2.11 (as n. 21), 1.80-4.
[45]Cap. 2, *PL* 207.815-16.   The work was dedicated to King Henry II.
[46]*Life of St Hugh*, 2.14 (as n. 21), 1.89.
[47]Wilmart, 'Maître Adam' (as n. 27), pp. 215-30, no. 1; *Life of St Hugh*, 4.11 (as n. 21), 2.52-4.
[48]Wilmart, 'Maître Adam' (as n. 27), pp. 230-1, no. 2.
[49]*PL* 153.799-884; see J. Hogg, 'Adam the Carthusian's *De quadripartito exercitio cellae*', in: *De Cella in Seculum* (as n. 1), pp. 67-79.

later middle ages, under the name of Prior Guigo II of la Grande Chartreuse, testifies to the need that it satisfied.

To summarize. Once Witham was founded under King Henry II and successfully set up by Prior Hugh of Avalon, the Carthusians found a ready place in England. The way had been long prepared by the Norman royal family's patronage of eremitical monasticism; the kings were accustomed to tolerate, and even to expect, such plain speaking from holy men of proven spiritual background as was justly to win for Hugh of Avalon the sobriquet *regum malleus*. The absorption of the Savignacs into the Cistercians, and the latter's loss of spiritual freshness and impetus, left room for the Carthusians to come to England with the force of novelty as the strictest form of eremitical monasticism. The zeal of the early Carthusians in England, and the fame of la Grande Chartreuse itself, won them ready acceptance. They enjoyed, for the most part, a favourable public response, both amongst writers and amongst bishops and magnates like Archbishop Hubert Walter. As bishop of Lincoln, Hugh of Avalon added greatly to their reputation. Yet his was not the only exemplary and widely noticed Carthusian life. Adam of Dryburgh, too, showed how a learned religious of exceptional spiritual qualities could find his home by transferring from another order to the strictness of the Carthusians. His *De quadripartito exercitio cellae* naturalized Carthusian mystical devotion into the spiritual heritage of later medieval England.

INDEX

Except in the case of Pope Gregory VII, this Index does not usually include an entry for a person or topic when a reference occurs in the title to an article. The following abbreviations are used: a. = abbey; ab. = abbot; abp. = archbishop; akg. = anti-king; ap. = anti-pope; b. = battle; bp. = bishop; c. = council; card. = cardinal; ct. = count; d. = duke; dss. = duchess; e. = eastern; emp. = emperor; emps. = empress; kg. = king; m. = monk; mon. = monastery; n. = nunnery; p. = pope; pat. = patriarch; pr. = prior; pt. = priest; q. = queen; St = Saint.